"I tell you on my divine authority:
I am the Ancient One,
I am the Lord of the Universe."
- Avatar Meher Baba

Christ Come Again
Volume Two
1926-1942

Ed Flanagan

CHRIST COME AGAIN

CHRIST COME AGAIN

CHRIST COME AGAIN

Acknowledgements / copyright

Times New Roman 12 pt.

ISBN 978-0-578-31402-0

Copyright © 2021 The estate of Ed Flanagan
All rights reserved

Editor and interior designer Susan McKendree
Cover design Karl Moeller
Line editor Irma Sheppard

All quotations, referenced text and images remain
the property of the copyright owners

Christ Come Again
Volume II

Ed Flanagan

The Life and Teachings of Meher Baba (1894-1969)
and the Avatar's revelations of his previous advent as Jesus,
compiled from books, journals, letters, tape recordings, online
and personal accounts of those who met or lived with the Avatar.

CHRIST COME AGAIN

CHRIST COME AGAIN
VOLUME TWO
by Ed Flanagan

I   About Ed Flanagan—Rob Findlay
V   Organization of this book—Karl Moeller
VI   Introduction by Ed Flanagan

1 Chapter 14 The Prem Love Ashram Blooms
Another Great War ~ Pure Gold from Mixed Alloys ~ Parents Break Their Word and the Master's Heart ~ True Love is Not for the Fainthearted ~ Uninvited Visitors ~ Baba's Second Catholic Disciple ~ The Prem Ashram Closes ~ The Perfect Boy ~ In Apparent Trouble is the Hidden Mercy of God

41 Chapter 15 Lust and Love
The Battle with Lust is a Necessity for Evolution ~ Abortion and Birth Control ~ Love, Lust and Divorce ~ Inviting Baba into One's Weakness ~ The Persians are Overwhelmed by Baba ~ Under the Radar ~ Baba's First Western Interview

77 Chapter 16 Secret Visits to Persia and the West
Sheriar's Fervent Prayer ~ Forgiving Treachery ~ A Third Visit to Persia ~ The Master Pulls another Charade ~ Hung on a Rusty Nail ~ Love Calls Me to the West ~ Baba Prophesies the Demise of the British Empire ~ The Mahatma Meets the Master ~ Western Shores at Last ~ "I am the Avatar—the Christ-Messiah"

107 Chapter 17 The Avatar Reaches America's Shores
The Harmon Retreat ~ The Dream Come True ~ Boston and New Hampshire ~ Back to New York ~ A Film on Spirituality ~ God Incarnates on Earth in Major and Minor Advents ~ "I am the Ancient One"

135 Chapter 18 Baba's Return to the West
Baba's First Messages to America ~ What to Make of Him? ~ Meher Baba's Spiritual Direction: Prayer—God is Always Listening ~ Satan and the Problem of Evil ~ The Blessed Trinity ~ The Occult ~ Perfect Masters and Spiritual Perfection ~ Silly Questions

165 Chapter 19 Realization through the Medium of Film
Philip White's Dream ~ Newsreels and Movies of the Avatar ~ There Will Be No End to My Photos ~ Hollywood Bound ~ Rolling out the Red Carpet for Meher Baba ~ Public Reception at the Knickerbocker Hotel ~ The Pickfair Reception in Beverly Hills ~ Meher Baba's Address to the Motion Picture Industry ~ False Promises of Romance and Happiness ~ Hollywood's Most Spiritual Actress

209 Chapter 20 Breaking His Silence in the Hollywood Bowl
Laying War Cables in the Far East ~ The Avatar as Divine Juggler ~ "Did Baba 'Brake' His Silence?" ~ Meher Baba and Albert Einstein ~

229 Chapter 21 Italy, Egypt, Spain and Switzerland
Seclusion in St. Francis' Cave ~ A Spiritual Cliffhanger ~ Cairo: "My Dear Old Place" ~ Portofino ~ Saints and Secret Agents ~ Home Work ~ Seclusion at Fallenfluh ~

265 Chapter 22 Hollywood — Take Two
De'Acosta and Garbo ~ More Frustrations in Hollywood ~ Weakness vs. Compassion ~ The Odyssey of Gabriel Pascal, Baba's Phoenix

293 Chapter 23 The Ten Commandments
"My Work in Universal" ~ The Next Voice You hear ~ Quentin Loses and Regains ~ Meher Baba Links Hollywood and Bollywood ~ "The Soul's Journey from Unconscious to Conscious God" from *God Speaks*

313 Chapter 24 Balancing East and West
Meher Retreat Ashram in Nasik ~ The Most Beautiful film of Baba ~ In One Ear and Out the Other ~ Cannes: A New Ashram on the Riviera ~ Mohammed Comes to Cannes ~ Vichy Water ~ The Master's Tomb ~ The New St. Peter ~ The Women's Ashram on the Hill ~ The Meherazad Zoo ~ A Traveling Ashram

355 Chapter 25 War Clouds
The Disease of Selfishness Leads to War ~ War as Divine Diplomacy ~ An Ashram Skit Foreshadows the War

369 Chapter 26 Baba's Wayfarers
The Search for *Masts* ~ Baba's Scribe, William Donkin ~ Five Types of *Masts* ~ The Divine Art of Contacting *Masts* ~ Meeting Two Secret Agents in Goa ~ The Last *Mast* for Now

391 Endnotes

400 Multivolume Table of Contents

404 Reference Codes and Copyrights

CHRIST COME AGAIN

About Ed Flanagan

Ed was born in 1936 and raised in West Roxbury, Massachusetts. After attending Catholic University, he entered the Maryknoll Missionary order of Catholic priests in the 1950s. Disillusioned with the Church after Vatican II and seeking further truths, Ed left his parish in South Korea, and soon the Catholic priesthood altogether, and moved to New York City in the late 1960s. Flanagan first heard about Meher Baba in 1975 but dismissed him as "just another Indian guru." It wasn't until several years later that he came to accept Meher Baba as "Avatar of The Age."

Ed was the youngest of four. He had three much older sisters whom he adored and who doted on him. Affectionately called "Champ" by his working-class father who was the owner of a small vending machine business and who worked closely with Ed's mother running that business, Ed often referred to himself as a "latch-key" kid who spent a lot of time as a child on his own, and he liked it that way. Ed had no desire or interest in sports or even school, and so at a time when most young boys' idols were baseball players, Ed's focus and passion was in film and music. At this time he was an award-winning child actor on radio performing theater on Boston's WMEX FM. From a very young age into adulthood Ed loved jazz and classical music and was a big fan of the early big band crooners and jazz singers. He once described his musical tastes as, "… anything out of The Great American Songbook." Fascinated by film and with a particular passion for the grand MGM musicals starring greats such as Gene Kelly, whom Ed would work with and befriend later in his life, Ed would go to the movies and then come home and re-create lighting, dreaming of one day working on a movie set. Ed attended High School at the prestigious Boston Latin School, the oldest existing school in the USA and the first public school in America, but admittedly did not excel because he was so preoccupied with music and whatever the new MGM movie was that week. At the age of seventeen he wrote to the head of production at MGM Studios, Dore Schary, who eventually became president of the studio during the 1950s. Dory was so taken by Ed that he wrote him back and personally invited him to take a tour of the studio to "see how movies are really made." His father traveled with him on train from Boston as far as Chicago and then got off for business, and a young Ed traveled the rest of the way by himself to MGM.

While there he visited the Pasadena Playhouse, a legendary acting school he had heard about and longed to attend after High School to study Directing. Upon graduation Ed's father insisted he attend college on the East Coast and so Ed attended The Catholic University of America along with actor Jon Voight. Ed graduated from CUA and much to his father's chagrin became a Maryknoll Missionary priest and worked in several parishes throughout South Korea.

After leaving the priesthood Flanagan settled in New York City and in 1970 he became a television and film producer. He initially worked on several Network specials for General Electric Theater and then worked producing documentaries, including one on jazz piano legend Mary Lou Williams, with whom he was intimate friends. Toward the late 1970s, with his lifelong, ever-increasing urge to seek the innermost truths about himself and the nature of God, Ed studied under Bolivian philosopher and teacher Óscar Ichazo and later became an instructor both in London and New York City for Ichazo's Arica Institute. Arica was dedicated to teaching a complete system of holistic mind-body techniques for consciousness-raising, as well as ideologies for one to relate to the world in an "awakened" way.

It was during this time in 1975 that Ed first saw a photo of Meher Baba at Pete Townshend's studio in London where his Arica school was invited to experience a lecture on Meher Baba. Ed reported being so moved by Baba's photo that he re-entered the room on several occasions to catch another glance, although at that moment in time he did not accept him as anything more than a spiritual teacher or perhaps a mystic or "just another Indian guru," as he often would describe his first impressions of hearing of Meher Baba. It wasn't until a few years later in his Manhattan apartment on 22nd Street in the morning during a quiet moment while looking at the sun's rays shining into the room through a hanging asparagus plant that he said "… it hit me instantly." He stated that at that point he knew, simultaneously, in both his heart and his mind, that Meher Baba was exactly who he said he was: "The Avatar of the Age."

From that moment on Ed was passionately compelled to absorb like a sponge as much on Meher Baba as he could and devoted his life to loving Meher Baba and seeking "Baba" in ALL things. This spiritual awakening and psychic change that Ed says he underwent that morning in his apartment eventually culminated into devoting the last 5 years of his life exclusively to writing this very book.

After the priesthood, producing, and his Arica work, Flanagan moved to Boston in the early 1980s close to his roots. There he made a living from his private practice where he conducted "Bio-Energy" treatments to clients with various forms of addictions, applying special (and very secret) techniques and philosophies he learned from the renowned Yefim G. Shubentsov, known to many as "The Mad Russian," whom Ed had worked under for a few years. While living and working in Boston Ed made several pilgrimages to Meherabad, Meher Baba's home in the East, where he came to know intimately Meher Baba's last living disciples and family members.

Ed moved to Calabasas, California, on September 10, 2001. He had been booked on American Airlines Flight 11, scheduled to leave Boston the morning of September 11, the very flight that was hijacked and flown into the North Tower of The World Trade Center. Two days before his trip, Ed had strong feelings that told him to "Leave Boston right away!" and so he re-scheduled his flight to be a September 10 departure instead of the 11th.

In Los Angeles Ed continued his Bio-Energy treatment practice and also pursued his childhood dream of being an actor. He appeared in many independent films all the while treating clients at his home office with quit-smoking and weight loss treatments. In his down time he began writing a biography on Meher Baba which eventually became what he repeatedly told me was his "true life's purpose," writing this book, *Christ Come Again*. It must be noted that Ed Flanagan was also a member of the first Board of Directors of the Avatar Meher Baba Heartland Center in Oklahoma as well as one of its major benefactors. This was a project, like this book, that was ever close to his heart.

In 2010 Ed retired from acting and closed his business in order that he could devote all of his waking hours to completing *Christ Come Again*. Ed Flanagan passed away at his home in Calabasas, California, on September 25, 2016 a few weeks after completing this book's final draft.

Rob Findlay November 2019

Organization of This Book

Ed was indeed Father Flanagan for many years. Make no mistake, Ed sees Meher Baba through the eyes and training of a Catholic priest. There are sixty-nine chapters in his manuscript, which took Ed much of a decade to write. This project will span five to six more volumes, and it will be one of the most thorough biographies of Meher Baba, second only to Bhau Kalchuri's monumental *Lord Meher.*

Susan McKendree, editor and layoutwalla, 2021
Karl Moeller, layoutwalla, 2019

Introduction

by Ed Flanagan

"Avatar" is a popular term in film titles, graphics and weekend workshops. It is actually a Sanskrit word meaning the total, direct descent of Reality into illusion—Personal God coming into human form on earth as the eternal Savior, the Highest of the High—the one and only Ancient One.

The Unity and Divinity of All Life
Meher Baba, Sept. 12, 1954

Age after age, amidst the clamor of disruptions, wars, fear and chaos rings the Avatar's Call: "Come all unto me!" Because of the veil of illusion, the Ancient One's call may appear as a voice in the wilderness. Its echo and re-echo nevertheless pervade time and space, to initially rouse a few and eventually millions from their deep slumber of ignorance. In the midst of illusion, as the true Voice behind all voices, it awakens mankind to God's newly manifested human presence on earth.

The time has come for me to repeat the call and bid all to come unto me. Regardless of your doubts and convictions, and for the infinite love I bear for one and all, I continue to come as the Avatar to be judged time and again by humanity's ignorance to help man distinguish the Real from the false.

The greatest greatness and greatest humility go naturally hand in hand. When the Greatest of all says, "I am the Greatest," it is but a spontaneous expression of an infallible Truth. The strength of his greatness lies not in raising the dead, but in his great humiliation in allowing himself to be ridiculed, persecuted and crucified at the hands of those who are weak in flesh and spirit.

Throughout the ages, humanity has failed to fathom the true depth of humility of the Avatar's greatness, gauging his divinity by mere religious standards. Even real saints and sages having some knowledge of the Truth have failed to understand the Avatar's greatness when faced with his real humility. History repeats itself age after age when men and women in their ignorance, limitations and pride sit in judgment over the God-incarnated Man as he openly declares his Godhood.

They condemn him for uttering Truths they cannot understand. He is indifferent to abuse and persecution, for in his true compassion he understands, in his continual experience of Reality he knows, and in his infinite mercy he forgives. God is all. God knows all. God does all. When the Avatar proclaims he is the Ancient One, it is God proclaiming his manifestation on earth. When man utters for or against the Avatar, it is God speaking through him. God alone declares himself through the Avatar and mankind. I tell you with divine authority we are not "we" but *"One."* Unconsciously you feel my Avatarhood in you; I consciously feel in you what each of you feels. LM 3552–53

Thus, every one of us is an Avatar, meaning everyone and everything **is** everyone and everything at the same time and for all time. He is the only Reality, and we all are one in the indivisible Oneness of this absolute Reality. When the one who has realized God says, "I am God, you are God, and we all are One," and also awakens this feeling of Oneness in his illusion-bound selves, then there is no question of the lowly and the great, the poor and rich, the humble and exalted, the good and the bad.

Pay heed. I say with my divine authority that the Oneness of Reality is so uncompromisingly unlimited and all-pervading that not only "We are One," but even this collective term of "we" has no place in the Infinite, Indivisible Oneness. Awaken from your ignorance and try at least to understand in the uncompromisingly Indivisible Oneness, not only is the Avatar **God**, but also the ant and the sparrow, just as one and all of you are nothing but **God**.

The only apparent difference is in the states of consciousness. The Avatar knows a sparrow is not a sparrow; whereas, the sparrow does not realize it, and being ignorant of its ignorance, remains a sparrow. Live not in ignorance wasting your precious life span differentiating and judging your fellow men, but learn to long for the love of God. Even in the midst of your worldly activities, live only to find and realize your true Identity with your Beloved God. 3554

When Religion goes, God comes.
—Meher Baba

One taste of Reality relieves an eternal hunger.
—Zen saying of Hakuin

The God you are searching for is not up in the sky. He is here on this plane! "I am That." I am in you, so search for me within yourself. I am not in any mosque, temple or church. 1006

God is Eternal Freedom, Bliss and Knowledge. Trying to put him within walls of man-made churches only proves our ignorance. To try binding fathomless God in narrow and limited dogmas, creeds and *churchified* conventions lacks the true perception of God's Omniscience. GG VI: 75–76

    Any religion, method, system or practice within the sphere of reason and intellect, if followed in the right spirit, can lead one to the real Path above reason and intellect, leading one to the Ultimate Goal of humanity – God-realization. The various ceremonies, liturgies and rituals which are part and parcel of every religion constitute merely their shadow.
    Dogmas, creeds and conventional ideas of heaven/hell and sin are total perversions of Truth. They confuse and bewilder the mind. Rituals and ceremonies instituted by priest-ridden churches have concentrated on outward forms while ignoring the real essentials of spiritual life – love, obedience, humility and sincerity. Man seeks life and is given a heap of stones. The mass of humanity confuses mere liturgical/ritualistic worship with religion. AW 2 (no. 4,): 5

    I bless you that the spark of my divine love implants in your hearts the deep longing for love of God. World religions proclaim there is but one God, the Father of all in creation. I am that Father. —Meher Baba, addressing five thousand at his historic East-West Gathering in Pune, India, November 2, 1962. 4863

Eighteen years earlier, as WWII entered its final year, a crowd of over thirty thousand Indian devotees came to be with Avatar Meher Baba from dawn till midnight, captivated by his divine personality, drowned in the Ocean of his light and lost to the world. He addressed them:

The organized religions of the world often fail to express the real vision of all those [Christ/Avatars] who have been the fountainhead of inspiration for their very coming into existence. Dogmas and beliefs, rituals and ceremonies can never be the essence of true spiritual life. When religion becomes a mere matter of external rituals and liturgies, it has become a cage for the soul.

Nor does it help to change one religion for another, like going from one cage to another. If religion doesn't help man to free the soul from spiritual bondage and realize God, it is useless. It is time for religion to make room for God, for *when religion goes, God comes!*

And so I am not interested in founding a new religion. The world is already divided by numberless sects, based on dogmas and beliefs. I have not come to give another cage to man, but to impart to the world the illimitable Truth. The world does not need mere verbal instruction.

It needs true awakening; it needs the freedom and the amplitude of divine life, and not the superficiality of mechanically pompous liturgies; it needs love, and not the display of power. The world task ahead of me is very creative. Really speaking, none of you need receive divinity from me. But what I give is the *experiential* knowledge of the Oneness of us all.

At the end of this 1944 discourse, Meher Baba was requested at midnight to bless all thirty thousand devotees who in their longing gathered there the entire day to be with him. The Lord of the Universe stood in his full glory and raised his hands, his face aglow. There was utter peace and stillness in a blessing that spoke secrets in everyone's hearing—a scene reminiscent of times in Judea, revived anew by the living Christ come once again on earth. 2440-41

May this book from one who was a Catholic priest help not only Christians but all in other traditions to make the leap from entrenched dogmas to new ways of understanding, as I myself had to. It is my real prayer that this book may serve as a bridge for them all.

I also ask the reader's indulgence for what will seem a long Introduction, for it sets the stage for a new proclamation of the greatest story ever told—the birth, life and death of the God-Man, Christ come again in the twentieth century. It took me seven years after resigning from the priesthood to even hear of the Master Himself—the Messiah returned—then thirty-seven more to distill his message and the exalted secrets he revealed as contained in these pages.

My experience of Avatar Meher Baba over those decades since his passing in 1969 is that he is very much alive and incredibly accessible as Christ, Master, companion, guide and most intimate friend. His Tomb-Shrine in India is a daily direct *inner-net* link to his living Presence beyond the limits of time, space and the illusory physical gross universe.

His statement on the unique position and function of the Avatar was unequivocal-that he was, is and always will be One and the Same–*Emmanuel*: *God with us*.

> *Lo I am with you always, even unto the End.*
> —Matthew 28:20

This one fact crashes down once and for all the Jericho-walls of theological differences and religious intolerance so dividing mankind.

If all men have been worshipping one and the same Avatar under his different guises and names in impersonal and personal aspects, then truly all religions are *One*. Their seeming differences are only in the false minds of men, not in the Divine Essence poured out by the Eternal Messenger. This is the "thread" on which to string those separative religious beads.

Needless to say, not just early on but over decades I met with serious opposition from family, friends and most especially my fellow priests and other Christians, over Meher Baba as "Christ come again." How could it have been otherwise? It also happened in Jesus' time.

Meher Baba's similar but infinitely greater humiliation was to be ridiculed by unbelievers for speaking the Truth. We have all experienced that in trying to share him with those who not only rejected him, but were embarrassed for us—the utter foolishness of those who should have known better.

In the tumultuous late 1960s, conditioned by years of rigorous theological training as a Catholic missionary priest in the Far East, I had just freshly emerged from religious life, courtesy of my petition to Rome for early retirement, only to then deal with the culture shock of being back in the "unreal" real world after thirteen years of being "out of it"—an expression many comically and perhaps accurately used to describe me in those days.

I transitioned back to life as an ordinary layman, barely skipping a beat, landing a job in the Madison Avenue television and film world. We were in the middle of producing a one hour network General Electric Theatre TV special with folksinger John Denver.

Robert Riger, my boss, and also a Catholic, walked into my office one morning and questioned me: "Ed, what do you think of Meher Baba?" He went on to ask if I thought it possible that Christ might have recently returned to earth in human form as promised.

It seemed his son had just returned from India, reborn and "buzzing" about a silent Master there called Meher Baba, believed by hundreds of thousands—Hindus, Muslims, Christians and even Jews—as the "return of the one and only Christ-Avatar" to earth.

"What?" I asked incredulously, then fired back facetiously, "Well, *I* certainly didn't catch it on the evening news!" I had to keep from laughing at his ludicrous question. For as a priest I knew far better about such nonsense; or so I thought. But when I began exploring, I witnessed the ecstatic charismatic movement, complete with tongue speaking and prophesy in the previously sober Catholic Church, which was experiencing a massive exodus of religious—priests, brothers and nuns—including myself.

It wasn't hard to make out the legend *Titanic* on the hull of the quickly sinking barque of Peter, having sprung a fatal leak in colliding with the icebergs of irrelevancy and denial as it neared the twenty-first century. The Pentecostal movement had burst forth among American Protestants at Meher Baba's birth in the late 1800s.

It was now curiously reappearing in early 1969 as I was transitioning from the priesthood and Meher Baba was finishing the final touches of his work on earth for this age. It was happening once again after millennia. His was the most significant life lived in this age, though few on this side of the globe were yet aware of it.

Once again we now had Pentecostals—*Catholic* ones, no less. They had first appeared following the crucifixion and the outpouring of the Holy Spirit. I was actually seeing it recur now in modern times—Catholics and Protestants praying together in each others' homes—popularly referred to in the late 1960s as the "underground church."

It was a brotherhood of unprecedented friendship beyond the urgings any official ecumenical movement could have ever anticipated. It made me realize something spiritually new and exciting was going on. But what was it? It was *some* kind of ecumenism; certainly not of ideology, but of shared, heartfelt experience. People were now—God forbid—bypassing their churches, as heart was finally winning the battle over mind. In its heyday from 1920 to the mid-1960s, Maryknoll, the missionary order I joined, had two thousand members at any given time. Today in 2015 it has fewer than three hundred, as all denominations cease being the magnetic centers of human lives. Clergy are now being looked upon as fossilized growths stubbornly clinging to decayed and crumbling walls.

People have become totally fed up with the various organized, racist religious "isms" and the wars they continually spawn, cataclysmically hurtling us uneasily toward a disastrous future. We are now becoming *the priests of our own consciousness*, thirsting for true spirituality and mysticism without lifeless, dried-up dogmas and the trappings of worn-out falsities.

Leaving the priesthood, I, too, was caught up in the outpouring of Spirit beyond religion. Swimming in it with countless thousands, I felt like those first astronauts in that same year of 1969. We were making a choice about the future of humanity.

We had to stop looking in the rearview mirror and trying to live by the tombstone-rules of past established religions with their rigid dogmas based on a kind of fear that divided humanity so as to control it. Without exception, all had lost the way.

The future was ominously approaching at lightning speed, challenging us before it was too late to understand who we are *now,* and not who we were *then*. We had to unlearn, painfully at times, all the false religious certainties that we had always assumed were true but are not. What we would—will—become is Meher Baba's New Humanity.

When the Lord came again into this world, people beseeched Him to *do something* about this mess religions have gotten us into. The unification of the world's major faiths, *"like beads on a string"*—Meher Baba's own term—is one of the single most real promises Christ gave for his work in this new millennium. Will it be accomplished before we destroy each other and the delicate fabric of Earth's mantle in the twenty-first century?

I had no clue about Meher Baba. He sounded like one of those Beatles' Maharishi fads I so disdained. How could I guess he was a manifestation of the living Christ come yet once again with his old yet new outpouring of the Holy Spirit? Later on, I was especially intrigued to see so many Jews having a strong affinity for Meher Baba beginning as early as the 1930s.

This is when he first came West to Europe and America. And it continued following the Holocaust with the evangelical messianic Jewish movement taking off in the early 1970s just after Meher Baba's passing. Groups like "Jews for Jesus" grew in major U.S. cities as well as in Russia and South Africa. What was happening here?

Since the 1960s there has even been a Meher Baba Center in Israel that Baba directly communicated with. Only later did I recall early Church fathers proclaiming the Lord's return at the Second Coming would occur only when Jews finally accepted Jesus as their own Prophet, said to be a manifestation of the gathering of the lost tribes of the Diaspora. This gathering was Jesus' final mandate to His Apostles:

Go not to the gentiles, but to the lost tribes of Israel.

But that so *many* Jews would make the double leap to accept Meher Baba for exactly who and what he said he was—the Messiah, the God-Man, Christ on earth returned, thereby also including and embracing Jesus—no, this was nothing I could have even remotely anticipated.

Whatever the religion, people had left God aside to worship instead their pet rituals—prayers, rosaries and dry scriptures which had supplanted true love for God. This caused a violent reaction of great unrest and deep social upheaval. Rituals once commanding respect had degenerated into routines that no longer spoke to the true spiritual needs of God's people.

They created a foreboding spiritual vacuum. When God became less important than scriptures, the world cried out with Buddha:

> *The oceans have dried, mountains crumble,*
> *the pole star is shaken,*
> *the earth founders and gods perish*
> *like frogs in dry wells.*

Meher Baba assured us he didn't come to establish anything new, but to do away with the *rust* of dogmatic religious ceremonies and rituals so long encrusted over the kernel of Divine Truth.

He stressed that God *needs no worship* and only values honest love, hearing not the language of tongue or mind, but only the language of love coming directly from the human heart. Listen to the universe's secret and its goal as embodied in these words of Meher Baba:

> The soul's existence is everlasting, and its Eternal Existence is one with God. Do not mistake soul's Eternal Existence with the mind or intellect. The soul makes the intellect work, but nothing controls the absolutely independent Soul. Intellect is but an instrument of the totally independent Soul. It is a means to attain the Original, Eternal Existence and to experience it. Love, service, devotion and dedication can make a person know God. 1375

> To know Himself, God *became* each individual Soul. He embodied himself in them, thereby becoming bound by his actions. And thus, it is the responsibility of the Avatar [the God-Man] coming to earth age after age to unbind man's actions, which then leads to God-Realization. 689

Consciously or unconsciously, every living creature fundamentally seeks one thing based on a memory—dim or clear—of its essential unity with God. For every living thing is a partial manifestation of God, conditioned only by lack of knowledge of its own true nature.

In fact, evolution is the evolution from unconscious divinity to conscious divinity, in which God Himself, essentially eternal and unchangeable, assumes an infinite variety of forms, enjoys an infinite variety of experiences, and transcends an infinite variety of self-imposed limitations. From the standpoint of the Creator, evolution is **a divine sport** in which the Unconditioned tests the real infinitude of His absolute knowledge, power and bliss in the midst of all limited conditions.

But from the creature's standpoint, evolution's limited knowledge, power and capacity for enjoying bliss is an epic of alternating rest and struggle, joy and sorrow, love and hate – until in the perfected person, God balances these pairs of opposites, and duality is forever transcended.

Creature and Creator then experience themselves as One. Changelessness is established in the very midst of change; eternity is experienced in the midst of time. God knows Himself as God, unchanging in essence, infinite in manifestation, and ever experiencing the bliss of Self-Realization.

He continually experiences fresh awareness of Himself by Himself. This Realization can only take place in the midst of human life; for only in the midst of life can limitation be experienced and transcended, and subsequent freedom from limitation be enjoyed. Di 266–67

These quotes tell us that evolution must necessarily be based on the development of consciousness; thus, ***consciousness drives*** *evolution*, and not the random survival of the fittest as Darwin would have it. Meher Baba's explanations are grounded in ancient eastern traditions, but nothing in terms of traditional religious or spiritual practices surround him.

There are no rigid meditations, initiation, membership, rituals, diet, dress or prayers. He cautions "Do not observe prolonged silence nor meditate. Do not serve yourself by doing so. You who are dedicated in my Cause have no need for such discipline." Aw 19 (no. 2): 1

Still, Meher Baba gave three extraordinary prayers to humanity in this Advent: the *Prayer of Repentance*, *You Alone Exist*, and *The Master's Prayer,* or *O Parvardigar*, all of which we will encounter in this book's ongoing pages. Meanwhile, there's no study course, or scripture to be read or mastered. False mind is now forever bypassed in favor of heart.

The Avatar was often celebrated in huge public gatherings of thousands. But he discouraged his followers from proselytizing on his behalf. He said:

> *Let your life itself be my message of love and truth to others.*
> — Meher Baba

There's no eternal damnation, or any need to be saved, for everyone without exception by their very existence is already saved. This means *everyone* is *God in human form*—no exceptions here:

> *There is no separation between you and God. Lover and Beloved are One. You yourself are the Way. You are God.*
> —3519

Failure in this game is no option, for any exception would be outside of God and therefore contradict His infinite state. But we are all temporarily veiled by a mind composed of false impressions from past-life forms not yet eliminated on our journey across creation's "seven days," meaning the seven stages of evolution—stone, plant, worm, bird, fish, animal and the first human form]—followed by a process of countless human reincarnations.

We have not yet experienced that glorious final state, the goal of every creature under God's sun. But the knowledge of such a certainty should cause joyous waves of optimism, even in the face of whatever earthly suffering we might still be destined to pass through from past incarnational mistakes, whether good or bad, funny or sad.

> God alone is Real. There is nothing but God; everyone and everything is God. To awaken this Truth in humanity, Infinite God periodically assumes a precious human form, known as the Avatar. Wholeheartedly loving the Avatar—the God-Man—is a most natural way of realizing the goal of life—union with God the Eternal. GG VI: 10

> Each earthly advent of the Avatar is a matchless mystery, and owing to his boundless compassion it occurs time and again. Age after age in His compassionate omniscience Infinite God chooses to become man. To quicken the life pulsating in everyone and everything, the Creator re-involves Himself in his age old game of creation. GG IV: 1

He is the *God-Man Messiah*, also called the Buddha, the Christ, the Rasul or the *Saheb-e-Zaman* (Arabic: Supreme Commander and Lord of the Universe). These terms refer to abstract God appearing on earth in solid, palpable three-dimensional human form.

From the beginningless beginning, the Messiah-Avatar is the *only* Perfect Master to take birth on earth again and again to awaken humanity to his sublime Truth which all organized religions have either forgotten or have carefully hidden.

And he comes to give the actual experience of it. The Infinite Consciousness of the Avatar is in no way affected by life or death. His awareness includes individual awareness of each being in creation. "Always aware, always on the air," carrying out his Universal work, God returns in human form again and again for the sake of his beloved children.

Except for the Avatar and Perfect Masters, all beings reincarnate back in the gross world to continue perfecting themselves after dropping their bodies. After leaving his body, a Perfect Master disconnects from the illusory creation and ceases the cycle of reincarnation. The Avatar alone is connected to one and all for all time and eternity, as he repeatedly takes new human forms.

Thus, Abraham, Zoroaster, Rama, Krishna, Buddha, Jesus, Mohammed and Meher Baba are all incarnations of that very same *Ancient One*—Adam—the Original Avatar from our endless past. As the eternally active source of God's limitless love and grace, the Avatar does not drop his body in the same way a Perfect Master does. Eruch Jessawala, who became the Master's newest apostle in 1938—his *new St. Peter* in this advent—explains:

> When the Avatar sheds his man-form, he continues to be infinitely conscious of his creation and its creatures, and mindful of his lovers who adore him in their hearts. Shedding his physical body, there is no lessening. He keeps exercising Infinite Love, Mercy, Compassion, Authority and Power. So, anyone seeking help at the Avatar's Tomb is not only assured of external benefits, but also derives spiritual benefits due to his direct and lucky approach to God for assistance. AO 201

The Avatar transcends the unimaginable gulf between Infinite Unconsciousness, Infinite Consciousness and God-Realization. From eternity without beginning, he is the only God-Realized being who ever reincarnates, repeatedly coming into the world from time to time every seven to fourteen hundred years. RD 147

> *Among the Perfect Ones, it is only I who does not preach,*
> *teach or tolerate any particular religion*
> *or allow any sectarianism.*
> —Meher Baba (*Lord Meher* 1580)

Our world has left the age of the word and has now entered the post-modern age of the image. And so, unlike his advent as Mohammed, Meher Baba fittingly left us his image in photographs and films, as well as drawings, music and poetry to convey to us his presence and teachings. This is a far more aggressive and universal advent than ever before—far more than his six previous advents in this last five-thousand-year cycle.

With the viral disease of selfishness gone global, Meher Baba travelled and worked all over the world as the only Avatar whose impact has been on *all* the nations, rather than on a limited Eastern region as in the past. The universality of Meher Baba's Avataric work is also seen in the infinite degree of attention given to details in written accounts of his life, activities and teachings, besides the countless photo images he left behind.

He used seven languages: English, Hindi, Marathi, Gujarati, Persian (both Farsi and Dari), Telugu. Following the beginning of his life-long silence in 1925, he developed an extraordinary array of gestures, hand signs and facial expressions.

Although birthless and deathless, the Avatar as Lord of the Universe is eternally bound by His Father's business to come down age after age. He returns in "swaddling clothes"—his bodily form to work for the sake of all creation. This means one thing only: *to suffer*. This duty not even the five Perfect Masters always on earth can accept on his behalf. In November 1952, standing with fifty of his closest male devotees prior to touring India to meet hundreds of thousands of his lovers, Meher Baba stated:

> I'm destined to take this body again and again. And so I *have* to come into the world. But you at least should be free from this unbroken chain of being born again and again—growing, marrying, procreating and dying. God is as soft as He is hard, as compassionate as He is harsh. Invoking Him, if He is touched even *once*, the work is done. The impossible becomes possible. 3146–47

And thus, the false illusion of "needing to be saved" is absolutely and irrevocably done away with once and for all. Guaranteed salvation is the absolute individual soul's Divine birthright, automatically emanating from its Divine Origin. This is the real *Good News*, at which narrow and limited fundamentalism in any form can only gnash its teeth.

And so there are no religious hierarchies, no priestly intercessions, no communities of worship or organizations. Those are now done away with. As Baba himself said, "Rome, go home!" No one has exclusive rights or inside tracks to Truth, as all are equally One with it. 1800

On January 9, 1941, with WWII escalating to brutality of a kind never before seen, Meher Baba stated that he gave no importance to creed, dogma, caste or performing religious ceremonies or rites, but to the *understanding* of the following:

The Seven Realities

1. The only **Real Existence** is that of the One and only God, the Self in every (finite) self.
2 The only **Real Love** is the love for this Infinity (God), which arouses an intense longing to see, know and become one with its Truth (God).
3. The only **Real Sacrifice** is that in which, in pursuing this love, all things – body, mind, position, welfare and even life itself – are sacrificed.
4. The only **Real Renunciation** abandons amidst worldly duties all selfish thought and desires.
5. The only **Real Knowledge** is that God is the in-dweller in good people and so-called bad, in saint and so-called sinner. This requires you to help all equally as needs demand, without expectation of reward, and when compelled to take part in a dispute, to act without the slightest trace of enmity or hatred; to try to make others happy with brotherly or sisterly feeling for each; to harm no one in thought, word or deed – even those who harm you.
6. The only **Real Control** is the discipline of the senses from indulgence in low desires which alone ensures absolute purity of character.
7. The only **Real Surrender** is when one's poise is undisturbed by any adverse conditions, and amidst every kind of hardship the individual, is resigned with perfect calm to the will of God.

And so this book might equally be called *Abraham, Zoroaster, Rama, Krishna, Buddha, Jesus and Mohammed Come Again*. Now in Meher Baba they have *all* come again. All are One and were never two. In 1927, Meher Baba said:

I am the Christ, and because of me the entire world exists! There is no time, space, cause, effect, duality, or anything besides me – only unity.
686

Baba had thousands of copies of this message sent out to disciples in various cities in India, instructing that it especially be given to priests and others in charge of "churches, temples, mosques and ashrams." Thousands were later sent to the West early on during the war, through which the Avatar directly guided human civilization behind the scenes lest it be destroyed. 2183

The Avatar's work is to uplift mankind's awareness to a new understanding of the nature of love and the very goal of existence, including the awareness that without exception every being in the creation is to be treated with great care and respect. For in reality, he said, *"We are not we, but One."* Regarding this particular age and the Avatar's role in it, Meher Baba said:

Avataric periods are the springtide of creation, bringing a new awakening of consciousness for all by means of a Divine Personality, an incarnation of God in a special sense —the Avatar who appears in different forms under different names at different times and in different parts of the world. His appearance always coincides with man's spiritual rebirth.

And so, the period immediately preceding his manifestation is always one in which humanity suffers from the approaching birth pangs. Man seems more than ever enslaved by desire and greed, held by fear and swept by anger. The strong dominate the weak, the rich oppress the poor.

The masses are exploited for the benefit of the few who are in power. The individual who finds no peace or rest seeks to forget himself in excitement. Immorality increases, crime flourishes, as corruption spreads throughout the social order. Class and national hatreds are aroused and fostered.

Wars break out while humanity grows desperate. There seems no possibility of stemming the tide of destructions. At this moment, Christ as the Avatar appears. Being the total manifestation of God in human form, he is the gauge by which man can measure what he is and what he may become. He trues the standard of human values by interpreting them in terms of the divinely human life. Di 269

Life after life, the principle of Illusion–*Maya*–beats man mercilessly. To save him from its clutches, the Compassionate One takes periodic human births. On New Year's Day 1951, prior to entering a hundred-day fast and deep seclusion during his historic *New Life*, characterized by total renunciation and annihilation, Meher Baba vowed, "My oath is so irrevocable that from today, January 1st, it's unlikely even one of you will remain with me as I expect something superhuman. I am in the soup with you. To be cheerful in all conditions is superhuman! So let's do our best to help each other."

Baba then offered a prayer to God with his disciples and companions in Jesus' name:

> Oh God Most High! Grant guidance to Baba and lift up his heart with Your love. O Christ, everlasting Truth, that he may live the New Life with faithfulness to the end! May the work of these 100 days seclusion be fulfilled to Baba's

entire satisfaction, and the desire of his heart come to pass with the aim of the New Life being achieved for all.

Grant his body be sound and healthy during this deep seclusion and give strength to him to bear whatever sufferings may befall him in the coming New Life! Grant, O Most Merciful God, these desires of Baba be fulfilled through the grace of Thy Son, Our Lord Jesus Christ! 2970

My salutations to all—past, present and future Perfect Masters, real Saints—known or unknown—Lovers of God and all beings in whom I reside. 4193

It is I who loves you. Remember this in the future. When anyone hurts you, it is I who hurts you; when anyone loves you it is I who loves you. If someone laughs at you, it is I who am laughing; when you love anyone it is I whom you love. I am in everything and in everyone. How can you realize my Infinite Presence if you shrink from me in those who hurt you and welcome me only in those who please you? Aw 8 (no.4): 9

Start learning to love God by beginning to love those you cannot love. In serving others you are truly serving yourself. The more you remember others with kindness and generosity, the less you remember yourself; and the less you remember yourself the more you forget yourself. And when you completely forget yourself, you find me as the source of all love.

Give up parroting in all aspects and start practicing what you truly feel to be true and just. Don't make a show of your faith and beliefs. You need not to give up your religion but give up clinging to the outer crust of mere ritual and ceremonial observance—Shariat.

To get to the fundamental core Truth underlying all religions, reach beyond religion. Through endless time, God's greatest gift is continuously given in silence. But when mankind becomes completely deaf to the thunder of His Silence, God incarnates as man to give a spiritual push to the world by his physical presence on earth. Then, the Unlimited assumes the limited.

He shakes Maya-drugged humanity to a consciousness of its true destiny, and gives a spiritual push to the world by his physical presence on earth. He uses his Universal body for his Universal work, to be discarded as a final sacrifice as soon as it has served its purpose.

God has come again and again in various forms, and spoken again and again in different languages the very same one Truth – but how many live up to it? Instead of making Truth the vital breath of his life, over and over again man compromises it into a mechanical religion as a handy staff to lean on in times of adversity, as a soothing balm for his conscience, or as a tradition blindly following the footsteps of the dead past. Man's inability to live God's words makes them a mockery.

How many Christians really follow Jesus by "turning the other cheek" or by "loving thy neighbor as thyself?" How many Muslims follow Muhammad's precept to "hold God above everything else?" Do Hindus "bear the Torch of Righteousness at all cost?" How many Buddhists live the "life of pure compassion" expounded by Buddha? Do Zoroastrians "think truly, speak truly and act truly?"

God's Truth cannot be ignored. Mankind's ignorance and weakness produces a tremendously adverse reaction, while the world finds itself in a cauldron of suffering—wars, hatreds, conflicting ideologies and Nature's rebellion in the form of floods, famines, earthquakes, and other "extreme weather events?" When the apex is finally reached, God manifests anew in human form.

He guides mankind to destruct its self-created evil so it may be re-established in Divine Truth. My silence and its immanent breaking is to save mankind from the monumental forces of ignorance, and to fulfill the Divine Plan of universal unity. Only the breaking of my silence will reveal to mankind the universal oneness of God and bring about the universal brotherhood of man. My silence had to be; and the breaking of my silence has to be.... 4448–51

This last, extended quote, from Meher Baba's final 1958 discourse *God Alone Is*, reflects the deepest universal truths of the Hindu Vedas, Buddhist discourses, Christianity's *Bible*, Muhammad's *Koran* and all known authentic spiritual traditions. Witness Jesus' words in St. John's Gospel 10:34:

> *It is written in your law, "You are Gods!"*
> *And the Scriptures do not lie."*

You cannot limit God by saying, "God is this or that." God is *God*. Illusion is God. God is not one or two, but just God. Nothing and everything are so merged so completely that you cannot say, "This is nothing," or "This is everything." Nothing, too, exists—but as total illusion. 1827

God is absolutely independent, infinitely independent and absolutely perfect within Himself. He is also beyond Perfect Independence, because when we call Him independent, then we have the contrary thought of *dependence*. When we say He is *without* attributes, we begin having thoughts of *attributes*. When we say He is *One*, we then have the thought of *two*. So, it's best to just say God is."

You must empty "is" of meaning,
while not taking "is not" as real.
— Zen Buddhism

One should call on His mercy from the depths of one's heart. If you go on praying for one hundred years without heart, you'll gain nothing; while a mere *second's* heartfelt prayer is instantly heard. So, with full inner devotion, just call on Him and you will experience the rays of His utter mercy. 3358

When we identify ourselves by saying "I'm an American;" or "I'm an Indian;" or "I'm a Russian," or a Christian, Jew, Muslim, Buddhist, Catholic or Protestant, we regress into the abyss of delusion where we've floundered for thousands of years. This is the realm of *separation, strife, war and destruction* and very opposite of the expressed teachings of all religions. Meher Baba sums up these ideas in the following words:

My cure for a worried world answers the questions, "*Whither and Whence*." The knowledge that all have the same beginning and end, with earthly life a happy interlude, will go a long way in making brotherhood of man a reality, and this in turn will strike at the root of narrow exploitation. I bless you all to realization this, the true aim of life." 1789

Over the years, Meher Baba's life was an open secret. He travelled extensively to the West, for which he claimed he especially came in this advent. On February 10, 1954, in an isolated part of north India, he finally and publicly revealed he was the Avatar of this Age.

He revealed that God, achieving manhood, descended as Himself, the Ancient One. He who had been each of the past Christ Avatars in man's endless history came again and again to bear full responsibility for the entire creation. Two years later, in July 1956, he repeated his truly unique Avataric claim in New York City, on NBC TV 4008

Writing this book for over a period of ten years, I was merely the pen in his hand. Perhaps not strangely, but clearly sensing my lowest worldly desires and previously acting them out on leaving the priesthood, I was surprised and grateful that they both virtually ceased when I began this writing. Then I came across this passage , which made it so clear:

> When one is absorbed in a subject concerning me directly, I can connect him with me by merely his thoughts on me. An opportunity is created to work spiritually—to dislodge the seats of low desires in the mental body of the person, making them impotent without being put into action by the physical body. This one is also being given the chance to serve me, whether he knows it or not—an opportunity he'll not get again in this lifetime. 1645

Still, we must be aware that even an exalted biography of God in Human Form, providing food for mind and heart in revealing the deepest spiritual secrets never before expressed as *Infinite Truth*, is only a book. And so it is only that—a book. As the Zen koan reminds us: pointing at the moon is not becoming the moon.

A week before his passing, Meher Baba instructed his nightwatchman, disciple and new St. John, Bhau Kalchuri, to write his biography, adding, "Make it interesting!" I hope, though a generation removed from that mandate, I too have made his life most interesting for you, dear reader. As Baba said, "Do your best and don't worry. Be happy, and I'll see to the rest."

Chapter Fourteen
The Prem Love Ashram Blooms

When Baba established Prem Ashram in 1927, he explained to the mandali:

> The Avatar can do all a Sadguru does. He has and prepares a circle as a Sadguru does, but he does one special thing also. The Avatar can make a person who is not in the circle or even "turned" to God [meaning on the inner planes], a God-Realized salik with special duty.
>
> If I get the whim, I may make a few selected boys of the ashram God-Realized at once, and then again bring them back for special duty. But for that the time—and also the whim. Krishna was the Avatar and he realized and brought down seventeen persons who were outside his circle; these seventeen were extra God-Realized *saliks*.
>
> Let me see who now gets the apple! . . .
>
> My wish at this time is advancing boys and turning them into saliks. I'm concerned mostly with them, and that's why all this trouble [the separate ashram school]. You'll see how many of these boys will be saints! The time is very near. And after this work is finished, I will manifest. But the whim from them must come, and it is difficult for it to come.
>
> But once it does, everything will be automatically done. I will show God to some and I will make some God!

> The boys' luck is so good that they have come near me.... I tell you, some will see me as I really am. Urge them to go on loving me more and more and more to be worthy of this. 878-79

Many years later he explained what he had meant about thinking of him and nothing else: "Like when we breathe, we pay no attention to it. It's our automatic constant companion, as in sound sleep. We put on pajamas and go to sleep without paying attention to the clothes, and in the morning take off the pajamas and put on our daytime clothes without attention except for a moment. So I am always with you. So start paying attention." 3587

In mid-December of 1927, Baba discussed advanced souls in other parts of the world. He revealed that a sixth-plane saint had just given up his body in Africa, and in that moment Baba had received a shock. There also was an advanced soul between the fifth and sixth planes in Baghdad who acknowledged that he was Meher Baba's disciple.

"There are three God-Realized persons in Persia [Iran] and one in Egypt. There's a very advanced soul stationed between the fourth and fifth planes in London—a telegraph-receiver who does as ordered, though I as his Master am unknown to him. In America, an even further advanced one knows I am his Master." 871-72

Meanwhile, Baba had been fasting for a year in semi-seclusion on Meherabad Hill in the underground crypt that would eventually become his tomb. He asked the women to send a cup of coffee up the hill twice each day in a small thermos bottle with a local boy named Lahu, hired to do the work. But instead of the full cups, Baba was only getting half a cup of coffee each time. Many years later he concluded the amusing story:

> When my year's seclusion was over, I went down the Hill to the women's quarters and asked why against my or-

der they were sending only a half cup of coffee instead of a full cup?

They said they sent up a full cup twice a day! Then I sent for little Lahu, embraced him [and] asked him to tell the truth without hiding anything. He confessed he was drinking half on his way up the Hill, giving me the other half. So for a year, I was actually taking only a half cup of coffee twice daily, and that, too, as the mischievous boy's *prasad*! [gift]" 3632-33

On December 26, 1927, Baba explained the deep significance of the number seven:

"The Divine Seven"

As I explained, there are an infinite number of worlds which have cooled down, and for each such world to cool down takes cycles upon cycles. Just try to imagine how long that is! But when a man attains Realization, ascending to the seventh plane, he feels only a second has passed; that is, no time has actually passed during the numberless changes of forms and deaths and births—8,400,000 times.

Now I know according to you that accounts for billions of years, and there's no limit to accounting. But my experience is this: *nothing has happened and there is no time spent*. There are seven worlds [planets in evolution], seven skies, seven suns, seven moons, seven planes and seven heavens [on the path of involution].

Sanskaric impressions are also of seven colors. Why seven? Because in the very beginning, when Primal Energy [Pran] clashed with Matter [Akash], it created seven divisions. Energy and Matter's explosive friction created seven dazzling colors. So, each individual is a total universe unto himself.

In the head are seven openings: two ears, two eyes, two nostrils and one mouth. In the body there are seven parts: two arms, two legs, one trunk and two openings [for excretion—front and back]. But all this explaining of the universe and creation relates only to the *hair* and has nothing to do with the head. So try to get hold of the head, because out of it comes everything. Let's say a barber shaves your head.

And here the barber is Mahapralaya! When that occurs, all the hairs—universes—on God's head are shaved off. It is said the universes pour out of the Godhead; they are like God's hair. Let your head symbolize God, and your hair the universes. 874–75

A year later, in January 1930, Baba continued his explanation of the number seven:

Evolution in creation has seven stages. There are seven [inner spiritual] planes and seven types of desires. However significant the number seven is, all these sevens should be eradicated once and for all—seven types of sanskaras, seven types of colors, seven types of flights of imagination and seven types of sounds.

The reason all these have seven variations is in the beginning of creation—with the start of the original whim in the Beyond, Beyond state of God—there was a clash between Matter [Akash] and Energy [Pran], and Energy's powers were then divided into seven forces. The original sound coming out of the Creation, or *Om* Point, also turns into seven sounds.

This higher music of the mental and subtle planes is indescribably sweet. Even listening to it for twenty-four hours without break, you'd never tire of it. It's so enrapturing one drowns in its melody. But remember, in the mental and subtle sphere, the sweetness of this music's sounds is but mere shadow of the Original Sound. The gross world shadow of this melody is again divided into seven parts.

Only expert singers can express these tones and octaves. Sound is created by contact between two things. When you speak, your voice passes through seven veils; but you don't notice this because the sound comes so quickly. Your physique—a by-product of your sanskaras—determines whether your voice is sweet or harsh. Everything is made up of seven—seven sub-divisions of the first subtle plane [the astral], seven stages of evolution, seven planes and seven heavens in involution. Can you grasp it? 1130–31

Meanwhile, on January 1, 1929, the twelfth day of Baba's confinement, Prem Ashram boys began breaking into tears throughout the day, whether in school, playing or having meals. They themselves had no idea why they were crying. Even the angels must have envied these children.

Matters climaxed that evening with every boy giving vent to overwhelming feelings of love. They were trying to lighten the burden of divine longing felt in their young hearts. They wept as if all their dear ones had been reported dead. For over an hour that evening this phenomenon held the mandali spellbound.

The boys' cries could be heard a quarter of a mile from the ashram. Those in charge tried but were unable to quiet them. All were crying out, "Baba, Baba, Baba!" When they were brought into Baba's close proximity and presence, suddenly all magically fell silent. LH 25

Late sixteenth century Persian ink drawing, *Man with ram*, by Riza, depicting an Iranian farmer with a striking resemblance to Meher Baba, and whose expression in reaching out toward his pet ram suggests he is kind and humane. But we can imagine the ram is about to be slaughtered, as a knife is concealed behind the farmer's back. It is a moment of tenderness and tension – illustrating the above narrative of Meher Baba's dagger: "My friends I kill and it is my highest mercy on them."

A Great War

At 8:00 AM on January 6, twenty soldiers came for Baba's darshan. When they left, Baba disclosed to the boys, "This is a sign of the great march to take place in the near future." No one had any idea of what he meant. Then Baba revealed that at about 2:00 AM, the Spiritual Masters had held a secret conference in his underground crypt.

It was decided that another massive world war would soon begin. The military's unexpected arrival that morning sealed its inevitability. Baba concluded, "A great war will take place, and when it is raging furiously, I will come forward and manifest as the Avatar!" 881

The boys' love grew over that winter and spring. On May 1, Baba told them, "Union with God is the ultimate end where lover, Beloved and love all become one." He quoted a Persian couplet:

> *The inmost core of my heart is so filled*
> *with thoughts of my Beloved*
> *that my own name and existence are obliterated*
> *in remembering Him.*

He urged them, "Create such love that you will actually *see* your Master. The Beloved can be loved even from a long distance. There's no question of time, distance or nearness; only love, awakened by constantly thinking of the Master." He was teaching them laser-like focus on his own Being—the key to utter transformation. 925

The boys were so focused on Baba that they experienced moments of divine madness. Not content with his companionship, they now also wanted his personal things. They stole his handkerchiefs, bed sheets, sandals—anything he used, so he gave them his handkerchiefs, cups and photos. At eleven o'clock at night some of the boys would run to Baba's room, loudly calling for him to come out. The mandali were upset at them for interrupting the Master's rest and spiritual work. But Baba took the disturbances lightly and came out, lovingly meeting with them for a while. Then he told them, "From now on, don't come before 2:00 AM. After that, it's ok."

These boys were following a path Baba had carefully chalked out for them and wanted them to follow even more than they did. He also began focusing attention on a boy named Bhiwa, calling him near, patting him with affection and kissing him sweetly and chastely.

Prem ashram students with Meher Baba and Staff, Meherabad, 1927

One day, Baba gathered all the boys, asking if they had problems meditating at night or in the early morning. Many replied no, but Bhiwa lowered his eyes as they filled with tears. When questioned, he answered, "While meditating, I don't see your physical form. Too many other thoughts assail me." Baba consoled him, explaining about the mind:

> The mind is such a terrible thing; it can be called a curse! Its business is to think and think and think—more so when we don't wish to think of a particular person or thing. For instance, when you sit down to meditate or concentrate on the Guru or Beloved God, other worldly thoughts of a thousand and one kinds which ordinarily you'd never even dreamed of, are sure to push into your mind. Thoughts are always creeping in with continuous onslaughts. . . .
>
> This isn't a sin, a defect or even the aspirant's mistake. Thoughts will come as long as that terrible mind is there. You have to persist in strenuously driving them away and trying to think only of Beloved God. He shouldn't give up meditation to be disturbed and disappointed by these attacks.
>
> Don't you sit down for hours till morning just to *meditate* on me while others are sound asleep? That's three-quarters of the work done right there! Now, only quarter is left; thinking of only *one* thing. Just try. If you're successful, all right; if not, don't worry over it, as three quarters of the work is done just by your waking and trying to sit. Don't worry or cry if you can't meditate due to disturbing thoughts. Getting up from your sweet sound sleep at midnight to meditate is half the work done already.
>
> Persevere and persist in your efforts. . . . Don't throw away the sitar because it's hard to tune. Try to adjust and tune each string persistently, firmly intending to make the

instrument *work*. Similarly, try to catch outside thoughts and throw them out by the ear.

Suppose there are countless mosquitoes buzzing around and some start biting you at night. What do you do to get rid of their annoyance? Do you just sit there and cry? No! You immediately get under a mosquito net. You resort to a real remedy and eventually it has the desired effect. Even though mosquitoes come in hordes, you don't feel disturbed, for almost all of them will be outside the net. Oh . . . a couple might get inside the net. Likewise, deal with these thoughts.

Like mosquitoes, they're sure to come to annoy you, but you've put up a curtain of thoughts "about me," having my divine image present before your mind's eye. Meditate on me so all other thoughts automatically stop pestering your mind. Let the mosquito net of meditation on me save you from being bitten by your false thoughts. Bring my image to your mind's eye by just thinking of me, playing games with you or listening to records, etc. No sooner you get this scene, don't lose it. Hold it firmly. Concentrate on it with all your heart's affection.

See my various activities—going here and there, discoursing, kissing and embracing the boys, reclining on my seat, on my activities will lead to concentrating on my form. Then, you can sit for *hours*, concentrating on it.
960-61

Baba then demonstrated three sitting postures, revealing, "When I was Jesus, I showed these methods to a thief." Nothing more was said of Jesus or the thief, but his instructions to Bhiwa are an excellent way to focus and develop an abiding love for God.
962

Pure Gold from Mixed Alloys

On New Years Day 1928, a sixteen-year-old Iranian student, Espandiar Vesali, became unconscious of the gross world and began experiencing subtle-plane consciousness, seeing "unimaginable light, hearing wonderful sounds, smelling indescribably sweet fragrances and other phenomena, such as feeling he was floating in space." RD 528-29

When asked to describe what had happened, he replied, "Baba broke my skull, and light began pouring from it." Espandiar asked Baba to exempt him from studies, as he just couldn't stop thinking of Baba or put his mind on his lessons.

"Before my eye is only *Baba*; in my dreams I see only *Baba*. Except for you I have no other interest in life. I want to go toward God—toward knowing God." Baba replied, "Okay, I'll grant it if you listen and obey me." He urged Espandiar to try concentrating on studies while beginning to observe silence. Then, in his astral form Baba began coming to Espandiar at night through the walls, instructing him on how to meditate.

Prem Ashram boy in meditation

The next day, Abdulla Rokneldin Pakrawan, a seventeen-year-old Muslim youth, arrived at Meherabad. He had seen an advertisement in his local newspaper for Meher Ashram, so he came to further his education. Having been raised a strict orthodox Muslim, only Islam meant anything to him. He wasn't the least bit interested in spirituality or gurus.

But shortly after entering Babajan High School, Abdulla's orthodox mentality became deeply transformed. One day the boys were seated on the platform outside his cabin. Baba was seated on the inside, discoursing through the window to the boys and to the mandali behind them. He disclosed, "To those worthy I shall attract to the mistress of love and offer them the elixir of life. Children, Truth alone is real—all else is worthless. Try to be diligent and *I shall make pure gold from your mixed alloys.*" At these last words, "*pure gold from your mixed alloys,*" Abdulla saw an extraordinary flash of light at Baba's window. Overpowered, he fell unconscious and had to be carried to the ashram hospital.

Baba gazed compassionately upon him, and though the weather that day was cold, Baba's chest was covered with perspiration and his long golden-brown hair spiked high, raised like a lion's mane as he worked inwardly to raise Abdulla' consciousness to the sight of God—the sixth plane of the mental world. Abdulla's eyes looked vacant. Having lost normal consciousness, he was seeing God everywhere! HM 38

On the third day of Abdulla's unconscious state, fellow-student Espandiar came to visit him. "Abdulla . . . do you recognize me?" Becoming semiconscious, the boy opened his eyes slightly and replied softly, "Yes . . ." "Who am I?" Espandiar asked.

"You are *Baba.*" A matchbox was lying nearby. Espandiar picked out a match and held it up. "Do you see this? What is it?" "It's *Baba,*" Abdulla answered. Whatever Abdulla was asked, he would answer with only one word: "*Baba.*"

Abdulla was seeing Baba everywhere. He was in this elevated state for four days. As he slowly regained some consciousness of his surroundings on the fifth day, he wept bitterly and uncontrollably. The pain filling his tears was indescribable compared to any suffering known in the world.

From his sixth plane state of consciousness he was coming back down into the gross world of illusion after blissfully seeing

God everywhere. Regaining gross consciousness, he was inconsolable. Baba later revealed that Abdulla had to return to normal gross consciousness.

As Baba brought him back down, Abdulla's eyes emanated a strange light. Inwardly experiencing Baba in his formless state, he now also saw him in his physical state. But the boy was so weak that the Master had him carried to his own underground crypt-cabin, where he dressed him in a new white robe, renaming him Chhota (Little) Baba. 883–84

Abdulla's inner experience of Baba's love was unique among all the Prem Ashram boys. One afternoon, Baba called a few of the mandali into his crypt with Abdulla. The following exchange occurred, as the Master questioned the boy about his experience of the sixth plane.

"Have you a mind?" asked Baba. "No . . . gone," said Abdulla. "Temporarily?" "Forever." "Any desires?" "None whatsoever." "Do you see me everywhere?" "Yes, even in the smallest particle." "Do you feel any pleasure or pain in the body?" "No, no sense of the body at all. I don't care if it remains or goes. It makes no difference to me. The sight is there while sleeping, awake—in all states—always." "So you see me always?" "Always! Without a second's break."

"How long will you see me?" "Forever." "Are you happy?" "Oh, yes, perfectly in unbounded bliss." "How long would you enjoy this blissful state of *anand*?" "As long as *You are*—forever. If You're everywhere and always, I too am everywhere and always with You; all twenty-four hours, I see you and nothing else." "You can't see anything else?" "What else is there to see but You?" "If left alone, where would you go?" "Where I am to go? Wherever I go, I am everywhere with *You*." "Do you feel anything walking here and there, coming or going from your room to here?" "Nothing whatsoever. No feeling—it's all automatic."

One of the men asked, "How can he read, reply, and go to the toilet without a mind?" Baba replied:

> It is *I* in him doing all this. His mind is completely gone. He has no mind, hence no desires. He still has a body, but no consciousness of it. He'd never speak without being asked. As far as his body goes, he wouldn't care if he went twenty-four hours without sleep. Even I'd be tired to sit like that, but he wouldn't, for he has no consciousness of his body nor does he want to have it. It wouldn't matter to him if thousands sat in his presence, or if he were kept in an empty room. He's absolutely indifferent. So perfect, so special is his case. None of the boys will be like him. He'll be a great help to me *if* he remains alive. 894

Baba was indicating that the boy's body was in danger of dropping over the next two months. When the mandali asked why he didn't protect him, Baba explained, "After giving the spiritual push, for certain reasons I can't interfere. But all outward measures can and are being taken to safeguard his body." Baba then moved Abdulla to an adjoining portion of the underground crypt sitting alone behind a curtain.

Turning to the mandali, Baba continued, "He has no feeling whatsoever of these movements from here to there or in the next room. This is *fana*—spiritual annihilation. In short, he's not the body; he's not the mind. He sees the Soul of souls." 893

The following is Abdulla Pakrawan's own account, given decades later, of what happened when the Master raised him to the sixth plane of consciousness:

> One day at the end of a discourse, Baba looked deeply into the face of each child, one by one. . . . I hadn't the strength to look into Baba's radiant countenance and low-

ered my eyes. He glanced at me, addressing me: "Try and be diligent, *for I'll make pure gold from your mixed alloy.*"

The profound effect this remark had upon me put me in a most bewildered state over that night and the entire next day. While playing field hockey, my mates were puzzled, noticing my manner of standing, running and the color of my face changing.

After just a few morsels at lunch, I felt a sudden change of extraordinary *heat* overtaking me. Everything began getting dark around me as things began vanishing. Suddenly, beyond my own volition, a weeping welled from the depths of my very being, and I began to wail. Within moments, I lost all consciousness of the people surrounding me and became insensible. In a short while, I found myself conscious again, repeating, "*I am far, far, far. Where is He? And where am I?*"

As time passed and weeks ended, the love for my Beloved exalted Master became more apparent, and the fire became hotter and more burning. Finally, even while doing normal things like eating and bathing, I'd be drowned in thoughts of Baba. There wasn't a moment I could forget him. Weeks passed, while I was being consumed in his intoxicating love.

Then by December 1927, desire for food left me. I'd abandoned care of my body and clothes, totally oblivious to my surroundings, lost in meditation and longing to behold only the beauty of my Baba. His name was my meditation, my remembrance of God. One night as usual, the children and mandali had gathered around Baba listening to him dictate a discourse. I found myself changed.

I began to see all around a radiant glow which betrayed the effulgence of the sun, quivering and flowing. I called out the Beloved's name and instantly lost consciousness. I was unconscious for five hours and taken to Baba. On regaining consciousness, he consoled me and asked me to sleep.

After that experience, whenever in Baba's presence I would kiss his feet, but no matter how much I would kiss and press my head on his feet, it could not soothe my burning heart nor help the turmoil which had so overtaken it. I was immersed only in the thought of the Beloved; without meditating, my soul was enjoying peace and bliss, as my eyes were fixed on his pure and noble face.

Shortly after this experience, the focus of my concentration was fully established in constant remembrance; so immersed in this natural meditation, that during this period I didn't care about food or whether I sat in the sun or rain. Many days were spent constantly weeping.

It was January 1928, when my inner state changed drastically. Sitting close to my Beloved Master, watching the sunset, suddenly I began to wail and scream. My external eyes closed and my inner eye opened. I saw my heart, chest, my limbs, veins, skin and bones were overwhelmed and ruled by a *Being* with such effulgence and radiance that it brightened the most hidden corners of my heart. Awestruck by the sight of that *Radiant Being*, I forgot the world and all that was in it. . . .

I spent five days intoxicated in bliss, while being totally unaware of the apparent world and people around me. During this time, the continuity of this vision remained unbroken, and I saw nothing but the glorious sight of His radiant and blessed being. I was in the height of bliss and joy, just in this sight of Him. Within my heart and soul these five days I enjoyed this unique vision of my exalted Beloved Master, Meher Baba in a blissful vision of *Reality*.

I understood the world, its belongings and luxuries are like a truly binding dream illusion. I realized holding a true Perfect Master causes eternal freedom and satisfaction. I was told Baba mentioned to his close disciples I had progressed to the sixth plane and called *Chhota Baba*, little Baba. The consequences of that state are so measurelessly mysterious if the gist of that joyous and blissful state of love were to be written, the pen would break and the paper tear in utter awe. 895–98; Rd 544

Parents Break Their Word and the Master's Heart

Drafting the Prem Ashram rules, Baba had made clear stipulations that with free room and board, clothes and books, etc., he'd put as many boys as possible in the spiritual line, giving them the benefit of his close contact to mold their morals and character in an ideal way.

But a very strict condition for admittance was that they must remain in the school until the completion of the course, whether it took two years or seven, and the option of going home during family emergencies was strictly at Baba's discretion; otherwise his very purpose would be defeated, destroying the purity of the boys' hearts.

Indiscriminate leave ran the risk of their becoming polluted and pulled back down into the company of worldly people, whether relations or friends. But once they'd passed through the long period of disciplines and restrictions in close contact with the Master, their character would become sufficiently molded on ideal spiritual lines.

Afterward they'd remain unaffected, even in the thick of worldly affairs. But that critical period *had* to be fulfilled before they returned immune to the world. The sole aim of the institution was spiritual training. Baba expressed the risk in this way:

> Allowing the boys to go home and mix with worldly people in the middle of their training, there's every chance the effect of the training will be wiped out clean . . . though the education imparted to them will advance India's political salvation.
>
> It will give spiritual advancement and material benefit to the country. Completing the course, these boys will no longer have prejudice against any religion, like today resulting in so much strife and slaughter [between Hindus and Muslims] all over the country. RD 409–11

During this period, Baba was fond of quoting a couplet from the Sufi Master Al-Hallaj. He later wrote the couplet out for the dedication page of a book written by his closest childhood friend- Bailey (Bairam Jamshed Irani):

> *I am He whom I love, and He whom I love is I. We are*
> *two spirits dwelling in one body.*
> *If thou seest me, thou seest Him. And if thou seest Him,*
> *thou seest us both!*

Other boys besides Chhota Baba experienced similar transports of divine love and expanded consciousness in lesser degrees. One of these was fourteen-year-old Sayed Ali Haji Muhammad, nicknamed Agha Ali. His father brought him to the school. The boy was deeply drawn to Baba from the start and under benign care began having glimpses of Baba's divinity. As one of the most ardent Ashram students Ali's spiritual nature was most remarkable, and his love extraordinary and inspiring.

But Ali's father had no spiritual understanding and in time succumbed to false rumors about the school, fearing that the boys had lost their mental balance and were also being converted to Zoroastrianism. No doubt the ashram's founder was a true Zoroastrian, but no less a perfect Muslim, Hindu, Sikh, Buddhist, Christian or Jew.

In short, Meher Baba belonged to every religion and he taught divinity in any form, or through any medium. He was not only "religion personified," but was also the embodiment of the deepest mystical union with God ever known to man—the alpha and omega of Creation.

Although at various times during his life Baba set up different headquarters and ashrams, he said that his *real* ashram was within every individual heart as well as in all of Illusion. Everyone and everything existing finds refuge in the heart of Baba, because, as Baba said, "It is a fact. I am the Lord of the Universe." 4168

Another chief complaint was that the boys were being detained against their will to extract ransom from their parents, that the food was meager and poor, and that they were being forced to bow their heads down to the feet of a Zoroastrian Master.

These complaints are fully documented in the written account. But there were more sinister accusations, un-delineated in historical records and simply noted in *Ramjoo's Diary*: "Besides these complaints were other very serious, but groundless accusations." RJ 480

The latter were clearly spelled out by Baba's youngest brother Adi Jr., who explained that some of these boys came from Muslim Mogul families, and in some Mogul sectors of India it was common for married men to express a special fondness for young boys.

Seeing the profound influence Baba had on Ali and others, some of these fathers projected wildly imagined scenarios onto him, suspecting something deeply sinister. They were judging the

Master in terms of their own old Mogul customs, especially in regards to the profound influence Baba had on Agha Ali.

Agha Ali's father feared he'd lose his son to this strange, unpredictable Master, who some of his friends had assured him was a black magician. For them to see beneath appearances to the real motives and spiritual reality their sons were experiencing was next to impossible. And so a few of the boys' fathers began appearing unannounced at the school, breaking their sworn signed agreements and abruptly pulling their sons out and forcing them to return home.

One is reminded of how Jesus was condemned for undesirable motives in associating with prostitutes and alcoholics, revealing the limited minds of those so falsely judging him. So it was no surprise that Ali was soon taken away from Prem Ashram, despite his father's signed pledge not to remove him from school before the promised time.

The train from Ahmednagar carrying Ali and his father passed along the railway tracks separating Lower and Upper Meherabad at the six-mile mark. Here it began gaining speed, and approaching the object of his love, Ali found it impossible to restrain the cries of his broken heart.

He leaned out the train window and gave free and wild vent to his sobs, drowned out by the noise of the fast-moving train. In that moment, confined in his crypt far up the hill, the Master granted Ali a glorious love-vision of himself which helped to give the boy strength for the desperate weeks to come. RD 443

But the magic of divine love is more potent than a father's ignorance and fear, and despite being kept under strict twenty-four-hour guard, Ali soon escaped. Undergoing severe hardships, he returned to his beloved Master. But it took only a few hours for his father to reappear, and once more Ali was taken back and made prisoner in his own home.

With Ali taken again, Baba cried that night—not for his own loss, but for that of the world. He lashed out with ringing words, "These Moguls are word-breakers and not to be trusted! As the Holy Koran states, Believers are those who keep their covenants." RD 510

Ali's love was the prototype for the outbursts of divine love to take place at the time of Meher Baba's Universal Manifestation. It seemed that the entire work of raising divine love in these chosen boys would now have to begin again for the sake of future humanity and the world.

Baba became deeply depressed, and he stunned the men by deciding to close the school and all other operations at Meherabad. Orders were given to start dismantling the buildings at once. But then two evenings later, as Baba approached the Dhuni fire-pit at Lower Meherabad, a blinding light suddenly flashed and those seeing it were dazzled. Baba left but later returned to sit very still by the fire for fifteen minutes. Then he cryptically spelled out on his board, "The Dhuni has passed word we should all continue our routine and go on with the school work as before." 913

True Love is No Game for the Fainthearted

Ali was wrenched away and forced back home by his father four times. It broke Baba's heart and caused him to shed tears. But in the end, the father gave in and finally convinced Baba's influence was not only potent, but truly beneficent. Ali was then sent back to complete his two-year stay at Meher Ashram.

Ali was later one of the few disciples Baba took with him on his first Western trip to Europe, New York and Boston in 1931. He was remembered fifty years later by Lettice Stokes, at whose Greenwich Village, New York home he had stayed with Baba. She said that the teenaged Ali had a dynamic spirit that was expressed in spontaneous humor and playful mischief, yet with a dignity and poise that made him a joy to be with. He was utterly devoted to his Master.

Ahmed Muhammad was a ten-year-old whose love also dramatically manifested, such that he too was removed from the school by his father around the same time as Ali and for the same wrong reasons. His family tried their best to reconcile him to the separation, but his young heart would have none of it.

After four months, Ahmed escaped and started out on foot without a blanket, food or money to make the long journey back to Meherabad. Selling three silver buttons from his shirt, he bought a train ticket to quickly take him out of his family's range.

Fearing they might come after him, he tramped cross-country in scorching Indian sun by day and hid during bitter cold nights by sleeping in the trees. After a fitful sleep with no covering or protection, he'd resume his journey, hungry in the pre-dawn cold.

As the bedraggled boy passed through a small village, an innkeeper took pity on him, giving him some bread and offering to secure transport for him in one of the passing buses. But afraid of running into someone looking for him, Ahmed continued on foot, spending his last *anna* on a meager midday snack. A European motorist gave him a lift to Poona.

The next morning, Ahmed found himself in the neighborhood of Hazrat Babajan and stopped to pay his respects and bow down to her, his Master's Master. She appeared to be sleeping, her head covered with her shawl. He tiptoed quietly to within a few feet and unobtrusively bowed his head down in deep reverence.

Instantly, Babajan's snow-white head emerged from its covering. Peering directly at Ahmed, she gave him a look of melting love, sending a thrill of delight through his being. Feeling totally recharged, he continued the eighty more miles he had yet to go.

At noon, an old man offered him bread and chutney, the first real food he'd had in two days. On the old man's advice, Ahmed took shelter in the village mosque that night. But it was so cold he could barely sleep. The next day, eating berries and leaves growing by the roadside, he attempted the sixteen remaining miles dizzy with fatigue and hunger.

Only by sheer willpower could he walk six more miles before reaching a railway station and having to rest. But the fire of hunger was so raging that he was driven to beg for food. A kind Muslim offered to buy him rice and curry, but he feared the curry might contain meat which he felt Baba didn't want him to eat.

He declined and just asked for some bread and tea. With his hunger appeased, he fell asleep on a railway bench until an officious policeman prodded him with his nightstick and drove him from the station platform. He then sought refuge under a staircase and was comforted by his Master's presence in a dream. The following morning he walked the entire day. At yet another railway station an older boy shared with him an unsolicited meal.

> Ahmed's story is freely adapted from Jean Adriel's book, *Avatar*. She met many of these boys later as grown men, still deeply dedicated to the Master's service. It would be natural to think such spiritual upheaval as Baba caused in these young lives might have had disastrous effects. However, from what she observed it was not at all the case: "I must say I've never met men more normal or balanced—mentally, emotionally and spiritually."

He set out at daybreak on the sixth day of his journey, again feeding on plants and berries along roadside fields. He begged one final time—not for food, but for flowers to be given as an offering to his Beloved. This was Baba's neighborhood, and as he was well known in these parts, a local gardener gave the boy an armful of red roses.

Sitting by the road, he soon forgot the weariness and hunger of his two-hundred-mile journey as he fashioned the roses into a crown for the King of his heart. Haggard and hollow-eyed, he climbed Meherabad Hill and with joy placed the crown on his Master's head. And so another saga of a child's love for the Ancient One was completed.

In the West we know little of such high states of consciousness and divine love and can easily dismiss them as fixations. But even granting this, what have we explained? What do we really know of the tremendous, almost super-human motivation that inspires a child to undergo such severe hardships and suffering for the sake of divine love?

Christian Leik, a Christian who will soon enter the narrative, also lived at Meherabad in these days and wrote of this phase of Baba's work:

> The Master's love knows no bounds. One must see him among his Ashram boys to understand the tie of affinity between Baba and his pupils. How touching it is to watch these urchins crowding around him when he's in their dormitory. They rush from their beds to embrace him, placing their tiny arms around his waist, while Baba, playing with them and teasing them gently, fills their hearts with such childish glee. Av 109–13; 1002

Many years passed before Abdul—Chota Baba—recorded his own story of what his Beloved had done for him:

> Although people constantly try to collect worldly belongings with the only purpose of having all the things that the world can offer, considering them the cause of happiness, I understood that collecting them, holding and keeping them is the real cause of misery and depression.
>
> Beholding the countenance of the Beloved with the inner eye and even with the external eyes [or in photos]—creates an immense joy and increases happiness. Then I saw that Blessed Being in myself, in others and all around me, continuously and without break. It is very rare great

fortune for a Perfect Master with his infinite grace, mercy and power to raise one to such heights.

In conclusion, I got a precious result from my life with Meher Baba during those years in the ashram. Even though I departed from him and lost the inner consciousness of what I was allowed to experience by Baba on the path, I was graced with character for life in the world.

I undertook a worldly life in trade, in business, in community with my neighbors, friends and dealings. Through it all, I've chosen the path of righteousness, truthfulness, sincerity, and have not a liking for material and worldly things as others do.

Though I could be wealthy and have land and houses in Iran, today I live so simply, renting a house without an inch of land or property. Whatever I have is spent to educate my children and for the care of others. I worked for Iran's Red Cross for twenty-seven years without pay serving humanity and offering the best aid that can be given to the needy in the times of disaster. The result I have is due to the life and love Meher Baba gave me. Printed *Lord Meher,* 1045

Baba also visited the Dastur Parsi High School in Nasik at around this time. But the cleric running it didn't appreciate his suggestions of how to give the boys both spiritual and religious instruction. He became indignant, insisting he gave "religious instruction according to the Zoroastrian custom." Baba criticized his attitude, saying to the mandali: "Intellectual training isn't enough. I know these priests' instructions. I attended a Catholic school. Priests are truly hardheaded with too much stress everywhere on religion. It's the root of all strife—internal and external and the cause of all wars in the world!" 4

On September 30, 1928, Baba said, "Last night was terrible throughout. I had a 105 degree fever. My limbs have gone limp.

My back is sore and aching, so aching. I had not even a second's rest. Had you been in my place, you'd have dropped your body."

Then quickly changing the subject, he turned to the youngest boy in the ashram, eight-year-old Pundit Yeshwant Mehendarge. "Now, tell me what you want; a car, toys, God, freedom, paradise—anything you like. Now's the time to ask, for today *I'll give it to you!*" Pundit replied, "Oh, Baba, I want your sufferings to stop. I want you to get completely well." 971

Such was this child's profound love for the Master. Baba explained further to his men about the Prem Ashram students:

> Throughout his life, Meher Baba's game was clearly one of construction and deconstruction. He had lit a fuse in the hearts of these young men for the tsunamic wave of divine love he said would appear for the sake of the entire world at the breaking of his Silence and his Universal Manifestation. 2069

I have a thousand and one thoughts about these boys. At this moment they are merged in me, and I must look after their health. They keep me awake all night remembering me. But this time, I'll give them the push. Have no doubt about it. But what I fear is parental interference.

If they put forth obstacles, the children will be neither here nor there. This path is no laughing matter – no joke. Some of the boys are quite good, but no immediate push can be given to them all at once, as they're only children. 976

And, they being children, Baba told the boys wonderful stories about the spiritual path:

> Once in the jungle, a tigress died after giving birth to her cub. The cub remained hungry for many days without food or water. Finally, a shepherd found and took pity on it. He reared it among his sheep, and the cub grew up thinking it was a sheep, not knowing he was really a tiger.

One day, a grown-up tiger saw the cub playing among the sheep flock, and was astounded. He approached the cub, doing his utmost to persuade it that it was really a tiger and not a sheep. But the young tiger just couldn't believe him. So the tiger took him to a pool of water and made the cub look at his own reflection there. The young cub was astonished, and at last was convinced of his true identity. He forgot the notion of being a lamb, and passed the rest of his days among glorious tigers.

The sheep flock represents . . . worldly people, profoundly ignorant of Truth. The tiger cub is an ignorant man. The *grown* tiger is the Perfect Master. The pool of water symbolizes the spiritual path; and recognizing the reflection is attaining God-Realization.

Though the cub was a tiger, out of ignorance, it took itself to be a sheep, as long as the grown up tiger hadn't show the cub its reflection in the pool of water. This false misconception continued. In the same way, man is potentially God. But being ignorant of his Real Self thinks himself to be only a man/tiger and passes through cycles of births and deaths in ignorance until the Master forces him to see his own true image. 998-99

Uninvited Visitors

In April 1928 Baba again entered seclusion in his underground crypt at Upper Meherabad, ordering that no one was to be sent up the hill. But one day, three groups of visitors came for darshan.

The first was a group of Parsis from Bombay. Having heard of the "Irani Saint," they decided to visit. A few were sincere, but the rest were mere sightseers. A Hindu couple also came. When all were told Baba was in seclusion and seeing no one, the Parsi sightseers laughed cynically and left.

The sincere ones stayed, but were disappointed when Baba didn't come down the hill. They sat with Chanji and listened to his Baba stories until they left at 4:00 PM. The Hindu couple sat alone and meditated until nine that night, in vain hopes of having Baba's darshan. Finally, believing it was God's will they not see him, they left with heavy hearts.

Then a wandering ascetic appeared, announcing forcefully that he'd have Baba's darshan before he would leave. He went to the well and washed himself in preparation for meeting with the great guru. Afterwards he sat under the neem tree near the Dhuni, silently repeating God's name.

It was a Meherabad custom to always offer a meal to travelers and mendicants coming from long distances. But the man insisted, "Without the Guru's darshan, no food or water!" That night he refused to sleep inside with the men, even after much persuasion. The next morning, the mandali found him fast asleep on their porch, concluding he'd finally given up his foolish behavior. But when the fakir awoke, he declared, beaming, "The Guru heard my voice and fulfilled my desire. I had the Guru's darshan last night!"

Thinking he'd dreamed of Baba, the mandali said that Baba often appears to followers in dreams. But the ascetic rebuked them, "Why are you talking about a dream? Meher Baba came in person and gave me his darshan and then went back up the hill." How could they be expected to believe him? Baba never came down the hill once he'd retired for the night. But the night watchman related how for some unexplained reason, Baba had walked down the hill at midnight and then returned a while later. The men gave the hungry fakir a welcomed breakfast, after which he left, happy to have met his great guru.

Baba later explained: "Yesterday, three groups came and reaped benefits as to their capacities. The most fortunate was the fakir. In his determination and intense devotion, I had to disturb my seclusion and come down the hill. There must be such true faith and longing to have God's darshan—to move Him down from the mountain!" 923-25

Then, in the late summer, a very odd Englishman named Meredith Starr; his consort, Margaret Ross; and her sister Esther arrived in Ahmednagar. They had heard of Baba in England when they met Rustom Irani, the first disciple sent to the West to locate English boys to bring to Prem Ashram. Starr would later divorce to marry Margaret Ross in 1930.

Significantly, Margaret and Esther Ross were Baba's first Western female disciples. Baba would later say that women would do his main work in the West. Thus, Margaret and Esther Ross were the link to all the Western women yet to come, but it would be a link fraught with difficulties.

The problems were rooted in Starr's mixed character. He was interested in Eastern philosophy and spirituality, but he was also involved with the infamous British occult magician, Alistair Crowley. Meredith, Margaret and Esther lived at Meherabad for six months, until Meredith's ways became such a nuisance that Baba told him to return to England.

Baba warned Starr that he was so "spiritually advanced" that he might drop his body if he stayed in India any longer. He also knew Starr was on the verge of committing adultery and wanted to save him from that. Compounding these issues, before departing the three were involved in an automobile accident, running up a hospital bill for which Baba had to pay thousands of rupees. Despite these problems, Starr was destined to play a major role in Baba's early trips to the West. Baba assured him that he'd come to England to stay at his retreat center in Devon. Those visits would take place in 1931 and in 1932. 1004; MM 1:211

Baba's Second Catholic Disciple

Christian Leik was a grey-haired, fifty-eight-year-old Russian pilgrim from Estonia. He had escaped before the Bolshevik revolution to become a wandering renunciate in India. He had also travelled to England and America to become a disciple of Ramakrishna, a Perfect Master of the nineteenth century, and he had heard of Baba through Meredith Starr.

When Leik arrived at Baba's Toka ashram in 1928, he realized that he'd found his true master, thus ending twenty-two years of seeking. Baba asked Leik to observe silence and instructed him: "Remain here with a totally free heart. Keep silence from tomorrow and don't worry. Whatever you need, ask Vishnu. Don't think of things that have bothered you. Have patience. I'll make you steadfast in the path. I'm pleased with you because despite so many hardships and sufferings, you've stuck to the path for so many years." 982–83

Leik was humble and unassuming, even to the point of washing his own clothes—unusual for a foreigner in India—and these things deeply impressed the mandali. He wrote in his diary:

> How utterly different I found Meher Baba and his Ashram to be. He is a personification of the highest spirituality and love; and the atmosphere of Meher Ashram reflects the deep peace and radiance of my beloved Master—Baba, as he is affectionately called by his devotees. There's nothing about him of the awe-inspiring solemnity attributed to the occult hierarchy....
>
> I have almost daily evidence the Master reads my innermost thoughts like an open book. When I'm worried, or someone touches a tender spot in my being to dishearten me, there comes a message of comfort and encouragement from Baba to set my mind at rest again. What a blessing!

That love, craved for all my life, I experience here more and more as the days pass on.

Baba said he'd help me one day by awakening in my heart the realization of his divine Presence, and later this truly happened. I became aware of the Self as the Self of all beings—and I know also that the One we call Baba has always been with me and will ever be, for all Eternity. . . .
Only by the Master's grace can one know his true greatness and realize who he really is. A 128

Baba was truly pleased with Christian Leik, explaining to the mandali that he was the very circle member he had told them of before his arrival. "He's a real man. There's a vast difference between Meredith Starr and Sadhu Leik. They're poles apart, though Starr was instrumental in bringing him here. The unreal goes, and the real one comes!" 1012

Baba sent Leik on pilgrimage throughout India to spread his name. But he also had other plans for him. Leik returned from one of these walking lecture-tours dreadfully exhausted, seriously ill and emaciated, and he died at 5:15 PM, October 29, 1929.

Leik was buried the next morning in grave No. P19 in the Christian cemetery in Bhingar, twelve miles from Ahmednagar. He was the second Western Catholic devotee to die in Meher Baba's service. 1120

Prem Ashram Closes

Completing his spiritual work with the Prem Ashram boys in 1928, Baba abruptly closed the ashram on Meherabad Hill with his now familiar words: "Temporary scaffolding is set up around a big building under construction, and upon completion the scaffolding is removed. My external activities and commitments are often only the external expression of the far deeper internal work I am doing."

The boys would eventually become God-Realized, together with Baba's circle members, while countless other humans would enter the spiritual path, as all kingdoms in creation get a spiritual push forward. What he accomplished in these boys became the prototype of what he would give to the entire world when the time was ripe. But for now, Prem Ashram students were on hold.

The boys were sent back home to do the work Baba had given them. Just before the ashram closed, Baba gave some final instructions to the boys:

> Meditate on me so as to forget everything else. Be merged in me. My disciple, Pleader, fasts and meditates, but is still not merged in me. Meditate spontaneously like inhaling and exhaling your breath which goes on automatically, like a clock's tick, tock.
>
> While sitting, eating, drinking, studying—in every act—meditate on me naturally. With the help of my mercy I'll lead you to the path and then to samadhi. Without grace, such meditation isn't possible. To meditate is to go deep within one's self and lose yourself in divine self-hypnosis. Forget false self and think of nothing but your *Real Self*. 988

The Perfect Boy

Even after closing Prem Ashram in 1928, for almost three decades Baba was on the lookout for what he called the "perfect boy" to accompany and attend to him. He explained this was part of his Universal work, molding the present and future youth of the world for the better by his direct contact with these boys.

But the perfect boy proved elusive, and over time, the mandali became frustrated because after bringing so many boys to him, Baba sent them all back home. To reconcile his men to the aggravation they underwent seeking out model youths, Baba explained, "My best work is done under these conditions: in the presence of children. I keep boys with me when music is played or songs sung; while playing games such as flying kites, cricket playing and marbles, providing them with all—food, clothing and money." 1138

Behind this work of mine is a great mystery. Through these boys, I forge links and work for chosen Prem Ashram boys who are now away from me. The work of preparing certain boys is a self-imposed extra duty beyond my work of preparing the circle for Realization. For that special duty, I opened ashrams for young children, prepared them and selected a few boys.

But what would happen to them after the ashram was closed? They couldn't just be discarded or set aside! Something had to be done for them once they came under the spell of my watchful gaze. Some had to stay near me for that. The best efforts were made, sacrificing so much expense, time, energy and labor to bring the boys near me. But then there were parental objections.

This kept them from remaining by my side. So, by an indirect method I called other boys to me, connecting their links with those few select boys of the ashram who are physically away. It cost thousands of rupees plus the trouble to me and the mandali. A boy was kept a few days, given good clothes, food and even paid an allowance; but then each was sent away. No one could understand it.

That's why even the best and oldest of my mandali laughed and ridiculed my work with these boys, which appears to them quite strange and without any meaning or substance. But my purpose was to forge links with the best of my selected boys who are now away from me. No one will ever grasp the significance of this work, as it is *univer-*

sal in its aspect. I'm discussing it with you now, but how can you know what I am doing in the universe at this moment? 1195

Baba even placed an advertisement *The Times of India*: "Boy, not above sixteen years old, wanted to serve as personal attendant to a Spiritual Master touring the world." Many applicants were interviewed, but none were satisfactory. So he changed his plan and looked for an intelligent, "perfect" girl to accompany him to the West. He sent to Quetta for Katie Irani, but her mother wouldn't allow her to go. Although he searched elsewhere, no girl could be found to suit his terms. Maya seemed to be frustrating him at every turn in this endeavor. 1357

Over the years it became a running joke with the mandali searching for this elusive boy, both in India and in the West. Never did they find one worthy to serve Baba for very long. And even finding him unsuitable, Baba would still bathe, feed and dress him in new clothes before sending him home. Printed *Lord Meher* 1245 and footnote

After nearly twenty-five years of searching for this perfect boy, Baba once kissed his own childhood photo in front of the mandali, saying, "I wanted a boy like him, but could never find one." There's no question that Baba loved the pure innocence of these boys without a tinge of lust as he was working toward the purity of world youth. 1114 and footnote

One time when Chhagan was looking for such a boy, he spotted a handsome youth working in a restaurant. After much persuasion, the manager allowed him to go with Chhagan. Baba liked him very much, but after a few minutes he noticed a small cut on the boy's leg and told Chhagan, "You'd better take him back to Meherabad. Let Padri treat his wound and then bring the boy back here it's healed."

It was such a minor injury that Chhagan was puzzled. Why was Baba making such a fuss taking the boy all the way to Meherabad —hundreds of miles from where they were—when a local doctor could treat him? But he said nothing. Baba also instructed him to stop in Poona on the way, contact Sadashiv Patel and deliver a message to him.

Chhagan left with the boy and was nearing Sadashiv's house when a Muslim woman filling her water vessels at a public well saw the boy and screamed out his name. She came running and embraced him in tears, "Yusuf, Yusuf! My dearest son, where have you been? I can't believe it's really you! I've been aching to see you day and night! It's been so long! Have you forgotten your own mother?"

Chhagan became alarmed. He forced his way out of the crowd, went to Sadashiv and described the situation. Sadashiv quickly came and approached the woman. Upon questioning, she said that her only son had disappeared from home five years ago, and searching for him had proved fruitless.

The grief-stricken parents had given up hope of seeing him again. Only then did Chhagan realize why Baba had sent him on this strange journey to reunite the boy with his heart-broken parents suffering for years over their lost child. 1166–67

After Prem Ashram closed, Espandiar Vesali returned to Tehran, Iran. He wouldn't see Baba for thirty-five years, but one day in 1963 he had an unusual experience. He heard a knock at his door. There staring at him stood a Muslim Mullah, who related that a voice in a dream told him that the eagerly awaited Imam Mehdi— Saheb-e-Zaman, Lord of the Universe, Rasool, the Christ Avatar, was again on earth, and he'd learn of him at a house in Tehran.

In his dream, the priest was guided to Espandiar's house, clearly seen in vivid detail. Searching the city, he found the house and knocked on the door. As the Mullah spoke, tears came to Espandiar, as his house served as the Avatar Meher Baba Center in Tehran.

CHRIST COME AGAIN

Weekly meetings were held there, though very quietly, as they were against Islamic law.

With this occurrence, Espandiar longed to have Baba's darshan once again and wrote expressing it to him. But he subsisted on a meager income from a cherry and apple orchard and had no money to travel to India. Most years, the winter frost destroyed the blossoms and there was little or no fruit. Baba wrote back that he could come to India only if he had a good crop this year and sold it, with funds leftover from his maintenance.

He also instructed Espandiar not to worry, but to walk around the trees, uttering these words: "It's thirty-five years since I have seen Meher Baba, and I want to go visit him. So you, my crop, are not allowed to freeze. I beg of you to bear abundant fruit so I might be able to go see my Lord. The frost and winter should not destroy my crop this year."

Certain now he'd not lose his coming year's crop, Espandiar borrowed money and flew to India, so anxious was he to meet Baba after more than three decades of separation. Putting his head on Baba's feet, he wept and wept. After a few minutes, he was lifted up and embraced by Baba. "In an instant I forgot those decades of separation. I no longer knew the meaning of separation. I felt so relieved and happy."

Then came the bombshell. Baba said he could stay only that day and had to return to Iran immediately. Shocked, Espandiar pleaded to stay three weeks. Baba said no, even if it meant he had lost his livelihood in coming. Baba was also with him back in Iran and was doing very important work there through him. What could Espandiar do? He returned to Bombay only to be told at the airport he'd have to have his return ticket sent from Iran.

It took exactly three weeks for that to happen, so Espandiar got his wish after all, spending all that time with Baba. When his fruit crop was later harvested, all the surrounding orchards had been severely damaged by harsh winter frost, while Espandiar's trees gave unprecedented rich yields, to the other local farmers' utter amazement. [1] 4981–82

In Apparent Trouble is the Hidden Mercy of God

Meanwhile, Baba's men were still complaining. "Staying with you is nothing but harassment. Our only thought in mind and heart is death. We look happy to others; we eat and drink with all who come, but who sees the dagger piercing our hearts?"

Baba responded, "It is my grace, my real mercy which descends on a very, very select few. These are my friends, my lovers to whom I give the gift of sorrow and distress; an incalculable gift much greater than gold and not given to all—only to my beloved children. So don't be anxious. . . . Were I to use my dagger on outsiders, they'd not dare approach me. . . My friends I kill, and it is my highest mercy on them. What is my mercy? What is my grace? It is your trouble and harassment." 1159

About his compassion, Baba would say, "When the lover offers himself in sacrifice, the Beloved laughs and the dagger weeps. The Beloved is the executioner." 3500

But it wasn't always harassment for the mandali. On occasion they were allowed special food, like the day Baba announced, "Today let's have a cooking contest between my uncle Masaji and Chowhary!" The two Meherabad cooks happily competed to outdo each other preparing a tasty vegetarian lunch. The mandali served as the panel of judges. Baba dished out the food and asked whose was tastier. The food was so delicious the mandali slyly replied, "Well you know, Baba, it's so hard to say; we'll really need to have second helpings to decide!" 729

In May 1929, Baba began the deepest six-month seclusion of his life until that time, entering a cave in the Tiger Valley region of Panchgani, named for its abundance of wild tigers. During this period of fasting, he kept aloof from everyone, even the four watchmen who had to be on duty at all times, day and night. Just before entering the cave Baba conveyed:

> If only my thinking of and planning for this seclusion has made these disturbances so abrupt, how can you have any idea of what will happen by my actually entering it. Be prepared to hear of bloodshed. There'll be severe tensions between the Hindus and Muslims. Antagonism between the higher and lower caste Hindus will totally prevail. Religious feelings will cause differences between the 2 communities, resulting in utter bloodshed. 1165–66

The First Idea for a Film

On July 11, 1929, confiding to Baba his intention of making a film, Rustom Irani said, "This film has been in my mind for a long time. Bombay movie director D. G. Phalke is willing to help with financing to portray spiritual themes through films. This is something the public has never been exposed to before. It will also be the best medium for spreading your teachings throughout the world." Baba liked the idea and let him to pursue it.

While Rustom was greatly encouraged and the mandali were excited about the plan, for now it remained only a plan. As we will see in future chapters, Baba would later carry over the idea and bring it to Hollywood. 1031

> Rustom Irani managed the Circle Cinema in Nasik. Declared open by Baba himself in February 1928, the venture was first called Meher Cinema, and the first film to be shown was Charlie Chaplin's *Shoulder Arms*. Rustom was married to Mehera's sister Freny.

With Prem Ashram closing, Baba felt impelled to re-visit the land of his ancestors. And so with ten of the mandali he prepared for a second journey there in October 1929. Once there, he planned to send for the three Muslim Prem Ashram students he had previously brought to Kashmir and worked with, afterwards sending them back home to Persia.

Before leaving for Persia, Baba was required to sign his name at the British Consulate to obtain a re-entry visa back into India for his return after a two-month stay. But he refused, because he had stopped signing his name in 1927. He had his passport issued as a Persian subject. This gave him easy entry to Persia but would be no help when it came to re-enter India later.

CHRIST COME AGAIN

Chapter Fifteen

Lust and Love

En route to Persia, Baba commented to his men about different nationalities—East and West: "Americans I like best, and for Italians heart is a must; but I don't like the way Arabs behave as they're so full of lust!" Arriving in Persia, Baba continued discussing the immoral ways of some Iranians:

> We should pity them. They're not to blame for their ignorance. Now that I've come to Persia, I'll finish this work of purifying the atmosphere here before returning to India. Meanwhile, tell me one thing and be frank; I have a special reason to ask about it. Today, I want you to disclose any [lustful] wrongdoings with an open heart and without the least fear – whatever it may be. . . . [After their confessing, he said] Now you don't have to repent for anything.
> You've been open with me and I've forgiven you for every wrongdoing. There are a few among you without any fault, but I have forgiven all the others. Just as I asked you today to openly confess your weaknesses, Jesus would meet daily with his disciples at a fixed time and forgive their weaknesses and advise them. From this act of Jesus, Catholics go to a priest for confession to this day. It's a good practice, but after confession and pardon, the actions shouldn't be repeated.
> If they are, where's the benefit? It does no good to commit seven hundred wrongs in seven days and then confess to a priest, only to repeat them later. Priests, mullahs

and preachers give ineffective, long-winded sermons—in one ear and out the other, while people continue committing the same wrongs.

Only a Qutub or Sadguru can really deal with the consequences of human offenses, underline their seriousness and influence the offender's mind. What impression can the words of a priest produce? It is the divine knowledge of a [Perfect Master] that creates a real impression, and it is his knowledge that has influence. So be alert; don't make mistakes for which you'll later repent. Lust's intensity has broken the penance and austerity of even people advanced on the spiritual path.

So, what about you? Your luck has brought you into my companionship and you've been forgiven with your confession. In fact, your hearts should turn to water by my loving forgiveness, for I am not in the least angry at your shortcomings. I've forgiven you under the condition you don't indulge in the offenses again. How fortunate you all are to I am the worshiper, I am the worship, and I am the One worthy of adoration. I am the fire, I am the spark, and I am the smoke—I am everything! I repeat this every night, praying and bowing down to myself that God may make worldly people worthy of emancipation. And who is God? I, myself! God as God alone is not consciously man, as man alone is not consciously God. 869

Later, in 1934, when someone asked Baba the difference between lust and love, he explained, "Lust is nothing but the desire for self happiness, while love is desire for the happiness of others." 1646 Then explaining the purpose of the human form, he startlingly explained that the original human form was a eunuch, and was never intended to beget children.

This tendency to cohabit is nothing but animal instinct. It is leftover from the previous lives of evolution from the stone to animal to human form. After evolving through millions and millions of forms from stone to ape, the first human form comes into being as a eunuch. The eunuch has no sexual desires. But due to overwhelming animal sanskaras, instinct takes control over the human mind causing the human form to become sexual. The human in its pristine form is perfect for realizing God. Baba explained:

"In its first birth, a human usually does not achieve Realization due to the propelling force of these animal sanskaras. In that first human form as a eunuch one does not have any sexual contact with its opposite sex. But after the sexual urge arises as a byproduct of the animal sanskaras, it cohabits in its successive births." 1691; EN 49

The Battle with Lust is a Necessity for Evolution

"One day, Energy and Lust had a fight," Baba told the mandali. "Energy was defeated, so Mind stepped into the ring and there was an even worse terrible fight between Mind and Lust. Mind was not easily defeated, but in the end Lust won again. Then *Soul* challenged Lust in a fight to the end. The result was that Lust was so completely defeated it never rose up to challenge a rematch." 1034

Baba now had each of his mandali promise never to touch anyone lustfully. His married disciples were not to touch anyone but their wives. Though happy to be forgiven, some still felt self-conscious and uneasy over past weaknesses. So Baba explained:

> Sexual intercourse is the highest type of sensual pleasure, but how long does it last? Only a few minutes. If this highest worldly pleasure is compared with the real happiness of eternal divine bliss, it is a mere shadow of a drop from the infinite ocean of eternal bliss. Once one is real-

ized, the bliss is enjoyed every second forever! So just imagine the hollowness of worldly pleasures. 352

Lust isn't bad. Because of it you've been born as human beings. And due to this very lust you will turn from men into God! But even if lust is in you, don't put it into action. From the spiritual point of view, lust is the worst possible weakness. The real hero is he who successfully fights it. Sex with a woman who isn't your wife [or a man who isn't your husband] is one of the worst possible sins. What had to happen has happened; but from now on beware of carnality.

Follow my orders and stay away from lust. . . . It can destroy your spirit and character, as well as infect the body. I know each and every thing, but still I keep on watching. You might think, "Knowing everything, why doesn't Baba save us from committing sins?" Before you do any wrong action, I already know you're going to do it! Then why don't I prevent you?

That's the secret of my work; though I know everything, I don't interfere. The fact is you *should* have this lust, but do your utmost not to fall prey to it. Put up a fierce fight. Even if defeated a thousand times, again be ready to continue to fight lust. If I wanted, I could destroy lust in you in no time.

But what would be the use of destroying it?

Inevitably, I will destroy it. Meanwhile, continue on with the battle inside yourselves. This is the law; it is necessary. Then joy will come in defeating lust. Without a struggle, there is no pleasure in fighting. The real pleasure lies in success after so many defeats. Wars won without obstacles, without sacrifices and untiring effort afford no pleasure. This should be a life and death fight!—a lifelong struggle, a conflict to the end of your days. It should be there to fight you.

And you should always be alert and ready for battle to kill it. Who loves me and has faith in me will try doubly hard to obey me. If you touch anyone with lust, tell me immediately. This is one remedy. Another is to think in your last birth you were a woman and had relations with a man.

Now you are a man and you want relations with a woman. You've had enough satisfaction in your previous births. What's to be had by more lust? Foremost, try to get rid of it, as all other vices are on account of it. For instance if a parrot's throat is cut, it dies.

But if its wings are clipped, it doesn't die; after some time the wing feathers grow back. Lust can be compared to the parrot's head. So, when lust is still present and we try to conquer other evils, such as anger, those evils again revive. Everything rises out of the head. But if lust is killed once and for all, every other evil is also destroyed—you've cut off its head.

Yet, in truth, lust is necessary for evolution. It starts developing in the vegetable forms. With the increase in lust, there is advancement in evolution, since lust means energy. And with the increase in energy, consciousness expands. But these are points on this path which you'll never understand.

There are thousands of points thinner than a hair. Remember it's not easy to eradicate sanskaras, and lust is the hardest of all sanskaras. But be heroes and fight lust; you'll defeat it. The real pleasure is to fight it and not succumb to it! Knowing this, I let it remain, but I will destroy it in you when the right time comes. Until then, go on fighting and never give up. 1099-1101

When asked to confess his misdeeds again, one man became peeved. Baba responded:

> You fool, you're an idiot! There's a real purpose behind it. How can you know why I'm having you confess again today? Everything can't be divulged. For my own reasons if I make you feel ashamed a thousand times, just remain humble and bow low. How fortunate if you feel naked in the world's eyes! The Master is always ready to give the treasure. But your vessel isn't empty.
>
> It's filled with filth! I want to give you love, but your mind is full of lust. Get rid of it or I can't give you love. So, conquer lust—drive it away! 1101

Baba explained in the Beyond-State of God only the One, Indivisible Existence prevails. There, sex does not exist. Only in the realm of the illusory phenomenon called the universe does sex assert itself. At another time when a man asked, "Can one express and develop love through sexual intercourse?" Baba gave him a surprising answer: "If you think you're expressing love through the sex act, you're sadly mistaken. Lust prompts you to engage in it. It's impossible to express pure love with intercourse; those sanskaric impressions clash." 1532

Decades later, Baba said to Dr. Hoshang Barucha:

> Lust means a craze. Some lust for power, some lust of the senses, etc. The whole creation came out of lust. The first whim was lustful. God had intercourse with Himself through the Om Point and the creation was the result of this act. Even a mother's love for her child is lust.
>
> There's never satisfaction in love; only continual longing and agony till union occurs. In lust there's satisfaction—for a time—then again dissatisfaction. As soon as the

child is sleeping, a mother can get to her other work. This satisfaction-non-satisfaction as to her child is a sign of lust.

Even in the lowest lustful life of the gross sphere, God experiences Himself as a lover; but a lover completely ignorant about his true nature or of God the Beloved; the lover's state is completely separated from the divine Beloved by an opaque curtain of non-understood duality, but still the beginning of a long process where the lover breaks through the enveloping curtain of ignorance and comes into his own truth as unbounded and unhampered Love. Aw 22 (vol. 1), 40 and 66; Di 401

Baba continued to speak of love and lust thought his life, and his comments were recorded by many of sources:

Love for one's wife, children or parents also isn't love. It's attachment. Love is a divine gift. When one has it, everything is sacrificed. Freedom is sacrificed—sacrifice itself is sacrificed! But from my point of view, obedience is higher than love. But obedience is impossible; more impossible than love because freedom is inherited, it is our birthright because originally we were free.

So when binding comes, freedom is refused to us. In such circumstances the easiest course is to resort to one binding to eliminate several bindings. But that too is difficult. Although out of obedience one may cut his own throat, he's motivated by the idea of freedom. 3328

When lust goes, love appears; and out of love comes longing but never satisfaction, for longing increases till it becomes an agony which ceases only in Union. Nothing but union with the Beloved can satisfy the lover. The Way of Love is a continual sacrifice of the lover's thoughts of "I," until at last comes the time when the lover says, "O Beloved! Will I ever become one with you and so lose myself forever? But let this be only if it is your Will."

This stage of love is enlightened by obedience. Now, the lover continuously witnesses the glory of the Beloved's Will. And in this witnessing he doesn't even think of union. He willingly surrenders his entire being to the Beloved; there's no thought of self left. This is the stage when love is illumined by surrender. Out of millions, only one loves God; and out of millions of lovers, only one succeeds in obeying and finally surrendering his whole being to God the Beloved. EN 4

Love lifts a man up, while passion or lust drags him down. Don't worry about being lifted up by love, but about being pulled down by lust. If you're not pulled down, you're automatically pulled up. To keep you away from lust focus at the root of the nose between your 2 eyes and think of me. But don't do this for a long time." Passion is very trivial – a few hugs and kisses and then the act.

After a couple of moments of pleasure, you realize you've been brought down by lust—but such realization is false, for it does not last eternally. Though a person may say to himself, "That was the last time," he never gives it up. The struggle is eternal, and only those who go through it successfully are fortunate to be "Realized" in the true sense. TGS 59

Higher love can emerge from the shell of lower love through constant discrimination. Real love also creates an arc, meaning love graciously given is also to be graciously received. Real love is tranquil—clearly different from lower infatuation and lust which obstructs real love. In infatuation, one is a passive victim of the spell of attraction. Love has an active appreciation of the intrinsic worth of the one loved without seeking anything:

> *Real love when given—*
> *to anyone or anything—*
> *always comes to me.*

Any worship or obeisance done to any deity, animate or inanimate, to any saint, guru, yogi or advanced souls eventually comes to me. Offering pure, unadulterated love to anyone and anything you will be loving me, as I am in every one and in everything, and also beyond everything. 3520

Love is so different from lust which relies upon a sensual object and consequent spiritual subordination of oneself to it, whereas love puts one into direct and coordinate relation with the reality behind the form. While lust is experienced as heavy, love is experienced as light. In lust life is narrowed down, and in love there is an expansion of being.
To love someone is like adding another life to your own. Your life is multiplied, virtually living in 2 centers. If you love the whole world, you vicariously live in the whole world; but in lust there's an ebbing down of life, a general sense of hopeless dependence on "another" form.
Thus, lust accentuates separateness and suffering, while love feels unity and joy. Lust dissipates; love restores. Lust is sensual craving; love is expression of spirit. Lust seeks fulfillment; love experiences fulfillment. In lust there's excitement; in love, tranquility. Di 112-13

Something else about lust and love: There's such a feeble line, sometimes lust can be thought of as love, and love as lust; and yet, love takes you to God, while lust binds you in illusion. The sign of love is one: love never *asks* for anything. The lover *gives* all to the Beloved. Lust *wants* everything. Remember, who wants nothing is never disappointed. He has everything. 3627

Of the seven colors of sanskaras, red is the deepest and the worst; it is the most lasting impression, and takes the longest to be wiped out. These red sanskaras are caused by the sex act; hence they are a great check on spiritual progress and advancement. . . . Thoughts of sexual desire may come, and even a rush of impulses, but one should not commit any action with another person.

Even masturbation is better, though it is physically harmful. Sexual intercourse has the worst consequences, attracting to oneself the worst sanskaras of ages past of one's partner; hence it is most difficult to wipe out. It incurs immense ineradicable damage to one's spiritual progress. 1889–90

If lustful, one tends to fasten it on several people. The ideal of celibacy won't allow even the *touch* of the opposite sex. Now, if the Master who is entirely free from lust wants to help a strongly lustful person incapable of abstinence, he allows marriage. This limits lust to one's spouse.

As lust diminishes, he may be asked to give up all acts of lust even with his wife, while maintaining married life. Then lust is gradually eliminated and the goal of brahmacharya [sexlessness] is finally obtained. 2275

In one sense, all are mad; deluded ones are always mad. For instance, if you think you're the body, you are body-mad, aren't you? Self has no sex, but when self treats itself as the body, the illusion of sex-duality appears. The Self in each of us is *sexless*, but thinks itself as a woman, and in another thinks itself as man—a subtle delusional difference coming from thinking ourselves as body.

The soul is to the body as a bald man to his wig. He puts it on going to work. When he sleeps at night, he takes it off. So, you learn to use the body when you need it for work, and to free yourself when you no longer need it. . . . *The Sexless Self is the highest experience.* 1779, 4546

British physician Dr. William Donkin would join Baba's ashram in 1939. He recorded in his diary that one day Baba told the men, "What is there in this life but eating, digesting and shitting—all filth under the skin, six layers of it to get to Baba inside these bodies." He then humorously went on to describe the various *jungli* (uncouth) eating habits of his men mandali.

"Ghani chews with his mouth wide-open; Baidul screws his food with his fingers on the plate, and on an Italian boat Vishnu couldn't eat spaghetti with a fork, so he checked around to see no one was looking and piled it in with his hands!" Baba continued:

For example, if you wear false teeth you use them to eat; they're in your mouth, but you know they're false and you can take them out; attached and detached, you make use of them. The dirty body, which I call the *walking latrine*, is used for the soul to realize itself.

Can you escape from it? No, so what you do is wash away the sweat and not go around brooding all day long, *"I mustn't sweat, I mustn't sweat."* You can't escape it, but you can become detached.

If you're married and love another it's all right; don't worry about it. But don't *act out* love except with your spouse. 1942, 3941

"If you have to marry, marry me!"

In married life the range of experience to be had in the company of the partner is so wide the suggestions of lust are not necessarily the first to present themselves to the mind. So there's a real opportunity for the aspirants to recognize and annul those limiting factors. By gradually eliminating lust and progressing through a series of increasingly richer experiences of love and sacrifice, they can finally arrive at Infinity. 1532

Each marriage incurs seven more lifetimes. So Marry Me! If you marry, you incur seven more new births [reincarnations]. That's why saints and Realized Masters advise their devotees to lead an unmarried life. These seven births go on multiplying as you proceed, lifetime after lifetime: 7 X 7 = 49 X 7 = 343 X 7 and so on.

How many former husbands or wives you have left in your past lives, and how many new ones you will come into contact with in the future! None of the past husbands or wives do you remember, nor will you know of those to come. So if you have to marry, *marry me!*

That means all regard, affection and love for me alone; that kind of remembrance of me demands a great deal indeed – far more love than even the yogis of ancient times. *So marry me!* Marrying me means love, peace and bliss, while ordinary marriage means fighting with a thousand other worries arising ["knife, wife and strife!"]. 906

Abortion and Birth Control

Baba was most definitely opposed to abortion. He would help a pregnant girl bear her child, and if she were unable to care for it, he would further help her to give it up for adoption rather than have an abortion. He advocated natural means and restraint or even abstinence rather than resorting to artificial means.

> From a spiritual viewpoint, birth control must happen through mental control and nothing else. Mental power is necessarily undermined by reliance on the physical means which is detrimental in developing self-control, and positively disastrous for spiritual advancement. It is unadvisable even for the best of motives.
>
> At the start of married life the partners are drawn to each other by lust as well as love. But with conscious and deliberate cooperation they can gradually lessen lust and increase the element of love. Through sublimation, lust ultimately gives place to deep love.
>
> "By the mutual sharing of joys and sorrows the partners march on from one spiritual triumph to another, from deep love to ever *deeper* love, until the initial period of possessive and jealous love is entirely replaced by a self-giving and expansive love." GD 31

Love, lust and happiness were ongoing themes in Baba's work. Once, when a man meeting Baba for the first time gave him a written statement describing the confusion in his life, Baba responded to take these things lightly:

> Life is beautiful and meant to be happy! I'll help you. Things will change. You'll see it! . . . Take things lightly. Say to yourself, 'I'm meant to be happy and to make others

happy.' Gradually you'll become happier to make others happy also. Don't ever suggest to your mind, 'I'm tired, haggard, depressed,' etc. That only makes it worse. Always say, 'All is your mind, 'I'm tired, haggard, depressed,' etc. That only makes it worse. Always say, 'All is well; I'll be happy.' I can and I will help you. You will actually feel it. . . .

When one is meant for spirituality one has either love or lust to the extreme. Lust must be converted to love. Lust is a craving of the physical senses, while love is the deepest craving of the soul. I know all about you and will help you spiritually.

Never ever think you've fallen so far as to never to rise again. PM 241

At another time when Baba was approached by a drug addict, he pointedly asked, "Are you happy?" "No, very, very miserable," the man responded. Baba similarly counseled:

Never think "life is dreadful, I'm tired of life." Such thoughts make life miserable. Life is worth living, and if you think it is, difficulties will appear insignificant. I'll help you to try to develop love. Never think, "I am alone, I have too much to do, I am poor," and so on. All are poor. The whole world is poor. Even millionaires are poor, because they have greed and want more. Love someone, and you will be rich. Don't worry, you have my Blessings! PM 249

The lower self makes you think you're small, that you're not satisfied, not happy. That makes others see you as small. Going against your lower self means transforming it in the opposite direction. Be what makes you look big and others see you as big.

Remain pleased and contented, happy and satisfied. When you're displeased, unhappy or upset and moody, it's only your lower self asserting its false itself. . . . I don't want any repression; I want transformation, and never say you mustn't get angry. Don't be confused. Get angry when the occasion so arises. But then at once get it out of your head, your mind and your life. 2143

Love, Lust and Divorce

People were often drawn to Baba when they needed help with personal problems. Once, a nervous woman approached him, saying she was in love with a church organist and asked if that friendship could be kept up if it remained pure. Baba responded, "Where's the harm in keeping it up?" She said, "Catholic law prevents marriage with a divorced man. The Church is against it. That's my conflict." Baba asked, "Do you love each other?" "Yes," she replied. "Then love is all that matters. If there's no lust, I see no harm in it. Let that love grow so it makes two souls. I'll help you both to make this love grow purer."

On another occasion, Baba was asked by a devotee about her failing marriage. Looking at her intensely, he put his two forefingers together and then broke them apart, indicating, "It's finished. . . . If there's no more love, then why stay married?" PM 242, 4368

He spoke at other times on the difference between love and affection or devotion:

> Love burns the lover. Devotion burns the Beloved. Love seeks happiness for the Beloved. Devotion seeks for blessings from the Beloved. Love seeks to shoulder the burden of the Beloved—it gives. Devotion asks. Love is silent and sublime, devoid of outward expressions. Devotion expresses itself outwardly. Love doesn't require the

presence of the Beloved in order to love. Devotion *demands* the presence of the Beloved to express affection for the Beloved. 4371

What then is the lover's duty? It is to make the Beloved happy without sparing himself. Without giving a second thought to his own happiness, the lover should seek the pleasure of the Beloved. The only thought a lover of God should have is to make the Beloved happy. 4392

Human love arises from ego-consciousness entwined with countless desires. Just as there are infinite shades of color in different flowers, so there are diverse delicate differences in human love. But human love is encircled by a number of obstructive factors, such as infatuation, lust, greed, anger and jealousy, all of which are either perverted forms of lower love or the inevitable side-effects of it.

In infatuation one is enamored of a sensual object; a lustful craving is developed toward it; and in greed one desires only to possess it. Thus a person is greedy for money, power or fame – instruments for possessing the craved objects. Anger and jealousy arise when these lower forms of love are thwarted or threatened. They obstruct the release of pure love which can never become clear and steady until disentangled from limiting and perverting forms of lower love. Di 112

Baba added that in the burning of real love "no smoke comes from the lover's mouth." It burns silently until the "otherness" of the lover is consumed. So a real lover never knows he loves. The moment love derives satisfaction from its expression it is not love but affection.

In a private interview on his first visit to his mountaintop center in Ojai, California, in 1956, Baba would straighten out a romance as he had done in many other cases. A young man had fallen in love with his friend's fiancée and she with him. Baba called the three together and explained to second the young man, "Your dearest girlfriend and your best friend love each other. They don't want to hurt you, so I'm asking you to release her." The young man was able to do so, though tearfully. At another time Baba said, "Love handled badly in jealousy is converted into hatred." 4069

A piece in the London *Daily Sketch* dated April 13, 1932, sheds light on how Baba viewed the spiritual role of women, marriage and celibacy. Observing Baba sitting for a sculptor, the interviewer began:

> "They say woman is a drag on man in attaining divine grace. All the saints . . ." But the prophet [Meher Baba] broke in, "Ah no, a woman can play a very important part in the development of divine grace. She is man's *equal*. And so long as she is true to herself all will be well. But once she surrenders to her surroundings, the function of marriage falls. Then come the divorces." "Then the vow of celibacy which the saints undertook . . ."
>
> "It is unimportant. Some men marry, others remain single, but a man isn't spiritually backward because he's married. A woman's love can inspire him to know the truth. But she must develop love, not lust. This is the key to happiness." Just then the sculptor took a piece of clay and once more the 'Messiah' looked heavenwards through the skylight." 1380, BG 128–9

Inviting Baba into One's Weakness

Although coming from the mouth of God Himself, how will humanity assimilate these words about traditional marriage? It's dizzying to even imagine it. Over fifty years later a young man approached Eruch Jessawala. The following exchange took place and maybe gives us a clue. The young man confessed his confusion: "Eruch, Baba said when you feel angry or have lustful thoughts to just *remember* him at once to prevent desires turning into unwanted actions. I keep trying, but fail most of the time, despite calling out his name." Eruch replied, "As you start indulging in your desire, invite him to take part in your weakness." The young man was shocked.

That doesn't seem right. Inviting a Divine Being to enter in a gross act you know is wrong? It sounds like blasphemy." Eruch said nothing. Then he proposed: "If you want to light up a dark room, you bring in a light. Bring in the Divine." Still puzzled, the want to light up a dark room, you bring in a light. Bring in the Divine." Still puzzled, the young man said, "You're serious? Invite him to take part in an immoral act?"

"Remember," Eruch said,

> He's present everywhere and at all times. There's not a moment he's not with or in you. When you invite Baba, he doesn't have to *come* to you. He's already there. Your invitation only increases *your* awareness of his constant Presence.
>
> He's never absent. It's your awareness of him that's absent. So create that awareness by inviting him into everything. By everything, I mean *everything*, for he's already present. You must create the *awareness* that he is already present." RT I, 44–46

This is how one shares in Baba's omniscience. He said that all spiritual advancement is accomplished by God's whim, and we do nothing. Adi Sr. once asked, "So one man is here, another there. The first has been doing penance and praying to God for years. The other man is one of the greatest scoundrels in the world. Can it happen in the blessings of the whim that instead of going to this righteous man it goes to the scoundrel, purifying him?" Baba answered, "Yes, for you only see the present life of the scoundrel. I see the millions of past lives and what he's done before. Perhaps the righteous man was the greatest scoundrel in his previous lives. So, when the whim flows, it knows exactly where to go and where not to go." JLH 78

When someone asked, "It's been said by fighting lust, one can develop true love. But you teach that by developing true love, one can break away from lust. Baba replied, "Love's method is direct. The other method is indirect and roundabout—like eating by reaching your mouth with your hand around your neck." The man countered: "If I meet a young woman, have undesirable thoughts and then avoid her, I feel I'm holding back my true nature." Baba answered, "Free mixing of the sexes as in the West is good on the whole, but if the aspirant feels the slightest of impure thoughts, he stands aside. But love he must! To avoid such thoughts, he should keep the thought in mind he is to *love me* in the other person." 1532

Baba further explained the purity required for the spiritual path:

> If a person wants to get a pearl from the bottom of the ocean, he doesn't shout at the pearl to come up while he sits on the beach. If he really wants the pearl, he tries his hardest to plunge to the bottom of the ocean to get it. Now, say the water of the ocean is Maya [illusion] and the pearl is God.

By spiritual law, it is essential the diver not get wet nor touch even a drop of water while diving! This means it's possible to dive and obtain the pearl, but it's impossible for him to not touch even a drop of water. This impossible aspect of spiritual things makes the diver worthy of the prize.

In order to not touch water, the diver must put on a full diving suit and an air tank. Only then can he dive and follow the rule of bringing up the pearl without getting wet. Comparing the above with spirituality, take the ocean water as Maya, the pearl as God and the diver as the seeker. The diving suit is love's willingness to renounce the world.
1591–92

> One morning, Norina Matchabelli, who will soon enter the story, woke up and saw Baba standing outside her bedroom window. "Tell me your dream," he said. She hesitated, thinking she couldn't, as it was a vivid dream involving sex. At last she told it. "Even on the sixth plane," Baba explained, "one still has lust. Aw 20 (no. 2): 17

Baba said that "fools don't get angry. Wise men get angry but don't express it. Eunuchs don't have sexual thoughts. Brave men have them but don't put them into action." Suppose you're having such thoughts. Don't try to stop them from coming or they will attack you again with double the force. So let them come and be spent away. There's no need to check thoughts from coming. But never put them into action. So what's the way out? Just to say don't put them into action?

But Baba proposed a more practical remedy.

There are two ways: lay at your Teacher's feet all the results of your actions. Let thoughts come and do things, but remain free by dedicating them to your Master. You will be free spiritually. But this is almost impossible, for we have to be quite honest.

The other way is to follow the Master's orders one hundred percent and let thoughts come, good or bad. Don't let them turn into actions; offset them by entertaining other thoughts. Think of the Master and his orders. This also is difficult because just when you're drowned in those thoughts, to have thoughts about the Master and his behests at that time is difficult.

Baba offered a radically graphic and instant remedy that involves using the mind's natural sensitivities and aversions to defuse a sexually-charged situation:

> So what's this remedy? Do one thing: when you have sexual thoughts, don't drive the picture away from your mind. Stare at it and think what a beautiful body, what a lovely face. But also what an amount of filth and dirt inside—urine, shit, blood, pus, all sorts of muck! The more you think like that, your former thoughts of that one's beauty are worn out. The moment you have these thoughts of filth in the body, remember the name of the Master. If he's a real Master, he'll surely help you.
>
> Don't worry. Let thoughts of lust, anger and greed come. They'll come. Fire must reach its zenith before it gradually subsides. . . . If I am what I am, you're safe. Even if I am not what you take me for, you're still safe! God will see to it. If in all faith you accept me as Perfect and obey my orders, your responsibility ends. In either case you're safe. But follow my wishes one hundred percent. 3304–06

Harry Dedolchow, an American merchant Marine seaman, was a Sufi under Murshida Ivy Duce in California. In 1960, when his ship docked in India he received permission to visit Baba. When he arrived with a suitcase full of gifts, Baba remarked: "This is unnecessary. All I want is your love. I appreciate what you do; I know it's the love in you compelling your actions. But all these things brought to me are illusory. Love alone is real." Baba embraced him and asked Dedolchow about his difficulties.

Dedolchow described the rigors of life at sea as a merchant marine and also spoke about the division he felt in himself between his impure thoughts and actions on the one hand, and his urge to go toward his "Father" Baba on the other, which he said he lacked the courage to do:

> Don't be afraid to come to me with all your impurities. Where else can you go to dispose of your dirt except in this Ocean? Throw all your impurities in this Ocean! Give them to me and be free. By surrendering to me both his good and bad, anyone can be free. But it is very difficult. Out of millions, only one can do it! Don't fear low thoughts.
>
> They harm no one if they come. Just don't put them in action or willfully entertain them. Nothing happens if a man occasionally thinks of taking poison, but if he constantly thinks of it, a time might come when he gets hold of the poison and swallows it. 4641-42

Baba gave the following discourse to his mandali. Its wisdom had never been shared before:

"Good vs. Evil"

> There really is nothing like "good" or "bad." As good is necessary, likewise bad is also necessary – just as positive and negative. Both are essential for action and evolution. If only good prevailed everywhere, life would end! Both good or bad done to extreme would lead to God-Realization; for instance, absolute evil with no trace of good, or absolute good with no trace of bad at all—both are equally conducive to the attainment of the goal of Self-Realization.
>
> If this is so, we can naturally ask, "Why is good preferable to bad?" Both good and bad are zero – nonexistent for the God-Realized. Both exist only in the realm of duality. But the Masters and Avatars give preference to and advo-

cate good over bad. This is only because spiritually speaking good is really easy for reaching the goal; though materially speaking, it's the reverse. . . .

Another reason for preferring and advocating good is in evil, although apparently easy to think about and actually commit a bad act, there's always a sort of torture in the mind coming after committing the act; for instance, illicit sex or murder. Whereas good acts, though apparently difficult, present nothing of the kind—no torture to the mind.

On the contrary, there's constant happiness in thinking and doing good, though it always seems harder to do good than bad. Besides, doing bad to the extreme would not succeed or endure until the end. A man's body however bold, indifferent, healthy and robust would not be able to withstand prolonged indulgence in vices—such as lust, drinking liquor, or extreme violence. 1721–22

The Persians are Overwhelmed by Baba

In October 1929 Baba embarked on a second trip to Persia, accompanied by ten mandali and three Prem Ashram boys. They reached Isfahan on October 27, and four days later they visited Mubarak, the hometown of Baba's beloved Agha Ali. The group came to the boy's home, but the family wouldn't allow Ali to travel any farther with Baba.

Although unhappy with the situation, Baba let Ali stay, and this led to his sending the other two boys, Ali Akbar and Abdulla, back to their homes as well. Agha Ali's uncle was violently opposed to Baba and, intending to kill the Master, hid a pistol in his shoe. But coming face to face with him, he completely forgot his intention, bowed down with tears in his eyes and took darshan instead. Deeply repentant, he later sent Baba a large basket of choice peaches.

Baba also wanted to visit Khorramshah, birthplace of his father, Sheriar. The Avatar was touching his very own roots. Arriving there in a splendid mood, he bought Chanji a new hat and Vishnu a new coat.

His next stop was Yzed, where he faced a challenge from the head of the Baha'i faith, who also had traveled to Yezd, and who claimed that Baba was not the Rasool—the Savior. But gazing at the Master, he forgot everything. With tears, he declared, "You are God Himself!" He bowed at Baba's feet, weeping inconsolably. Running outside, he exclaimed to the people, "Today I have met God!"

In Baam, a Persian Army general came to Baba's residence in full uniform with a sword hanging by his side. He asked the mandali about Meher Baba but was told no one of that name lived there. The general requested, "Please go and tell your Master a beggar is standing on his threshold." When so informed, Baba permitted him to enter.

The moment he came into Baba's presence, he saluted in military fashion, and taking out his sword, placed it on the floor. He fell at Baba's feet while kissing his hands. After calming him, Baba asked, "What's your rank?" "It's nothing before your venerable self," he replied. "I mean your army rank." "I'm a general in the Persian army."

Baba patted him lovingly on the head and remarked, "To die in the service of one's country is indeed great, but to die in the service of God is far greater!" The general nodded, "I understand, and implore you to grant that my devotion to God may increase." "I will help you," promised Baba. In adoration, the general closed his eyes and bowed down again.

"If I am permitted, your Holiness, I would like to say the salvation of my country does not lie in its military strength, but in the birth of spirituality by the grace of Masters like you. It is my humble prayer you might be pleased to shower your grace on my unfortunate country and its illiterate people." Baba smiled and gestured: "That's why you see me here this very day." The general responded, "It's a great privilege for this country. May your blessing sanctify the soil of this land!" The general then walked reverently backward, step by step, never taking his eyes off Baba—a touching scene for the mandali to witness.

Later, Baam's police chief also came to inquire about Baba. Persian law authorized the police to record the name, business and purpose of all foreign visitors traveling in the country. The commissioner himself had now come to gather the pertinent details. Chanji laid the facts before him. But the commissioner had other intentions and openly stated them.

"But I wish to meet your leader, the honorable Merwan in person." He was told Baba was not meeting anyone, but he persisted, "By government regulations, I must interview him in person." He was told again it was not possible. He replied, "I cannot tell you how much it would mean to me to see Hazrat Meher Baba." Then apologizing, he confessed, "I've used my authority solely to gain entrance and have his darshan today. It was all pretense."

Baba called the man to his room, who humbly kissed Baba's hands and was allowed to sit with him for a while. Baba remarked to him, "I'm going to Quetta soon, and will return to break my silence and manifest in Persia." The police commissioner said, "I am so happy to meet the Revered One so many talk about. Hazrat, I'm ready to carry out your wishes." Then turning to the mandali, he commented, "You're so fortunate to have the Master's constant company." 1108–09

Despite the mandali's great precautions, a local resident, Rustom Sohrab Irani, somehow came to know of Baba's presence. Though he entreated Baba to stay at his luxurious home, Baba refused. But assuring the Master of a totally secret entrance to his house, he convinced Baba to make a short visit. However, rumors spread far and wide and great crowds gathered outside the man's gate, so that police had to be summoned to disperse them.

Soon after this, mandali member Raosaheb hired a bus to drive Baba to Zahedan, a frontier station bordering Persia and British India. It was imperative Baba get there as soon as possible; otherwise they would become stranded in the Persian desert and miss boarding the last train from Zahedan to India. It was leaving in just a few days and would be the last for a month.

The drive proved a long and harrowing trip across a landscape plagued by highway robbers, at the end of which Baba's party was held up at the border where questions arose about his visa for reentry into India. Baba had entered the country as a Persian subject, so re-entering India now became a huge headache.

When Baba had left Baam on November 1, Hafizji, the hired driver, was explicitly told, "Do not load any other items on the bus!" When Baba lost his temper taking his seat on the bus, the mandali were unable to account for his sudden change in mood. Then after only a mile the bus had two flat tires.

The driver, Hafizji, became frightened, as the tires were brand new and there was no apparent cause for punctures. After the tires had been repaired, they drove on to the next stop and rested. The next day, Hafizji noticed steam spewing out of the radiator. Again, he couldn't figure out what was wrong. He put cold water into the radiator and restarted the bus.

But within minutes the radiator was as hot as before. Opening the hood and checking the engine, he found a small crack in the bottom of the radiator. He filled it with more cold water and drove slowly to a nearby village, muttering, "Allah, Allah, protect me! I've never had such trouble before. What have I done wrong?"

But after only a few miles, the radiator again boiled over. By now Hafizji was at wit's end. He tried repairing the damage but was despondent with fear. When Raosaheb approached Hafizji to comfort him, the driver suddenly remembered what was wrong. He told Raosaheb. "Now I understand why all this happened. It's so clear to me now. I broke my promise to your Master. Before leaving Baam, I loaded two gunnysacks of almonds on the bus against his orders. How can I ask his forgiveness? I'm so ashamed of my ignorance and folly. Kindly pray to him on my behalf to forgive me."

Raosaheb sympathized, "I warned you bad luck accompanies those who break their promises to Meher Baba, but you failed to heed my advice. Well . . . ok, I'll take you and entreat him to forgive you." Hafizji was taken to Baba, and of course he was forgiven.

But Baba also spelled out, "Never disrespect a Master's word or break a promise once given. Now don't worry; drive back to Baam carefully and return with another bus." Hafizji was afraid the bus wouldn't make it back, but Baba assured him, "Don't worry. I'll see it arrives safely." Baba and his men awaited the new bus in Fahrej village.

The headman there was greatly drawn to Baba and declared to his townspeople, "I've been in the service of fakirs, lords and nobles, but never come across such light as I find in Meher Baba's face!" Meanwhile, following Baba's advice, Hafizji reached Baam safely. But he was too exhausted and shaken to drive any farther and so he sent a new bus with another driver. He was blessed in learning a lesson he'd never forget.

So the Master spent the day in the isolated desert village of Fahrej. There was little to eat, and rampant thieves threatened to steal from them. The mandali wondered why Baba had chosen this dreadful route through such dangerous deserts and mountains, with severe privations on the entire journey, and three of them became seriously ill. Finally they arrived at the border station of Zahedan where they were to cross back into India.

Baba explained, "It will take a long time to get visas. Go to the government office today and start on the paperwork. If we're stranded here, we won't catch Sunday's train and will have to spend a month or more here with more headaches getting visas and passports."

There were only two trains a week leaving Zahedan for Quetta —Thursday and Sunday, and then no more for the rest of the month. To get the required visas before Sunday was beyond improbable. Still, Baba warned Chanji and Raosaheb of the need for a speedy return and demanded they do whatever they felt necessary to get the documents in time.

In the meantime, a man named Dinyar Irani had come for Baba's darshan but was turned away, as Baba was seeing no one. Dinyar left disappointed, but what he would accomplish for the Master would make his story immortal. Raosaheb and Chanji both did their best to get all the paperwork done, but despite their labors they only got visas from the Persian Consul.

They still had to get the more difficult British re-entry visas for India. The British Consul's office closed at 1:00 PM on Saturdays, and Baba wanted to leave the next day on the last train that month. Getting travel documents at this point seemed impossible. Still, relying on Baba's inner help they went the Consul's office under strict orders not to disclose his identity. So the information they offered was deliberately vague.

Without satisfactory replies about the party's plans, the British Consul refused to issue entry visas back into India. Baba was disappointed when told, but then he sent Raosaheb and Chanji directly to the Consul's residence. Again they returned without the visas. Now he asked them to go back to the British Consul. They balked.

"It's not a question of following orders, Baba. We have to work according to the ways of the world. We're told not to disclose your name and all this trouble is due to that; but we continue to faithfully carry out your wish."

Baba declared:

You're both useless. So what if you're driven away from the office? Forget the world's ways. Just keep my orders in mind. Don't I understand this? Am I mad? Just follow my orders. What good is there in doing something easy? If you do the impossible, your manliness will shine forth!

True discipleship means complete, implicit obedience to the will and word of the Master. If you don't want to carry out my wishes, what's the sense in remaining with me?"

Meanwhile, Dinyar Irani had returned, and, standing on the doorstep, was again prevented from entering. He pleaded, "I've come on an urgent matter. I must see Meher Baba." Baba was told and called for Dinyar. "Why have you come?"

"I've brought you a letter." Surprised, Baba asked, "For me?" "Not you personally, but a letter addressed to the British Consul on your behalf from the Governor of Zahedan to allow you and your party to cross the frontier on tomorrow's train." Baba's face lit up as he slapped his thigh, signifying "*Shabash*! Well done!" He beckoned Dinyar closer.

After patting him on the back, Baba rested his hand on the man's head—a true blessing. Dinyar had been so anxious to see Baba, and here he was meeting him in such an extraordinary way. The mandali were dumbfounded. After some moments of quiet, Baba looked with disdain at Chanji and Raosaheb who were now feeling humbled. He explained:

This shows what real love can achieve! Look at this man—a poor merchant in this town with no influence in government circles, yet he manages to approach the highest official here and persuades the Governor himself to write a letter to the British Consul to permit our crossing the frontier unhindered. This is no small work or service! And he did it all unasked on his own, without even telling us about it.

Such selfless, spontaneous service rendered, with no hope of reward except my blessings, must succeed. Why? Because of the love inspiring him to do it. That love brought him success. I'm so happy. He deserves my blessings!

So Chanji and Raosaheb arrived at the Consul's residence at the crack of dawn on Sunday with the letter and full information on Baba and the other men, explaining that Baba's departure today was imperative. After a short wait, the Consul called them into his office.

But unsatisfied even with the Governor's letter of recommendation, he just placed it on his desk and gazed at it. Exasperated, he said, "At least tell me who the hell you people are." Chanji admitted, "Merwan is our Master, and we are his disciples." Taking their simple statement to heart, the Consul directed his clerk to fill out their visas.

Under the Radar

Due to the emerging Communist movement's public call for India's full independence from Britain, the British Consul in Zahedan had to be extremely cautious with visas. Here he was, faced with a party of unemployed Iranis, Hindus and Muslims. He could only fear the worst. His neck was on the block if Baba's companions turned out to be Communist agitators whom he had permitted to cross into India to add to the disturbances there.

In fact some time earlier, Bombay's British Consul had sent a memo to all Consulates in Persian coastal towns: "Do not to allow Meher Baba to return to India, as he refused to sign his name and has only a Persian passport—not a British one." Unknown to the mandali, it was for this very reason Baba selected the hazardous route to cross the border at Zahedan, because he knew this Consulate had not received those instructions.

Some months after returning to India, Baba sent Chanji to see the British Consul in Bombay to obtain a passport for one of the mandali. The Consul asked him, "You mean your Master has returned from Persia?" "Yes, months ago," Chanji replied. "Oh . . . okay; so he's started signing his name again."

Chanji denied it. "Then how the hell could he enter India with no visa?" Chanji simply stated, "Nothing's impossible for a Master." Puzzled, the Consul asked, "By what port did he leave Persia?" "The land route through Zahedan." The Consul slapped his forehead. "Now I truly believe he's a Master—and a Perfect one, too!" 1109–17

Earlier, in July, just before Baba entered his first seclusion in Kashmir, Raosaheb had brought a young Kashmiri boy to him, Pandit Muhammad Dukandar, who lovingly asked for Baba's darshan. So Baba called him and observed, "His heart is so pure; he's clever and innocent." Baba then inquired if Pandit wanted to ask him anything. "No sir, not now," the boy said. "I'll come back some other time." "All right," Baba said, "But make sure you do!"

Then instead of leaving, Pandit sat down. So Baba asked, "Do you want to finish school? How about a job or do you want *mukti* [liberation]?" "I want devotion to God!" Pandit exclaimed. "That's the best choice," replied Baba. "I'll give it to you; don't even think about it." Pandit then touched Baba's feet, and on departing said he'd surely come back. He would turn out to be Baba's magic link to Agha Ali, who was sill held captive by his parents in Persia. 1062

Frustrated by being unable to retrieve Agha Ali from his parents, Baba sent a telegram to Pandit's father in Harvan, requesting Pandit be sent to him in Nasik. He then confided to the mandali, "If Pandit comes, my work will be done; otherwise, I'll have to return to Kashmir just to see him. Pandit is the link, and by my holding fast to this link, Agha Ali will be able to rejoin me from Persia."

But due to school exams, Pandit couldn't leave to travel to Nasik. Meanwhile, Baidul, who had remained in Persia, wrote a letter to Baba about Ali's condition: "Ali is very troubled. He's stopped eating and is so anxious to come to Baba at any cost." This was the longing of real love. Baba only commented that he'd take care of it. 1186

He then sent Raosaheb to Bombay to see Agha Ali's father, but word came back that Ali was still unable to return from Persia, this time because of his mother's persistent unwillingness. So, as Pandit was unable to travel, Baba had to travel to him.

The group reached Kashmir on June 23. Early the next day, Baba sent Vishnu and Raosaheb to Harvan village to bring Pandit to him. Baba again cryptically repeated, "Pandit is the link to bring Agha Ali back. Through my contact with Pandit, Ali will return from Persia." The Master's work with the children had been a serious preoccupation since Meher Ashram days, and he was connecting all the dots between these important links.

Returning to Meherabad, Baba celebrated the fifth anniversary of his silence on Thursday, July 10, 1930. He allowed his Arangaon village and Ahmednagar devotees to meet him on Meherabad Hill, where the mandali washed his feet.

Almost miraculously, a telegram arrived that very day from Baidul, conveying good news. After much pushing and pulling, he was finally able to return to India with Agha Ali happily at his side. Baba explained that the result of his two-thousand-mile trip to Kashmir "to instruct Pandit in meditation" for just five minutes, was really to bring Aga Ali back from captivity in Persia.

But Baidul and Ali were blocked at the border, detained at India's frontier without passports. On August 1, Baba cabled Rusi Irani in Quetta to do all he could to help: "Exert all influence. Boy's presence here most essential. Consider this my greatest service. Leave nothing undone to help them come here." The next day, Rusi replied that Baidul and Ali had been "inexplicably" cleared to enter India. Baba cabled in return: "So pleased you've done such a great service for me about which you have no idea, and for which you have my special blessing." 1192

When Baidul arrived in Nasik with Agha Ali, the boy was moved to tears in the Master's embrace. He had been away for nineteen months. Baba was also happy, explaining to the men:

> To make it clear, through Pandit I established Agha
> Ali's link in my first visit to Kashmir [August 1929]. Total-
> ly uncalled by me, Pandit suddenly appeared on the scene,
> coming on his own with full love and devotion. He actually
> wanted to stay with me forever.
>
> Although all my other direct efforts failed to bring Ali
> back from Persia, after our return from Kashmir, corre-
> spondence began with Pandit—Ali's new link, as Ali
> couldn't be brought due to parental resistance. When I
> again contacted Pandit in Kashmir during our last trip, Ali
> returned. That's why I went so far to Kashmir, 'wasting' all
> that time and money! With a bit of understanding, you'd
> see this was as great as raising the Himalayas! 1195

Soon after this, Baba discussed his finances with the men: "Expenses will really be difficult from now on. So what should we do?" Raosaheb offered to raise the needed money in Bombay. "Great idea—Splendid! But—and this is important—you must return tomorrow. Bombay. Can you do it?" Raosaheb assured Baba he'd surely return tomorrow and then left for Bombay.

When he didn't return the next day, Baba paced up and down, asking about him. Finally, on the third day, Raosaheb appeared. Baba wasn't pleased. Scowling, Baba asked Raosaheb, "Why weren't you here yesterday? Why did you disobey me?"

Raosaheb silently placed a bundle of currency notes at Baba's feet, thinking surely to satisfy him. But Baba sent for Chhagan and ordered him, "Pick up that money and burn it!" Raosaheb was aghast to see Chhagan burn the money. Baba explained: "What value has money for me? Even if you placed the whole world's treasure before me, it's nothing but shit to me! But by breaking my order you broke my heart! I don't want lucre; I want love!" Baba then forgave Raosaheb, adding, "Always follow orders. No other gift however valuable can ever compare to your obedience." 1161–62

Baba's First Western Interview

In November 1929, Baba was approached by a man named Raphael Hirsch, whoso pen name was Paul Brunton. Brunton was traveling throughout India, meeting with Spiritual Masters. In Baba's first ever interview with a Western journalist, Brunton began by asking if his present state was at all due to his schoolteachers or college professors. Baba responded:

Paul Brunton, author of *A Search in Secret India*

>What has education got to do with *Truth*? I will change the history of the whole world. As Jesus came to give spirituality to a materialistic age, so I have come to impart a spiritual push to present mankind.

There's always a fixed time for such divine workings. At the ripe hour, I'll reveal my true nature to the entire world.

I'll break my silence and deliver my message, but only when there's chaos and confusion everywhere and children in the streets cry out for mercy. For when the world is rocking, I shall be most needed. There will be upheavals, earthquakes, floods and volcanic eruptions when both East and West are aflame with war. Truly, the whole world must suffer, as the whole world must be redeemed.

It is now enmeshed in sensual desires, in racial selfishness and Godless money-worship. God is forsaken. True religion is abused; man seeks life and the priests give him nothing but stone. God must send his true prophet among men once again to establish true worship and awaken people from their materialistic stupor. My mission follows the line of earlier prophets; God has given me a mandate. Once I openly announce myself as the messiah, nothing will withstand my power. 1207

Baba ended his meeting with Brunton by urging him, "Go to the West as my representative! Spread my name as the coming Divine Messenger. Work for me and you'll be working for the good of mankind." Totally startled, Brunton responded, "Oh . . . I don't know if I can do that; the world will think I'm totally mad." Baba assured him he was mistaken, promising "I'll help you to render service to me in the West." 1209–10

Brunton didn't know that by using a masterful Avataric ruse Baba was turning the key so that the journalist would turn against him. After touring India in search of true Masters, Brunton returned disappointed to Baba, who now was in Nasik, and asked why he looked so distressed. Brunton replied, "My mind is troubled. I'm thinking of the twelve holy men encountered in India who all claim to be the Messiah!"

Baba smiled and gestured, "Yes, I've heard of some of them." "How do you explain it?" Brunton asked, very agitated. Baba replied, "If they're honest, then they're simply deluded. If they're dishonest, they're deceiving others and will have to suffer terribly. Don't worry about it. These men are unconsciously helping my work. I know who I am. When the time comes for me to fulfill my mission, the entire world will know who I am."

Again, Baba's secret motive was to aggravate him so he'd write negative attacks against him. Just as Baba had wished for Col. Irani to oppose him in India, he now wished for Brunton to oppose him in Europe and America. 1215–16

The work Baba wanted to accomplish through Brunton's antagonistic critique of the "so-called Messiah" was revealed in Brunton's book, *A Search in Secret India*. While censuring the Master, it drew countless Westerners to take great interest in Baba.

Even Brunton's later secretary, Louis Agostini, became a devoted follower. Visiting Baba in India in 1960, Agostini said: "In Brunton's last letter to me from New Zealand, he said he felt his original statements about Baba had been written altogether by another person, and certainly if he had to do it over again he'd write it all very differently: "My earlier books were written too soon, too impulsively and too immaturely. I should have waited several years. The time has come to put right the errors of my past."

Brunton never publicly rectified the misrepresentations of Baba made in his book. But when he finally wrote a letter of apology to Baba in 1954, Baba had a signed copy of his seminal work, *God Speaks*, sent to him.

Chapter Sixteen
Secret Visits to Persia and the West

Meanwhile, Baba had shifted his ashram from Meherabad to Nasik in June 1928. He was entering a period of travel and he wanted the women to be in a safe environment near the home of Mehera's sister Freny and her husband Rustom. In January 1930, in-between trips, he entered seclusion there. One evening during Baba's usual stroll, people on the street began to gaze at him, taken with his long hair and flowing white sadra. The mandali were walking behind him, which made the people wonder why he was being followed by such a motley crew of characters.

They concluded that Baba must be the lead actor in a traveling theatre company, and the mandali were other cast members. A few of them actually tried to find out where and when the show was starting. 1121

Sheriar's Fervent Prayer

Mehera contracted malaria while the women were living in Nasik. As Baba was away, Gulmai and her sister Soonamasi, skilled at nursing, began taking care of her. Baba's elderly father Sheriar also was not well, and wanting a change for him, Shireenmai brought him to Nasik, hoping that with Soonamasi's care he might soon recover.

Though he was weak, Sheriar sat each morning in a corner of the porch, continuing his practice of silently repeating his favorite name of God—Yezdan, with all his heart. Knowing Mehera was suffering from intense fevers, he asked to be brought to her room.

"I can bring her temperature down. I know a special prayer that will break her fever."

He was led to Mehera, who by now was only semi-conscious. He stood, softly repeating the prayer in mixed Persian and Arabic – four lines taking only moments to recite. But Sheriar said it with such fervor and love that by evening Mehera's fever was gone from that day forward. "From that day, I never had fever or an illness again, she said." Though she later learned the prayer by heart, in later years she said she had completely forgotten it. MM 1:229–30

Forgiving Treachery

Some years earlier in Poona, Baba had met a man named Mulog who was helping Sheriar with his toddy shops. After a time, Mulog convinced the Master's aging father to turn over the running of his chain of shops on the ruse that Sheriar might comfortably retire. 451, 635–36

Mulog was to take over only as a manager, and he presented a blank contract to Sheriar, saying, "Don't worry, I'll bring it to a lawyer to have it properly drawn up." All he needed was the old man's signature at the bottom. Sheriar was trusting and signed on the dotted line.

Mulog's treachery was revealed later when the document was filled in with totally false statements transferring complete ownership of all of Sheriar's shops to Mulog. The case dragged on for years. Sheriar could have told the court that his signature was forged, but as a true Zoroastrian, he refused to lie. It was his signature. To Shireenmai's chagrin, the family lost everything. But Sheriar was resigned to God's will and sent Mulog the following note: "I forgive you fully for what you've done. If a time comes to ask my forgiveness, I may be dead. I'm already an old man. So remember, there'll be no reason to ask, as today I have completely forgiven you. The matter is now between you and God."

Decades later, as he lay dying, Mulog deeply repented having defrauded Sheriar and begged Baba's forgiveness. His wife sought out Baba and fell at his feet. Bursting into tears, she said Mulog was on his deathbed, and though he'd already received Sheriar's forgiveness, he couldn't go until he received God's direct forgiveness for what he'd done.

Looking into the distance, Baba touched his chest with his right hand in a closed fist. Reaching out and spreading his fingers and opening his hand palm down, he gestured, "All right, I forgive him." Mulog died peacefully a few hours later. 635–36 and footnote; LL Mani 1:6

A Third Visit to Persia

On April 26, 1931, Baba embarked on a journey to Quetta. On June 1, accompanied by Agha Ali, Chanji, Behramji, Raosaheb and Gustadji, Baba left Quetta by train for his third visit to Persia—a secret one. This time also Baba refused to sign his name for a British passport, and he traveled on his previous Persian one. He chose the same route he had used on his previous trip and again he and the men were plagued by trouble. They reached the now familiar Zahedan five days later and drove on to Mashhad, near the border between Russia and Afghanistan, arriving at noon on June 6.

There was a large Shiite mosque in Mashhad where fifteen million Muslim pilgrims came to pray each year at the tomb of the great eighth-century Perfect Master, the eighth Imam Reza, who had been martyred when he was poisoned by the caliph. He was the only Imam buried in Iran.

Baba entered the mosque at midnight on June 6 for three consecutive nights, where he spent two hours in seclusion each night while his mandali kept strict watch outside. Due to prevailing orthodoxy, this arrangement was prohibited and therefore very difficult to secure. It was made only through the intervention of the Muslim priest-caretaker of the mosque who had dreamed that the greatest of Holy Men had entered Persia, and the Imam Reza, Ali ar-Ridha himself, instructed him to let Baba sit next to the tomb to fulfill his vigil.

Baba kept Agha Ali by his side at all times in Mashhad. He had once remarked to the mandali, "If Ali remains pure, I will make him a *salik* [a God-realized one who regains normal worldly consciousness to work for the upliftment of humanity]!" Ali was now serving as Baba's personal aide, reading his alphabet board, and he would soon travel to Europe, New York and Boston with the Master.

While in Mashhad, Baba went to see several movies. He also walked daily to a garden, and one day after strolling there, two women followed him to his residence. Baba beckoned them inside, asking what they wanted. When they told him they were prostitutes, Baba explained to them about leading a pure spiritual life devoted to God. Just looking at Baba's face, the women began to weep. "O Holy One! How can we make up for our sins? Our lives have been so immoral; we are beyond salvation." Baba consoled them, explaining:

> A true Holy One is like the ocean, so vast that if you throw dirt or sandalwood into it, it assimilates both, leaving its waters pure as before. In the same way, the Holy One also takes upon himself the good and bad of both the virtuous and the sinful, merging them in his Oceanic Love.
>
> In this way even the worst sinner is purified. So from now on, avoid your present way of living and realize you've been forgiven and made pure!

Both were deeply moved by Baba's silent words. He had them sit beside him and their hearts cried out, "O Holy One! We dedicate our new life at your feet!" They shed tears of repentance before him, and their sins were washed away. 1225–26

> *In his form are all —*
> *Who to take as a sinner —*
> *Who to take as saint?*
> *~ elf*

Regarding Mashhad, in 1943, during WWII, Baba made one of the most significant declarations of his Avatarhood: "The tree of my Divine Manifestation is planted in Mashhad where it will grow and spread, ultimately covering the whole world!" 2361

He was implying that humanity's spiritual transformation would be cued from the Muslim world and it was likely connected with his deep spiritual work with the Muslim Prem Ashram students from Persia. He also explained how archetypal acts connected with his Universal work were linked with his mission of giving all of creation a spiritual push forward. We infer that when Baba takes simple schoolboys and raises them to the pinnacle of divine love, he's working to accomplish that in all of humanity at the time of his Manifestation. 2069

The work that Baba conducted on a small scale in Prem Ashram will thus have a Universal effect on the world, raising direct awareness and love for God without priesthoods and the external rituals of lukewarm faith. He also explained:

> The world is laboring under terrible economic chaos.
> To follow the spiritual path material needs must be partly satisfied.
> So with my own hands as I clothe and feed the poor the world gains economic and material welfare. When I wash

> Meher Baba visited Mashhad three times; in 1924, 1929 and 1931. After his last visit he declared, "You'll see what happens to Iran. I am sowing the seed of Love there; I have sown it. Now when it becomes a tree, you'll see how many Iranis come here." Years later, the fire of the Avatar's love is igniting in Iran. As of the writing of this book, its pilgrims to Baba's tomb exceeded those from the United States, the past leader of non-Indian nations. Baba said after his Manifestation, Iranians would flock to Meherabad. They are coming, and as he said, even without passports. 4885

the mad and lepers, it helps those of abnormal consciousness to regain normal or supernatural consciousness, and lepers get cured or their future births are much lessened. 1786–87

The Master Pulls Another Charade

With his work completed, Baba was driven back to Zahedan, and from there he again quietly re-entered British India again without a passport. The men were completely taken aback by his rundown condition. He was still wearing his old coarse wool blanket coat which had become shabby and dirty. His cotton pants were frayed and stained, his hair disheveled and tangled and his cheeks covered with dark bruises.

With dark circles under his eyes he wore a haggard expression. Seeing him in this state brought the men to tears. He tried to console them, explaining:

> This is my condition now—dying every moment! I don't know what's ahead. I have so much work to do in the future, but my body has grown weak. If you want to stay with me, do so; otherwise, you can leave.
>
> I can't maintain anyone now. Our money is finished. How can I see to others when I myself am in such dire straits? The pressure of the work lying ahead may make me drop my body. You should now decide once and for all whether to continue with me or not.

But who could abandon him? Moved by his pitiful condition, the men forgot their own troubles and begged him to take care of his health. They were ready to undergo any and all hardships that might befall them. It was a truly touching scene, and Baba's woeful appearance was so dramatic that the mandali were deeply moved. Bidding them farewell, he stated, "I have great work before me, but I doubt this body will bear the burden. If not, it will soon drop. You may be seeing me for the last time." Then conveying resolve amidst tears, they bowed to Baba—perhaps for the final time. 1229–30

Topping it off, most of the men and women never even knew he had just been to Persia, never mind that he soon would quietly set sail for England and America. The mandali returned to Nasik in a sorrowful mood, forgetting their own troubles and complaints against him in light of his unbearable sufferings. This is why even though he was truly suffering Baba maintained his role of showing them his deplorable condition.

Meher Baba on his return from Persia wearing his patched kamli coat, which he called his most spiritually charged possession in this Advent, Meherabad, 1931

Hung on a Rusty Nail

Hammered into the trunk of Babajan's neem tree in Poona was an old rusty nail. A cheap little picture frame hung on it, containing a faded image of her Beloved son. She looked at it every now and then, nodding and softly talking to him, and was once seen leaning over to rest her forehead on the picture of her own Divine Beloved.

She now began murmuring about her Merwan, longing "to go to my child's place." Astonishingly, she left her seat beneath the neem tree in Poona for the first time in thirty-two years to be driven eighty miles to Meherabad. Early that same morning, Baba was seen walking barefooted up on Meherabad Hill—most unusual for him. The reason became clear just before noon.

As her car pulled up in front of the school bearing her name, Babajan got out and stood by the railway tracks between upper and lower Meherabad. Baba quickly walked down the Hill and stood fifty yards up from the tracks. As she and Baba gazed at one another, the men offered her water. After a few moments she left without words or physical contact. The women were peeking around their bamboo screen, watching the silent meeting.

Regarding her visit, Baba concluded, "Today is the most eventful, significant day of my life!" What he may have meant was that this was the signal that he was now to take his Avataric mission to the West and even farther, around the world, the mission for which he had incarnated in this Advent. He returned the visit the next day.

Babajan was sitting with a crowd under her tree in Bund Gardens. Baba stood at a distance on the opposite river bank a hundred yards away. After sending his mandali over the bridge for her darshan, he returned to Meherabad. This contact between the two was their last. 920–21

It happened that Babajan needed an operation on one of her fingers at Sassoon Hospital, but she said, "It's time for me to leave now. The work is over. I'm closing the shop. Nobody wants my wares or can afford the price. I've turned my goods over to the Proprietor," meaning the Saheb-e-Zamaan—Avatar Meher Baba. She would leave her body on September 21, 1931, while Baba was in England.

Babajan's presence on earth had lasted between 127 and 141 years. Some reports recorded her birth date as 1790. Hindus, Muslims and the people of Poona were speechless and heartbroken. Her funeral procession was a grand affair, rivaling those of the highest royalty in India. As Babajan herself once had said, "Cycles change, the worlds rotate, but Qutubs never their seat vacate."

Babajan's obituary appeared in the *New York Times*. She was laid to rest beneath her old neem tree, where she had sat dispensing Divine Grace for thirty-three years, crowning the new Avatar just as Buddha had been crowned under another neem tree. *Lord Meher* tells the amazing story of her early life:

> Hazrat Babajan was the daughter of one of the chief rulers and Ministers of the Amir of Afghanistan in Kabul. In Her teens, She was exceptionally beautiful, and from Her childhood had a natural inclination toward spirituality and realization of Truth. With growing age, this inclination turned into a deep-rooted desire for things other than mere materialism.
>
> This brilliant, beautiful, promising young girl on the threshold of Her glorious youth was a confirmed non-materialist. Things of the world, however attractive and bewitching, could create no impressions on Babajan. In short, Maya, with all her powerful implements of lust, greed and anger, was totally helpless against this future Power House and Emperor of Spirituality—even at that early age. When she was hardly fifteen, Babajan's guardians began to arrange for Her marriage on a grand scale.
>
> But disinclined to involve Herself in family affairs, She boldly left the family shelter and disappeared in the thin air! For fifty years She led a life of complete resignation and renunciation! Her only aim was to find the One who would reach Her to Her Ideal. After wandering from place

to place for fifty long years, She at last came across Her Master, and became God-Realized at the age of sixty-five.

After Her Realization, Babajan lived for some time in the Punjab where many began respecting Her as a Saint—some even worshipped Her. This worshipping and Babajan's occasional remarks declaring Herself to be God—An-al-Haq—naturally upset the Mohammedans, for this was nothing but blasphemy according to common interpretations of Islamic teachings.

Some of the most fanatic amongst them, certain Baluchis of a local military regiment, were so infuriated they could think nothing short of a "living grave" as punishment for Babajan's so seemingly blasphemous but true remarks. It didn't end with a mental resolve. One dark night they succeeded in capturing and burying Babajan alive! It was through Her own miraculous super-natural powers that She safely emerged from the grave. She soon left that place and headed for Bombay.

After many years and during the Great War [WWI], that Punjab regiment was transferred to Poona. Imagine their wonder and amazement coming face to face with Her on a street corner in Poona! But now their fanaticism turned into great devotion, and as long as the regiment was stationed in Poona, its members often came to pay their deep respects to Babajan.

Their rush was so great special facilities were granted by their superior officers to enable them to come see the Person whom they had once thought proper to murder in cold blood for claiming equality with God! Allah be praised! Afterwards, this whole regiment was killed to the last man in war at the Dardanelles. Who knows what significance and eternal blessing this battle became for these soldiers whose cowardice had turned into such spiritual bravery and Truth?

Despite advanced age, She defied nature with a vengeance, sitting so many years under the shelter of a mere tree through the intense cold, scorching heat and torrential rains of different seasons. The moral: always to aspire for the Real—for Spiritual Advancement. Marriages and other festivities appear nice and inviting, but they're all material and liable to be destroyed sooner or later, ending in nothing. Even after marriage, aspire only for true Spiritual Advancement! 6-7; CD part 130

Babajan's marble tomb-shrine was built by her beloved Merwan, who gave four thousand rupees to the Muslim devotees who would be in charge of its care. However, sixty years later, well after Meher Baba's own passing, the Muslims who maintained Babajan's tomb tore down the one Baba had constructed in her honor. They erected their own monument, removing Meher Baba's photo at the same time. With this over-zealous act, they mistakenly thought to honor their Master, Babajan. On the contrary, it would have been against her wishes.

These Muslims never knew her. They were veiled and never witnessed the Divine Light shining from the eyes of Meher Baba, their Zaheb-e-Zaman. They tried to protect her Muslim status from what they falsely perceived as a "mere Parsi saint," the one she herself called "*Mera piarra beta!* Oh my beloved son! This is my beloved son. One day he will shake the world, and all of humanity will be benefited by him."

Love Calls Me to the West

Babajan's death signaled that a new phase in Meher Baba's public life was to begin, with a beneath-the-radar trip to Europe and America. It was imperative for him to personally contact his chosen circle members in the West before the start of WWII. Most would be women, destined through the ages to be his earliest Western disciples. They would work intimately with him through the crucial war years and beyond.

Baba had told the Prem Ashram boys he was being "pulled" to the West as his new Avataric priority: "My work for the circle is almost complete and only a little bit remains. When that's over, I'll journey to Europe and America." Anticipating this exciting event, the Prem Ashram boys cleverly dressed Baba up in a stylish western suit and shoes and took his picture. Aw 20 (no. 2): 2

After Baba returned to Nasik, he shaved his beard and secluded himself for three days. This short seclusion set in motion preparations for the his first Western visit. He knew his men would have to endure difficulties during his four-month absence, and he acted in such a way that they'd be willing to face even the fires of hell to help him in his work and ease his suffering. Meanwhile, he cabled Meredith Starr in England: "*Make all preparations for my coming. Love calls me to the West!*" 1229-31

Baba In 1922, traveled to Karachi to see the city's mayor, Jamshed Mehta, a dear friend and personal advisor to Gandhi. Mehta had also spent much time in Baba's close company and became an ardent devotee. Baba was very pleased with the mayor's selfless service to the poor of Karachi and assured him he'd take Gandhi to England safely under his wing.

Baba had asked Mehta to obtain passports for Chanji, Agha Ali and himself. But even he had trouble convincing the British authorities to issue a passport without Baba's signature and had to exert pressure and use his strong political influence, but to no avail.

Baba Prophesies the Demise of the British Empire

Baba's silence meant that he neither read nor wrote. As he repeatedly refused to sign his name on his British passport form, the authorities simply kept turning him down. But he needed to board a certain ship on a certain day. So with great reluctance he signed his name on the form, ominously declaring: "The British empire hereby compels me to sign its own death warrant. This is the end of their empire." He grimly signed, "*M.S. Irani.*" Britain had unwittingly dug its own grave, as from that day forward, its rule in India began to topple. In 1927 Baba had observed:

> Sending the Indian army to fight in a foreign war is a bad British policy. If it continues to do such things it will lose its prestige all over the world.
> If these frictions and hostilities in China do not cease soon and a reconciliation arrived at, the British will be the greatest sufferers, losing everything—their name, fame, and empire throughout the world. Their underhanded dealings and diplomatic policies have made almost the whole world their enemy. They will suffer for the injustices they have done to innumerable people and many countries with their policies.

For the rest of his life, on the rare occasions when Baba consented to sign his name, it was always with that same signature, "*MS Irani.*"

The Mahatma Meets the Master

While in Karachi, Chanji had booked berths for Baba and his party on the SS *Tevere*, but as no second-class accommodations were available, Baba told him to cancel the reservation and book on the SS *Rajputana* instead. It was extremely difficult on such short notice to get a refund and then book tickets on a different ship. Chanji wondered why this last-minute change was necessary,

as it created more problems for him. Jamshed Mehta in Karachi was also at a loss to understand it.

However, a Round Table Conference on India's independence was scheduled to take place in London in September, and while it was uncertain whether Gandhi would boycott or attend, he agreed to go at the very last moment. When it was announced that he'd be sailing aboard the SS *Rajputana*, Chanji and Jamshed Mehta instantly grasped why Baba had switched passage to that ship at the last minute.

In 1922, Baba had prophetically remarked that he and Mahatma Gandhi would travel together on the same ship to the West. [2] Gandhi told newspaper reporters, "I must go to London with God as my only guide." And so he did, literally, and unknowingly, aboard the same ship as the Avatar. Both were making their first voyage to the West.

At the dock, thousands turned out to see Gandhi off. If they saw the Avatar it was only inadvertently. No disciples, family or friends came, and except for the three men accompanying him, only Mehera knew he was even leaving India. All was done under a cloak of secrecy.

Baba would be gone for four months. The men who stayed behind were told only after the ship had pulled anchor. If not, all would have been screaming to go with him. Brother Jal commented, "That was some charade Baba pulled." His brother Beheram added, "Were it not kept secret, we'd have pestered him to death to take us."

Devotee K.J. Dastur was shocked: "I can't believe Baba went to England without me; I have an M.A. and law degrees. How could Baba leave behind such an educated person as me?" He couldn't tolerate this affront and spent his later years writing negatively about Baba. 1231–35

The world could not know what precious cargo was sailing on that ship or how these events would change the destinies of the East, the West and the entire world: This was the just the first of Meher Baba's many Western visits and world tours.

As usual, he carried great quantities of luggage, much of it never opened. Changing plans and keeping his companions guessing were Baba's ways of working, or as he once put it, "I never make plans or change plans. It's all one endless plan to make people realize there *is* no plan." 839

Baba boarded the SS *Rajputana* on August 29, 1931. His first port of call was Port Said, Egypt, after which he continued on to Marseilles—the Avatar's first touchdown in the West. After a ten-day voyage, Baba's journey resumed, overland by rail, to London via Paris. As the ocean follows certain currents, so the *barakath,* or divine grace of history, follows specific currents channeled from East to West, and then from Europe on to America. These three regions have been spiritually connected since ancient times. Meher Baba simply followed the route established by the Masters in ages past, as did the Nordic Vikings in the tenth century, and, later, by St. Brendan and America's Pilgrim Fathers.

By now, Gandhi's popularity in India had risen greatly. Though he knew little of Meher Baba, he did want to meet him after briefly glancing through an article in the *Meher Message* magazine that he read in his jail cell serving an earlier sentence in Ahmednagar.

However, he later had an unnerving encounter with one of Baba's Masters, Upasni Maharaj, who shouted at him and roundly

CHRIST COME AGAIN

chastised him, asking, "Have you no shame for daring to call yourself a great soul—a Mahatma?" Maharaj then exposed his genitals to further show his contempt for Gandhi. The Mahatma retreated, visibly shaken by Maharaj's rudeness, thinking him a total madman and certainly not a Perfect Master.

Sometime later, Gandhi was taking a leisurely stroll with some political leaders on the road in Ahmednagar leading out to Baba's Meherabad compound. When informed of it, and also that Meher Baba's master was Upasni Maharaj, Gandhi remembered his terrible experience, did a quick about-face and returned to Ahmednagar. Now, aboard the *Rajputana,* steaming toward Europe, he was unaware of Baba's intimate presence.

After a few days at sea, Baba was getting impatient for Gandhi to make his move. "It's always like this. When I don't allow visitors, people complain. And now when I want to see someone, they don't even show an inclination. We should just forget about trying to contact Gandhi. It's too late now. . . . He's a good man, but it would be better and to his great benefit if he sees me. I love him dearly and would like to meet with him for his own good."

Gandhi didn't act until receiving a cable from Jamshed Mehta informing him of Baba's presence and urging him to seek contact with the Master without delay. Finally, with this prod from Mehta, Gandhi's secretary contacted Chanji to arrange a meeting on board for September 8 at 9:00 PM.

Baba traveling incognito aboard ship to the West, in 1931

That evening, Gandhi began a halfhearted search for Baba. Leisurely strolling the deck, he glanced at cabin numbers until he came to the right one. As the door opened, Baba stood up, and Gandhi suddenly beheld the Master's form. We can only imagine what passed between them in that destined moment. Baba had been drawing him for lifetimes, though veiling him from that realization.

Gandhi got right to the point: "Baba, I've come only because I received a telegram from Jamshed Mehta. I'd never come on my own. I'll see you for five minutes and then go." Baba asked him to have a seat. Those five minutes would extend to three hours that first night. Gandhi continued, "I've read about you and wanted to see you one day, God willing, but I never expected it to be so soon!"

"Now I suppose you know Upasni Maharaj is my guru," Baba remarked. "Oh, Baba," Gandhi replied truthfully, "I got such a bad impression from him." Baba replied, "Perfect Masters have their own ways. It's impossible for anyone to understand them." [3863–64

Actually, Upasni knew Gandhi's work was with Baba and not him, so he had soundly and deliberately put him off with his crude behavior. Gandhi was astonished at what he encountered and recognized Baba was a true Master. Baba spelled out on the alphabet board, "I hold the key to the three worlds."

Gandhi implored, "Baba, do something about it! Why not give me the key of the gross world just for India's independence?" Baba assured him, "I will, but only on one condition. After India gets independence, you must give up all politics and come to stay with me and do as I ask. Do you agree to that?" Gandhi promised. "Yes, if India gets independence," but it was a promise he'd eventually break. He then expressed regret over the time he had wasted by not contacting Baba sooner. He even suggested that they share the same cabin. Baba declined but said they could meet next day.

Baba then spoke of his secret book, saying that it would one day be "like a new Bible for the world." Gandhi asked to see it. So Baba handed him a few chosen pages, warning him, "Be careful. Up to now I've not even allowed my mandali to see it. No one else is to read it."

Gandhi returned the pages the next day, remarking how well written and touching they were, adding: "Baba, enough now of this tyranny! Please break your silence and proclaim yourself to the world." Baba indicated that the time was not yet ripe. Then came discussions on spirituality, politics and a strategy to liberate India from the British. 1240-4; V 218

Baba also discussed their mutual acquaintance, Col. M.S. Irani, who was defaming him among Parsis in India, and about whom he would later say: "Honestly, I love Colonel Irani. I know he is within me and is doing what I *want* him to do."

> Everyone works as he is intended to work, and God is in all. No one is at fault. Parsis defame me; call me 'Shaitan'—the Devil, simply because I don't eat meat and fish. I don't drink liquor and have never been to a brothel.
>
> Their definition of a Parsi is he should be a non-vegetarian, drink wine and lead an immoral life while wearing the religious symbols of the sadra and thread, visiting the fire-temple and paying heed to those priests. It's the priests who are responsible for all this.
>
> The priest class totally impedes everything. If independence is gained, arrest all the Hindu, Parsi and Muslim priests! Don't use violence, but deal with them firmly and vigorously. It's a hugely important work and unless you send all the priests to Yerawada Prison, they won't improve; they'll just become worse!" 1248

Baba asserted that the church and priesthood had totally ruined religion: "Catholic priests are the same as in every religion the world over. Out of selfishness, they create and propagate their own customs, tenets and practices, crippling religion. All these rituals and ceremonies are the dry husk of the corn." 1272

Baba would later observe, "Religion as a living force has become obsolete! To resuscitate religion today's urgent need is to dig it out of its narrow, dark hidings and coverings, and let the spirit of man shine out once again in its pristine glory." 2568

During subsequent meetings onboard ship and at later, Gandhi continued to express his desire to join Baba's ashram as an intimate one. But Baba kept putting him off, repeating that he had to end his political activities for good, and only then would he be called. Of course, Baba was secretly using Gandhi's invaluable work to rid India of Britain's oppressive presence, as he himself publicly could have nothing to do with it.

On their tenth day at sea, nearing the port of Marseilles, Gandhi spied Baba on the upper deck and approached him reverently with folded hands. Suddenly, reporters swarmed like bees out of nowhere, snapping pictures. "The photographers won't allow us even a moment's rest. Promise we'll meet again secretly in London," Gandhi asked, and Baba agreed. 1239–48

As they docked at Marseilles, the press clamor worsened. Countless reporters, newsreel cameramen, radio and wire services were on hand to greet Gandhi. What likely happened next is in none of the official accounts, nor has research found the news account of the following story, and so it is strictly anecdotal. Early Baba lover and former Pakistani intelligence officer, Minoo Kharas, claims this story was directly relayed to him by a close friend who read it in a Karachi newspaper published the day the *Rajputana* docked in Marseilles. [3]

According to this Karachi news report, before he stepped up to the microphone, Gandhi's first words to the gathered press corps were, "Gentlemen, tarry a while." Then pointing behind him, he repeated, "Tarry a while, my brothers. Behind me is one traveling incognito. I'm not equal to the dirt under his nails. If he so desires, he can make the sun rise in the West and set in the East. It is he you should be interviewing, not me!"

Western Shores At Last

But Baba wanted to arrive unobtrusively, so his party quietly disembarked toward the rear of the ship, far from the reporters and the Gandhi hubbub. Baba stepped onto the shores of Europe at 8:00 AM, September 11, 1931. Three people were waiting to receive him: Meredith Starr, Kitty Davy and her brother Herbert.

Kitty and her brother hailed from London. They had heard of Baba from Meredith and were anxious to meet him. They had invited him to stay at their parents' home in Kensington.

Much correspondence had been exchanged between Baba and Meredith Starr since he'd left India in 1928 to establish Baba's link with the West. Baba must have made a humorous picture dressed in a white sadra, a brown fake-Chinchilla coat and a pink scarf wrapped around his head. 1253; Gl, May 2006: 23

Despite his quiet arrival, however, the press named Baba as Gandhi's Spiritual Master, causing both men unwanted publicity so that they became fodder for the tabloids. Neither acknowledged the other on the train to London via Paris, as Gandhi was in "protective custody," surrounded by Scotland Yard guards. By the time he reached the West, his political stance had undergone remarkable strengthening in India, taking the British completely by surprise. For security reasons, his guards took him off the train at Folkstone and he was driven the rest of the way to London, as they were wary of a demonstration at Victoria Station, where huge crowds had already gathered.

CHRIST COME AGAIN

The crowds hadn't come to meet the Avatar, but when Baba arrived they gazed on him in awe. They had never seen a human being like him. those gathered at the station were stunned by what they saw. His thunderous silence spoke a mystery only an awakened heart could begin to hear. Baba was reviewing pages from the books of their past lives. 1254

By the time Baba, his mandali and three English disciples had loaded the luggage and driven away from the station, they found the streets lined with crowds waiting to receive Gandhi. As Baba's car passed, they began waving and cheering wildly in an unintended welcome. As the Master of illusion drove past them incognito, they craned their necks to get a glimpse of Gandhi's presumed motorcade, now on its secret back-street route. Britain had just given a grand welcome to the Lord of the Universe.

Kitty had made arrangements for to Baba to stay in her parents' home at 32 Russell Road, Kensington, where he, Chanji and Agha Ali were taken. Gandhi telephoned Chanji there two days later, saying, "I'm very eager and must see Baba. Please bring him tomorrow, on your shoulders if you must, for even a few minutes!" Baba agreed to meet Gandhi at a community center in East London. 1285

Baba with Prem Ashram student Agha Ali, Devonshire, 1931

Also destined to contact Baba in England was Thomas A. Watson, Alexander Graham Bell's collaborator in the invention and manufacture of the telephone. Watson had accumulated great wealth by the time he retired and was now a spiritual seeker. So responsive was he to new ventures that ten years previously he had set sail for England to study acting and to travel with a Shakespearean road company and perform for several years throughout rural Britain.

Back in America, he was associated with groups of spiritual seekers in New York City and Hancock, New Hampshire, many of whom were destined to be among the Master's first American disciples. Through these contacts, Watson learned of a retreat center in Devonshire, England, and he returned to England to seek out Meher Baba, scheduled arrive there very soon. Watson would be the medium for arranging and financing Baba's coming trip to America.

The day Baba was due to arrive at the Devonshire retreat, Watson awoke to find his pillow wet with unaccustomed tears streaming from his eyes. In his heart was an indescribable joy. Baba arrived later in the day, reaching the country farmhouse after a mile-and-a-half hike across muddy English moors.

After greeting everyone who had gathered there to meet him, he went up to his room, pausing just a moment to reach over the banister and place his hand gently on Watson's head. Watson was so moved by Baba's divine touch he began weeping like a child for fifteen minutes, his heart overflowing with love. He was taken to the library and after some moments of silence said, "In my 78 years, today is the first time I've experienced divine love with just a touch from the Master."

The Devonshire retreat where Baba launched his work in the West was run by Meredith Starr. True to form, Starr immediately began to issue orders to the mandali. And although Meher Baba was surely a most honored guest Starr even expected *him* to follow the rigidly scheduled daily program, carefully drawn up for silence and meditation. One day, Baba came to sit with the group who were seated in the library during one of these enforced silent meditations. When he casually pulled a book from the shelf and showed them the title, *All Quiet on the Western Front*, they all but burst out laughing. Meredith then made Baba smile and pose for pictures outside in the bitter cold for an hour, wearing only his thin white sadra without his coat. 1269

How could God possibly feel cold? Baba later recalled the scene: "I alone know how the cold bit to the very bone." He was fed only a piece of bread and butter, while the mandali had full meals. Baba commented, "Although I'm the Master, I follow Meredith's behests. And if you do that, too, what harm is there? Meredith hasn't even allotted time for me to be with my mandali, so I have to meet with them at 5:00 AM to be ready by six for Meredith's "program!" Baba soon became bored, fed up with the cold and Starr's routine. 1387

Still, Baba tolerated the behavior because he wanted Meredith there for his own purposes. Through him certain key persons in England had come to Baba. But that work would be completed, after the Hollywood contacts to come within six months. Then Baba would cut him loose. So until it was finished, Meredith's presence was grimly endured.

"I am the Avatar — the Christ-Messiah"

In a splendid mood after interviews, Baba walked the group to a valley where they sang songs about him. He also mentioned his mission for the world, candidly revealing that he was the Avatar— the Christ-Messiah for whom the world had long waited. His Eastern devotees called him a Perfect Master. So although God appeared in physical form in the East, it was here in the West where he first revealed himself as the Avatar. Not until 1954, twenty-three years later, would he reveal his Avatarhood in India. 1264–65

With great goodwill Watson appeared devoted to Baba, expressing, "America is the country for a great spiritual worker like you. You must go there. On behalf of its people, I extend my heartiest invitation to you to come to the United States." Of course, this had been Baba's intention all along. Watson wanted to pay passage for Baba and his party to America.

Although Baba's pockets were nearly empty, he refused the offer and accepted only after persistent entreaties. Watson and his wife went on ahead back to America to prepare the way. However, Watson's ardor and devotion proved short-lived. With such a positive initial reaction to meeting Baba, he would later become strangely indifferent. 1273

After Baba had been at the Devon retreat for a few days, he received a telegram informing him that Hazrat Babajan had dropped her body on September 21, 1931. Baba commented, "With Babajan dropping her body, numerous difficulties will crop up. Circumstances will now change as I go directly to America. The Round Table Conference, the precarious English economy, chaos in Russia, Japan and China, rumors of war—all convey rapid change." Baba cabled disciple Ghani Munsiff in India to donate four thousand rupees on his behalf to erect a marble tomb at Babajan's perennial seat in Poona, where she had bestowed God-Realization on him.

After eleven days, Baba had had enough of the Devon Retreat and wanted to leave. He departed with Chanji and Agha Ali, returning to London to stay at the Davy family home again for nine days for a far more relaxing visit than Devon. Baba's routine was to arise at six, and after breakfast at 7:30, read the paper, and then prepare for visitors at nine.

On Baba's second day in London, Kitty's mother Helena came to him, puzzled about understanding and loving him. He told her that when she prayed, she should simply place his photograph before her. She hesitated a moment. "But when I pray I keep Jesus' picture in front of me." "Continue gazing at His picture. It's one and the same. Christ's love is the supreme ideal. Don't worry, I'll help you inwardly." Helena called her daughter's Master "Mr.

Baba." She was fortunate to have this time with him, as she died the following year.

Meanwhile, Baba was taken out on sightseeing excursions through London where he made hurried visits to the Victoria and Albert Museum and Regents Park Zoo. At Westminster Abbey and the Tomb of the Unknown Soldier Baba remarked, "Those buried here are fortunate I've been here." He was especially intrigued by the underground subway system and its humorous names for stops, like Oxford Circus, Shepherd's Bush and Piccadilly. 1270–71

Quentin Tod was an American comic and dancer working on Broadway, the London stage and later in a few early British TV shows. He said of his first meeting: "I was so engrossed looking at him everything else faded away. I was impressed with his wild quality, something untamed, and his truly remarkable eyes. He took my hand, from time to time patting my shoulder. We sat for several minutes in silence. There was a great feeling of love and peace emanating from him and a curious feeling of recognition, as if I had found a long lost friend." 1272

After a short while, Baba took Tod's left hand and it felt as if an electric current of pure love passed between them. Tod knew immediately that he must serve Baba in some way. His mind became still before Baba's silence as all questions faded away. He understood that Baba had always known and loved him.

When Quentin's brother Malcolm was introduced to Baba, he mentioned he'd been drawn to Catholicism but concluded that the Church had commercialized Christ's mission and was leading people away from his teachings. Baba commented, "It has always been the case with religions everywhere." 1564

One day a wealthy British woman entered the room and inquired in an imperious manner, "Are you the Christ?" Baba looked at her softly and nodded yes. She turned around in a rage and walked out. He said nothing. When she returned later, he refused to see her. She waited until late in the day, and when he finally came out of the room, she approached him meekly and said, "Forgive a silly old woman." PM 274

Baba held many other brief interviews during this visit. One of them was with Christmas Humphreys, a Christian convert to Buddhism who had founded the London Buddhist Society. When Humphreys expressed doubt about instant God-Realization, Baba conveyed:

> Realization can be gained within a second. All actions can be annihilated and the experience of God instantly given. Bondage to illusion (*Maya*) is always there, and karmic bondage is due to actions. But once actions are destroyed, there's no bondage.
>
> Perhaps you think you can't obtain Realization in this birth. Why not? Actions can be destroyed by the grace of the Master. If that isn't so, the Guru is useless. What value is grace if everyone has to await his laborious turn and time?

Humphreys later said of Baba:

> For the first time in my life—and I have not met another like him—I found myself in the aura of a man who literally radiated love. He combined the profundity of mystical experience with the guileless candor of a child, and his smile was as infectious as the words he used were immaterial.
>
> He radiated such a pure affection that one wondered when all religions praise the value of pure love, it's such a memorable experience to meet one actually *practicing* it. Were there more Meher Babas in the world, wars would end.

But Humphreys was stuck in the old Buddhism and he was unable follow the direct guidance of the "new Buddha returned." 1274–75

Besides Quentin Tod, many other early English disciples were connected with the theatre. Margaret Craske was a ballet dancer and instructor. [4] Minta Toledano was an actress, and Delia DeLeon and her brother ran a theatre in Kew Gardens. Delia recalled her first meeting with Baba: "It was like I was in a dream, stunned at the wonder of Baba. Nothing else existed for me. I had no questions. I had implicit faith and trust in him. I wanted nothing, but gave my life into his keeping and knew my search had come to an end." GG V:79

Kitty Davy had had choral singing lessons with world renowned composer Gustav Holts, though she was unaware of his great love for Indian mysticism. She brought him to meet Baba. Holts was distressed because there were times when he couldn't compose. Baba consoled him. "Don't worry or be anxious over it. As there's nothing in the world to worry about! This is weakness. Never worry. I will help you spiritually and not just with words!" 1281–82 and footnote; LA 262

Despite the Master's divine personality, not everyone collapsed in tears or took adoringly to him. He had his share of doubters and detractors. One of the doubters was Helena Davy's oldest daughter, May, who was visiting from Canada. She was quite outspoken in her rejection of Baba, declaring, "I believe in no other Christ, and no other in the future. Jesus is the one and only Christ forever. Christianity predominates in the West and is superior in religion and spirit to the East." Her feelings reflected those of most Christians in the West. Baba replied, "To explain will take time, but I'll convince you I have gained the state of Christhood and am that *very* Christ."

May spoke back to him quite forcefully, "That's impossible! I don't believe you or even understand what you could possibly mean." Baba continued: "Were I to explain it, you'd instantly understand everything. Truth is above religion, and far, far beyond intellect. It can only be reached by love. Christ attained that state of divine love. I am in and always ex*perience* that same Christ state of everlasting bliss." His answer and smile erased only a small bit of May's roiling skepticism.

Baba went to the photo studio of London-based Japanese photographer Hisae Imai to pose for pictures taken on Wednesday September 30. The six portraits were superb, capturing the Master's ever-changing moods.

The next day, May confronted her sister Kitty and faulted her for weeping over Baba: "Such hypocritical tears; you're weeping like this just for show. That's not love, but a total sham. This hypocritical humbug totally unnerves me!" Upset, Kitty went and told Baba.

He called May, explaining to her, "It's not pretense. The tears you see are the outcome of Kitty's love, which even she can't prevent." Baba then slyly warned May, "You'll also start loving me within two days." May laughed, not at all believing him. But the next night along with the others she suddenly burst into uncontrollable tears for three hours, holding onto Baba's feet, kissing and touching them with her forehead and cheeks. 1282–83

Baba also kept his promise to Kitty's mother Helena, when he visited a home for the old and needy where many were blind and deaf, accompanied by Helena, Margaret and his newest devotee—May. Baba spoke inwardly to them for a long time, communicating directly to their hearts, which he deeply touched. No words could describe God's love coming directly to them that day. Baba had comforting messages for the residents of the home. To one old deaf and blind man Baba conveyed, "At night, drink a glass of warm water, while recalling the feel of my hand on yours, and you'll be better." That man was soon well enough to return home. Baba gave another woman a rose petal, telling her "keep it under your pillow." On their way back from the home, Baba remarked, "Here in the West, I've so far enjoyed most my visit to this home for the needy." 1284

As his eyes had been set on America long before this journey he was feeling a great pull, calling it "his country too," predicting that it would become truly spiritual and not merely a "religiously-minded nation. . . . What's needed is love for whatever God one likes. In the form of Jesus crucified God can and will do it. The time is near when this spiritual upliftment takes place. It must, and will be. Be sure of this: America is destined to lead the world, *spiritually*." 3082

But not wishing to go there directly from England, Baba made a side trip to Turkey, saying life there had degenerated alarmingly. Needing to do deep Inner work for its people, he crossed the English Channel from Dover to Calais by ferry and boarded the famed Orient Express on October 6, passing though Milan, Venice, Trieste, Belgrade and Sofia on his way to Istanbul.

There he visited, Hagia Sophia, the great Blue Mosque, as well as another mosque that had been converted from a Catholic church, but which still displayed a mural of Christ and the Twelve Apostles. Entering Istanbul's poorest slums, his mood changed, as he silently dispensed his love and compassion to all.

Just as in London, great crowds inadvertently greeted the Master when a raucous military parade marched through Istanbul. Little did they know the Real Emperor was there among them. All were struck by Baba's flashing eyes. His great spirit and beautiful face captured their hearts. He worked for nine days in this cradle of early Christian and Muslim religious civilizations, returning by rail to Nice, where he boarded the SS *Roma*, bound for America. 1291

CHRIST COME AGAIN

CHRIST COME AGAIN

Chapter Seventeen

The Avatar Reaches America's Shores

At 2:00 PM, Friday, November 6, 1931, the SS *Roma* passed the Statue of Liberty and sailed into New York harbor, docking at the West 57th Street pier. But even after two hours, Baba and the men were still not allowed to disembark. An insolent immigration officer was kicking up a storm, unnecessarily delaying them from disembarking.

He was dissatisfied with the answers Meredith and Chanji gave to his questions. He was especially suspicious of Baba's silence and his alphabet board, which he even tried reading himself. When he couldn't, he challenged Baba directly.

"You've come to teach people in America, and you don't even speak? How on earth can you teach with this foolish board? Who gave you this silly idea?" At this, Baba spelled out one of his most famous replies: "I have come not to teach, but to awaken." The officer glared at him scornfully. Still, Baba remained serene and calm and meekly submitted to questioning.

This harassment went on for two hours, until suddenly, out of nowhere, a ship's officer dressed in an immaculate starched white uniform appeared on the scene and severely reprimanded the immigration officer, saying he saw no sense in the man's rudeness. He insisted Baba and his party be allowed to leave the ship.

Their paperwork and references were in due order. In fact, the officer said he himself would stand guarantee for the party if needed. His commanding tone and crisp uniform led all to believe he had to be the ship's highest-ranking officer. Of course, this dressing-down upset the red-faced immigration agent. He had no recourse but to issue landing permits.

Sitting at his table and grumbling under his breath, the agent filled out their landing cards. Chanji then searched the ship to thank the officer. The man couldn't be found and none of the ship's staff had any idea of who he might be. 1300–01

The Harmon Retreat

With funds already collected, and additional help from Thomas Watson, Baba's first American disciples made arrangements for his month-long stay at Harmon-on-Hudson, located forty miles north of Manhattan at 80 Old Albany Post Road South, near Briarcliff, in Westchester County. The property was owned by Margaret Mayo, a successful Broadway playwright who graciously loaned Baba's group her home when she heard of their need for accommodations.

Cath Gardner and Lillian Wardell met Baba and his party at the docks to drive them up to Harmon-on-Hudson. Cath and her friend Alice Green had previously established a small school in California for people wishing to lead "a simple spiritual life." But their years of labor were fruitless. Cath was searching for a true spiritual guide, and upon meeting Baba, she exclaimed, "Waiting for the Master, I've now found him!" Baba later explained to her:

> People make a great mistake talking of leading a simple life. Such a life is infinitely difficult. Outwardly, one may wear plain clothes and have a simple diet, but this isn't living a simple life! The spiritual life is lived by being free of *all desires*.
>
> One must be open and guileless. Why only outwardly live this way? The elaborate dress of desires and longings is still there side by side with that feasting ego! To really lead

a simple life is to be totally desireless—impossible without feeling true love for God. 1305–06

Baba, Chanji and Aga Ali rode with Cath, while Lillian drove the rest of those who had come to greet them at the dock. By 5:30 PM they had all arrived at the retreat. The large, secluded, four-bedroom fieldstone house with red window frames was located in a wooded area on the east side of the Croton River. Baba's private master bedroom on the second floor ran the length of the house and opened onto a deck where he could look out over the treetops to the Hudson River.

Among the many Westerners meeting Baba at Harmon were Jewish poet Malcolm Schloss and his common-law wife, Jean Adriel. Jean was a tall, regal blonde with an otherworldly air. A New York journalist, she had met Malcolm at his bookstore, The North Node, at 114 East 57th Street. Here they made many contacts with other spiritual seekers during the late 1920s and early 30s. Their network was an invaluable channel for Baba's visit.

The Christmas card they had sent out to their contacts the previous year had read, "Blessed are those who can rest from speech to dwell in holy silence. Blessed are those who can rise from thought to the fullness of pure knowing. Blessed are those who, detached, can rest in their own true being." Aw. 19 (no. 1): 45

Both well read in metaphysics, Malcolm and Jean were seeking a spiritual path. Later authoring the first American biography of Meher Baba, Avatar, Jean recalled:

> A most outstanding impression of that meeting was of peering into bottomless pools of infinite love and tenderness as his eyes met mine. With tremendous excitement my heart pounded, and for a while I couldn't even speak. I felt *he* was the reason for my very existence. I had never really lived till this moment. At the same time, he was deeply fa-

miliar and precious to me, just as I was no stranger and so very dear to him. 1301–03

The small group of new devotees at the evening dinner were wonderstruck in Baba's presence as he loving looked back at them from the head of the table. Many claimed the experience of having met the Master before. Some who were Christians already had been contacted by him in remarkably lucid dreams where he appeared as the most loving Jesus.

Meeting the Master, they instantly recognized him as the Christ of their dreams. When asked, Baba replied: "Many in the multitudes are connected with me from past lives." 3415

Later, Malcolm described being in the presence of super-consciousness at Harmon:

> Could it have been a dream that November, 1931 when we lived in the old stone house over the Croton River near Harmon, New York? With that beautiful being from India, we learned so quickly to love and have yearned so ardently ever since to serve him in any way? Was it a mirage on his arrival, when he sat at the head of the table in the soft glow of candle-light, looking for all the world like a Rembrandt painting of Jesus come to life, dispensing Christ-like potions of love.
>
> Or those three-minute periods of silent meditation we were called to the following day, and repeated almost daily until he left? Those precious moments crowned with the gift of tears, welling up mysteriously from depths we had never plumbed before, while we were pervaded with bliss —were those illusions? And the differences which had led so easily to conflict some months before when we who had gathered to greet him at Harmon had spent the summer together in New Hampshire.

Did his radiant love dissolve those differences? Did we actually go about feeling we wanted to embrace each other—we stolid, unemotional, self-sufficient Anglo-Saxons? Did all three hundred fifty people that month find deeper bonds of friendship, greater consecration, quicker response to the call of selfless service, while his love spread like divine contagion? Or was it all a dream? Aw 19 (no.1): 51

The Dream Come True

With the Emperor holding court in America, two women from Russian aristocracy came to stand before him—both well-bred, with strong personalities and social connections. But their egos would be ground down over time and they would remain deeply devoted disciples for the rest of their lives.

Russian Countess Nadia Tolstoy was the daughter-in-law of Count Leo Tolstoy, author of the epic Russian novel, *War and Peace*. She attended the University of Petrograd, studying psychology, logic and philosophy. She later continued her studies at Lausanne University in Switzerland. She also studied piano at the Moscow Conservatory.

Nadia had mystical inclinations, and one night she was astonished to see the Count, whom she had never met, in three dreams after his passing. In the third dream, a man resembling the Count appeared to her. He was in a big boat approaching the shore as if to invite her on board. Later, at a friend's house, she met Count Ilya, Leo's oldest son, and she understood the dream's significance when she realized that he was the man in the boat. They soon married, emigrating from Russia in 1917 to live in the United States, just outside New York City.

A sincere spiritual seeker, Nadia was not satisfied with reading books. She was searching for a living Master. When she learned of Meher Baba's visit, she came to Harmon for his blessing. The moment she set eyes on him she exclaimed, "My search is over!" She describes their first meeting:

> As I climbed the steps to his room, I chanted *Om* and entered. There, stretched on the couch at the far side of the room, was that mysterious, long-expected Being, the Divine Enigma—the True One! I saw Christ before me seated on the couch in the expression of his entire figure and his divinely lit-up face, his eyes beaming total love . . . the fulfillment of a long-awaited meeting.
>
> It was the climax of my life . . . I declared loudly: "*Jesus Christ!*" With the solemnity of those great words something within me recognized in this dear form of Meher Baba, the incarnation of Jesus. So the unbelievable became a revealed fact. I gave my will to his Will, my life to his cause of truth and love, knowing to love the truth means to live it.
>
> The next day Ilya decided to come and meet Baba also. He asked Baba a question troubling him much of his life: "How can one love when there is so much evil in this world?" The Master, eyes beaming with that very love, answered on his alphabet board: "You must take love in your heart." And then added, "Ilya is such a fine man." Aw 20 (no. 2): 31

When Nadia began to tell Baba about herself, he put up his hand. "I know all and will help you." She was practicing kundalini *kriya yoga* under Swami Yogananda. Baba warned, "This is *not* for the West nor for you." Aw 22 (no. 2): 33

She later wrote:

> During the short meditation with Baba, I knew he was reading and helping me. I felt his eyes seeing into depths beyond which we can see, reading the open book of my life

and working within me. I *knew* he was my Master and the shining sun we never question. He simply and naturally entered into my life and into my hidden being.

It was suddenly clear he was Krishna. He immediately recognized my soul, creating a feeling of absolute confidence my path was found. I already knew he was the True One who knows and who can help . . . The Supreme One was here. 1318-19

Although Nadia was her Russian name, Baba called her Nadine. Ilya also met Baba, and afterward he said to his wife, "This is the first time I've met a man who has Divine Love." Before his death he experienced a great spiritual transformation. In her article appearing in the July 1941 issue of the *Meher Baba Journal*, Nadine expressed her sorrow that the great Count Tolstoy himself had not had the unique opportunity of being helped by a living Perfect Master. GG1:142

> Nadine became ill in the early-to-mid 1940s. Kriya yoga exercises likely led to her diagnosis of Lou Gehrig's disease, which destroyed her throat muscles. She died on April 14, 1946, at Roosevelt Hospital in New York, at age 61.

Also meeting Baba at Harmon was the famous Italian silent screen and stage actress Maria Carmi, whose real name was Eleonora Cecilia Erna Gilli. Her greatest performance was in the renowned London pantomime play, *The Miracle,* written by her first husband, playwright Karl Vollmöller, when she was cast as the Madonna. [5] Following their divorce she married Russian war hero Prince Georges V. Matchabelli in 1917. The couple immigrated to America in 1924 and settled in New York City, where she was known as Princess Norina Matchabelli. The Prince was an amateur chemist who had an amazing ability to detect an "astral" perfume and then chemically duplicate it. He and Norina established the iconic perfume company bearing the family name.

A few weeks before Baba's arrival, as Jean Adriel was preparing to leave for the Harmon retreat to get things in order for his visit, Norina happened to stop by her apartment. She had just returned from Europe where she had socialized with royalty and the rich and famous. With searing sarcasm she challenged Jean with all sorts of questions about what on earth she was getting into.

"Who in God's name is this '*Master*' at whose feet you'd worship? Are you mad? Women like ourselves—who've had such deep inner experiences—don't need any man to show us the way to God. How can you allow yourself to be drawn into such foolishness?" 1307

After this torrent of disapproval had run its course, Jean quietly told Norina she was following her deepest inner promptings—the intuition of her life. One thing she mentioned to Norina was the phenomenon of tears Thomas Watson and many others experienced on meeting the Master. Norina laughed sarcastically, "Well darling, when your '*Master*' arrives, I must meet him, as I too would like to weep like dear old Watson!" 1308

Norina was among the earliest to arrive when Baba began his Harmon interviews. Something extraordinary had happened to her during those intervening weeks. Tears were already in her eyes, as she walked in unsteadily like a puzzled child. Drawing Jean aside, she whispered, "*Tell me about him.*" Jean replied, "You'll see for yourself in a few minutes." Norina confided that since the moment Baba's feet had touched America's shores, she'd done nothing but weep and was forced to cancel all engagements. Her old sophisticated hauteur gave way to a bewildered, child-like perplexity. Then word came that Baba would see her. She climbed the stairs and entered his room.

Blinded by the intensity of his radiance, brighter than the sun streaming through the window, she staggered across the room with the help of one of the mandali, and falling to her knees, gazed at him with tears of ecstasy rolling down her cheeks.

Baba greeted her, with the words "I am man, woman and child. I am sexless . . . Have no fear." She pleaded, "Take me out of this. Oh, take me away from it all!" Baba gestured, "It's yet too soon." Norina felt she could have died of grief hearing these words. Av 179

About ten minutes later, as Malcolm was passing the stairway leading up to Baba's room, he caught sight of Norina coming down, clutching the banister. Appearing on the verge of fainting, she fell into his arms. She wept as if her heart were breaking in an ecstasy of pain, crying out, "*Oh, Jesus!*" It seems she had a considerable number of psychic experiences in her life. Baba had appeared to her three times in visions and dreams when she was but a child of twelve and it was only natural that meeting her Lord face to face might evoke her memories of them: "He came as Jesus and spoke to me. He explained to me in words of sublime wisdom this love which had begun to surge within me was an imperative for fulfilling the highest form of spiritual love. He spoke the unforgettable words: 'I am your first and last love.'" These words were now fully realized seeing Baba at Harmon and recognizing him as Christ personified. Without her mentioning her dreams, Baba had spelled out, "It was I who came to you in the form of Christ to lead you to the goal."

She didn't know then that over the next three years she would have to go through the outer motions of her accustomed way of life, while being inwardly prepared for a radical new one; nor that her husband would soon pass and release her to devote her time, life, and energy in total service to the Avatar. Baba told her that she had been his father and his mother in two of her past lives. Aw 20 (no. 2): 16

Norina recalled: "When I saw him it was as if I had always known him. He was an old, old friend. It was instant recognition. His silence didn't seem strange or awkward." Over the years, both Norina and Nadine Tolstoy would spend much time in the Master's

Meher Baba and Princess Norina Matchabelli during the mid-1930s

company in America, Europe and India, together with a third one destined to become a member of his American circle, Elizabeth Patterson.

Elizabeth came from a wealthy, well-connected New York City family. She was an insurance broker and the first woman to work the floor of the New York Stock Exchange. Elizabeth had also circled the globe on a world cruise, joined a North Pole scientific expedition, and driven ambulances transporting wounded soldiers from the New York City docks to hospitals for the American Red Cross Women's Motor Corps in WWI.

Baba would call these three women to India in 1933 and again in 1938 to join him for the Blue Bus Tours. In 1941 he would send them back to the West to work together "spreading his message of love and truth," as well as locating property in the United States for a spiritual center.

Baba revealed to them his plan to establish five centers in America, hinting at work that only time would reveal. The first center was to be located on virgin land with freshwater lakes beside the ocean and offered to him as a gift from the heart. It became the Meher Spiritual Center in Myrtle Beach, South Carolina. Of the other four, one would be in a big city (Los Angeles), one on

Anita de Caro (Vieillard), Elizabeth Patterson and Norina Matchabelli at Croton-on Hudson, New York, 1932

a mountaintop (Meher Mount in Ojai, California), and one in the heart of the US (the Heartland Center in Prague, Oklahoma.) The last center, located in the desert has yet to be established as of the writing of this book.

Still, Baba expressed reservations about organizations and societies:

> I want neither an organization, nor any society—*exactly* what I fear could happen. If such centers are allowed, they form themselves into organizations or societies. That's why I build structures and then demolish them. The more

changes I make, the more unchangeable I become! Organizations are like the foam which brings unwanted things up to the surface of the sea, letting the real substance lie submerged beneath the depths. 1908

These three women became close companions in Baba's love and lived in a duplex on East 67th Street in New York during the 1940s. Filis Frederick, another of Baba's Western disciples, wrote that Elizabeth quietly paid the bills while Norina gave lectures about Baba to countless hundreds at Steinway Hall, adjacent to Carnegie Hall. Nadine's work welcoming individual seekers would bring many people to the Avatar. [6]

Baba later called this trio of extraordinary women the "three pillars" of his work in the West. He explained that due to the predominance of male energy in the West, these women would do much of his work there, whereas in the East, where feminine energy prevailed, men would do much of his work. He added that Eastern souls were now reincarnating in the West and vice versa.

Malcolm Schloss captured the essence of Baba's hectic stay at Harmon:

> From the moment Meher Baba set foot in the house at Harmon, there continuously flowed from him a love which can only be called divine, spreading through us all, and seeing as never before what the love-feasts of the early Christians must truly have been like.
>
> We saw the relationship of Jesus and His apostles re-enacted in a modern setting. Though silent, not even a cyclone could have been more active or more devastating. Men and women came from Baba's room after a five-to-ten-minute interview with this *Speechless Being,* so exalted they wanted to be left alone to absorb the experience. Here was an incarnate being like Jesus, whose presence over-

whelmed the soul with love beyond comprehension. 1332–34

Accompanying Norina that first day was a talented young art student, Anita de Caro. Raised Catholic, she was nervous about meeting this great religious man. How should she behave? In her own words:

> The only proper thing to do was to kneel, make the sign of the cross and say, *"Bless me, Father,"* then maybe kiss his hand. My heart was pounding with fear. When the door opened, Baba was sitting crossed legged. Looking at him, I burst into peals of laughter and threw myself on him. "My heavens! It's actually *you*," I cried. "You made me go through all this masquerade and fear, when it's *you*! Incredible!" I laughed and laughed.
>
> Baba opened his arms. Enraptured, I felt a tremendous joy. My whole being was as if in a furnace. Words can't describe it. It was like meeting someone I always knew and had come back to my real home. I experienced such great beauty and joy.

Baba asked Anita about her interests. When she said she was an artist, he gestured, "Could you paint me?" "Oh no, Baba, you're much too beautiful—too difficult to paint," she replied. Still, a couple of days later, Anita returned to Harmon and at Baba's request painted a small portrait.

Baba loved having Anita around because she was so full of joy and she always made him laugh with her spontaneity. When he remarked "I am eternally happy," Anita interjected, "Oh, you don't have to tell *us*! You *must* be with this face of yours. What bliss! Just look at his eyes. They speak more than words—so radiant and penetrating, understanding and compassionate. Without doubt, you look eternally happy." 1310–12

Malcolm Schloss, Prem Ashram student Aga Ali (standing), Meher Baba, Meredith Starr and Chanji in foreground, at Greenfields farm, Hancock, New Hampshire, 1931

Another artist who met Baba at Harmon, Julian Lamar, exclaimed, "How radiant your eyes are! What a glow is on your face! I'd like to reflect your true beauty in painting your portrait if you'd consent to a sitting." Baba pointed to himself, "This is not the original picture! My real portrait is something different, and to portray it accurately you must first wipe out your own image." 1306; S 84

Lamar's oil portrait was later taken to the Meher Spiritual Center in Myrtle Beach and is on view at Baba's House there. When Baba saw it in 1952, he gestured to the painting, "This artist has captured the *star*"—the star-shaped mark between his eyebrows, adding, "I always have that mark when I come."

A few days into Baba's stay at Harmon, an adjacent building housing several in the group burned down. Luckily, it was well-insured. Some thought it fortunate as everybody then had to move into the main house—that much closer to Baba. After making sure no one had been hurt, he remarked that fires often sprang up where he went. He told them that since no one had suffered severely, it was a good sign that those who had lost their few belongings in the fire would begin a new life, while those who had managed to save their possessions might have to wait a bit for their new beginning.

Also meeting Baba at Harmon was Graham Phelps Stokes and his close friend Spencer Kellogg, Jr., heir to the Kellogg cereal empire. Graham's secretary, Ann Clark, knew that Graham was a spiritual seeker and told him about Meher Baba's trip to America. A few years earlier Graham had bought books at Manhattan's North Node Bookstore, where he met Malcolm and Jean, as well as Thomas Watson, after store hours. All had been involved in planning for Baba's arrival.

Stokes, a wealthy philanthropist, well-known architect and housing reformer for the poor, owned a pink double townhouse in Manhattan's Greenwich Village. [7] He was so impressed upon meeting Baba that he invited him to stay at his house. Baba indicated that he might accept the offer. The next day Graham brought his wife, Lettica Sands, to meet Baba. 1306-07

Graham Stokes would play an important role in Meher Baba's work in America. Born into great wealth, he had graduated from Yale University in 1892, two years before Baba's birth. The Phelps-Stokes were prominent in the Social Register and traced their roots back to late eighteenth-century New England. Stokes' father was co-founder of the New York Metropolitan Museum of Art.

Stokes obtained an medical degree from Columbia University in 1896 but never practiced medicine. Instead, he was active in the early Booker T. Washington Civil Rights Movement, and for all his wealth and privilege, he led a truly admirable life. He held Monday night "spiritual meetings" in his home and co-celebrated Baba's birthday with his own each February until failing health in home in the mid 1940s, but at the end he drifted away from Baba. [8]

Boston and New Hampshire

Departing Harmon-on-Hudson, Baba was driven to Boston by Cath Gardner, who had brought him from the New York docks up to Harmon. Jean sat next to Baba. Also with them was May Cluse, Kitty's sister, who had traveled to Harmon from Canada. Meredith Starr, Chanji and Ali rode with Malcolm in another car driven by Julian Lamar.

Baba accomplished some Inner work on the trip. Jean said he had a blue jacket and would put it over his head, and then his body would go limp. Cath was alarmed the first time it happened, but five minutes later Baba became animated again. This happened a dozen times during the drive as he attended spiritual work in other parts of the world. Baba later indicated. "In this state the eyes turn back—very disconcerting for you to see." Thus, he'd cover his eyes by putting the jacket over his head. Av 28; Aw 12 (no. 1): 25

Among Cath's friends was a Norwegian-born actress named Asta Fleming Case, age 37. She lived at 279 Newbury Street in Boston. Having seen Baba in a dream two years earlier, she invited him to come up to Boston. The group stayed for two days at the Vendome Hotel, where about twenty-five people eagerly awaited Baba's arrival.

Another person who met Baba at the Vendome was astrologer Dane Rudhyar. Casting Baba's chart, he saw him as "the Age's great World Teacher." Also meeting him was Richard Mayer, 59, a German immigrant cotton merchant who exclaimed to Baba, "You alone know how to suffer!" Baba spelled out, "I am infinite bliss, yet I feel compassion for all who suffer and help them through my knowledge and power. Thus, my mercy is my suffering."

Yet another awaiting Baba's visit was an Indian yogi, Swami Paramananda. As the youngest disciple of the saintly Indian Swami Vivekananda, he invited Baba to visit his California ashram. He also brought some books he had written, but on seeing Baba and recognizing his startling spiritual status, he hid all his books away, prostrated himself full-length at the Master's feet and implored Baba for deep spiritual help. 1320-21

Baba visited Asta's home on Saturday, November 21. There he met a few more people before taking a late-morning, hour-long sightseeing tour of the city. He asked to be driven around the nearby Christian Science Church headquarters. Its foundation stone, was inscribed 1894, the year of his birth.

On Baba's last day in Boston, Cath drove him out to see some property she had just given him, a few miles north of Peterborough, New Hampshire. It was a hundred-acre wooded estate called Greenfields, on beautiful land surrounded by low mountains and meadows. It was located on Norway Hill Road between the towns of Hancock and Elmwood. Baba loved it, especially as it was being given to him from the heart. The deed was recorded in his name.

The original idea prior to Baba's arrival in America was to create a New Hampshire center to be named *"The New Life Experiment."* It was an offshoot of Malcolm and Jeans's North Node bookstore, but the plan never fully materialized. The mortgage and roof-repair costs for the ten-room farmhouse were beyond Baba's resources, and though it was sold years later, this was the only property Meher Baba ever owned in America, in New Hampshire, whose state motto is "Live free or Die."

Back to New York

Returning to Boston, Baba boarded the SS *George Washington*, a 5:00 PM ferry taking him back to New York City. There, he checked into the Hotel Astor in Times Square at Broadway and 44th

Street, a very expensive hotel frequented by wealthy clientele. Though Baba was a distinguished guest, Norina still had to use her influence, as they were reluctant to accommodate an "Indian Guru."

Because he was still carefully avoiding the press, Baba conducted private interviews in his room. Among those meeting him was Rev. Dr. Robert Norwood, 57, a well-known Canadian poet who held a doctorate in theology, but while searching for the truth he had lost hope in organized religion. Baba explained:

> Religions and cults just don't cut it. I'm preparing a way for people to be able to live a life of Truth. Love is the only way leading to Truth and God-Realization. There's no religion higher than trying to see and experience God. The first thing is Reality.
>
> The second is Unity. Love is truly the quickest shortcut on the long path to God-Realization. Love is the only *real religion*. People are so tired of theories, doctrines and principles. They want the real deal, which explanations can never give. They must *feel, see and experience Truth*. Only then can one find harmony within everything and and everyone, remaining in the world, but not of it. I am eternally happy.
>
> I see only my own Self in everyone and everything. I neither preach nor belong to any creed. Religions, dogmas and rituals all hinder on the path to all-pervading, infinite Truth. I teach nothing, and in fact make the learned forget. I have come not to teach but to awaken. Going to church may help, but a church nourishing sectarianism renders no help. 1323

Dr. Norwood was very happy hearing this and said, "I'm so glad we agree!"

Leopold Stokowski, noted orchestra conductor of the first half of the twentieth century, came to see Baba as well. A Christian of Irish and Polish descent, his concern was creating unity between the East and West. Baba told him it not only could happen but would, and that he himself would bring it about in this Advent. Stokowski then asked, "Is outward beauty necessary for inner?" Baba asked. "Only the internal matters, not the external. On reaching enlightenment, the soul experiences Oneness."

Stokowski replied, "I've asked so many wise people this same question, but none has satisfied me like your clear-cut answer." Baba further explained, "It's not a matter of thought or feeling. I know and I do. From your standpoint as an artist, you see all that is outwardly beautiful in nature and through it you see the internal. That's good, but once the inner perception is gained, nothing remains of external beauty or ugliness. All is absolutely and blissfully alike."

> "Vivekananda can be said to have done the first 'spiritual spade work' in the West by establishing his American headquarters in New York City in 1895, just a year after Meher Baba was born. Vivekananda referred to New York as the *'the head, hand, and purse of the country'* As a worldly metropolis it was a 'wellspring of new ideas' . . . the center of the arts, rich, generous and throbbing with vitality—everything was there." 1300

Baba loved walking through Times Square at night, sometimes seeing a movie. On the evening of November 25 he went to The Roxy Theatre on 50th Street and 7th Avenue, where he saw *Monkey Business* with the Marx Brothers, whose zaniness he loved. Mehera later said Baba did a fabulous take-off on Groucho Marx's slinky, stooped walk. 1320–26

A Visit to Sing-Sing Prison

After a few days in the city, Baba returned to Harmon and within a day or so asked to be driven to Sing-Sing, America's oldest prison. They departed Harmon that night at ten o'clock. Baba

> The prison was five miles from Ossining and a mile from where the author would attend seminary and be ordained a priest thirty-three years later.

wanted to contact a prisoner whom he said was God-mad. As the car circled the prison in the dark, Baba gazed at it, blowing kisses. Stopping by the high entrance gate, he sat motionless for a while.

As on the drive up to Boston, Baba threw a shawl over his head and went limp, leaving his body to enter the prison. Upon returning to his body, he communicated, "There's a man in this prison who is my agent—an *abdal*, doing very good work for me. When I speak, I will free him."

Baba seemed sad on the drive back, so they suggested next day that they request permission for Baba to visit the prisoner. He remarked wistfully, "I don't need to go physically into Sing-Sing, as I've already made contact with him." 1330

*The caged bird, the man in prison—
the free and consciousness soul transcends the body;
can a prison capture that abdal's spirit?
His cell was but a seat from where he worked invisibly.*
~ elf

A Film on Spirituality

Baba was interested in filmmaking as a potent vehicle for raising mass consciousness. Invented the very year of his birth, he considered it his medium. He frequently attended movies, using the concentrated attention of the audience to conduct his Inner work. He stated as early as the 1920s that motion pictures portraying soul-stirring dramas would be the most effective means of arousing the higher emotions.

During his second visit to America, Hollywood would be his primary focus. At the end of 1934 he'd spend three weeks of very intense work attempting to get his films made in the movie capital.

It was here at Harmon where the topic of making a film on spirituality initially arose. Baba's theme was "the purpose of creation, the outcome of the universe, and our spiritual journey through many repeated reincarnations."

Margaret Mayo told Baba that she could draw up a detailed scenario if he gave her some points. He immediately took her aside to work on the theme. Within an hour the entire plot was dictated—the beginning of creation in developing stages of evolution, reincarnation, and the stories of three characters over five lifetimes reaching Realization. When it was read to the group, all declared it to be splendid.

After it was typed out, Margaret's movie producer friend, a Mr. Artkin, came by and Baba's story was read out to him. Very impressed, Artkin assured them, "It's a grand story and surely can be worked into a movie." They further discussed the film's possibilities. The project would develop over four years with Baba's return visits and his upcoming trips to Hollywood in 1932 and 1934. Baba titled his scenario *A Touch of Maya*, and it was later used as the basis for several screenplay proposals.

As it turned out, the Harmon retreat had had something of a reputation during prohibition as a "speakeasy and bawdy house." Graham Stokes felt it totally inappropriate for the Master's work. He again offered his Manhattan double-townhouse in Greenwich Village as Baba's temporary headquarters, urging him, "Leave Harmon as soon as possible."

That the house had a bad reputation might not have bothered Baba in the least. But he had more work to do with Graham, and also saw it as a wonderful opportunity to return to the city he loved. So he graciously accepted the offer, and the whole entourage moved in a caravan of cars from Harmon to Greenwich Village, staying there two days before he and his party boarded a steamship to return to Europe.

The venerable old house would host the Master during two future visits to New York, one six months later and again in 1934. It was also the Monday night meeting place for the New York disciples for many years. Graham celebrated Baba's birthday each February 25 with John Bass, Agnes Bourne, and Darwin Shaw, as well as Nadine, Norina, Elizabeth, and others. After dinner, Graham would stand in the dining room doorway and give a little talk. Aw 21 (no. 1): 33

Just before leaving Manhattan, Baba was driven around the Wall Street financial district. It was just two years after the stock market crash, ushering in the Great Depression. As it was a Saturday, the streets were practically deserted. Jean Adriel was also in the car and mused, "How ephemeral and unreal all this money madness is!" Pointing to the skyscrapers, Baba smiled, saying, "It's all a bubble; so easy to prick!" His very words would be echoed forty years later in the Wall Street housing crash.

Following a month's stay in America seeing over 350 people, Baba returned to Europe on the SS *Bremen*. He remained secluded in his cabin and avoided going out so as not to be recognized during the rough Atlantic crossing. Passengers stayed inside as sixty-foot waves crashed over the decks, but Baba enjoyed the rough ride. After his strenuous work in America, his coat pockets bulged like what he called his "post office," filled with love letters from those left behind. Pulled by their love, he'd soon return.

On December 10, Baba allowed a news crew to make a brief film of him. Docking in Le Havre, he and his party were met by a group of English disciples, whom he had called for a two-week stay in Paris before he returned to India. That night they saw the new Charlie Chaplin film, *City Lights*.

But Meredith Starr's overbearing behavior once again rose to the surface, causing Baba to warn him that Paris held "hidden dangers" for one so "spiritually advanced" as he. When Baba said he should leave immediately, Meredith quickly returned home to his

Devon retreat in England. To everyone's relief, the atmosphere now became normal and relaxed. But Baba still needed this strange Englishman for his work when he returned to the West. After that, Meredith would be cut off from the Master.

Among the sites the group visited on December 13 were the Eiffel Tower, the Louvre, the Arc de Triomphe, the Cathedral of Notre Dame and the Gare de Lyons. They ended the day with a walk along the Seine. They also drove down the Champs Elysees, where Baba went into the Galleries Lafayette to purchase a new coat. That evening, they saw the MGM movie *Trader Horn*.

Meher Baba with the mandali and several Western disciples, atop the Eiffel Tower, Paris, France, December 1931

On December 15 they drove to Versailles in a Rolls Royce limousine to visit the Hall of Mirrors where the treaty of Versailles was signed, ending the first World War. After seeing Marie Antoinette's suite, they held hands in the gardens, skipping happily in a line, followed by tea in the café—chosen ones enjoying Baba's unrestricted company.

Here Baba explained to them for the first time about reincarnation. Then he spelled out: "You do not see me as I really am. I am not this body; my Real Self is far more beautiful. I am Infinite Truth, Love, Infinite Power and Life Eternal. I was Krishna, Buddha; I was Jesus and now Meher Baba. In the East people worship me; here in the West, I have their love." 1338-40

With Baba preparing to leaving Paris, the women began packing. Kim Tolhurst observed that the great city now seemed like a "casket without a jewel, a rose without scent." Returning to India, Baba wept aboard ship, listening to Paul Robeson's recording, of *Feed My Sheep*, recalling his lovers left behind and their grief at his parting. Chanji later recorded in his diary:

> How the West received Baba: thousands from all vocations and walks of life saw and adored him. Among them were humble farmers, artists, poets, philosophers, scientists, politicians and journalists. They loved him as no one else before. His graceful figure, charming personality and spirit captivated all hearts.
>
> It wasn't a passing infatuation. Divine inspiration literally transformed the lives and affairs of all who approached him with open sincere and loving hearts. Their experiences were related verbally and in letters full of divine love in words that would make the reader cry at the very depth of their feeling and love. 1448-49

Returning to India, Baba told his men about his work in the West:

> You'll never be able to understand my Universal work. In this Avataric period, I have to cleanse the world completely. This overhauling will last a thousand years. During

this advent the greatest work will be achieve— the union of the East and West.

I am the Universal Avatar and not just an Avatar for the East as in previous advents. I threw out the net and the fish were caught. I belong to the whole universe. This is why the Westerners were so easily caught in my net and now these fish don't want to free themselves from the net. 1357

God Incarnates on Earth in Major and Minor Advents

Baba spoke many times and gave many explanations of his seven Advents on earth. He said, "Becoming Realized, I came down as the Avatar innumerable times—5,329 times just in the last major cycle—and once more after 450 years. The end will be the 5,330th time, though the universe is never finished." At other times he said he'd be back in seven hundred years.

But he also said that he comes in minor Advents in which he is born with full consciousness of his divinity, but without any Avataric responsibilities or duties. In December 1938, during the first Blue Bus Tour, Baba would escort a group of female disciples to Mandla. It is a place that tradition claims to be the exact center of India. He would bring them on a river to a place called A Thousand Waterfalls, where the great philosopher Shankara had his seat over two thousand years before. Baba came here in a minor Advent when he didn't fully reveal himself before his next major Advent as Jesus. He also said that he had been a Buddhist monk in Burma, living as a hermit during a minor Advent. He further disclosed that he had once been a "sweetmeat seller" in northern India. 1174.

Baba later revealed that in the seventeenth century he took birth as the great Hindu warrior, Shivaji, from whose companions in war all his present inner circle members were drawn. Jean Adriel wrote in *Avatar*:

In Avataric periods, the one Avatar continues unbroken his successive births. But the positions assumed on earth are then of less Universal spiritual significance; though always his role is one of beneficial help to humanity. There are times when world conditions demand his occupying many bodies during one and the same period:

As a genius of the arts, he quickens man's higher sense; as a master poet, he unfurls yet another petal of the cosmic rose; as an inspired scientist, he reveals hidden secrets of nature to humanity; as a leader of Church or State, he gives man a broader concept of life.

As a nameless wanderer, he cheers the disheartened to ease man's burdens. No generation is without his physical manifestation in one form or another, though often his true identity remains hidden and his presence on earth unknown to man. Av 50

Baba may even have taken birth as an Egyptian pharaoh, possibly as Akhenaton (1364-1347 BCE), who turned Egyptian religion away from the worship of many gods toward worshipping the One God, symbolized by the sun, thus introducing monotheism to Egypt.

Minor Advents were unknown before Baba's revelations. Even in a minor Advent, the Avatar is always aware of who he is, though he doesn't disclose his true identity.   Printed Lord Meher, 1308; footnote

He can also incarnate in a minor Advent as often as he pleases. Baba later remarked, "When I manifest, I will be seen at a thousand places at once!" There are many other instances where Meher Baba spoke of some of his minor Advents in such detail, commenting that the Avatar may take birth in several minor Advents between each of his major ones.

A devotee once asked, "Baba, why don't you reveal yourself now?" His answer: "It's so easy to reveal myself. Concealing myself till you're ready to perceive me is far more difficult; like when one has to pass wind, how easy to let it go. Holding it till the right time is not only difficult, but uncomfortable and can be painful. That's my state." 4531

Baba declared himself to be "the Ancient One," another recurring theme throughout his life.

"I am the Ancient One"

Believe me, there's no doubt about it. I am not this body that you see. It's only a cloak. I am *Infinite Consciousness*. I sit with you, play with you and laugh with you; but simultaneously I am working on all the planes of consciousness. I have before me yogis and saints who all are me in different forms, for I am the core rooted in everyone and everything. An infinite number of branches spread out from me. I work through you all, and so suffer for you all.

Understanding has no meaning. *Love* has meaning. Obedience has even more meaning. But holding my daaman has the most meaning. I know three things: I am the Avatar in every sense of the word. Whatever I do is the expression of my unbounded love. I suffer infinite agony eternally through your ignorance. What sustains me in my Universal suffering is bliss and my infinite sense of humor.

The amusing incidents arising at the expense of none lighten my burden. So think of me and always remain cheerful in all situations, and I am there to help you. 4441

"God is not to be lured, but loved," he said on another occasion. "God is not to be preached, but *lived*. Only those who live the life of love, honesty and self-sacrifice can truly know me as the Ancient One." PL 20

Chapter Eighteen

Baba's Return to the West

On March 24, 1932, a little more than three months since returning to India, Meher Baba embarked on another trip to Europe and the United States. Unlike that first, strictly private visit, this one was going to be highly publicized and he was pulling out all the stops. After a week of enduring Malcolm's directives at the Devon retreat he spent five days in London, after which he invited a group of disciples to join him for an excursion to Lugano, Switzerland, for a nine-day holiday in the Swiss Alps. There the weather was much warmer and more comfortable.

Even there, however, Meredith told officials and hotel staff that Baba was his friend and Chanji and Agha Ali his personal servants. He also told people about Baba, who wished to remain incognito. Chanji was harassed with constant curious inquiries.

During a scenic boat ride heading to Mt. Generoso from Lugarno, a humble old Swiss laborer sat opposite Baba for an hour. When the boat stopped at a small harbor, the old man smiled at Baba, and getting off, almost danced along the road. Baba told those with him:

> He is my agent. I'm here for complete rest and must temporarily hand over the work to someone else. This morning, I've done that with this man. I had to raise him from between the second and third plane to between the forth and fifth so he can take on the work given him.

Transferring my work must take place either in a thick jungle, on a high mountain, on water or in a crowd. That's why he looked at me, smiled and got off looking so happy. Did you notice he answered with his stick on the deck with taps timed in reply to mine?

Baba used Ghani's walking stick to demonstrate the code-tapping. The group then returned to London for six more days before Baba traveled to Southhampton to depart for America on the SS *Bremen* on May 14.

This time the Silent Master would have much to say. During this second American visit, he wished for his work to be reported by the press. Malcolm Schloss gave a statement to Henry Forman, which was printed in the April 24, 1932, edition of *The New York Times*, in anticipation of Baba's arrival in the city:

Roughly, every 2,200 years, the sun enters another zodiac sign. We are now entering a new solar epoch. The critical condition of the world is due to this fact. An old age is dying; a new age is being born. The world is convulsed by the birth pangs of a new civilization. Now, as always, when the need of mankind is most pressing, a great spiritual push will be given to the world. But first a great darkness will fall upon it. This darkness, however, is only the shadow cast by a great light.

This is both a wonderful and a terrible time. It depends on how you look at it. Everywhere old forms, mental as well as physical, are breaking up. The wise see in these changes the bursting asunder of the chrysalis that frees the golden butterfly. During the last two thousand years, the lower human mind has developed to its zenith. The divine Universal mind is stirring from its age-long slumber.

And a new era which we're about to enter will mark the unfoldment of the divine mind. This implies a manifestation of a new type of Universal mind is now stirring from its age long slumber, and the new era which is about to enter man's consciousness—a higher synthesis of heart and mind. [8]

One week before Baba's arrival, the May 2, 1932, issue of *Time* magazine had published a preview article of Baba's visit along with his photograph:

"Bringing the Infinite State to Harmon"

At Harmon, close to Briarcliff, stands a retreat called Meherashram [*sic*] (Home of Compassion), where the pious of any and all sects may soon meet with a long-haired, silky-mustached Seer who is called Shri (Honorable) Sadguru (Perfect Master) Meher (Compassionate) Baba (Father). To his Indian followers, the Parsis, Meher Baba, thirty-eight, is the "God-Man" or the "Messiah." To many other followers he is simply the "Perfect Master." His U.S. sponsors are Malcolm and Jean Schloss.

They await him at Harmon, think and write of him in uppercase—He, Him, His, Himself. Next week the God-Man sails from England, arriving at Harmon's Meherashram on May 16th. At nineteen, Baba met a holy woman, Babajan—One with Infinite Consciousness—who died lately in India at a reputed age of 125. Meher Baba soon had a vision of his divine nature and for nine months lay in a coma, coming out of it merged in God. He explained many are in such a super- conscious state.

But few remain in touch with the world like Baba to be able help others attain divinity. For almost seven years Meher Baba has uttered not a word. Arriving at his U.S.

retreat here Meher Baba's lips will be unsealed with much ceremony. Meanwhile, he carries a small board with letters to which he points when he has something to say. He'll establish retreats in New Hampshire and California.

Meher Baba is supposed to have performed many miracles. Now he wishes only to "make Americans realize the infinite state which I myself enjoy." His method of accomplishing this is cryptic, yet reassuring, "Let God flood the soul. What I am, you are." [15] 1410

Meher Baba aboard the SS *Bremen* in New York harbor, giving his first message to the West on the alphabet board at 1 PM, May 13 1932

On May 19, the day of his arrival, with about forty miles to go, Baba had a special message printed out to be given to the swarms of reporters, each of whom wanted to be the first to meet him. It included his now iconic statement: "I have not come to establish any cult, society or organization, nor even to establish a new religion. The religion I will give teaches the knowledge of the One behind the many. The book which I shall make people read is the book of the heart, which holds the key to the mystery of life." 1406-07

This was a difficult time for America. In the depths of the Great Depression, its unemployment rate was at thirty-three percent. Franklin Delano Roosevelt had just been elected President in a landslide victory over Herbert Hoover, while a struggling America was whistling in the dark and finding it hard to be optimistic. Baba's message was coming at a time when people most needed hope.

Despite having the printed message on hand for reporters, Baba was besieged at the 58th Street pier in Brooklyn, where he allowed himself to be photographed with his alphabet board before being whisked away by the disciples who had come to meet him, having reawakened the hearts of all those who had previously met him and so missed him over the past six months. His visit began with a three-day stopover at the Stokes' Greenwich Village townhouse with a reception for over three hundred mostly new people.

Meanwhile, Norina and her husband Prince Georges had agreed to a divorce, but she pleaded with him to meet Baba just one more time. He reluctantly agreed, despite the fact that he had been unable to accept Baba as Christ after their first meeting in 1931. But even though it only lasted two minutes, something happened at this meeting. Baba lovingly embraced Georges, telling him, "Just before you die, you'll experience who Baba *really* is."

Baba's words had a profound effect. Georges told Norina, "You were right. Meher Baba is real!" Norina also recalled, "He told a friend of ours, 'That man has done something to my heart!' He began . . . truly practicing Baba's message." Three months later the prince caught pneumonia and Norina, who was in Hollywood with Baba at the time, flew across the country to be with him at the end. Georges passed away at age forty-nine, but moments before death, as the Master promised, he had a beautiful experience of Baba as the Eternal Christ. 1654; Gl Int. Winter 2013:19

CHRIST COME AGAIN

Baba's First Messages to America

During this second, short visit to Manhattan, Baba agreed to a press interview with American reporter Frederick L. Collins, who was invited to afternoon tea with Baba at the Stokes residence. Collins' candid interview was published in the May 19, 1932 issue of *Liberty* Magazine. Baba was quoted as saying:

> My work will embrace everything and permeate every phase of life. Perfection would fall far short of the ideal if it were to accept one thing and reject another. The general spiritual push I shall give to the whole world will automatically adjust these problems such as politics, economics and sex, even though not directly connected with the original theme. New values and significance will be attached to things which appear to baffle solution at the present moment. 1408

"I Can Hardly Believe It — Portrait of a Happy Man, Silent for Seven Years"

"You must come to tea with Sadguru Meher Baba," said my friend. "With *what*?" "The new Perfect Master from India." Well, I'm not much on Perfect Masters *or* on tea, but my friend was insistent. So off we went to visit her globetrotting Parsi. In the cab my reluctance turned to terror when I asked, "What language does your friend speak?" "Oh, he doesn't speak at all," was the reply. "He hasn't spoken for seven years." The interview was looking sourer by the minute.

"What did you say his name was?" I asked in desperation. She was very patient. "*Sadguru*, which means *Perfect Master*, *Meher*, which means *compassionate*, and *Baba*, which means *father*." Perfect Master, Compassionate Father! That was a pretty large order.

But I must say despite dressing up for tea in an imitation chinchilla fur coat and light gray flannel slacks, Meher Baba looked every inch the part—not very many inches, to be sure. Now Baba—what I decided to call him—was small in the oriental way, yet somehow strangely impressive. In such a get-up, how he managed to be anything but funny was more than I could see.

He sat draped over the soft red fabric of Mrs. Phelps Stokes' best square-backed couch. What kept me from laughing out loud—though I'm loath to admit it—was the man himself. Pouring Baba's tea was a stunning ruddy-blonde woman [Jean Adriel].

She was on her knees before the Sadguru. Baba is not married. At thirty-seven he even flirts tentatively with the doctrine of celibacy as a sort of world sedative. But his disciples made it clear he did not prescribe celibacy for his followers. I asked if he were married. "Married? No. Sex for me does not exist. Modern marriage is too much of a business affair. No wonder it often ends in divorce.

"Spouses should put each other foremost. For a happy family life it is essential that selfless love should predominate over lust." "Americans have other problems now besides sex," I interjected.

"Yes, things have been pretty messed up here by a lack of understanding," Baba commented. "So what are you going to do for this messed-up country of ours?"

Baba smiled, spelling out, "It's my country, too." He then explained his mission in coming to the West. I asked, "Will you break your silence by radio?" "*Certainly not by radio!*" Meredith Starr cried out, horrified. "Why not?"

Baba spelled out. I then questioned him on America's problems.

Baba stated, "America has great energy, but a great deal of it is misdirected and produces destructive complexes which in turn, produce fear, greed, lust and anger, resulting in moral and spiritual decay." "Is your aim to help us with our spiritual problems or our practical problems?" Baba responded: "Our spiritual problems *are* our practical ones!"

"And just how do you intend to help?" "The help I will give will produce a change of heart in thousands, and right thinking will then automatically result." "Will that solve the depression problem?" "It will solve every problem." "Prohibition? "Yes and even the problem behind prohibition. It should never have been put into effect the way it was." "All at once?" I inquired.

"Yes. Hard liquor should have been barred, but not beer and wine. We might then have had a law that could have been enforced. As it is, we have a law which makes money for dishonest officials and increases vice everywhere. I believe in self-control, not coercion. Coercion based on oppression results in fear and hatred. Self-control requires courage and may be induced by love.

"A person will do many things for those he loves which he wouldn't ordinarily have the strength of mind and power to do. How many habits has a person been able to break through love he'd never have the strength to break without love? And when the love is Universal love, all habits which are detrimental either to the individual or to the social order will be dissolved in its light.

"It's the same with the economic situation you were asking me about. There's a very close connection between a man's character and his circumstances, between his internal environment of thoughts and desires and his external social environment. 'As within, so without' is the law. A man is dissatisfied with his environment because he doesn't know how to properly adjust himself to it.

"Instead of becoming discouraged and depressed, thinking how can I get out of this, one should think, what's the lesson here to learn from this experience? Providing one does one's best to find work, poverty cheerfully endured develops humility and patience and greatly aids spiritual progress. It is a test of character. I know it's difficult to be cheerful when starving, but all worthwhile things are difficult. Even millionaires are unhappy until they've learned to think and live rightly."

"Would a general acceptance of your doctrine of love bring about a more equitable distribution of money?" "It must," Baba emphasized. "Suppose we all loved each other as deeply as we now love the one whom we love best. The most natural desire of love is to share what one has with the beloved. The desire to share with everyone would produce a condition in which it would be a disgrace rather than an honor for anyone to possess more than anyone else."

Taken aback, I asked, "And you expect to do all this at once?" Baba replied, "No, but sooner than you think. People will respond because they'll *have* to." After thinking over what Baba had stated, I asked, "What will you do initially?" Baba replied, "Go to China and then come right back. I'm only staying there for a day to lay a complete cable between the East and the West. . . .

"The world will soon realize neither cults, creeds, dogmas, religious ceremonies, lectures nor sermons on the one hand, nor ardent search for material welfare and physical pleasures on the other, can ever bring about real happiness. Only selfless love and Universal brotherhood can do it."

Fredrick Collins was deeply impressed and found himself drawn to Baba, even though he was so skeptical before meeting him. The interview occurred on May 18, the same day Nadine Tolstoy came for her second darshan. She only had her interview when Collins left. Seeing Baba again, her faith was confirmed, and she accepted him as her Master forever.

What to Make of Him?

At many press conferences characterizing Meher Baba's second American visit, there were as many as fifty reporters and photographers on hand firing away. They didn't know what to make of him. He was a totally new phenomenon, against which they had nothing to compare. A Meher Baba devotee later put it this way: In terms of how Avatars are envisioned and remembered by humanity, the case of Meher Baba greatly differs from Avatars Rama, Krishna, Buddha, or Jesus. Meher Baba's was a twentieth-century Advent—a period when the modern photography and cinema were growingly established and became commonplace as part of our worldwide culture.

Devotees of Rama, Krishna and Jesus might generally rely on imaginative paintings when seeking to picture and envision their beloved figures, while devotees of Meher Baba enjoy a special boon of authentic photos and numerous short films of our modern-day Avatar, encouraging meditation on his divine qualities to seep into the viewers' hearts.

Baba may have been a big news item, but he loved nothing more than stealing away to walk through New York's city streets, as he had done on his first visit, just to be with the crowds, with which he was fascinated. He went out incognito, wearing sunglasses, his collar turned up and his long hair tucked under a beret.

Even so, as he was walking through Times Square or down 5th Avenue people would stop and stare, some bursting into quiet sobs, not being able to fathom the Presence passing them by, or locking glances with him they'd turn completely around and walk backwards. They'd stare at him so as not to lose his gaze, stirred by something primordial in the depths of their souls. Without the mind's interference the heart broadcasts on wavelengths secretly tuned to resonate in the presence of Compassion Incarnate.

On Saturday, May 21, Elizabeth drove Baba through Central Park. At East 110th Street he had her stop the car. He got out and walked toward the park lake with the others following him, wondering what was going on. No one was around except a nurse pushing a baby carriage. After only a glance at the woman, Baba turned and walked back to the car. None would know the significance of Baba's stroll for a year.

As it would turn out, disciple Josephine Grabau, who had been with the group, was in a New York City hospital when a young woman asked her whose photograph it was by her bedside. Josephine told her it was Meher Baba. The woman remarked, "It's the same man who looked so like Christ whom I saw walking in Central Park by the park lake a year ago. I'll never forget his face!"

That evening, Baba went to a movie in Times Square with a group of eighteen tagging along. The next morning, Sunday, May 22, a Fox-Pathé news crew arrived to film him giving a silent message on the alphabet board in the Stokes' back garden. [9] 1414–15

People living in the adjacent apartment buildings above and around the garden were hanging out of their windows that Sunday morning, intrigued by the scene below. Everyone wanted to see him. [10]

Later, in the middle of a program at the Stokes' home, Baba suddenly stopped to point out a woman far back in the crowded room, gesturing that Norina bring her to him. The woman was embarrassed, explaining that she was just here with a friend but really didn't feel inclined to meet Baba. He kept signaling her to come forward.

CHRIST COME AGAIN

At this, her attitude changed. As she approached, Baba's stretched out his hand to her with obvious joy. He had found a needy soul who was due to meet him. The woman's embarrassment grew to confusion, but Baba consoled her in his compassionate way, saying, "Don't worry; I know everything. I'll take care of it and help you." With that she began to shed tears and disappeared back into the crowd as the reception continued.

About a week later, just before driving to California with Elizabeth to meet Baba in Hollywood, Norina got a phone call from that rescued soul. "I'm the woman you so graciously induced to meet the Master. May I come to see you? Something so wonderful has happened to me!" And so the woman came to Norina's apartment, narrating a sorrowful tale with an extraordinarily beautiful ending:

> My daughter and I have hated and persecuted each other for twenty years. I've never been able to understand why, as she was born in love. But I was never able to overcome a detestation for my child. I had never even kissed her! I had no idea why the Master was calling me that day. Unhappiness was such a part of my life I didn't even know I was in need of help. The Master greeted me with such kindness; I wasn't impressed in any way, and didn't even look at him closely.
>
> I was like in a dream and woke up suddenly as if I'd been carried off somewhere by an invisible friend for some good reason. The next morning, I woke from an unusually deep sleep and found myself bathed in an ecstasy of love and bliss! It was so powerful it made me function without my will and without thinking. I walked straight into the room of my sleeping daughter.
>
> Drawn by irresistible love, I stretched myself near that despised child, and for the first time in our lives we felt a bond—a bond far more than a mother and daughter's love!

It was an almost was superhuman experience. It sealed our hearts together, and has begun a new life for us. My experience contagiously felt by her, and a tender relationship today reflects happiness for our whole family.

On another occasion, an alcoholic friend of Norina's came to meet Baba in New York. For years, she'd been in and out of one hospital after another. She lived with her mother, greeting her each morning with such cruel words: "Why aren't you dead yet?"

Norina aroused her curiosity about Baba, and her friend finally agreed to see "that man." When the woman was brought to Baba, Norina tried to tell him about her. But Baba cut her short, motioning, "I know her very well." The woman sat at his feet, and after a few moments of friendly chat, Baba mentioned alcoholic beverages and drinking.

With intense interest they discussed different types of drinks, and Baba mentioned a wine he'd heard was really excellent. The woman was overjoyed to talk on a subject so familiar to her. It was a lighthearted meeting, jovial and full of humor. After a while, she turned to Norina, "You know, your Baba isn't as bad as I thought; he's a real human being!"

A week later, the woman invited Norina over for tea. As she entered the woman's apartment, Norina at once noticed she hadn't been drinking. Her friend immediately disclosed her determination to change her life. "I no longer drink, nor will I ever again. I was such a fool!" 1418–19

Herbert Davy brought his friends, Arthur Rubinstein and wife Nela, to meet Baba. Rubinstein was a Polish pianist and an agnostic. Baba explained, "Music is one of the mediums for the expression of the Infinite, and musicians are more inclined towards spirituality, as spirituality touches the heart." 1558

Meanwhile, during this second American trip, Meredith Starr, who had accompanied Baba from England, continued to imply that he was Baba's "right-hand-man," claiming to know all about the Master's ways and preferences. It was time for Baba to begin bringing this one, who raised himself to the heights, crashing down. Though he had allowed him a loose rein in the beginning, Baba now stopped pampering him and began tightening the leash, deeply cutting into Meredith's ego by denying him access. It was a great shock. Meredith couldn't bear being excluded, and after this trip he'd leave Baba forever.

After a three-day stay with the Stokes, Baba revisited Harmon, north of the city, where a Paramount news crew filmed him exiting the stone house and drinking from a well. A few of the new women spent a day with Baba at Harmon before he left for the west coast. After lunch, he led them out to the stone terrace and into a field. Spying wildflowers, most ran on ahead to pick some, all except for Elizabeth. Baba gestured, "Don't you want to pick flowers, too?" She smiled and said she'd rather stay with him. He bent down, picked a small pink flower and handed it to her.

He then spelled out on the alphabet board, "Always keep this flower and write down today's date—May 24, 1932. One day you'll know its significance." She later pressed it in her New Testament and added the date. She forgot about it for twenty years, when the wildflower's meaning was revealed. 1421

Meher Baba's Spiritual Direction

No matter where he was—East or West—Baba freely gave spiritual direction to those seeking it, inviting and answering questions, without pause, on every topic one could imagine: prayer, the Blessed Trinity, Satan, "Real Light and False Darkness," spiritual perfection, ghosts and the occult, Krishnamurti and the Theosophical Society.

Prayer — God is Always Listening

God is always listening, Baba explained, and if one remembers God sincerely and wholeheartedly, one's cry is heard and the connection is instantly made. There's no question of distance, as he is the center of the entire universe.

But how can the prayers and calls of millions be heard at one and the same time and bring immediate connection with the Avatar? As the possessor of infinite and unlimited powers, to him there's no question of one, twenty-one, thousands, millions or even billions, as everyone is equally present regardless of distance or the number of voices on the line.

Baba also said that prayers, however long and loud, are meaningless and are mere show if they don't originate in the heart. He decried offering hired prayers through priests as worse, as nothing short of sheer hypocrisy. 1043

> Attend to your worldly duties as now, but with this difference – dedicate your inner life to loving God. You must give up nothing. But know within you only God is real. . . . In silence and secluded all alone in your room with all your heart, cry out, deep down within and say, "Baba, let me see God who is in me! Baba let me see God *in Me*!" Cry out with such longing that during this time you want nothing else but to see God [and] you will see him.
>
> If you really carry this out, then you will see God. Do it honestly, as if your life depended on it. Nothing more, nothing less. If you want to see God, as he ought to be seen do this, and I will help you. But do it very honestly. Cry, cry, and cry! God wants us to see Him, longs for it more than we ever long for Him. It's the truth. I know it. So do it honestly as if your very life depended on it. 3080

Baba characterized most people's prayers as invariably asking for something material or spiritual. In fact, God is merciful and bountiful even without their asking. He always gives much more than His lovers can receive. He deeply knows their needs. And so, asking for something from God is not only superfluous, it mars the inner love and worship which a prayer tries to express: God is not to be learned, studied, discussed or argued about. He is to be contemplated, felt, loved and lived. 3047

You praise God, not in the spirit of bargain but in the spirit of self-forgetful appreciation of what He really is—because He is praiseworthy. Your praise is a spontaneous appreciative response to His true being—infinite light, infinite power and infinite bliss.

It's futile to take a standard prayer and hold it up as an ideal for all people at all times. The Almighty's glory transcends all human understanding and defies all verbal descriptions. Eternally fresh and self-renewing in its unlimited amplitude, it never fades nor is confined by any limits.

The best of all hymns and prayers reach out to God's eternal Truth only to merge you in silent and unending adoration. If by ideal prayer to the Lord is meant a set formula, any search for it is a wild goose chase. All real prayers ultimately initiate the soul into an ever deepening silence of sweet adoration, where all formulas are dissolved in direct perception of divine Truth. . . .

Praying for someone's good, your prayer may bring about good both to him and to yourself.

Some pray for the spiritual benefit of those who have wronged them. Here too, they help spiritually. But all prayers with any kind of motive fall short. The ideal prayer is totally without motive. B 74-76

Once, while traveling in India, Baba and his men were staying near a mosque. As customary, the Call to Prayer and God's name were shouted in a loud voice from the top of a minaret each morning and then five more times throughout the day: "Allah! Allah! Allah!" At another time in a room next to the mandali, a Brahmin priest got up at four o'clock every morning to loudly chant Hindu verses, waking everybody up and driving them crazy.

"Is God deaf?" Baba asked. "God is never fooled by church-going, prayers, bell ringing or minaret shouting—He's deaf to it all; not fooled. Only love, *true love* moves Him." HT, Letter 382, March 10, 2011.

"What is the necessity of shouting His name so loudly from minarets? It makes one's heart skip a beat! God doesn't listen to such bleating. He has an ear only for the voice of the heart, of which the world has no idea." 1170–71

> Everywhere in the world in the name of prayer or worship this useless babbling goes on without substance, and those who practice it derive absolutely nothing from it. Do they think for a minute such loud noises can bring any kind of result?
>
> For years on end it's been happening. And it will go on for years to come, especially in the Muslim culture. The priests of *all* the various religions have been muttering hired prayers—actually *paid* for such drivel, while not the slightest advantage has ever been gained by anyone as a result. The reason is none of them does it sincerely or with the totality of their hearts. It's sheer hypocrisy if prayers are nothing more than the vocal chords' useless prattle with no heart or feeling in it.
>
> Their attention wanders here and there with this idle mumbo jumbo. One's prayers go straight to God only with an honest, open heart, with a clear, sincere mind and not the

outward show of meaningless chatter. Heartfelt remembrance of God from anywhere of the world, even by the worst sinner or the lowest of the low, instantly reaches God's ears. I am deaf to the sound of that Brahmin priest's chanting, though it is so near. I can't hear it as it neither touches nor has any effect upon me. Any type of loud, insincere prayer from any quarter leaves us Masters unmoved, as it is only noise and carries absolutely no heart. Such dry flat prayers, however loud or lengthy, or done over a long period of years, have no effect on us Masters. 1042

    I love and adore all religions; but I belong to no religion, nor do I seek to establish another one or add to the numberless illusory cages dividing man against man. No religion was ever intended to be anything more than a stepping-stone to God as Truth.

    People pray to me to solve their difficulties, saying they love me; but there's a vast difference between love and prayer. In Persian, to pray means to *beg, want or desire something*—even God's blessings. But when a person *really* loves, he gives himself completely without any expectation of receiving any reward. This is true love—no begging, no wanting, no room for desires.

    Only longing to unite with the Beloved remains. Love renounces the self; prayer means *selfishness*, no matter how high that prayer may be. So there's a vast difference between one who merely prays and one who loves. 1228

Baba remarked upon this theme throughout his Advent:

    Every religion has been converted into a total *veil*, obstructing the undimmed perception of the One Truth. As soon as the Truth of direct inner Realization is intellectualized or formulated, it is covered in the act of trying to express it. This comic/tragedy reveals itself in all world religions. 3499

Satan and the Problem of Evil

Baba also said that humanity has been so brainwashed by their religious leaders and by misunderstanding their scriptures that many actually believe in beings like Satan, Lucifer and Beelzebub. He taught that these are not entities, but purely symbolic images of the forces of Maya's evil—meaning the ignorant false workings of the limited human mind, and strictly speaking there is no such thing as "evil," except as a lingering relic of an earlier good.

The tendency is due to sanskaric impressions—necessary and inevitable at a lower, animal phase of consciousness, but carried over and persisting in a higher phase of human evolution where they are now obsolete. They persist simply due to their heavy inertia. Baba has assured us: "Everything happens according to divine will, and it's a mistake to think that God has any rival in the form of a devil." AW 322; Be 57

The only devil is the deluded human mind. That's the Frankenstein-like monster that we have built up over millennia by our lower tendencies and desires. Baba described the current orthodox views of heaven and hell as nothing less than grotesque and macabre. Baba also offered another explanation of the relative existence or non-existence of evil:

> Evil is not utterly evil, but merely goodness in its lowest degree; weakness is not mere incapacity, but strength in its lowest degree; and vice is not pure vice, but virtue at its lowest level. In other words, evil is a minimum of good, weakness a minimum of strength and vice the minimum of

virtue. All aspects of duality have minimums and maximums with all intervening degrees; and perfection is no exception. The whole range of humanity is included within these double extremes.

Perfection and imperfection are seen by comparison, contrast, and their relative existence. Perfection in the domain of duality is only "relative" perfection. It is only when one compares it with imperfection that it even appears as perfection. . . . [On the other hand] the Perfection of the spiritually realized souls has no parallel in the domain of duality and is entirely beyond the scope of intellect. When one becomes spiritually *Perfect*, he directly experiences that nothing exists but God.

What seems to exist in the domain of duality and capable of being grasped by the intellect is nothing but pure illusion. For the spiritually Perfect, God is the only Reality. Hence, science, art, music, weakness, strength, good/evil are all nothing to him but our false dreams. God's perfection is the experience of One Indivisible Existence totally beyond our false dreams. Di 78–7

The Blessed Trinity

Baba was also asked about the Blessed, or Holy Trinity. Between the fourth and fifth centuries, huge controversies arose around the nature of the Trinity. Yet the Gospels never once mention the Trinity. And it is hard to believe most Christians even a hundred years after the crucifixion would have bothered themselves with such arcane Trinitarian subtleties. Yet the relationship between cosmic power and the individual soul is uniquely triangular.

Baba said the relation of a Perfect soul is reflected in the idea of the Trinity as the three aspects of God: first the Father as Creator and Preserver; second, the Son as Redeemer and Savior; and three, His continuous, unending presence in creation as the Holy Spirit of Grace and Truth.

This allegorical triune mirrors the spiritual fabric of the universe. Meher Baba made clear on many occasions that the Son of God as the Avatar is the Divine indwelling presence in everyone and everything, traditionally known as the indwelling of the Holy Spirit—even where He is unknown or perceived as unwelcome due to the false mind's inherent ignorance, as in the so-called atheist. Be 14–15

When asked about different kinds of healing, Baba explained:

> Real healing is spiritual. When free of desires, doubts and hallucinations, the soul enjoys the eternal bliss of God. Physical healing may retard more important spiritual healing.
>
> If borne willingly, physical and mental sufferings are God's gifts and when accepted gracefully, they lead to everlasting happiness." 3046

Baba also offered a discourse entitled "Real Light and False Darkness":

> God is the real Infinite Light, and infinite subtle gas is the real Infinite Darkness. The nebula is created by the clash of Space [Akash], Energy [Pran] and subtle gas. The indescribably huge and innumerable pieces into which the nebula breaks up are so dazzlingly bright that each of them surpasses the light of billions of suns put together.
>
> But they are not hot. Each piece of the nebula is so dazzlingly brilliant equaling the light of hundreds of millions of suns, and its size equals a thousand million suns. And

there are millions and billions of such pieces of nebula, all originating from the tiniest Creation Point!

To sum it up: God is the Real Infinite Light; infinite subtle gas is the Infinite Real Darkness; the nebula is false light; the sparks or heavenly bodies are the shadows of the false light; and our world is totally false darkness." Meher Baba's Early Messages to the West, 166

The Occult

Many disciples wanted to know about occult phenomena. Baba said that such things as stigmata, telekinesis or objects like a communion wafer flying through the air, and bodily elongation and levitation may amuse or astound people, but they have nothing to do with the spiritual path for uplifting, healing or anything even remotely resembling spiritually. They are an illustration of how the overriding laws of nature can be suppressed by preternatural laws of the inner spheres and planes.

The real lover of Truth passes beyond such manifestations. A real lover doesn't even get entangled with the occult. Ones on the real path cannot afford to be diverted from the real goal—union with God and experiencing his radiant purity and love. Baba spoke of this disastrous misuse of energy:

> One can derive such powers by gaining tantric knowledge—mystical formulas for magical powers. Such powers may then be utilized for good or bad; good if used for removing evil spirits and ghosts from people, and horrific if used for self-aggrandizement.
>
> They have nothing to do with the Spiritual Path or inner-plane powers. Miracles done with such powers are childish. Even Vivekananda got into a terrible predicament

craving such powers. His Guru, Ramakrishna, saved him in the nick of time. 4966

Also, occult powers have nothing to do with ghosts. Ghosts and occult magic [both black or white] are quite different. Spirit [mind and energy] as in ghosts, is a power . . . but occult powers are caged and covered. If a tantric magician or sorcerer seeks to acquire such occult powers, his spirit contracts horrific sanskaras—worse than the worst sins, and reaps the fruit accordingly.

Never fall prey to such madness. It has no connection with the spiritual path to God or the inner planes. On the contrary, one following such falseness is far, far off the spiritual path, while accumulating the worst possible sanskaras, proving an obstacle to his further progress on the path.

The least said about these occult powers the better. This type of tantric spirit, in comparison to ghosts of suicides, is even more terrible, and neither receives nor gives benefit from his efforts. He gains occult powers through various studies and very undesirable practices—like eating excrement, drinking blood and other such obscene acts. These practices take a very long time.

The person may acquire only the power of making his body large or smaller than an ant's—and then assume his normal bodily size again. But when he changes into another form for some material gain or objective he can enter another's body by making his body small, but his own binding gross body sanskaras are with him even in his tiny form.

Ghosts, unlike tantric spirits, are those who have committed suicide and have no body. They enter another body and then influence the body of whomsoever they enter do as they wish. But he who has gained occult powers never does this; he can only make his body big or small, and thus his bodily sanskaras are always with him. In this action, there's also the danger of some accident.

He may be trampled on by someone while in his little body. In short, after long and hard study, such tantrics benefit in no way, but on the contrary risk contracting some of the worst possible sanskaras imaginable. So there's no use in playing such a worthless game of magic—sorcery! 870–71

Perfect Masters and Spiritual Perfection

In reply to a Westerner's question about an infallible method for recognizing a Perfect Master, Baba explained that an ordinary person has great difficulty distinguishing different stages up to the sixth inner plane of consciousness:

> Perfection includes all perfections, but there's no need to express them all. Krishna was spiritually perfect in everything. But he never showed his perfection materially, as the material manifestation of perfection has no meaning in the realm of illusion. He could have shown himself a perfect drunkard, perfect sinner and a perfect rogue. But that would have shocked the world. So he didn't express that. But he *was* a perfect drunkard, perfect sinner and a perfect rogue. 2002–03

So an ordinary person might suspect someone to be advanced, but one never really knows the degree of attainment. A Perfect One is simultaneously on the level of the lowest and the highest, and at the same time beyond both. But when a sincere and patient seeker of Truth contacts a spiritually Perfect One, there are three outer signs inseparably associated with that spiritual perfection. They are delineated in Meher Baba's *God Speaks*:

> The first sign of Perfection is not only "Oneness with God," but the continual, uninterrupted experience of "Oneness in everything." A Perfect Master continually without break experiences and realizes his own Self as the Self in all. This inner experience objectively manifests itself in the spontaneity of love such a one feels and expresses towards all Creation.
>
> To him nothing is attractive or repulsive. Good and bad, saint and sinner, beauty and ugliness, wisdom and idiocy, health and disease—all are modes of his own manifestation. When embodied Perfection loves, fondles or feeds any living creature, it feels and enjoys as if it were loving, fondling and feeding its very own Self. In this stage no vestige of "otherness" is left.
>
> The second sign is that the atmosphere of bliss Perfection radiates in its immediate vicinity, an atmosphere a stranger in search of it cannot help feeling. A Perfect Master not only enjoys infinite bliss, but experiences Universal suffering. But the sharpness of suffering is nullified or subdued by the overwhelming feeling of bliss. So, Perfection can appear blissfully calm in the face of every kind of suffering and persecution. The third sign of Perfection is its power to adapt to any level of humanity.
>
> It can be as nonchalant on a throne as in a gutter. It can very naturally be thrifty with the poor, extravagant with the rich, regal with kings, wise with the learned and simple with the illiterate and the ignorant. Just as a Master of Letters teaches English in different ways to beginners and graduate students, so also a Perfect Master adapts himself to the level of those he wants to uplift spiritually.

As the Perfect Master Ali Shah Qalander said in a spiritual discourse, "Giving perfection to a disciple is a matter of a fraction of a second. A word in the ear is enough to lift one instantly from finiteness to infinity. Such a transformation is not dependent on prayers or fasting." GS 246–47

Theosophy

Someone else asked Baba about about the Theosophical Society, headed by Annie Besant and her protégé Krishnamurti, acclaimed as the "modern Messiah." Krishnamurti himself was not so self-deluded and renounced all such claims. Baba observed: "These Theosophists deceive themselves. Their chief wire-pullers are said to be somewhere in the Himalayas—Tibet. You'll find nothing there but dust and stones. Besides, no real spiritual Master ever required someone else's body for his own use. Such thinking is ridiculous!" 628–29

"Krishnamurti is not as advanced as some think. Yes, he does good and will come to me one day. I'll help him advance on the path. . . . He has real possibilities within, but he'll not fulfill himself or become truly great as long as he does not come to visit me." 1305

But Krishnamurti as a "New World Teacher?" God forbid! You cannot compare the Sadguru Ramakrishna of Calcutta with Krishnamurti. Ramakrishna was Rama and Krishna personified! Krishnamurti is living in all majesty and splendor, pomp and power and is moving about England in aristocratic, fashionable circles, playing tennis and golf, leading a most comfortable life.

He doesn't have the faintest idea – not even a wisp of Real Truth; so is it with these funny, showy "theosophists." Their greatness lies only in editorship—writing and speaking high-sounding words about planes, powers, colors, secret doctrines, society and caste. Truth is far, far beyond this. If you aspire for Realization, you should hold your very life in the palm of your hand, ready to give it up at any moment! Then alone will you be deemed worthy and be able to experience Truth. 679–80

When Malcolm Schloss wrote to Krishnamurti about Baba's first visit to America, he wrote back that he'd like to meet Baba and conveyed his greetings. Though he may have had the intention, sadly he never took the opportunity to meet the Avatar. Baba stated he was on the fifth plane and would remain there until he died.

When asked about the popular spiritual teacher George Gurdjieff, Baba commented, "He has some, but certainly not all the Truth." Then in 1933, Annie Besant's daughter, Mrs. Vincent Scott, came to see Baba in London. Discussing her recently passed mother, Baba revealed she was now born as a man in India. 1379; MM 1:366 side note

Then one day the topic turned to the American Christian Mission and the Salvation Army—two groups which were doing their utmost in India to convert people to Christianity as the only road to salvation. Baba sadly shook his head and asked:

> Why mislead people into leaving their religions? Is religion the Truth, as well as the way to the Truth? Religion has nothing to do with Truth. Truth is far away and beyond the tenets and principles of any religion. Truth is naked, unrestrained and experienced only by cutting loose illusion—Maya's limbs of lust, anger and greed. . . . If it's not a sin to make others doubtful of their religion, it's surely a great weakness. What advantage is it to expand a religion's numbers to millions?

This is the horrific Kali Yuga! Just see the horror done in the name of religion. Look at the massacres born of ignorance and cruelty between Hindus, Muslims and Christians, all for the sake of religion. At the same time, many false prophets have appeared and hypocrisy runs rampant.

People now want religious doctrines to suit their *own* ideas of life, and the crafty leaders who observe all this and fulfill their wishes find thousands of followers. So, as I've been telling you, control your mind, live a pure and clean life, discard desires and follow a God-Realized Master.

Then alone you will be safe. Following a Master doesn't mean giving up your religion. You should renounce your *mind*! If you try to set green grass on fire, it won't burn. But if you set a match to dry hay, it will immediately catch fire and burn to ash. The hay symbolizes sanskaric impressions accumulated over lifetimes. To dry out green grass keep it near a fire.

So to destroy one's sanskaras, a person should stay near a Sadguru in whom the fire of divine knowledge is always burning. In his contact and company, sanskaras accumulate, but also dry. Finally, the flame of his grace descends as he sets fire to and uproots all one's sanskaras. Even the deep red sanskaras of lust and anger, the fastest growing and most deeply rooted, are nothing to worry about if you have contact with a Sadguru. 680–81

When the topic of beauty arose, Baba said, "I like beauty in everything. Real beauty is immortal and never perishes." But then he continued with an unexpected explanation:

Look at the human body so full of filth and dirt. The mouth, nose, rectum, urinary tract are all filth! Still, people run after beautiful women and chase handsome men. This is not beauty but foul lust.

Suppose the face of the beautiful one you love gets misshapen by acid thrown on it, rendering it ugly. What will become of your love? If your heart is clean and your mind pure, you'll remain unaffected, even surrounded by thousands of beautiful people. As it is, you don't love beauty, but dirt, as you yourselves are unclean. Get rid of your own foulness and find out what real beauty is. Beauty can never be enjoyed without rooting out the dirt. 1353

Silly Questions

But sometimes people asked Baba ridiculous questions like, "What time should I go to bed at night?" He would just raise his eyebrows as if to ask, "Is he an idiot?" He later commented:

> They ask questions about every little thing: should I go to the toilet? Should I wipe myself? Should I pass gas? Should I piddle? They don't ask if they should get married and have children, but they'll pester me about all sorts of other insignificant things and then think they're taking my advice. Whatever I don't want them to do they'll do on their own anyway. They don't ask about real things.
>
> Suppose I say, "Don't marry so and so." "Oh, but I'm in love," they say. That's their answer and that's why I don't allow these people to live near me. If I act lovingly, they follow Meher Baba; but once they start experiencing pain, they won't stay for one-half hour with that Baba. They'll run away. They're not ready for that. Whatever's in their share is exactly what I give to them. GuG 237

Chapter Nineteen

Realization through the Medium of Film

Unlike during his Advent as Mohammed, Meher Baba very much wanted us to see his image in photographs, movies and videos. This was the first Advent in the last five-thousand-year year cycle of seven Advents where he would leave behind his dynamic, living physical image for his lovers in posterity, adding that he would accomplish Universal work through his photos. But he also said, "What use is my photo on paper if you've not first established me in your hearts?" Aw 5 (no. 3): 1

When people would bring Baba's photos for him to touch, if one accidentally dropped in the midst of the crowd, he'd have it picked up, touch it to his forehead and then return it to its owner. It was a lesson for us all that his photos were to be cherished and treated with the greatest reverence, love and faith—as a representation of him worthy of worship. Baba's Mehera had this to say in a 1982 letter about his photos:

> To me each and every image of the Beloved Baba is very precious. It is a portrayal of the Divine coming amongst us in human form. True, no photograph or painting can do justice to the Godman who is the personification of love, perfection and beauty. . . . But his photos are a ray of the Sun of His Being.
>
> Gazing at them we feel the warmth, light, and comfort of His presence. For those who were with Baba, and those who were not, Baba's photos and videos are all the more

meaningful now that He has dropped His human form. This treasure will be a continuing source of joy to all hearts where Beloved Baba eternally resides. 5112

If viewed with love, Baba said at times he'd come alive in his photographs and at the time of his Manifestation even bestow God-Realization through these images upon souls that were ready, or at least help liberate them from illusion's bondage. Such "coming alive" was true for many, whose lives were changed by seeing a photograph of Meher Baba.

Philip White's Dream

This story from Philip White shows how Baba used photographs to answer an ailing child's prayer:

> When I was four years old in 1952, I remember getting down on my knees in front of our red couch at home as I broke down weeping. I was shocked at the depth of my weeping, because at age four, I had never had any kind of experience of myself; its depth frightened me. I blurted out, "I want to find God!" It is the most poignant memory of my childhood. Little did I realize then it was to bring me so close to the incarnation of the Godman Himself.
> In early 1965, at age sixteen, I was diagnosed with terminal cancer and given about six months to live. Well, I was upset and frightened as any sixteen year old would be, feeling regret about what I wouldn't live out in my life. A part of that was feeling something was missing about God.
> One day after surgery, basically sewn-up and left to die, I was sitting in my room reading the Bible. I remember saying, *"Not my will, but Thine be done,"* and having a really profound experience of such magnitude that I lost con-

sciousness of it for eight years, until I was twenty four.

It was then I wanted to go live in France, but was unable to. Instead, I went to New York City, cut my hair, decided not to be a hippie anymore and got a job. Then I happened to meet an old Chapel Hill, North Carolina, friend and Baba lover named Bill. He had a "Don't Worry, Be Happy" photo of Baba on his dashboard. Seeing it, my heart pounded and I went into utter terror breaking out in a cold sweat. Now, I always prided myself being tolerant of other's religious beliefs.

But this photo terrified me. I became instantly unaware of my body and found myself sitting before a huge chess board with this man in the photo on the other side,

Meher Baba, much as he appeared in Philip White's dream

sitting there waiting for me to make my move. I was petrified. If I made a move, he was going to nail me and it'd be over.

He got impatient and gestured. "Make your move." So I moved. He instantly made his play and through his look said, "Checkmate. Game's over." Then His image sort of faded and I was back sitting in the car sweating, with my heart pounding. I felt like I'd just been through *The Lord of the Rings'* fire or something. So there it was, and Bill said, "What's up? Anything wrong with you?" "No, nothing . . . but who's that guy in the photograph?" "Oh, that's Meher Baba."

"That's enough. I don't want to hear any more, thanks." I can't believe I said that, but I was that terrified. Of course Bill said nothing else, but I became literally obsessed with Baba from that moment on—fear/fascination. There was a clear pull and I was in utter agony over it. So this was my introduction to Baba, just through that photograph!

Then one night I had a complicated dream of Him. At one point Baba pulled an old hat and cane out of thin air, and humped over walking, perfectly mimed an old man. Now, that's something I used to do as a boy, miming an old man! As I watched Him, it was utterly hilarious. Years later I ran across a photo his sister Mani had taken of Baba dressed in a white top hat and cane and wearing white shoes—just the way He looked in my dream.

Later on, Baba showed me numerous lifetimes and my personalities of those lives – an entire panorama of opposites, but with the continuity they were all me. . . . And then Baba looked into me and telepathically said these words. I'll never forget: "Nothing is as it appears, for I am the One true light." I thought, "What do you mean 'Nothing is as it appear—I am the one true light?'"

As I asked him in my mind, his body began to melt and finally condensed down into a little ball of light. I thought, what's this ball of light? I've seen it before, but where? I woke up and went to work, only this time with an elbow in my brain. I couldn't get this haunting light out of my mind. So I finally quit my New York job and went back to North Carolina – my version of Walden Pond.

It was [at a] farmhouse with a pond where I began reading a set of Baba's *Discourses*, because now I really had to know who this Meher Baba was. Reading Volume Two I remember this incredible moment, an epiphany really, where I just knew Meher Baba was the state of God, and he was not just some guru or spiritual adept or Oxford scholar writing about mysticism; he was actually God in human form. When I realized that, I lost consciousness of my body for how long, I don't know.

After that, I began to recall the time when I was pronounced dying of cancer with only a few months to live. I began to put together how I was allowed to stay in the body for a while. I remembered having been in that room years ago and reading the Bible, looking up and saying, "*Not my will, but Thine be done.*" And it was at *that* moment I remembered what I had seen it at age sixteen.

It was that little ball of light in the doorway. With my eyes rolling up, I slumped back on my bed. It was the most beautiful light I had ever seen . . . totally beautiful. It pulled me into it and I came out on the other side, knowing things and experiencing things about my future I had no way of knowing before. It showed me different parts of my life.

Then I was slammed out of the light and back into my bed. Then the light got bigger and came closer to me, again pulling me into it. I felt like a giant overlooking the United States, just knowing the whole country and everything in it that needed to be known.

Then I was slammed back into my bed. The light got bigger and pulled me in yet again. This time I was in outer space and saw the earth. . . . I had never seen the earth like that, but when they landed on the moon in 1969 and sent back pictures of earth, *that was it*—just how I saw it in 1965.

Once again the light got bigger and pulled me through, and I experienced myself as being in everything. From that glimpse I got just a shadow of an idea of what Baba means when he says, "I experience myself as everyone and everything." That glimpse was humbling and so incredible. Then once more, I was thrown back into bed and the light encompassed everything.

I remember thinking about . . . me and this light. And it gets down to just this subject and just this object. I was pulled into it again and experienced a merging with the light in which there was no separation—just this unfailing, ineffable, inviolable blissful knowing.

When I came out of that experience, I was blissful for months; no worry, no fear, no anger, experiencing being in the will of God. It didn't matter if I stayed in my body or not. I knew if I died it was meant to happen. There was no worry, concern or doubt. So people would come in to pray for me, but coming into my room their knees would literally buckle and they would just begin to weep.

They'd come to my bed and I'd console and hold them. I remained in that state for about a year, and then gradually it waned. Oh, what a great loss. I still grieve over it, but feel wonderfully fortunate that in answering a four-year-old's prayer; Baba gave me a glimpse of His infinite state. [11]

Newsreels and Movies of the Avatar

Of the three newsreels of Baba mentioned earlier; the first was shot by a London Paramount news crew in early May, 1932. Then two weeks later, a second film was made on Sunday, May 22, by a Pathé news crew in the back garden of the Stokes residence in Greenwich Village. J[12] Just days later, a third newsreel was shot on Baba's second visit to Croton-on-Harmon.

Five years later an extraordinary film was shot for an Indian newsreel on Baba's forty-third birthday, called *Nasik 1937*. Mehera and the other women, cloistered in Baba's ashram at Nasik, as at

Meherabad, did not attend this celebration, and they didn't see the film for many years.

Aside from one short film made in 1948, no other footage taken during the 1940s seems to exist. However, the 1950s saw a sudden abundance of films made with home movie cameras, both at Myrtle Beach and in India. Several home movies were shot in 1953 during Baba's stay in Dehradun. On October 11 of that year, Bombay filmmaker Bal Dhawale shot footage of Baba, intending to produce a film about him. Baba later agreed to see him and discuss the film's completion. He also wanted Bal to go to Sakori to film Upasni Maharaj's ashram, as well as in Meherabad and various other places associated with this Advent.

Baba conveyed to the Bombay filmmaker that those who had never seen Baba before in person would be helped spiritually just by seeing him in film: "It will help them to be liberated from the bondage of Maya." With Baba's encouragement, work on this film continued over several months. In November 1953, Adi Sr. viewed some footage at an Ahmednagar theatre. But for all the interest, it seems no finished film was ever produced. This was true of many other film projects Baba initiated in the 1930s, despite Baba's time-consuming and meticulous involvement with the making or planning these films—especially in Hollywood from 1932 to 1934.

Baba's work was aimed at making motion pictures a channel to reach the hearts of his lovers in future ages. He said that he would contact people through his image in photos and films. But he also warned that it was of little use to have his photo unless he was established in the heart.

In the mid 1950s, another young American who had heard of Baba was invited by a friend to attend a Baba gathering. He went, but with reluctance. He was a bit put off by some of the other people there and decided to leave early. But something happened each time he got up to go, resulting in his staying, as he explained:

They finally showed an Indian film of Baba's visit to Andhra in February 1954. That's when I started becoming really interested, seeing him walking with thousands of people following him around. I thought "This Meher Baba must be very special. Just look at these countless people following him around as if he's Christ."

I started really paying attention to the film when suddenly his face came out of the film, showering me with a huge ray of love. Internally I exclaimed, "Oh, my God, *that's God!*" I knew instantly Baba was God the moment he gave me that glance.

Meher Baba, dressed in his faux-chinchilla coat, India, 1930s

A young Westerner living at Meherabad once said that she was watching a film taken of Baba at Meherabad, walking past the room where she was staying. As he passed, a thought came to her. "Baba, did you know I'd be staying here?" The moment this thought occurred, Baba took a step backwards in the film, looked inside her room, then turned to the camera and smiled. Baba responded to her unspoken thought as clearly as if he had physically been there with her in that moment.

At a film showing in Argentina, people were so moved by Baba's images that although no one understood the English soundtrack, Baba spoke personally to each one in their hearts. Someone later related, "The room was so silent you could hear an ant walk."

In many films, Baba looks quickly to the left and right and then very fleetingly at the camera. In that instant, looking directly into his eyes we feel him looking directly at us as individuals. People spending time in his presence said his eyes rarely stayed put or focused in one place for a moment—that his glance darted constantly from here to there.

With such light coming from his eyes one might be burned in the sheer ecstasy of his glance, drowned in the bliss of his gaze. But surely he knew in those fleeting moments of eye contact that one day he would intimately touch people viewing these films or photos, down to the individual identity of each person. Gazing at him live or in film or in a photo is a kind of meditation. In the film *Nasik 1937* and in others, when Baba suddenly glances at the camera, those who meet his eyes even for a split second so vividly experience his presence.

Meher Baba, Meherabad Hill, early 1930s

The Beloved's glance imparts his direct protection and intimate blessing. But he also said, "You still don't see me as I really am. This body is not me. My real self is far more beautiful. You'd lose your senses if you caught even a glimpse of it." 1574

Most people in Baba's presence—even strangers—couldn't take their eyes off him. Countless thousands of people in the East and in the West experienced a spontaneous flow of tears, simply by being in his physical presence. It didn't matter if they knew him or not.

At other times, if Baba didn't want people looking at him, he withdrew his magnetism. Don Mahler once observed Baba standing on a street corner in New York when none of the passing crowd gave him so much as a fleeting glance, even though he was dressed in distinctive Indian garb.

Baba wanted the atmosphere around him to be natural. He didn't want people gaping at him with ostentatious adoration. But sometimes he'd grant that intimate glimpse that went straight to the heart. He often reminded his lovers, however, repeating it three times just before he dropped his body: "Remember, I am not this body." Still, his physical form was enormously significant and beautiful as the medium through which the God-man appears on earth, allowing us to see and embrace him in the body in which he suffers while bearing the burden of his Universal work.

With total adoration his beloved Mehera tenderly touches and kisses each image of Baba she sees throughout her day. A clear and distinct image of Baba's face appeared in the tree bark outside Mehera's bedroom in 1969, giving her great solace shortly after he had passed. Baba encouraged his lovers to meditate on his photograph with love and pray to it.

There Will Be No End to My Photos

"Now that you've seen me in this coat, this form," Baba said, "keep my photos or whatever reminds you of me and helps you to continue remembering me. Keep my picture in your house—even in your toilet—so even there you can remember me all the time. Starting and ending your day, remember me." AO 97

> A time will come when my photograph will be taken every day, in great numbers, in different poses and sold everywhere. They will appear in different world newspaper languages, in books and magazines, in residences, businesses, religious places, government and private offices. Wherever your eyes look, my photos will be seen as the Ancient Eternal Beloved come once again.
>
> It will be on lockets around necks, coat buttons, on rings showing my face, small and big photos will adorn the walls, life-size oil paintings of me, also. Over and above

that, my image will be seen on movie screens—sitting, standing, sleeping—in all postures; smaller than the smallest pea and bigger than life-size. There will be no end to my images and photos. 2258

"You'll see my pictures in filthy places," he further stated, "even in back alleys. It will be on badly defaced postage stamps, on matchboxes and the labels of cheap brands of goods. So why be disturbed? I also live in the filthiest of places and am in the filthiest of things and beings." [13] 4344

Hollywood Bound

But Baba had in mind an even more potent means to spread not just his image, but his message. On May 25, after a brief return to Harmon, Baba and his entourage boarded a train, ultimately bound for California. Swarms of reporters met Baba's trains at major stops across the country, and he always had a message for them, but sometimes the message didn't make it into print as intended. An example of the frivolous publicity he received in allowing such press interviews can be seen in a front-page article in the Kansas City *Evening Star*:

"Baba, the 'Persian' Messiah, Hollywood-bound"

Shri Sadguru Meher Baba, claiming to be of God—in the sense Jesus, Buddha, Krishna, Zoroaster and other mystics claimed and taught—was in Kansas City today en route to Hollywood to break an *alleged* seven-year silence, and speak words to restore the world's peace and happiness.

Travelling with Baba are nine disciples. He will soon be giving up his *"uh,"* and then his fingers will get a needed rest. He who has transcended the world of illusion and is of

God and heaven, walked in the *flesh* today at Union Station under a $15 depression suit and an extra pair of pants, smiling timidly under a mustache the size of Buffalo Bill's and black as the ace of spades.

The Holy One, *"Perfect Master, Compassionate Father,"* is Hollywood bound where he will break a seven-year silence and lead all men to happiness and peace. On July 13 at seven P.M., Baba will cease pointing his fingers, and grunting *"uh"* to reporters in response to questions. He'll then break forth in full bloom of his *"messiahship,"* and his speech will transform the consciousness of humanity. 1422–25

Not just the *"grunting,"* but the whole tenor of this press caricature shows how America misperceived the Master, traveling incognito through her heartland. On his first visit Baba had travelled through New York, Massachusetts and New Hampshire. Now crossing the American continent, he passed through Pennsylvania, Ohio, Indiana, Illinois, Missouri, Kansas, Texas, New Mexico, Arizona and California—ten fortunate states. When the train arrived in El Paso, Texas, Baba got off and took a brisk twenty-minute walk before continuing on to Tucson, Arizona, where his party changed trains and boarded a Santa Fe Railway passenger train bound for California.

Meanwhile, Norina and Elizabeth were bravely driving cross-country from New York to Los Angeles to help arrange Baba's busy Hollywood schedule. He had expected that they would accompany him on the train, but they looked forward to the adventure of driving across the west, so he let them.

In the 1930s, before interstate highways, two women traveling alone across America's Dust Bowl was a truly remarkable undertaking. But in the featureless Western desert they became lost. Suddenly, a man in the car ahead of them beckoned them to follow him. They did, and he soon got them back onto another road. They stopped to thank him, but his car had vanished into thin air! They later learned that a bridge had washed out on the road they had planned to use, and had they continued on they'd have likely been killed. Baba said he sent one of his agents to save them—the vanishing stranger. Aw 20 (no. 2): 29

While much of the Avatar's Inner work is done by secluding himself away from the world on mountaintops or in caves, his Universal work is accomplished among throngs of people and crowds, utilizing their tremendous energy. So it's no coincidence that Meher Baba's visit to the film capital coincided with ongoing preparations for the 1932 Summer Olympics.

Los Angeles was an international beehive preparing for a gathering of fifteen hundred athletes from thirty-seven nations—just the sort of milieu in which Baba loved to work. The idea was to bring the world to Los Angeles. Little did the city suspect that the Avatar of the Age was included in the package of bustling preparations for this major world event.

Hollywood was about to enter a Golden Age of film in the 1930s and was "ruthless in its pursuit of excellence. Its great stars —Greta Garbo, Jean Harlow, Clark Gable, Cary Grant, Claudette Colbert, Gary Cooper and Marlene Dietrich, to name a few—are still household names. Studio by studio, director by director, film by film, the riches of the 30s have never been equaled." John Baxter, *Hollywood in the '30s*

Anticipating Baba's arrival, reporters were on hand with flashbulbs popping as soon as the Santa Fe Express pulled into Old Pasadena Station at 8:30 AM, Sunday, May 18, 1932. Baba stayed at the home of Priscilla and Marc Edmund Jones on 2400 North Gower Street in Hollywood. Jones was a renowned astrologer and friend of Malcolm and Jean. Quentin, Meredith and Chanji also stayed with him at the Jones's. Kaka and Baba's brothers Adi Jr. and Beheram stayed at another private home nearby, while Jean and Malcolm, Margaret Starr and the others on the Hollywood

The home of Priscilla and Marc Edmund Jones at 2400 North Gower Street where Meher Baba stayed for a week during his first visit to Hollywood, May 1932

junket stayed at the local Mission Hotel.

The first thing Baba wished to do was to get out to see his surroundings. He was anxious to drive through Beverly Hills to begin making silent contact with specific film industry personnel with his silent radar. During the drive-through of this exclusive neighborhood, he was drawing the spiritual life-blood of those in the film industry destined to meet him now and for his subsequent longer and more focused working visit to Hollywood in 1934.

At a press conference that afternoon Baba gave his first direct message to Hollywood, and he didn't mince his words.

Baba's First Message to Hollywood at the L.A. Press Reception

So much has been said and written about the Highest Consciousness and God-Realization that people are bewildered as to the right process and immediate possibility of its attainment. Wading through such literature, the philosophical mind only ends up learning intellectual gymnastics.

The highest state of consciousness is latent in all. The Son of God is in everyman, but requires to be manifested. The method to attain this great consciousness must be very practical and adapted to existing mental and material conditions in the world.

The rituals and ceremonies instituted by priest-ridden churches have made the process too dry, accounting for the lack of interest felt all over the world toward religious things in general. India, in spite of its high state of spirituality, at the present moment is very caste-ridden due to various cults of mindless rituals and ceremonies, maintaining the form but killing the spirit.

Forms and ceremonies, instead of diminishing the false ego, only strengthen it. The stronger the ego, the more aggressive it becomes. In the anxiety to become conscious of a separate self through *thinking* thoughts such as 'I am in the right' or 'I am the favored one' or 'Only I have the right to live,' one becomes destructive.

The furious arms race within the Christian world shows the utter disregard of Jesus' commandment if one cheek is smitten, the other should be offered. This shows clearly what I mean by the ego. In the evolutionary ascent from the mineral, vegetable and animal life, the latent mind gradually expands and develops until full consciousness is reached in the human form.

To create this consciousness, the universe emanated from the Infinite Ocean of knowledge and bliss—namely, God the Absolute. In human form with mind fully developed, a difficulty is confronted which prophets and spiritual masters have visited this earthly plane to remove.

Alongside the development of full consciousness in human form as a result of previous conditions of life, the ego—the false 'I' has evolved. This ego is composed of fulfilled and unfulfilled desires and creates the illusion of feeling finite, weak and unhappy.

The soul can only progress by general suppression of this finite ego and its transformation into the Divine Ego—the One Infinite Self—retaining full consciousness of its human form. When man realizes this state of divine consciousness, he finds himself in everyone—actually *sees and experiences* all phenomena as forms of his own Real Self.

The best and easiest process for overcoming the ego and attaining divine consciousness is to develop love and render selfless service to humanity in whatever circumstances we are placed. All ethics and religious practices ultimately lead to this. The more we live for others and less for ourselves, the more the low desires are eliminated and this reacts upon the ego, suppressing and transforming it proportionately. The ego persists to the very last.

Not until all six out of the seven principal states [inner spiritual planes] on the path are traversed, culminating in one God-Conscious state, is the ego completely eliminated only to reappear on the seventh plane as the Divine 'I'—the state of Christ Consciousness to which Jesus referred saying, "I and my Father are One," and which corresponds to the state of Perfection—living in the Infinite and finite at the same time. This is for one who works on his own initiative without coming to a Perfect Master.

But with the help of a Master, the whole affair is greatly simplified. Complete surrender to the living will of the Perfect One with unflinching readiness to carry out his orders, rapidly achieves a result not possible even by practicing the entire world's ethics for thousands of years.

The extraordinary results achieved by a Perfect Master are due to his being one with the Universal mind. He is present in the mind of every human being and can therefore give just the right help needed to awaken the highest consciousness latent in every individual.

To achieve the greatest result on the material plane, Perfection must possess a human touch and a keen sense of humor. I eternally enjoy the Christ state of consciousness. When I speak in the future, I shall manifest my True Self.

Besides giving a spiritual push to the whole world, I shall lead all who come to me toward Light and Truth. In short, this is my mission to the world. 1426–27

A *Los Angeles Times* reporter asked Baba, "What do you hope to accomplish in America?" Baba replied, "A general awakening which will affect the whole of mankind and eliminate the depression and dissatisfaction existing in today's world." 1428–29

Before retiring after his busy first day in Hollywood, Baba was outwardly restless and ill-at-ease with Meredith, who insisted upon sharing his room. Baba reluctantly allowed it for two nights, but Meredith's supercilious persona was a constant irritation.

Meredith did have some virtues, but they were more or less nullified by his pretentious behavior—giving orders to the mandali and forcing Baba to follow his own peculiar ways of doing things, just as he'd done in England. Baba had patiently endured the aggravation, which had been building since 1928 in India. But Meredith's behavior these last two nights became the final straw, and Baba decided that the time was approaching to get rid of him once and for all. 1428

When Meredith had become a pompous nuisance in Paris, Baba told him of a particularly negative energy there and that it would be best if he returned to England at once to save himself from its bad influence. He had departed Paris immediately.

Now, the same behavior in Hollywood proved his undoing. Baba warned him, "There's a *very bad* influence here in Hollywood for one as spiritually sensitive as you." It was suggested that Meredith and Margaret travel up the Pacific coast to a beach colony near Santa Barbara called the Dunes. There they could contact some honest bohemian seekers—early "hippies" living in a seaside commune. Baba would follow up with a visit there shortly afterwards.

This was the beginning of the erosion of Meredith's external contacts with Baba. The internal link, however, would always remain intact. No one can say what was going on inside, or what work Baba was doing with him.

Baba remained in the movie capital for seven hectic days packed with interviews and receptions. The mandali barely had four hours of sleep a night.

Rolling Out the Red Carpet for Baba

With the lightning speed typical of his work, the next day Baba began contacting Hollywood's reigning luminaries—writers, directors, producers and stars. In a bustling round of meetings with executives at various studios—MGM, Paramount, Fox and Universal—he indicated that he was laying the cables for a totally new kind of motion picture.

Baba was a welcomed guest, ushered onto sound stages to meet casts and crews and to closely observe the movie-making process. There can be little doubt filmmaking was very much a group activity, with so many creative contributors under the supervision of a director—just like the Avatar's circle was minutely directed by the Master himself.

Hollywood may have treated Baba like royalty, but getting it to understand his project was another matter altogether. His daily itinerary was carefully laid out, but he would make last-minute changes to be flexible for the many who truly sought him out.

Only three years had passed since the beginning of the Great Depression, which provided the backstory to Baba's ambitious film project. With all its glamour and bravado Hollywood was desperately trying to mask the real human toll from which it was reeling. Initially unfazed by the market crash of 1929, Hollywood naively calculated that Americans now more than ever needed escapist entertainment. And so it blithely slated more and more high-budget films to fill their productions rosters.

This cavalier, if not downright reckless disregard for economic realities had brought about a terribly rude awakening by 1932. With theatre attendance falling drastically, there were massive movie house shutdowns. Production simply had to be slashed. Even film executives were forced into deep salary cuts, mandated across the board by President Roosevelt's economic recovery plan.

The Avatar was also facing these box-office realities. By worldly standards, 1932 was probably the worst possible year for Meher Baba to make his Hollywood pitch. But who knows what he was really doing behind all these scenes?

America's national shrine, MGM, was the only studio to turn a profit that year—$8 million. Paramount, Warner Brothers, RKO and Fox were in danger of toppling into bankruptcy. Desperate theatre owners were scrambling to lure movie patrons with bingo games and dish give-aways between double-features.

On his first working day in the film capital, Baba was driven through the huge, stately gates of the failing Paramount Studios on Hollywood's Melrose Avenue. The Starrs hurried to take their places on both sides of him, as usual.

Baba was taken to a soundstage where *The Devil and the Deep* was filming. Quentin Tod knew its co-stars: acclaimed British actor Charles Laughton, and the beautiful, feisty young actress, Tallulah Bankhead, daughter of a U.S. congressman. After Tod introduced them to Baba, they in turn introduced him to Gary Cooper. After watching several scenes being filmed, Baba posed with Bankhead, who instantly fell for him. With her husky voice and articulated British/Southern accent, she was known for her outspoken risqué language and persona.

Other visits that day included Universal and Fox Studios. When word got around Meher Baba was at Fox, several more stars quickly emerged from sound stages to dance their own fox-trot

> In 1935 Fox merged with 20th Century Films to become 20th Century-Fox, with a bigger studio lot. Gone today, the former studio is now known as Century City, a high-rise commercial center near Beverly Hills.

across the lot to meet him. Tom Mix, one of the most popular stars of the day, was filming scenes for one of his Western cowboy features. He spent an hour and a half with Baba on his former ranch, where Fox had established a movie studio.

Later that day Quentin returned to Paramount to pick up Bankhead. She had asked for a private interview with Baba at 5:30, just before she was to head over to visit Greta Garbo. Bankhead assured Baba she'd tell Garbo about him. 1429

Meher Baba and Tallulah Bankhead, with brother Adi Jr., Quentin Tod, brother Beheram, Chanji and Kaka Baria, Hollywood 1932

She and Baba talked for an hour and a half. When she brought up the subject of alcohol addiction, he told her there soon would be a program for alcoholics. Shortly after this, the twelve-step Alcoholics Anonymous Program began spreading, following what may have been its founder Bill Wilson's silent encounter with Baba in an elevator at the Astor Hotel six months earlier.

Ironically, Bankhead had stated in the June 1932 issue of *Photoplay* magazine that the only reason she had come to Hollywood was to meet the "Divine One"—a popular reference to Greta Garbo, who had starred in MGM's *The Divine Woman* in 1928.

Public Reception at the Knickerbocker Hotel

During the evening of May 31, a large public reception was held for Baba at the landmark Knickerbocker Hotel on Hollywood Boulevard. Over a thousand people from the film community and surrounding areas flocked to what was later described as a "spiritual love gathering."

All visitors were kept outside the main ballroom, to be admitted one by one to meet Baba in silence and receive his firm handshake and radiant smile. The dazzling light of Baba's figure, dressed in his white robe and hair loosely falling to his shoulders, immediately captivated people's hearts. His instructions were that no one was to ask questions, but leave after his handshake. After two hours, everyone was ushered back into the ballroom where his message was read out:

> Since arriving in America, I've been asked many times what solution I've brought for unemployment, prohibition and rampant crime to eliminate the strife between individuals and nations, and pour a healing balm of *peace* upon a troubled world. The answer has been so simple it's been difficult to grasp. The root of all our difficulties, individual and social, is self-interest.
>
> Self-interest causes corruptible politicians to accept bribes and betray the interests of those they have been elected to serve. This causes bootleggers for their own prof-

it to break a law designed, never mind wisely or not, to help the nation as a whole.

People further connive for their own pleasure to break that law, causing disrespect for law in general and tremendously increasing crime. Other forms of self-interest cause the exploitation of great masses of humanity by individuals or groups seeking totally selfish personal gain.

This impedes the progress of civilization by shelving inventions which would have contributed greatly to the welfare of humanity at large. Their use would mean scrapping present inferior technologies. When people are starving, this causes wanton destruction of large quantities of food, simply to maintain market prices. This in turn causes hoarding of large sums of gold when the welfare of the world demands its circulation.

But the elimination of self-interest, even an individual's sincere desire to accomplish it, isn't so easy, and never completely achieved except by the direct aid of a Perfect Master. Because self-interest springs from a false idea of the true nature of the Self, this idea must be eradicated and the Truth experienced before elimination of self-interest is even possible.

When I speak, I will reveal the One Supreme Self [who] is in all. With this accomplished, the idea of the Self as a limited, separate entity will disappear and with it self-interest will vanish. Then cooperation will replace competition; certainty will replace fear; generosity will replace greed. Exploitation will disappear. It has been repeatedly asked why I have remained silent for seven years, communicating only by means of an alphabet board, and why I intend to break my silence shortly.

And it might well be asked what relation my speaking will have to the global transformation of human consciousness. Humanity now uses three vehicles for expressing thoughts and experiences for three distinct states of consciousness. These three vehicles are: the mental body (the mind), in which thoughts arise as the result of impressions from past experiences. These thoughts may remain latent in the mental body as mere seeds, or may be expressed through actions. If expressed, they take the first forms of *desire*, and pass through the subtle, or desire body which is composed of the five psychic senses.

They may rest there, as dreams or unfulfilled desires, or may be further expressed in *action* through the physical body with its five physical senses. These three states of consciousness corresponding to the three vehicles mentioned are: unconsciousness [mental body at rest] as in deep, dreamless sleep; sub-consciousness [subtle body's energy] expressed in dreams or obscured, unformed, unfulfilled desires; waking consciousness [physical body's movement] as in active daily life.

The inner process by which thought passes from the mental through subtle into physical expression is called the expression of human will. In order for thought to be expressed effectively, all three expression vehicles must be perfectly clear, and the interaction between them totally harmonious. Head and heart must be **absolutely** united with intellect and feeling balanced, and material expression understood as the fruit of Spiritual Realization. The God-Man neither thinks nor desires.

Through him the divine will inevitably flows into perfect manifestation, passing directly from the spiritual body, which in the human is undeveloped, into physical expression. In him the super conscious state is the normal state of consciousness. From him there continuously flows infinite love and wisdom, infinite joy, peace and power.... When he speaks, **Truth** is powerfully manifested.

More than when he uses either sight or touch to convey it. For that reason, Avatars usually observe a period of silence lasting several years, breaking it only when they wish to manifest the Truth to the entire universe. So, when I speak, I shall manifest the divine will, and the worldwide transformation of consciousness will then take place.

Had humanity ever before received such a summation of Incarnate Truth? At the program's conclusion, everyone was asked to leave. But they were so enthralled that no one could move; they just stood there entranced, gazing at Baba. Repeatedly asked to leave, only slowly and reluctantly with heavy hearts did they begin walking backward with their eyes fixed on him. The following declarations were overheard:

> If Christ were alive today, he'd look just like him . . . What a divine glow on his face. He doesn't seem to belong to this world. . . Can any man be so utterly beautiful . . .
>
> He's the living Christ . . . How marvelous his divine attraction . . . I feel like looking at him forever! My eyes are dazzled by his beauty . . . I just can't leave. For the first time in my life, I've seen divinity!
>
> What a sweet face! How holy his divine purity! . . . Nothing can be said about him. My tongue is stuck . . . How electrifying was his touch! I felt such a shock pass through me. My God! I was totally senseless . . . What's happening to my heart? . . . Oh, how wonderful is his form . . . What brilliance! What beauty! What a smile! Seeing him, I'm so amazed!

It was an evening to be remembered by each one for the rest of their lives, and it would undoubtedly have repercussions in many of their future lifetimes as well, for they had now entered the orbit of the Avatar by receiving his most personal touch.

The next morning, June 1, after meeting executives at MGM in Culver City, Baba was brought onto a soundstage to watch actor Lewis Stone film some scenes. There he also met Virginia Bruce, one of the leading actresses of the day.

From there he was taken onto another stage. The filming of *Mata Hari,* with Ramon Navarro and Greta Garbo, had just wrapped. Garbo had already left the set, missing Baba in a karmic pattern to repeat itself with two more missed appointments with the Master in Hollywood. Baba especially wanted to meet her.

Down the block from the Culver City MGM lot was Hollywood's laugh capital of the world—the Hal Roach Studios. Baba's favorite comedians next to Charlie Chaplin were Laurel and Hardy, who were busy filming their next feature film. Baba was a great fan of their high-jinks comedy, and he might well have sought them out.

On Josef von Sternberg's set for *Blonde Venus,* Baba watched Marlene Dietrich. He later commented that he didn't care for the role she was playing, but very much liked the director—one of Hollywood's greatest. Von Sternberg was so taken by Baba that he didn't want him to leave the set. 1429–32

Several other stars met Baba during his visit, thanks to Quentin's help. These included actress May Beatty and Florence Vidor, the former wife of MGM director, King Vidor, and a brilliant film comedienne. Flo Vidor was now working under Ernst Lubitsch, a director who perhaps more than any other of this era perfectly echoed Meher Baba's vision of what film could be. Lubitsch said, "I always felt impelled to use film as an expression of hope and faith with positive ideas and ideals rather than negative ones. I've strayed from this resolve with nothing but total regret." David Robinson, *Hollywood 1920s*, 112

Among the many others whom Baba met that week was Boris Karloff, to whom he gave a very warm embrace, as well as John Gilbert, Bruce Evans, Charles Farrell, Johnny Mack Brown and Cary Grant. How amazing to realize, when watching these actors in their classic films, that they had unknowingly met God in Human Form.

One might reflect on what influence these actors may have on future audiences. It's hard not to feel that the Master was working through them as indirect agents, knowing that millions of fans would watch their performances over the years, making them an indirect medium for his work. It was as if they, and the many others Baba met, carried a kind of "radioactive conductivity" that was subtly transmitted to everyone they contacted or influenced, whether in person or on the screen. [14]

The Pickfair Reception in Beverly Hills

Douglas Fairbanks and Mary Pickford in front of Pickfair, Hollywood, California, c. 1930

Many Hollywood personalities Baba had met earlier on sound stages wanted to see him again. So a formal dinner party was arranged for the evening of June 1, at the home of Douglas Fairbanks and Mary Pickford, who were thought of as Hollywood's royal couple. Pickford was America's sweetheart, and Fairbanks the idol of every American man.

By 1919, Pickford was already a Hollywood millionaire. He, Fairbanks and Charlie Chaplain, silent film's three greatest stars, joined forces with producer-director W.D. Griffith to form their legendary film company, *United Artists*. When they went on to build their own studio and sound stages in 1928, four years before Baba's arrival in Hollywood, the word around town was, "The inmates have now taken over the asylum." Mary Pickford was America's first superstar, appearing in over two hundred feature films, many with Charlie Chaplin. She was the world's most famous woman at the time.

Pickford and her husband invited Baba to Pickfair, their lavish twenty-two-room mansion at 1143 Summit Drive in Beverly Hills, which had also played host to the world's royalty. Every American president from the mid-1920s to the 1960s would visit. Pickfair's priceless china had been a gift to Empress Josephine from Napoleon Bonaparte. [15]

The Pickfair reception was attended by many key industry players, happy to be invited to such an august reception for the Silent One who was taking all of Hollywood by surprise. Marc Jones drove Baba, Meredith, Margaret and Quentin to Beverly Hills. Norina, Elizabeth and the men followed in another car. After greeting Baba at the front door, Pickford led him to the spacious hall where she invited him to sit on a sofa. She sat on the carpet at his feet, with her husband beside her, as Baba's silent love began speaking to their hearts.

Before dinner, one of the mandali read a message as Baba tapped it out on the alphabet board:

> I have created the whole universe and its structure as *my* cinema. While the audience is absorbed witnessing a drama on the screen. It engages their emotions, swaying their feelings by its influence, causing them to forget it's not real.
>
> In this way, spectators, charmed by this worldly film show, forget themselves and take it as real. So I've come to tell them this absorbing worldly cinema is not real, and to turn their focus toward Reality. Only **God** is real; everything else is a mere movie! 1433–34

Communicating this very point about the illusory nature of false consciousness might well have been the real reason for Baba's Hollywood visit. Later that evening, he would offer a far more detailed message, one meant to uplift and focus the Hollywood community's awareness of how important their efforts were, and how he intended using their work for the sake of humanity.

He said the motion picture—invented in the very year of his birth, was planned by the Perfect Masters especially for his Avataric work in this age, and he emphasized just how urgent it was for filmmakers to use the medium responsibly. He urged them to portray stories emphasizing the divine themes of *life* and *love*, explaining how movies and other future means of mass communication were God's channels in the modern world to spread recognition of the common bonds of humanity to unite people across the planet. They would provide a blueprint for the later spiritual globalization to occur with his Universal Manifestation in the mid to latter twenty-first century.

Baba's analogy of laying cables offers insight into how the Avatar worked in this particular age, specifically in Hollywood. He intended film to rally humanity to higher, altruistic goals based on their mutual divine origin and unity. The best aspects of the American dream as a synthesis of all the races were to be presented to the world so as to uplift and inspire.

Baba had at least three of his own personal film projects in mind dealing with the divine theme. He wanted to illustrate how both good and bad sanskaric impressions and bindings between people were the reason why they kept cropping up in each other's scenarios, life after reincarnating life.

The Pickfair reception would be known today as an "A-List" affair with over a thousand guests in attendance. Many were Hollywood luminaries seeking Meher Baba's company, some feeling that they were on the same level as he was in terms of celebrity status.

Baba had attained certain renown in the tabloids by now, as well as being hailed in newsreels and newspaper and magazine articles in London, New York and Los Angeles. These included a *Time* magazine article as well a feature story on the front page of *The New York Times*. His photo had been scheduled to appear on the May 2, 1932, cover of *Time* magazine, but it was pre-empted by the kidnapping drama of the Lindbergh baby.

For all the publicity, however, Baba never descended into trivial celebrity status. Only after meeting him did these film personalities understand that their attraction to him wasn't superficial; rather it was something far deeper.

Needless to say, the mandali had entered an entirely new social milieu. When packing for their journey, each of the men had been allowed to bring only two flimsy dress suits and one pair of shoes, which they had to wear continually. In contrast, Baba would change his attire as needed, wearing a stylish Palm Beach suit to the Pickfair reception. In contrast, the mandali looked like paupers—which is exactly what they were.

As if poorly tailored suits weren't bad enough, the sole of Adi Jr.'s shoe became loose and flip-flopped comically as he walked around like Charlie Chaplin's little tramp. Baba refused to let him get a new pair, wryly joking maybe this would keep him away from the ladies. So Adi tied a string around his shoe to hold it together. Celebrity crowds dressed in formal attire mingled throughout the Pickfair mansion, schmoozing all evening long, while Adi sat mortified, huddled in a corner to keep his worn shoe out of sight. 1433

Partway into the evening, sensing Adi's discomfort, Pickford quietly approached Baba to ask what she might do for his brother. Without losing a beat, Baba replied, "Bring over Gary Cooper." Baba knew Adi especially admired him. Pickford dutifully brought the immaculately dressed Cooper over to Adi.

Self-conscious of his shabby attire and shoes, Adi was hardly able to greet his favorite star with much enthusiasm. But Baba's ploy to bring the actors to Adi eventually seemed to work, although the only guest Adi felt comfortable commiserating with was Boris Karloff. The actor was depressed over his career and being typecast in horror films in which he was never happy, calling it his "unfortunate destiny."

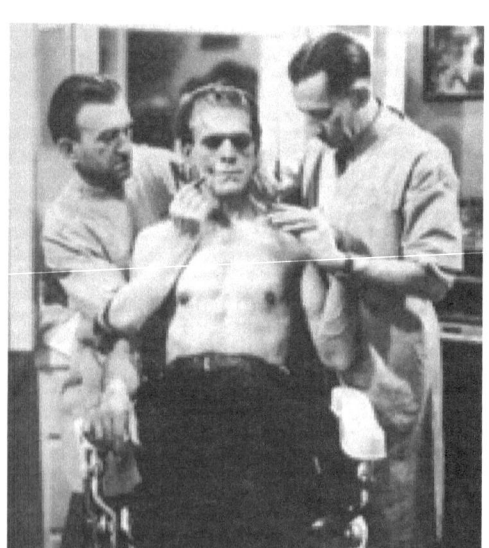

Universal Studios' top star, Boris Karloff, being transformed by makeup artists into his famous monster character, Frankenstein.

Despite being Universal Studio's top-billed star in their enormously successful horror-film genre, he regretted that even in his personal life people often treated him unnaturally, confusing the man with his film roles. Nobody made him feel happy. Nobody engaged him in humorous or lighthearted talk. But marvelously, after meeting Baba and getting his embrace, he felt his life utterly changed.

He now understood that all was illusion—Maya. Baba's advice inspired him thereafter "to play his horror roles to the hilt." This simple encouragement was a great help in changing Karloff's assessment of his work and career. Aw 18 (no. 1): 3

Adi Jr. later said that the outcome of that evening was a friendship with Karloff and an exchange of correspondence them lasting for decades, until the actor's death on February 2, 1969, just two days after Baba's own passing. It seems that Adi's loose sole helped seal Karloff's soul's connection with Meher Baba. 1433

Cecil B. DeMille and his wife also attended the party. In 1927, five years before meeting Meher Baba, DeMille had made the acclaimed silent film, *King of Kings*. Little did he suspect he was now meeting that very One in person. It was DeMille's stern Episcopalian father who had instilled in his son a reverence for the Ten Commandments. Later, DeMille's now-classic film of the same name would become the occasion of renewed communications with Baba in the 1950s.

Pickford's younger sister, Lottie, as well as Charles Farrell, Countess Carla Denise di Frasso, and the woman who wrote Pickford's film plays, also attended the Pickfair reception. Born Dorothy Caldwell Taylor, the Countess was an American multi-millionaire socialite and gossip. Here at Baba's reception, she was in her milieu.

Meher Baba's Formal Address to the Motion Picture Industry

After dinner, Baba gave the gathering a prophetic discourse on the power of motion pictures, emphasizing the impact of films and their value in turning people toward spiritual goals. He made clear how he wished the film industry to play its part both then and in the future to help awaken humanity to the truest meaning and purpose of life:

I was very glad to come to California for the opportunity to contact those making or appearing in motion pictures; and I'm delighted this gathering could be arranged tonight. I needn't tell you all, engaged in the production and distribution of motion pictures, what power you hold in your hands. Nor do I doubt you are fully alive to the great responsibilities which you wield.

It involves so much power. He who stimulates the imagination of the masses can move them in any direction he chooses. There's no more powerful instrument for stimulating their imagination than motion pictures. People go to the theater to be entertained. If the story is strong, they come away transformed, surrender their hearts and minds to the author, producer, director and stars, and follow the example which they see portrayed before their very eyes.

It is more than they themselves could ever realize. Both press and radio may influence thought, but both lack the power of *visible example*, which is the greatest stimulant to action, which the motion picture offers better now than any other medium in the modern world.

We find ourselves today in the midst of a worldwide depression affecting everyone, rich and poor alike, and from which all are groping blindly for deliverance. No doubt the film companies, theaters and stars alike have suffered from this depression. And if they could help to end it, I am sure they'd be so glad to. Let's see how motion pictures can help in this respect.

You must understand this economic depression is neither an accident, nor purely the result of overproduction and inflation. Those may be the immediate causes, but are merely the instruments used to bring the depression about. The depression *itself* was caused by those entrusted with the evolution of humanity. Man has to be utterly stripped of his material possessions so he may realize through actual experience his *true base* is spiritual and not at all material.

Only then will he be ready to receive the *Truth* I have come to bring. This Truth consists of knowledge that man, instead of being a limited, separate individual, completely bound by the illusion of time, space and customs, is eternal in his nature and infinite in his resources. This world illusion is a total dream of his imagining. It is a play enacted in the theater of his consciousness—a comedy in which he is at once the author, producer, director and star.

But his absorption in the role he has chosen to enact has made him forgetful of his true self, and he stumbles now as a creature through the path he himself has created. Man must be awakened to his true nature to see that all material expression depends upon and flows from a spiritual being.

Then he'll be steadfast and serene under any and all circumstances, with no further need for this depression which will totally disappear. Now, how can the motion pictures help man attain this realization? The character of film need not be changed. "Love, romance and adventure" are key.

They should be portrayed as thrillingly, as entertainingly, as inspiringly as possible. The wider the appeal the better. What needs changing is the emphasis, or stress. For example, courage is a great virtue, but if misapplied may become a vice. So with love; the mainspring of our lives leads to the heights of Realization or to the depths of lustful despair.

No better example can be given of the two polarities of love and their effects than of Mary Magdalene before and after meeting Jesus. Between these extremes are many kinds of love, all of which are good, but some better than others. I use the terms *"good" and "better"* simply to designate the degrees of liberation which they lead to or confer.

Even the love which expresses itself through physical desire is good to the extent it frees one from the thralldom of personal likes and dislikes. It makes one want to serve the beloved above all other things. . . . Every human relationship is based on love in one form or another, and endures or dissolves as that love is eternal or temporal in character.

For example, a marriage may be happy or unhappy, exalting or degrading, lasting or fleeting as to the love inspiring and sustaining it. Marriages based on sexual attraction alone can never endure, leading inevitably to divorce or worse. But marriages based on mutual desire to *serve and inspire*, grow continually in richness and in beauty. They're a benediction to all who know of them.

To lead men and women to the heights of Realization, we must help them to overcome *fear, greed, anger and passion* – the result of looking upon the self as a limited, separate, physical entity, having a definite physical beginning and definite physical end, with interests totally apart from the rest of life. Real life truly needs preservation and total protection.

In fact, the self is a totally limitless, indivisible spiritual essence—eternal in nature and infinite in its resources. The greatest of life's romance is to discover this Eternal Reality in the midst of infinite change. Once a person has experienced this, one sees oneself in *everything* living and breathing. One recognizes all of life as *his life* and everybody's interests as his own.

The fear of death, desire for self-preservation, the urge to accumulate substance, the conflict of interests, and the anger of thwarted desires are then all gone. One is no longer bound by habits of the past, no longer swayed by hopes for the future. One lives and enjoys *each present moment* to the fullest. There's no better medium to portray this than motion pictures.

Screenplays which inspire to greater understanding, truer feelings and better lives needn't have anything to do with "so-called religion." Creed, ritual, dogma, the conventional ideas of heaven, hell and sin are perversions of the Truth and confuse and bewilder, rather than clarify and inspire.

Real spirituality is best portrayed in stories of pure love, of selfless service, of Truth realized in home and business, school and university, studio and laboratory—everywhere evoking the heights of joy—the purest love, the greatest power, producing everywhere a symphony of bliss.

This is the highest practicality. Portraying such circumstances on the screen makes people realize the spiritual life is something to be ***lived***, not just talked about. That alone will produce the peace, love and harmony which we seek to establish as the constant of our lives. 1434–36

Baba would be filmed thirty years later in 35mm color sound film to expand upon this theme, saying: "The film world has magnificent scope to tell the world spiritual things they must know. Those who see films forget themselves, putting their hearts and minds into the show. They forget worries, the world and most importantly forget themselves to realize God."

False Promises of Romance and Happiness

Even as early as the 1930s, the divorce rate in Hollywood was the highest and most media-covered in the world. It is thus befitting that in this spontaneous Pickfair address Baba commented on relationships based on love, which he contrasted with lust, saying marriages based on sex could never last and inevitably ended in divorce or worse.

The Master tried to get up a few times after dinner, but the hosts and their guests just wouldn't let him go. When he finally stood, everyone else stood and surrounded him as he continued conversing with them on his alphabet board. After a few minutes, his glance fell on a young woman standing alone at the end of the room with her back to him.

When he called her, she turned her face toward him but remained aloof. She was called again. Then slowly coming forward, she stopped at a distance. Norina encouraged her, "Don't hesitate, dear, come near and meet Baba." "How can I touch him?" she asked. "Why not?" Norina replied, "All can meet Baba!"

This brought tears to the woman's eyes, and she replied, "But I'm a sinner! How can I touch a holy being like him?" Baba went over and passed his hand over her head and shoulders. At this, she experienced a tremendous release and began weeping.

Baba gestured to her, "I am the purest of the pure. I can purify the worst sinner. Now you've understood your mistakes and acknowledged them faithfully in the presence of others, so you are totally forgiven. This penance from the depths of your heart is enough. You are now cleansed. Don't fear in the least, and don't repeat past mistakes.

"I give you my blessings!" Baba lovingly embraced her, as tears which he had drawn from her heart wiped out all her past mistakes. Several people in the room, deeply moved at this scene, had tears in their own eyes. Before departing, Baba again embraced all the guests. And again putting his hand on the girl's head, he smiled and consoled her, "You've received forgiveness for everything! Forget the past and don't worry at all." The girl pressed her face to Baba's hand, kissing it.

Through the mother of an actor, Baba sent the following private advice to her son:

> Art is a source through which the soul expresses itself and inspires others. But to express art thoroughly, one must have inner emotions thoroughly opened. If you feel something checks you expressing yourself then you must do one thing—adjust your mental attitude. Just before you do anything, think, "I *can* and *will* express it thoroughly."
>
> And every time you act, you'll find you're more convinced. It's the mind that's closed. Many actors through feeling inferior or nervous feel they cannot express; and this [negative] feeling in the mind totally checks their expression. Think you're the greatest actor in the world and express yourself so. I'll help you spiritually. Just think you're the *greatest* actor. What harm in thinking it? It's not pride, but for bringing out the best you can do; then there's nothing wrong. Aw 18 (no. 1): 21

Baba stayed at the Pickfair reception for three hours before returning to his hotel. All eyes followed him as he left. They couldn't help feeling that the evening was over too soon, wishing it to go on and on. Mary Pickford and Douglas Fairbanks depicted scenes of deep human love, but tonight they witnessed pure divine love from the Master in a heart-moving experience.[24] Aw 18 (no. 1): 36

Baba would later reminisce:

> Douglas Fairbanks and Mary Pickford invited me as an honored guest to their home. Many came to shake hands as Mary welcomed me: "We're so honored by your presence in our home," and then introduced me to all the industry guests she had invited.
>
> This included Gary Cooper, Charles Laughton, Marlene Dietrich and Will Rogers who spoke to me for a half hour,

and of course Tallulah Bankhead. I especially remember Marie Dressler taking to me like mother to son, inviting me to her home for dinner, caressing my face and saying: "My child, my child!" 4893

Hollywood's Most Spiritual Actress

During his second visit to Paramount Studios that week, Baba met Maurice Chevalier and Jeanette MacDonald, along with director Rouben Mamoulian, on the set of the musical *Love Me Tonight*. Also starring in this film were C. Aubrey Smith, Charles Butterworth, Charlie Ruggles and Myrna Loy.

On this visit to Paramount Baba again met Tallulah Bankhead. She ran up, hugging and kissing him like an old friend. Baba quietly asked her if she'd arrange a small dinner party at her house that evening. He specifically wanted her to invite Greta Garbo, without revealing why. Though known to be difficult and temperamental, Garbo was considered by Baba the "most spiritual" of the Hollywood actresses. She was later called "an inexplicable legend beyond analysis."

> With rare photogenic quality, despite an ungainly body, she appeared as the most graceful creature to ever move. She never made a move or delivered a false or miscalculated line. She worked with the good and bad.
>
> But no one ever affected her extraordinary radiance. With Garbo you were aware less of an actress than of a soul exposed to life and mankind. The depth of her acting—her very being—transformed anything she played." David Robinson, *Hollywood in the Twenties*, 202

Though Garbo herself was veiled, Baba commented that if you really wanted to see spirituality portrayed on the screen, simply watch any of her films. Director Ernst Lubitsch described her as the most naturally uninhibited person he'd ever worked with.

And so a dinner party was arranged by Bankhead for Baba to meet the actress, who was due to arrive at 6:00 PM. Earlier that same afternoon, Mary Pickford came to see him for a private interview at 3:30 and meditated in his presence for five minutes.

Baba and Quentin were then driven by Lubitsch in his sports car to have tea at his home in Santa Monica. "Lu," as he was known around town, was famous for his sophisticated humor, "the Lubitsch Touch," and was very drawn to Baba. With his sly sophistication, Lubitsch become one of the most admired European directors in town. The films he produced between 1931 and 34 were as great as any the cinema produced. He would eagerly reach out to contact Baba again in 1934. 1939

Greta Garbo, from the Picturegoer Series, London, 1930s

When Baba arrived at Tallulah Bankhead's home that evening, Garbo had just phoned from her home at 1201 San Vincente Boulevard in Brentwood. She'd stayed out the night before drinking champagne and coffee—things she usually never touched—and was not feeling well, and she regretted having to skip the evening dinner party. Baba was disappointed as well. But she'd get another chance a year a half later during his 1934 Hollywood visit.

Despite her absence, Baba still had his evening with Garbo—at Grauman's Chinese Theatre on Hollywood Boulevard—at the special invitation of owner Sid Grauman. The mandali, usually kept in the background, were also invited. There was an excellent stage show with variety acts, a stand-up comedy routine by Will Ma-

> Rom Landau was another writer who had also traveled to India and met Meher Baba just prior to his visit to Hollywood. He had written introduction letters for his friend Quentin Tod to both directors Lubitsch and Josef von Sternberg. And although in his famous book, *God is my Adventure*, Rom Landau was critical of Meher Baba, he also was a link to many renowned Hollywood personalities, a link bearing fruit not only in this life, but likely in their succeeding lifetimes as well. 1403–04

honey, and a screening of Garbo's latest film, *Grand Hotel*. The movie quickly became known as MGM's triumph of style, and in it Garbo delivered her historic line, "I want to be alone." Baba praised her performance as being extraordinary, and the film went on to win the 1932 Academy Award for Best Picture. 1439

On June 4 Baba had lunch with Marie Dressler at her 801 Alpine Drive, Beverly Hills, home. Dressler had co-starred in many Charlie Chaplin movies and had won an Academy Award for Best Actress the previous year. Dressler also had been nominated for MGM's best actress competition, winning first place in coveted industry box-office polls three years in a row. Some years earlier, Baba had seen her with Chaplin in *The Kid* and enjoyed her keen wit and great sense of humor. They were soon sharing stories, laughing and joking like old friends.

During lunch Dressler remarked, "Baba, if you'd allow me, I'd like to take you out to the woods and *dance* with you. And even if you want to speak a few words to me, I promise not to tell anyone!" Baba laughed silently and spelled on his board, "Before breaking my silence, it's essential I go to China for just a day. On returning, I'll break my silence July 13 at the Hollywood Bowl." Dressler said, "When you break your silence, I'll be at your side." 1440

Tallulah's "Love Spell"

Adi Jr. had many memorable experiences during his Hollywood travels with Baba, like observing the mistaken impressions some stars had of Baba. At Pickfair Adi had been morbid with embarrassment. Seeing him alone at one point, Bankhead sat down next to him to cheer him up, but she had an ulterior motive. As other stars came over, Bankhead introduced them to Adi, who politely but shyly shook hands.

Bankhead invited Adi to her house the next day for lunch, as she had something very important to talk about with him. Adi warned her to please not touch him. She explained she just wanted to talk. Adi told her that he would have to ask Baba's permission. He did, and Baba replied, "Fine, but don't touch her and don't let her touch you." Adi assured him that nothing ill-intentioned would happen. And so, the following day Adi went there for lunch.

As soon as he entered Bankhead's home, he nervously blurted out, "I'm happy to be here, but please don't touch me." She said not to worry; she wouldn't embarrass him. During lunch, Adi asked what she wanted.

Bankhead confided that she was in love with an actor (very likely, Gary Cooper), but he neither returned her love nor showed any affection. She wanted Adi to persuade Baba to cast a "love-spell" on him; thereby he'd fall in love and be hers. Adi was taken aback, explaining that Baba didn't do such things, and she was greatly mistaken about the kind of spirituality Baba taught. Still, she insisted that Adi at least *ask* his brother if he'd cast such a spell.

Adi said, "Well, I suppose I could ask, but I highly doubt Baba would ever do such a thing." He returned to the Jones residence feeling disturbed but said nothing until he met with Baba later that afternoon. Baba sternly inquired, "Did you touch her!?" Adi assured him that he had not, and then he explained why she invited him and what she wanted Baba to do.

Baba threw up his hands with an eye-roll, gesturing "Hollywood!" It seems that many of these movie stars thought that Baba was a spiritual magician, a yogi or swami with occult powers who

Meher Baba with some of the film luminaries
he met during his first visit to Hollywood in 1932

was a spiritual magician, a yogi or swami with occult powers who could influence people's minds. Hollywood's understanding of real spirituality or what Meher Baba's Avatarhood truly meant was in many cases utterly lacking, as in Bankhead's comically absurd request. 1438

Tom Molinari, known as Tommy Marlow on stage, was a talented Broadway dancer and long-time student of Margaret Craske. Tom danced twice for Baba in the mid 1950s, receiving two embraces for his extraordinary performances. One was a silent Charlie Chaplin routine performed at Longchamps Restaurant in New York City, which made Baba shake silently, pink with laughter. The other was in the Barn at the Meher Spiritual Center in Myrtle Beach. Later on during the 1950s, Marlow was working with Bankhead in a Broadway show. They sometimes went out for drinks after the show and exchange "Baba stories." And one of the first things she asked was, "Did he ever break his f****** silence?"—the exact words she had used with Norina Matchabelli when they ran into each other at a New York function in the 1940s. Bankhead was true to form—pulling no punches. She called herself "pure as the driven slush."

The Big Show was an hour-and-a-half live variety program, the best ever heard on American radio. Broadcast by NBC, the program was hosted by "the glamorous and unpredictable Tallulah Bankhead, with scenes from top Hollywood films and Broadway shows recreated on radio with their original casts." Broadcast from 6:00 to 7:30 every Sunday evening, it was the top weekly radio show in America—and radio's last gasp. Today it would cost close to a million dollars an episode to produce. But between November 1950 and April 1952, people listened to *The Big Show* as surely as they attended weekly religious services. [16]

Bankhead had a terrible memory for names, calling everyone "*Da-a-h-h-ling*" in her sweet southern Alabama drawl, exchanging one-liners with Hollywood and Broadway's finest. And although her double entendre jokes went about as far as censors would allow, she became totally transparent and childlike as she sang her signature theme song at end of the show, "May the Good Lord Bless and Keep You," composed by Meredith Wilson in 1950.

> *May the good Lord bless and keep you*
>   *whether near or far away.*
> *May you find that long awaited Golden Day.*
> *May your troubles all be small ones,*
>   *and your fortunes ten times ten.*
> *May the good Lord bless and keep you,*
>   *till we meet again.*

Bankhead said that she always sang this song to Baba, knowing that somehow, somewhere, he would hear her. [17]

Chapter Twenty

Breaking His Silence in the Hollywood Bowl

Meher Baba took Hollywood by storm, with the depth and power of his messages and silence, coupled with his extraordinary energy and emanation of divinity. Striding across movie lots, he was as graceful as flowing water. Stars and technicians stopped in their tracks just to watch his unfamiliar movements in their familiar environment.

At the same time that he was meeting key film personalities about his projects, Baba also announced a specific date when he would break his seven-year silence in a widely celebrated venue, The Hollywood Bowl. His message would be broadcast on radio from the famed amphitheater, and he was to be introduced by Mary Pickford.

That Baba would actually speak created quite a sensation. All of Baba's verbal communications with people had been through his alphabet board. [18] In fact, Baba's announcement had the effect of uniting the east and west coasts, creating a national media scramble to establish the very first live, coast-to-coast radio broadcast between New York and Los Angeles. It was specifically engineered by NBC and other networks to cover the widely heralded event.

This first west to east coast radio hookup was far more important than might meet the naked ear. Hollywood had just taken America and the world out of the silent movie days. Established Hollywood actors initially panicked at the impending arrival of the talkies, fearing it would be their undoing. It was said at the time,

"Adding sound to movies is like putting lipstick on the Mona Lisa." It was an extremely risky business venture that they pulled off with absolute finesse, when everybody had been saying it was doomed to fail. So the jump from silence to sound was a novelty in the culture's mind. People were already enchanted by Meher Baba's "silent movie," imagine now what the "talkie" would be like. The promise of the "Eastern Messiah" to break his silence even inspired a 1950 movie, *The Next Voice You Hear.*

The mandali continued to manage Baba's busy appointment schedule, which included more visits with studio bosses as well as preparation to get Baba's films off the ground. Quentin was world famous for his musical comedy stage work in America and in London's West End as a talented female impersonator. He had used his connections to bring Baba to Hollywood and now he managed Baba's appearances like a line-producer.

It was Quentin's persuasive enthusiasm that convinced some of the women to have fancy dresses made for the occasion, assuring them that they would receive God-Realization in the Hollywood Bowl. Many of Baba's female disciples, including Kitty Davy and Delia DeLeon, made their own preparations, scurrying up and down Rodeo Drive haute-couture shops with established female stars to be fitted for their "God-Realization" designer gowns.

They planned to wear them again in a wildly envisioned ticker-tape parade riding in open-air convertibles as Baba waved to the cheering crowds down New York's 5th Avenue. Of course, Baba himself never remotely implied such bizarrely ludicrous things. 1440

Laying War Cables in the Far East

Earlier that week Baba had casually announced that he had some urgent business to attend to in the Far East before breaking his silence. He had already sent his brother Jal and cousin Pendu, as well as Vishnu, Raosaheb, Gustadji and Rustom, who had stayed behind in India, to China, where they would rendezvous with Herbert Davy, who was teaching English there. The group expected to accompany Baba back to Los Angeles in time for his silence breaking.

It would take "just one day," he said, and then he'd return in time for the Hollywood Bowl event on July 13. After cancelling a trip to San Francisco, Baba and party were driven to the Port of Los Angeles at Long Beach on June 4. A large group of followers came to see him off for an 11:00 PM sailing. He then dropped out of sight, slipping off the West Coast on the *Monterey*, making its maiden voyage on Baba's first Pacific crossing.

By stopping in Hawaii before proceeding to Japan and China Baba planned to lay more cables in the Far East. The Imperial Japanese Army would soon be invading Manchuria, heralding the Pacific Rim hostilities that would escalate into the Pacific Theater of World War II and the bombing of Pearl Harbor. Baba again stated that the Masters had had this war in mind for a long time, and there was no avoiding it. This was Baba's first revelation that he was setting the scene for the outbreak of war in the Pacific, and after completing his work in Hollywood and the Far East, the coming war would be the focus of much of his work.

After four days at sea, Baba reached Honolulu. Hs was met at the dock by Rustom Irani, whom he immediately sent to Australia and New Zealand on the *Monterey*, which was sailing from Honolulu to the Lands Down Under, where he was forging more links.

After checking into Honolulu's Moana Hotel, Baba and the men relaxed for two days. Like proper tourists, they visited the coconut grove gardens at the Royal Hawaiian Hotel where they watched a performance by traditional Hawaiian dancers, before taking a long drive out to tropical groves, where they drank freshly pressed pineapple juice to their heart's content. More sightseeing in

Honolulu followed, including visits to the Huimalu Hotel and a sea aquarium.

But after two lighthearted days of relaxation, Baba quietly drew Quentin aside , telling him,

> I want you to return to California and inform them of a change in plans. I must return immediately to India from China. So tell everyone in Los Angeles I'll not be breaking my silence in the Hollywood Bowl on the radio as announced. Then you must go to Italy and rent a villa for me to stay at the end of July and meet me there with the *gopis* [Baba's name for his female disciples]. Give Meredith and Margaret Starr tickets to New York and five hundred dollars for passage back to England, and tell him I want him to continue his work at Devonshire.

Tod dreaded his return as the bearer of such grim news, but it deepened his faith in Baba, as he reasoned to himself, "No ordinary man could possibly behave like this." Arriving back in Santa Barbara, Tod cabled the disciples to inform them of Baba's change in plans. He said that Baba had to sail directly for India without returning to Los Angeles, thus postponing the breaking of his silence in the Hollywood Bowl. Everyone was stunned.

Baba also asked Tod to tell his close ones to pay no heed to the media hazing that would inevitably ensue, but to simply hold onto their faith in him, assuring them, "The whole world will know and welcome me as Jesus returned once I speak."

Needless to say, the news caused deep grumblings with some people calling foul. The sting was impossible for some to bear—especially Meredith Starr and Marc Jones, but it was the opposition that Baba was deliberately creating for the fulfillment of his work. The following front page item appeared in major papers:

"Silent Hindu Defers Radio Talk"

(Los Angeles, July 13th 1932 AP) Meher Baba, who came here recently, heralded as the East Indian holy man who has not uttered a word for seven years, will after all *not* deliver his "message" to the world over a planned national radio broadcast from Hollywood. Quentin Tod, the mystic's secretary, telegraphed from Santa Barbara that Baba has decided to postpone the word-fast breaking until next February, because "conditions are not yet ripe."

The New York Times picked up the story with a similar headline: "Silent Mystic Defers Coast-to-Coast Radio Talk."

Meanwhile, Baba set sail on the *Empress of Japan*, accompanied by Beheram and Adi Jr. and two of the other mandali, bound for China and Japan. As the ship left Honolulu harbor, a jazz band played as native Hawaiians sang and danced, waving handkerchiefs and throwing flower leis. Little did they know the Emperor of Creation was on board, working invisibly to unite the East and West in divinely enigmatic ways, which would include the bombing of their own Pearl Harbor. Most of the crew members of the ship were Japanese.

Baba's planned ports of call in Japan were Kobe and Yokahama. [19] While in Yokahama, Baba and the men took a sightseeing side-trip through Tokyo before re-boarding and proceeding on to China. After meeting Baba in England the previous year, Kitty Davy's brother Herbert had accepted a teaching job in China and was also giving lectures to those interested in hearing about and awaiting the Master's visit.

Baba spent June 22 through 28 in Shanghai and Nanjing, just as Japanese troops began occupying Shanghai and warships reached Nanjing—all part of his laying of cables for the upcoming war in the Pacific. Dressed in a stylish suit and a Panama hat, Baba disembarked and was taken to Shanghai's Palace Hotel. 1442–44

After tea, Baba wanted to visit the city's crowded markets and narrow lanes filled with bustling activity. He spelled out to Herbert on his board, "I want to go and mix with the Chinese. Take me to where there are thick crowds!" The first places they visited weren't busy enough, so he was taken deeper into the alley slums in a hand-drawn rickshaw. Baba got out and walked for three hours, striding through the squalid alleyways and drawing fascinated stares from its humble dwellers, some of whom

The Shanghai Palace Hotel where Meher Baba stayed in 1932

were not especially friendly. The long-awaited Chinese Buddha, Milo Fu, was here in their midst, but no one recognized him.

Nor were they aware of the fun he was having trying to eat with chopsticks. When Baba wanted a bottle of seltzer, he made the sign for popping a bottle cap off. The mandali asked directions to a restaurant to get such a drink, but the Chinese man misinterpreted Baba's popping gesture and took them to a lavishly decorated brothel. Later Baba went to a movie to conduct his work with the audience. MM 3:242

Baba was met in Nanking by many of Herbert's young Chinese students, as well as older men and women. In this city, too, he wandered about the dirty, run-down lanes of the poorer neighborhoods where Chinese peasants gazed at him with curious wonder. After viewing the Great Wall of China, he was driven up Purple Mountain to see the memorial to China's great revolutionary leader, Sun Yat-sen. At last he boarded the *Kaiser-i-Hind*, the ship returning him to India. 444–46; PM 180

During the voyage, Baba read and re-read the letters from those left behind, and he wrote touching replies:

> I know how you all feel missing your Beloved Baba. But be assured this will all end after six months. I want you all to give serious attention to the film work I've entrusted to each of you, and not feel sad or dejected. You know how I love you. I want you to be always happy and have you with me. But for the work ahead, all must put up with some pain.
>
> And the separation you all feel and suffer for me now will make much sweeter our happiness in six months. So, dearest sweets, be good darlings, and in thoughts of a happy reunion and the great work you'll all have to do under me, be happy and keep cheerful. There's no need to tell you I am always with you, as you are with me forever and ever. You know that. My unbounded love and laughter go with this, my so dearest darlings. [signed] Baba 1575

Baba's last ports of call included Hong Kong and Ceylon (Shri Lanka). The *Kaiser-i-Hind* docked in Bombay harbor on Friday, July 15, 1932. But less than twenty-four hours later Baba left Bombay, again on the *Kaiser-i-Hind*, now sailing for Marseilles, accompanied only by Chanji and Kaka.

When Baba had earlier announced the breaking of his silence in Hollywood, Adi Jr. had boldly spoken up in protest. "Look Baba, you're not going to break your silence in the Hollywood Bowl. Why all this fuss with radio and papers, making people go to all this trouble? They'll be furious, very angry if you don't speak— and I know you *won't!*"

Baba scolded, "No, no, you don't know! Keep quiet! This time, I'll do it!" Adi held his tongue, but he knew in his mind and heart Baba would never, ever do such a thing. He actually feared they'd be beaten by angry mobs once Baba's other plans were discovered

What kind of ploy was this on the Avatar's part? If not naïve, how gullible the Hollywood people were. Was there any necessity to employ material or mechanical means for the Avatar's voice to be heard throughout the world, with a sonorous Coast-to-coast radio announcer proclaiming, "Ladies and gentlemen, the next voice you hear . . ."

But this manner of working is the Avatar's game-play, his *leela*; and there is divine humor in how he plays it. Knowing all, while pretending to know nothing, he carries out such a fantastic ruse. Baba remarked seven years later:

> Don't you know me *yet* even after so many years with me? One who doesn't care for the world or publicity, who declares in America, "I will come here and speak," and doesn't—don't you understand him yet? What do I care what the world thinks or says.
>
> I'll do anything for my work. Even if the whole world goes against me, I'll teach and strike—both! I'll do what I have to do; but all in its own time. India nowadays is sadly remiss. By indulging in too much politics and Maya, India now lacks spirituality. The old spiritual glory is gone. It's sad, yet it's a total fact. 2060

But it didn't end there. Baba now announced he'd break his silence, this time in London that coming February, 1933, and of course, once again it was a non-event. However, he stated so many times in his life that his promises would come about "in my own way, in my own time." Meher Baba's work for humanity was at times incomprehensibly enigmatic, but he never undertook anything without divine purpose.

Regarding this apparent public humiliation, we really have to give him the benefit of the doubt. Perhaps he was borrowing from his Avataric mischievousness as Lord Krishna, because he delighted in turning the tables on his disciples' expectations, pulling the rug out from beneath them before they could even ask what the heck had happened.

But something deeper was going on here as well. *Lord Meher* asserts, "It's certain Baba will 'speak' in Hollywood from where the melody of his Word will spread one day throughout the world through films. Only Hollywood will be able to delineate Baba's life story to the world, which then will listen to his Song's resonance. His Song, though echoless, merges within itself all the echoes of the world and in him are all the images of the world!" 1441

After laying cables in the unseen to bring on World War II, he would later re-contact many of these spots, using in a seemingly accidental visit by a disciple or giving a direct order that someone should go to a certain place. A letter or cable might also do the job. For example, Baba himself never went to Germany, but he did send certain disciples with social or business connections there, as he did just a few days before the signing of the Munich Agreement, when he sent a close "disciple-agent" to the city. DL 153

The final results of this cable-laying would only manifest when the hostilities of WWII subsided, solidifying unanticipated ties between the East and West. This was a vital aspect of his work in this Advent, to break down the selfish isolationism of world powers that would persist into the twenty-first century.

The postponement of his silence breaking goes hand in hand with a characteristic of the Avatar in all of his Advents—a constant change of plan, an effective means of wearing down the mind's ego-centric expectations—very much a part of his obligation and responsibility to disciples, devotees and others who come into his contact. In this way, a Master shatters his disciples' binding impressions. This is his main duty, the real work, which is accomplished through disappointments and small daily events as well as cataclysmic ones on humanity's path to God.

Later on in London, following the Hollywood uproar, Baba joked with his British disciples, "Now you really didn't think I was going to break my silence in the Hollywood Bowl, did you?" Then to ultra-sophisticated Norina Matchabelli he pointedly remarked, "When I really break my silence, even your eyes will totally pop!"

In the end, they all had a good laugh over the Hollywood Bowl charade, minus the few like Meredith and Herbert, who deserted Baba for not breaking his Silence after so much publicity. Meredith demanded either to be paid the four hundred pounds he felt owed to him for expenses he had incurred from Baba's visits, or be given instant Illumination! "Otherwise," he threatened, "I'll leave and expose you as a fraud!" Baba had his letter read out to the group, then threw up his hands, gesturing "the West!"

Though Meredith's claims were ridiculous, he actually filed a Scotland Yard report. But the investigator just scratched his head, unable to find anything to question about Baba. In fact, the reports on Baba's work were quite excellent. After all this time, Meredith had grasped nothing of the Master's ways. But for Baba's own reasons, Starr was chosen as the first link between the East and West. Whatever his faults, he will always be remembered for that. 1533

Herbert was experiencing similar turmoil. "Baba, you promised to speak! Now what will the world think of you?" Baba spent two hours replying to Herbert to address his concerns, yet despite Baba's great patience, Herbert was simply unable to grasp the Master's ways of working, and so he also eventually left him.

> It's good, even essential mankind adhere to religious and moral principles, observing religious bindings; but for the spiritual path, they're totally unnecessary. I am beyond all principles, laws, bindings and matters pertaining to worldly duties. I am Perfect and there's no restraint or binding for me. I've broken all barriers and gone beyond all laws!

According to the world's moral code, mankind considers one's word or promise to be absolutely sacred. But he who's gone beyond time, space, cause and effect is limited by *nothing*. For him, there's no such thing as bondage. The infinite cannot be bound by anything finite, however sublime its aim may be. This means that one *cannot limit the limitless!*

For this reason, and without your asking, I give you promises. And your aim will be fulfilled at the proper time. But I also know a promise can also be a "time-serving device." It may not be meant for fulfillment, but necessitated by circumstances – purely a demand of the situation.

And so I don't care for its resultant reaction. I don't worry about the world's criticism or its terrible slander and harm to my work for not keeping my promises. I purposely create and court opposing reactions – even nurture them. Such opposition is needed to give my work a great punch. I am beyond all praise and slander. They affect me not in the slightest. Those who care for name, fame and worldly success, fearing criticism and scandal, are only ordinary human beings.

They must preserve their prestige at any cost. Their "name and fame" alone matters above money, life and everything else. I am Truth incarnate and no amount of voluminous praise will raise me higher, nor can any carping criticism pull me down. I am what I am and will ever be. Whatever I do, I do for my work which encompasses and sees to the welfare of all. 1555–56

The Avatar as the Divine Juggler

But who can ever truly leave him? Baba called the Avatar "the master of broken promises"—a divine juggler who teaches his

close ones to live every day by the very seat of their pants: "It's the work of Sadgurus, their profession and wish to keep those of past connection near them by giving them false promises to make them hold on to them. . . . Since eternity, I am a past-master at not keeping promises. The very first promise I gave to God I kept, and now this whole creation is 'round my neck.' The last promise, when I speak, I will fulfill." 948, 3462

>Vagueness, building plans in the air, regular shifting
>from one place to another, changing from one plan to another, are the principal traits and characteristics of all the

Avatars. Just read the lives of Avatars Ram, Krishna, Buddha, Jesus, and Muhammad.

If one minutely marks the trend of events throughout their lives, you'll find they had no definite program or organized scheme, except to spread their teachings and impress on humanity the utter worthlessness of the world and worldly life through the very vagueness of their own plans and schemes. The Avatar's methods are strange and peculiar; quite opposite the world's. They never plan a thing. If they do, it's nothing but an outward show—a bluff, without any basis or firm foundation.

Like provision of funds, etc. It's all in the air, with risk of apparent failure at any moment. Yet, they take the risk and indulge in the game. But their schemes hang in the air by a mere thread! And even if they're going well and on a sound basis, they may turn around and destroy them at barely a moment's notice. Such plans and schemes are created for a definite purpose. How can you know it?

Such plans are a means to a certain end. No sooner is the end achieved, the Avatars and Sadgurus stop running them—however flourishing they might be. Once their purpose is served, they're dropped—meaning *dropped*! If they prepared their schemes on a safe, firm, sound, permanent basis, they'd be no different from the rest of ordinary human beings.

None of the past Avatars like Ram, Krishna, Buddha, Jesus or Muhammad ever did this. Their lives and work are all full of utterly hectic movements and gestures entirely vague and with no sound basis behind them . . . except the great purpose which every Sadguru and Avatar has.

Their mission in life is to depict and prove the transitoriness and falseness of the world and all its things, through the very vagueness of their moves and schemes . . .

proving this changing world and everything in it is a total illusion. . . . Krishna either played cowboy or thought of war. Jesus too—no definite plan. Re-read the Sermon on the Mount. Muhammad—absolutely vague; always on the run— a marriage here, another there, and so on; all vague; but with a precise purpose behind it.

I too, am like them. I build on sand or in the air, planning schemes without at times even a penny in my pocket, or without any definite arrangement for future maintenance if started at all. And even when started, I break it up or abandon it. Plans were laid for Meherabad, the school, ashram . . . all were so well planned and running smoothly, but all were broken up and *pulled down* the instant their purpose was served, as I alone know.

But people can't remotely grasp it, and instead totally misunderstand. That's how the Avatar's work is always misunderstood and misjudged by the world. During his lifetime the Avatar's work always goes unappreciated, and so it is with mine. 1908–10

This was Baba's classic exposition defining the vagueness of all Avataric plans. No one has calculated the number of times Baba promised to break his Silence throughout his lifetime, and it was something that irked and puzzled his disciples until the very end. Indian disciple Dr. M.S. Moorty received a letter from Eruch, dated August 21, 1963, containing another now-classic explanation of Baba's continuing Silence.

"Did Baba 'Brake' His Silence?"

[Eruch wrote:] "Baba wants you to note and relay to people wherever you go [that] the breaking of his Silence would be after nine months after his return to Meherazad from Poona, and Baba returned to Meherazad on July 1,

1963." Accordingly, I visited various places relaying that important message of Baba breaking of His Silence. People took it from me as an exciting piece of fresh information, eagerly waiting to see when and how Baba would break His Silence.

When the stipulated period was over, we all expected the divine delivery of the "Word." And just as I looked at the calendar hanging on the wall in front of me, I noticed the date April 1 circled in black—the day when those nine months were exactly over. It instantly struck me I was played an April Fool! That night I dreamed Baba was laughing so hard at me while showing the calendar and repeatedly putting His finger on April 1 date again and again. So, what to do? I enjoyed his joke.

A few weeks later, I visited Meherazad and sat before my Beloved in a perplexed state and asked Baba to please tell me why he didn't break his silence after those nine months as he promised. The only reply I got was he is not bound by any promises. . . .

Well, I have my own esoteric interpretation to offer: If instead of breaking his Silence, Baba is *breaking his promise* of silence-breaking, then that for me shall mean *The Brake* is still necessary. I spell it as *Braking his Silence* in order to save the uncontrollable speed of destruction.

Hence, Baba's Silence is a kind of "Working Brake" in Sound Conditioning which when applied shall definitely check the speed of destruction. May Baba *not* break his Silence, but keep *The Brake of Silence* intact. And so, the question of breaking promises doesn't even arise. The world, which is produced in his Maya, is in itself a big "bluff" of reality, and so as we must exist on this planet, Baba must carry on His bluff eternally. Dr. D.S. Moorty, *The Wonders of Silence,* 132–135

Meanwhile, Hollywood hadn't seen the last of Baba, as he would return for an even longer stay, continuing to pursue his film plans and oversee preparations for his spiritual screenplays. But his presence would be kept a secret so that the usual pestering media and crowds wouldn't distract him from his essential work.

Before a planned reunion in Europe with his key Hollywood players, Baba sent Quentin and Norina to Venice, Florence, Verona, Munich, Basel, Zurich, Halle, Berlin and Budapest. As Norina spoke English, German, Russian, Italian and French, her wide acquaintance among Europe's elite intelligentsia was invaluable. 1480

These were the aristocrats, artists and avant-garde who would prove useful to Baba's work in bringing about and managing WWII. This had been his focus, as well as that of the Perfect Masters, from the very beginning; it was never mere movie making.

Meher Baba and Albert Einstein

Norina and Quentin's most notable contacts made during their travels included Dr. Carl Gustave Jung and theater producer Max Reinhardt, both in Vienna, and physicist Albert Einstein in Berlin. Norina was friendly with Einstein's stepdaughter, Marian, who had met Baba in 1932 at the Stokes' home in New York. The Italian Princess now met Einstein himself:

> It was through the courtesy of Professor Luders, a famous professor of Sanskrit at the University of Berlin who had met Baba, that I had the unusual chance of visiting Einstein. I say unusual, because he hates inquisitive visitors, unless they come in direct interest and value to him.
> Professor Luders, who had already met Baba, graciously wished to give him hospitality in Berlin and arranged my meeting with Einstein with only twelve hours' notice.

Baba's name, I suppose, magically opened the door for the visit, as I personally had no excuse to be interesting.

At two the next afternoon, I stood before the glass door of "the most intelligent man in the world." Through the door of his very modern bungalow at Caputh, I could see him sitting before a pile of manuscripts on a narrow table in his office and writing intensely. When the bell rang, he got up and opened the door. Our meeting immediately became one of intimacy and warmth.

He said, "Oh, my daughter Margot [Marian] loves you very much; so by reputation I already know you. I hear through Luders you'll tell me of a great spiritual man." His direct way of addressing the point of my visit put me at ease. Within seconds, Baba was the topic of conversation.

It's very difficult to repeat Einstein's conversation literally. It was so subtle, sophisticated and intricate. The first point seeming to puzzle him most was how it was possible for a man who is silent to influence others. He said, "*Everything* I've achieved was through the power of thought expressed by language. What can Meher Baba touch in other individuals but their minds?

Jesus, Buddha, Krishna, Plato – they left words in the mind of man. And these words created thoughts and thoughts make man!" I answered, "Has man ever realized the innate God within him? Has he ever experienced the Truth through books, words, or schools of thought?" He then looked somewhat wonderstruck but reverent, at the age-old statement that God *Is*—and is to be *Realized*.

After a few moments of silent concentration, he continued, "How do you recognize such a man? Was Jesus a popular figure in his time?" "Such a man expresses Truth," I replied. "These men create facts of a deep, re-ordaining order. Facts are results. The results these omniscient, omnipotent Pure Beings created have endured. Truth is its own witness."

Einstein's humor suddenly turned the course of thought. With the smile of a wise child knowing how to evade dangerous ground, he said, "Well, tell him for me if he's able to transmute the consciousness of my cat's vulgar instinct to eat birds, I'll believe in him!"

We discussed matters for a little while longer. Einstein realized whatever exists is created by God's love and no one is in possession of the pure, omniscient and omnipresent power unless merged in God. As this is beyond Science, in the end Einstein found the subject a bit too much to grasp.

He apologized for having to finish the last page of his new book, but before leaving he added, "Should we ever have the privilege to be in the same place, in the same town in some part of the world, do you think Meher Baba would see me?" I replied, "When you wish it, he *will*." 1481–82

Although no meeting ever took place, Einstein did receive a copy of *God Speaks*, signed and sent to him personally by the Avatar himself. In the mid-1950s, shortly before his death, Einstein was reported by Norina to have said after reading the book, "All I know is *nothing* compared to what Meher Baba knows." In the end, Einstein's vision of compassion in the universe resonated deeply with the Avatar when he wrote:

> A human being is a part of the whole called by us "the universe," a part limited in time and space. He experiences himself, his thoughts and feelings, as something separate from the rest—an optical delusion of consciousness. This delusion is a kind of prison for us.
>
> It restricts us to personal desires and affection for those few persons nearest to us. Our task must be to free our-

selves from this prison by widening the circle of understanding and compassion to embrace all living creatures and the whole of nature in all its beauty.

Everything is determined by forces over which we have no control—determined for the insect as well as the star. Human beings, vegetables or cosmic dust all dance to a mysterious tune, intoned by an invisible piper. Quoted by H. Eves in *Mathematical Circles Adieu* (Boston, MA:1977**)**

Chapter Twenty-One

Italy, Egypt, Spain and Switzerland

Before returning to the United States again in 1934, Meher Baba would make four more trips to Europe. Two included visits to London to see his established disciples. The other two were what we can only call Italian holidays. These four journeys would also include visits to Zurich, Cairo, Rome, Venice, Paris, Assisi, Madrid, Avila, Barcelona and Colombo. Along the way Baba would pass through Dover, Southhampton, Marseilles, Boulogne, Calais, Trieste, Pisa, Florence, Genoa, Naples, Brindisi, Milan, Lausanne, Lugano, Port Said, Aden, and non-stop through Yugoslavia.

The men and women left behind at Meherabad sorely missed him during his trips to the West, but after just three days at home he shocked everyone by re-boarding the *Kaiser-i-Hind* to set sail for Marseilles on his way to the seaside resort of Santa Margherita.

It would be his first Italian holiday, and he called ten of his closest English disciples to join him on the Italian Riviera. They settled into Villa Fiorenza, a small pension between Santa Margherita and Portofino. There they spent seventeen idyllic days.

Seclusion in St. Francis' Cave

While in Italy, Baba was intent on completing a twenty-four-hour fast and seclusion above Assisi on Mt. Subasio, in a hidden cave that St. Francis himself had used eight hundred years before for his own seclusions. Baba had planned this work long before his actual visit by sending Herbert ahead on a mission to find the cave. Herbert had been instructed to disguise its entrance with branches and to meditate there for several hours each day before Baba's arrival.

Baba explained that before he could do his work in Assisi, one of two things would happen: "Either there will be a horrific storm or I'll fall ill." The storm held off, but Baba suffered stomach cramps that made him painfully restless the night before. As he tossed and turned in anguish he said, "My pain is like a mother giving birth." His expression was said to be like paintings of Jesus suffering on the cross.

At 2:30 PM, August 6, with Baba still in great distress, he and four of the men drove toward Assisi, passing the famed Leaning Tower of Pisa. They stopped for lunch in Sienna, birthplace of St. Catherine, who received the stigmata of Christ's wounds in the fifteenth century. She was one of Baba's favorite saints. Reaching Assisi at 5:00 PM, they had a light meal and then drove partway up Mt. Subasio. They made the rest of their way on foot. It was a difficult climb for Baba, who was still feeling ill.

Baba told two of the men to attend Mass the following morning at St. Francis' Basilica below and then bow down and kiss St. Francis' tomb before returning to the mountain. The others were left with strict instructions not to come near, touch or even look in Baba's direction, for his working outside his physical body in the realm of high energies could greatly endanger them. Then at 7:30, just as the sun set and birds headed for their nests, Baba entered the cave, carrying a string of large Franciscan rosary beads. 1454-56

The men kept watch outside the cave till 5:30 PM on Sunday. Baba was radiant at the end of the seclusion, but emerging from the cave he seemed not fully aware of his body. Approaching them, he gestured, "How lucky you are to be the first to speak to me after this seclusion." 1457

He said that he had held a meeting with the spiritual hierarchy, the likes of which had never been held before. As Baba explained:

> Besides the fifty-six God-Realized souls on earth at all times, five of whom are Perfect Masters . . . there are also seven thousand and one souls in the spiritual hierarchy traversing from the first to the sixth inner plane. Very few can recognize these souls. . . . They are indifferent to the world's happenings, sorrows and comforts, living in, with and for God alone, unaffected by climatic conditions, insufficient food or lack of sleep. They're healthy, despite being deprived of all life necessities. 2967–68

Baba told the men that during the meeting the next two thousand years of human history had been exactly laid out, adding, "It had to do with the greatest upheaval of all times that is coming upon the world, and also the greatest spiritual revolution of all times." MM 1:243

Then they all had a simple supper outside the cave, seated on a wooden plank—bread, butter, cheese, salad, sardines and fruit. The men collected dried leaves, twigs and stones lying in the cave and took them back to be preserved. Descending the mountain afterward, Baba was dazed and the men had to support him, at one point laying him down on the road to rest. This exalted experience had drained his energy, and now he had to focus on coming down from higher planes to reconnect to his physical body. 1459

Baba explained that St. Francis of Assisi's love was unique and unparalleled. "He'd not seen or met Jesus physically, though his longing and love were so great, excelling even Peter the Rock." Baba also revealed for the first time that Francis wasn't merely a saint, but a God-Realized Perfect Master, a fact unknown to Christianity. 4757

Baba said of St. Francis:

He began his uniquely impulsive spiritual quest in the thirteenth century. After four years of immense sufferings, he contacted a European saint who gave him Divine Love with just a glance of his grace. After remaining three more years in a love-stricken state, Francis came to India in search of God. He finally contacted a Hindu Master who gave him God-realization. He then returned to his native place attracting hundreds of thousands of followers. 860

St. Francis told Brother Leo, "Then I was in the light of contemplation, seeing the abyss of the infinite goodness, wisdom and power of God . . . and in the flame you saw was God, who spoke in such a manner to me just as of old he had appeared to Moses." On Mount Sinai God appeared in a thick cloud with fire. The house of clouds are symbolic expressions among mystics for the six inner spiritual planes. QA 12

Brother Leo described the vision of St. Francis. "A light descended, resting on the head of St. Francis; and out of the flame there came a voice."

St. Francis suffered such headaches that he dashed his head against stone, just as Baba did, coming back down into the illusory universe after his own Realization. He healed some of his followers by the touch of his hand. Bowing at his tomb in honor of Francis' extraordinary love for Jesus, Baba remarked, "This is the least I can do. Nobody loved me like Francis." SOF 195; 1454 footnote

During these early Western travels Baba was often asked about the life and words of Jesus, including about the Second Coming described in the Bible. The Gospel of St. Mark, Chapter 9, verses 2 and 7, record that Jesus' transfiguration occurred when he ascended Mt. Tabor. There was a cloud overshadowing him, and a voice came of the cloud, saying *"This is my beloved son, hear him."* Mark 12:16 continues: But in those days, after the great tribulation then shall they see the Son of man coming in the clouds with pow-

Above: Meher Baba with local Italians on the beach, Santa Margherita, Italy, August 1932; Below: Baba with his arms around Herbert Davy and Quentin Tod, Santa Margherita, Italy, August 1932

er and glory. And then shall he send his angels to gather together his elect from the 4 winds, from uttermost part of the earth to the uttermost part of heaven."

Baba explained the gathering of the elect:

> This refers to the reincarnation and final assembling of his close disciples and followers at the time of his second coming.... It's wrong to associate the Second Coming with the imprisonment of the devil and a thousand years of peace, or a literal interpretation of the last Day of Judgment. All the great mystics have understood "clouds" as symbolic for the inner-plane states of spiritual consciousness.
>
> When Christ descends from the infinite seventh plane, he brings with him to earth infinite goodness, wisdom, power and love, and also the powers, signs and experiences of the six lower planes. In the words of a great Sufi saint: "Behold the sky, the clouds and the world. First is meant God, then the planes, the last is earth, but all three are linked."

A Spiritual Cliffhanger

Baba rejoined his disciples at Santa Margherita, where he stood in the sun on the balcony outside his room watching them swimming below in the calm blue sea before breakfast. Delia and Margaret recalled the wondrous times:

> It was a very intimate vacation with such an extraordinary atmosphere. Chanji said it amazed him, because until then only a few of the women in India had had such a close a relationship with Baba. It was like an enchanted dream. We sat on the sands of the crystal blue Mediter-

ranean and wandered the wooded hills with Baba in a dream filled with his sweetness. He was so happy here, repeating to the group, "Just love me and don't worry."

As word of Baba's presence spread, boats would row back and forth in front of the villa. Italians from local villages came to sit quietly near him, delighted to be in his presence. In the evenings Baba and his devotees sat out on the balcony playing records and games like charades and cards or else went out to the local movie theater so that he could work with the audiences. Later they might visit Lena's open air cafe by the bay to sip coffee or eat Italian ices. Kaka and Chanji were made to eat fish after years of being strict vegetarians. 1452–53

One day, as directed, Chanji playfully took Baba's hand and led him to Margaret, introducing him as "Thomas," a little boy having his first dancing lesson. "Come along, Thomas," Margaret said, taking him by the hand:

> I showed him a simple 1-2-3 hop step. No obstacle. He took to it at once. Hand-in-hand we then flew around the garden. *And I mean flew!* He moved like no one else has ever moved with such joy, freedom and rhythm. The steps weren't difficult, but Baba's sense of rhythm was really quite extraordinary. We spent a truly lovely and extraordinary afternoon. Not having to intellectualize it, I knew dancing was and always will be a part of God. 1462

Baba took the group to Venice, where they visited St. Mark's Square. Baba entered the cathedral with only the men, who customarily enter a church bare-headed. Church regulations barred women from entering if they had no head coverings.

When they came back outside, Baba explained the church's architecture and its spiritual significance. He had them count and write down the number of pillars, domes and arches, which came to exactly 120. Baba indicated, "This church is one of the four great spiritual centers of Europe. The whole structure corresponds to the Avatar's twelve inner-circle members and the 108 disciples of the outer circles. He then made an astounding revelation: "I was here as Jesus with two of my apostles a month before my crucifixion, and sat on the exact spot where St. Mark's was later built."

Dressed now in his stylish white suit and fedora, Baba posed for photos with each of the Westerners. With his arms around their shoulders, Baba sat, beaming, while pigeons fluttered about feeding from his hand. His recollection of having been in that very spot not long before the crucifixion struck a poignant contrast to the carefree joy of the moment. 1463

At night, the group went out to watch the crowds and listen to a concert in the square. Later, at an outdoor café, Baba remarked, "I was here 620 years ago," perhaps in another minor Advent coinciding with the lifetime of St. Francis.

Baba then suddenly turned sad and told them he sometimes allows his disciples to share in his suffering. "I am eternally crucified. When the burden is especially heavy, I sometimes let my disciples share it, giving to each as much as they can bear." Then his mood lifted and they went to see Charlie Chaplin's latest movie, *The Gold Rush*.

Cairo: "My Dear Old Place"

Having finished his work in Italy, Baba sailed from Venice to Alexandria, Egypt, accompanied by Kaka and Chanji. Watching him board the SS *Ausonia* at 4:00 P.M, his English lovers wept at his departure. Baba's eyes also filled with tears as the ship sailed away. They sent him a cable on board, and he pressed it to his lips and eyes, wetting it with his tears.

Baba's eyes remained tearful until he retired that night at ten o'clock. Never before had Kaka and Chanji seen Baba so sad over a departure. As if in agony, he spent a restless night. They wondered why he should suffer so. What sort of love could cause the Master of Bliss to be so restless?

For the next three days, Baba showed no interest in meeting anyone or even going for a walk around the ship, as he constantly remembered each one of those left behind and their ways. He spelled out on the board: "Kimco, my heart. How they all love me!" Then he dictated this short rhyme to be sent to them: "Kimco, my heart, now as ever and ever as now. How I love you! How I miss you! Just wait four months, when I come and kiss you!" 1466

Meher Baba with Quentin Tod and Herbert Davy, St. Mark's Square Venice, Italy, 1932

"Kimco" was the abbreviation Baba used when referring and writing to his earliest English female disciples. "Kim" was, of course, Kim Tolhurst, who had met Baba at the Devon Retreat in 1931. "Co" referred to the rest of the women, who also included Kitty, Margaret and Delia.

The SS *Austonia* docked in Alexandria on August 23 and Baba continued by rail to Cairo for a six-day stay. There he rode a donkey on an excursion to Giza to see the Great Pyramids and Sphinx. He also wished to visit the Coptic Church, telling Kaka and Chanji, "The Coptic Church contains a cave where Mary and Joseph stayed after fleeing Herod. The reason I came to Egypt is to visit this church." Baba convinced the church warden to let him go down into the cave. Afterward he said that he had come there as Jesus with his Apostles, adding, "This is my dear old place." And, as with nearly all the places he visited, he went to the zoo, as well as the Museum of the Pharaohs, several Islamic mosques, and the Citadel. 1466

Baba returned to India on the MV *Victoria*, arriving September 5. He spent four months in the Nasik ashram—months filled with the exchange of telegrams and letters with his Western disciples, to whom Chanji wrote:

> Letters and cables from the West . . . pour in almost daily with the same common tone and tune of all—the tune of the heart. . . .
>
> And now, before I close, some good news—of his advent to the West! From the trend of events, it appears he might leave here by the beginning of November for Italy, and then . . . sweet dreams of January to be realized! So I'll let you dwell in those glorious dreams of love when the Darling Beloved of your heart stands physically in your presence with you all, while you are trying always to find your blessed moment to be with him and in his arms, thinking always of things that would make him happy, and of the surprise you have in store for him. 1479

Baba departed for his fourth trip to Europe on November 21, 1933, on the SS *Conte Verde*, bound for Venice. From there he continued to London for an eight-day visit before traveling to Zurich, Switzerland, for his first visit there, accompanied by a small group of disciples.

In Zurich Baba met with a group of spiritual seekers at a reception held in his honor. Among them were Walter and Hedi Mertens and Hedi's friend Helen Dahm. Walter was an architect and both of the women were artists. All three became life-long disciples. From Switzerland Baba returned to Egypt for a nearly-two-week visit before sailing on the SS *Baloeran* for Colombo, Ceylon (now Sri Lanka). There he spent eighteen days before returning home to India.

Portofino

In February 1933, Baba decided to obtain a British passport instead of a Persian one. Forms were filled out and his photo taken. In the column for "visible distinguishing marks" Chanji wrote, "Scar, center of eyebrow"—from the stone thrown by Upasni Maharaj in 1915, blessedly returning Merwan to gross consciousness. 1504

Then in June, after less than four months at home, Baba again sailed for the West, this time on the SS *Conte Verde*, for a second Italian holiday that would include both European and American disciples meeting for the first time. This time they traveled to Portofino, which they had first visited the previous summer.

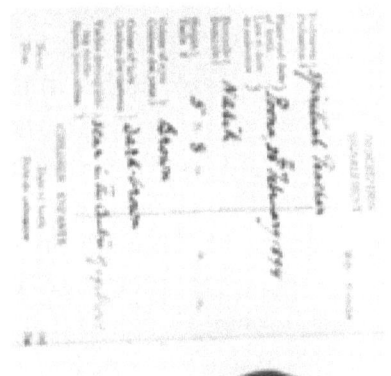

Meher Baba's passport, February 1, 1933

There, Elizabeth had rented Villa Altachiara, a beautiful retreat with elegant Victorian interiors surrounded by a large park overlooking the sea. It was another idyllic, love-filled time. The thirty-room hilltop villa had breathtaking cliff views and had been the home of Lord Carnarvon, sponsor of Howard Carter who discovered Tutankhamen's Tomb.

Meanwhile, Baba's circle of female devotees continued to expand, composed of upper-class, cultured, well-educated, strong-willed and courageous women. All surrendered their lives to him, and "love," as Kitty once noted, "was the keynote to their character.) Aw 20 (no. 2): 49

Ruano Bogislav, stage persona for a woman whose name was Elfrida Klamroth, was a singer, actress and businesswoman living in Paris. When Quentin Tod had returned to England from India in June 1933, he stopped off in Paris to tell her about Baba.

Baba called her to join him in Portofino. She later recalled: "It seemed to me as if I had been looking for ages. I put my hands over my face and cried and cried. I'll never forget the kind, gentle way Baba led me to a sofa and had me sit beside him as he patted my hand. Through my sobs I tried to tell him how sorry I was I couldn't stop crying." Baba spelled out on his board to Quentin, "Tell her it's just as it should be." 1525

Baba explained to the group that he had visited Portofino in another Advent and that there were "spiritual reasons" for His returning there. He went on to name four places of "great spiritual significance" in the West: Avila in Spain, and Portofino, Venice, and Assisi, all in Italy. He would soon have visited all four of them.

Baba and his party traveled to Rome on July 6 for a quick overnight visit packed with activities. But he appeared not to be happy there and proclaimed the city "spiritually dead." As Kitty recalled, "After breakfast we drove around Rome's Seven hills and went to St. Peter's. Baba wore a small beret to hide his flowing hair. Walking in the midst of the party, he was able to enter without taking it off." Inside, he stood in the center beneath the dome of the huge basilica. "He turned, signing toward each of the four quarters. Then, without letting us linger over the exquisite paintings and statues, he turned and walked rapidly along the left aisle back out the west door, passing Michelangelo's *Pietà*". LA 10

Later, the group went to the Aragno al Corso in the city's center, a famous sidewalk café where Rome's intelligentcia gathered to discuss the day's issues over espresso. Suddenly a heavy-set blond man drove slowly by in a red Fiat sports convertible. Baba explained that this man, named Christiano, was his chief European agent. His family never suspected his spiritual advancement. He went on to say that there were four such direct agents functioning on the fourth plane, one each in Europe, Africa, Asia, and one for North and South America, wielding occult powers for others. 1394, 1524 and footnote

Baba's group also visited the Lateran, several Roman fountains, and the Vatican Museum. After practically racing through the galleries, Baba sat down for a moment in the Sistine Chapel. They also visited Capitoline Hill and the Forum and walked in the Coliseum. Baba then asked to be driven twice around Benito Mussolini's office. Afterward he declared, "Now my work in Rome is finished." 1521–25

While in Portofino Norina brought a worldly young philosophy professor to Meet Baba. He came under duress and was outright rude as he fired intellectual questions at the Master. Baba answered each one with simplicity and brilliance. This antagonized the young professor all the more, making him unreceptive to the obvious truth, beauty and wisdom in Baba's direct answers.

Prompted by uncontrollable inner anger he interrupted Baba. Turning to Norina he said, "Tell your so-called Master he's given me no new answers, but merely repeated all the old, worn-out formulas for Truth!" Baba smiled kindly and put his hand on the man's head, looking deeply into his eyes. The mental storm subsided. The professor began breathing deeply as his reactive mind stopped and his consciousness instantly expanded.

Suddenly, he was a transfixed receptacle of grace. With the look of a newborn soul christened by divine waters he said, "I know love is the only answer to all questions. Love is Truth, and you know, you actually just made me realize that. I now know only love solves one's problems of duality and the battle of life." He then knelt before Baba and said, "Take my whole life and use it."

Baba replied, "Don't be confused and don't struggle to change your life, but try with all your heart to create *longing* to be one with God. This longing will make you see your Real Self. The glimpse I've just given you won't last, but you'll now understand more of the Truth, going deeper and deeper, and in time you'll be of great service to humanity."

Norina recalled that "leaving the room, the man stood before the closed door. With tears in his eyes he said to me, 'To think I didn't even want to *see* God! I thank you for making me come. Please let me know whatever I can do for him. I am at his service.'" 1522–23

One day Baba led the group down the cliffs to the sea. On the treacherous climb back up the cliff two of them became stuck and were in extreme peril, needing immediate rescue. Baba gestured to bystanders, "Quick, get a rope!" No one grasped his gestures except Tino, a young boy who understood instantly, quickly running to fetch a long rope. Meanwhile, Baba enjoyed all the excitement

Anita recalled her rescue: "Baba's tremendous beauty was amazing, like seeing for the first time what beauty was. As I was pulled up, Baba looked at me, and there he was against the sea, the cliffs and the sky like a tremendous Byzantine figure with the most beautiful smile. In that moment, I thought, 'Never again will I see beauty like this.'" 1528

In the early 1980s, Baba lovers visiting Portofino met a local ferryman who was amazed to see Baba's photo buttons on their jackets, exclaiming "He's the Baba! That's Baba!" Through halting conversation he told how he witnessed the cliffside drama with "the silent Baba." He was Tino, who as a boy had alone understood from Baba's gestures that he needed a rope.

Tino's family owned Lena's Cafe, where the group often had refreshments. He took them there in his boat to meet his mother, now bedridden. She had made a little altar with Christ's photo surrounded by pictures of saints. She remembered Baba very well. Her son explained to her that "the Baba" was now loved and followed all over the world. OL 63–64

Baba recalled an event from ages past that had taken place nearby. He told them of a minor Advent in Portofino when he incarnated as an unknown spiritual figure who was with a group of disciples on those very cliffs. "There was a violent struggle, and two of my men were seriously wounded."

One evening at the villa, Baba got up at midnight. Kaka was on night-watch and followed him downstairs in pitch darkness. Baba sat on a step for a few minutes, then returned to his room. When Kaka asked him what that was all about, Baba explained, "There was a spirit here who's been trying to get free for five hundred years. Tonight, I've relieved him." 1521

Interspersed with adventure and ghostly encounters, there was much laughter. One day Baba spelled out on his board to Anita, "You do know I'm both God and man." Shocked, she thought, "I've no idea what God is." Then she said, "Baba, I don't grasp you as a man; how can I understand you as God? Oh never mind, it doesn't matter. We all make mistakes. Call yourself God—call yourself whatever! I love you just the same." Baba almost fell over rocking with silent laughter.

Calling Chanji, he shook his head, gesturing, "Anita's really so amazing! You know what she just told me? It doesn't matter, it's not important I may have made a mistake saying I'm both God and man. She's absolutely and totally indifferent about it!" 1519-20

Saints and Secret Agents

Baba's sixth trip to the West in September and October of 1933 included thirteen days in London and his first visit to Spain. There he felt very much at home, saying that it reminded him of India. Among those accompanying him were Norina, Herbert and Quentin, as well as the mandali who had been traveling with him.

His first stay was in Avila, the home of St. Teresa. Baba took the group to visit her house. He said that St. Theresa had loved him deeply: "She devoted her entire life to Jesus—to me. I feel at home here. Like in Assisi, the spiritual atmosphere you feel gives value to the shrines of these saints. . . . Saints are like the nerves of my body. They work for me and I guide their lives." [20]

They then returned to the hotel and had their last meal for the next twenty-four hours. He explained, "I have very special work in Avila. You must all fast and we must walk together over the hills, although no one should touch me." The following morning he took the men to the cathedral on a hill above Avila, and they felt as if they were walking with Jesus through the hills of Galilee. Baba revealed to them about yet another minor Advent. "Long ago, before the cathedral was built, I was here in Avila. I would walk on this hillside and quietly rest and meditate here. There were no trees here then." LM 1567

After visiting the cathedral, Baba instructed that the sacristan be given four silver coins. The group then walked in the surrounding countryside as Baba continued explaining: "In Europe and other continents, are holy places connected to great spiritual work . . . four holy centers of Europe are Saint Mark's in Venice, a place on the Ligurian Coast of Italy [perhaps the Portofino-Santa Margherita seaside Baba had visited with his disciples], Assisi [Italy] and Avila [Spain]. I have now visited and revisited them all. From their holy grounds have sprung many saints!" Baba instructed Herbert to return to Avila ten days later and sit every day for a week on the rock where Baba had sat.

Baba's entourage left Avila the same day, arriving in Madrid that night, checking in at the Hotel Principe Don Juan on Calle de Recoletes. Baba told them, "The rest of our time in Spain will be pure rest and relaxation." As Baba also wished to contact the masses, they strolled along the crowded streets of Madrid with its cool, brilliant air. He especially liked the Puerta Del Sol—Gate of the Sun, and would come to this square several times a day.

Despite attempts to fit in with his European clothing and beret, Baba found that the Spaniards would turn, staring irresistibly at him. He revealed to his companions, "It is due to the internal work I'm doing, as I can move about quite unnoticed when I wish to at other times."

That night they went to a seedy cabaret frequented by prostitutes. Baba especially enjoyed the gaiety of the gypsy flamenco dancers. Besides taking in the show, he was no doubt working for the welfare of this class of humanity in unseen ways. The group went to another movie late that night—the iconic *King Kong*.

Baba told the men, "Madrid is the last place of my present visit to the West and I do not intend to return to the West for another year. Hence, I have much work to do before I leave," reiterating, "It is due to my special working that people's attention is attracted toward me everywhere I go. I worked intensely this morning, standing for ten minutes in the very big, busy square, while Quentin and Norina were inquiring about certain information that I sent them to gather. All the while, one very old man was intensely gazing at me." 1569

The next morning the group shifted to the Gran Hotel Londres overlooking the Puerta del Sol. That evening they all went out for music and watched another Flamenco dancer. During the following days they toured the Prado (the National Museum of Art) and Royal Palace, and went out to movies or the ballet in the evenings.

They also attended a bullfight, where the Westerners who wanted to go had told him there would be a great crowd for him to work with. But Baba was bored, and his companions were overcome at the brutish killing of the two bulls. He said the whole thing was childish, and now his work there was finished. They quickly left, with Baba adding, "Those two bulls were fortunate to be killed in my presence. They'll now incarnate as humans and rapidly advance on the path." 1571

Baba sent all the Westerners home except for Herbert, and on November 1 he and the remaining men boarded a train for Barcelona. Arriving the following morning, they were met by a huge military escort of officials and a brass band, presumably, to greet officials who had been on the train, but it appeared as if all the fuss was for the Lord of the Universe Himself. Only Baba and the men were aware of the connection between the two events. 1567-72

Earlier, before they had de-boarded, Baba had told the men, "My agent knows I am coming [to Barcelona]. He is unique among my agents, as he is a policeman in ordinary life." During their short stay in the city, they visited an amusement park, taking in the sideshows, and made an excursion to Mt. Tibidabo. Afterward, at the Plaza de Cataluna, they observed a policeman glancing at Baba in a very direct manner. He was the agent Baba had come to contact.

Baba took the opportunity to talk about his work with these advanced but frequently veiled souls who worked for him in the gross world and in other spiritual dimensions. These souls are found all around the world, internally connected with the Avatar and or the five Perfect Masters on inner planes to receive his commands. The agents then carry out these instructions to further the Avatar's or the five Perfect Masters' work. Direct agents are few—one for each continent. They receive instructions directly from the Avatar. Indirect agents, also few, receive their orders from the direct agents. Borrowed agents are many and they get their orders from indirect agents.

Direct agents are always on the fourth plane, and act for the Avatar through the powers they wield on that high inner plane. They may even carry out miracles for him, since the Avatar almost never performs miracles himself; but if he wished to, he would have to station himself on the fourth plane at that time, just as Jesus did. These agents are on the fourth plane only because of the necessity of using certain of their powers for the Avatar's work. 1573

> Agents are of two types: with and without bodily form. The latter not having undergone the process of evolution are a different order of beings. But they are very powerful. They have no mind, no desire and no form, and have no connection with agents in bodily form.
>
> These spirits appear like sparks. An illumined person can see them even with the physical eyes. Here about me now are *so many*. Without mind, they do whatever they hear and see, because they *feel*; then through feeling they pass it on to the unconscious Ocean in the Creation-Point.
>
> Everything these millions of agents see or hear goes directly to the Perfect Masters. There are four different types of agents in bodily form: *Avtad, Abdal, Afreed,* and *Afsoon.* They have minds and are very powerful, though not yet God-Realized. The first type [*Avtad*, appears externally mad] gives and receives messages to and from the Perfect Masters, somewhat like a wireless [or the Internet]. The second class of agents can also appear and disappear at will thousands of miles distant from their physical bodies.
>
> When the first type of agent, *Avtad*, has a message to transmit to the Perfect Masters, they must relay it through the second type, the *Abdals*, who then instantly go wherev-

er their service may be needed. Even greater work is done by the third and fourth categories, *Afreeds* and *Afsoons* who always appear sane, whereas *Avtads* always appear mad. The former two types are most powerful.

They can create living forms; still, they are not perfect. Only one thing — the Infinite Ocean of Love is real. Billions of messages every day pass over me as that Ocean. I deal with important ones myself. You are all one with the Ocean, yet still separate in consciousness. Gl (Feb. 1996): 2–3

In exchanges with agents, Baba rarely used words. With just a momentary glance or a gesture his work with a conscious agent was done. Once in a while, seemingly bizarre actions or arcane verbal messages might be employed, given directly to Baba or to one of the mandali. For certain Universal work involving long-range planning for humanity, Baba would set up what might be called spiritual summit meetings with agents and the Perfect Masters on the inner planes who did not need to be in his physical presence, like spiritual teleconferencing in his subtle body.

Baba explained how the extensive network of agents on the inner planes have duties and are interconnected with Perfect Masters beyond the limitations of time and space. "With the help of their universal mind and body, Perfect Ones can approach and contact anyone at any time, anywhere. Time and space do not exist for them. In fact, all souls traversing the inner planes, and not just those few who are agents, are also directly under the protective radar of the Perfect Ones. This is especially needful for anyone who is crossing the unbelievably dangerous fourth plane." 2091

The Masters often veil such a one to prevent misuse of the fourth plane's enormous energy and dangerous occult powers. One mishap using these miraculous powers even in a slightly selfish way for personal power can return one's consciousness back to stone, so that the transgressor would have to go through the entire evolutionary journey all over again.

Baba often met physically his direct agents, who were generally found in the West, because there are no advanced or God-intoxicated souls on the higher spiritual planes in that part of the world to act in that capacity. But unlike *masts*, agents are aware of everything. They go undercover, unrecognized—true, divine secret agents doing work in the West that masts do in the East.

Home Work

Baba sailed home to India, arriving on November 14. It would be seven months until he returned to the West, longer than any of his previous returns to his ashram. He immediately picked up with his work in Nasik. After meeting with his mandali to check on their work and states of mind, Baba was told that Gulmai's daughter Dolly had been feeling very depressed during his absence. So he traveled to Ahmednagar just to see Dolly, giving her a discourse that afternoon on mental depression. He had it typed out and distributed for everyone to read:

> You say you're tired of living life in this body. Unwelcome bad thoughts disturb and make you unhappy. But life *is* thoughts, not body. When you're asleep you're body is there, but you don't feel the need then to end your life . . . So why should you be so unhappy?
>
> You're neither too tall nor too fat. You're healthy, you can read and write. Think of the poor, the paralyzed, the lepers and disabled. The paraplegic or leper knows he's heading toward a sure death and likely to die in a far worse state than he is in presently. Yet, there are thousands like these silently dragging on through their days, dragging, dragging on through their endless days and nights.

If you compare your lot with the dumb, illiterate millions in this country, you're most fortunate. You live with and move in the surroundings of a Master. What's there in the Himalayas and the jungles? Didn't you see the *Tarzan* movie; how the jungle is life full of strife and struggles?

Despite bad thoughts, you don't indulge in bad actions; so, what higher life can you live than this?

It's normal to have bad thoughts; *just don't act them out!* Then you get an opportunity to exercise control. If no thoughts assail you, then what's the difference between you and a stone which has no thoughts at all? Mind is like a wound-up alarm clock. At the appointed time it will ring, but only as long as it is wound. Just take care to not wind it again by indulging in bad actions. Still, if you want to die, die in my *naad*—my infatuation – by holding on to me firmly. There lies salvation.

That's real dying. Worldly death isn't the thing. However, nobody has so far captured me. If one really catches me, I try to free myself. But so far, I've not even had an opportunity of freeing myself. On the contrary, it is I who have been trying to catch hold of you people. Remember this much: the whole world is nothing but a zero, and everything connected with it is without sum or substance. [False] mind is the universe, the man, the woman, the beast. 1576–77

To further console her, Baba brought Dolly with Gulmai to Nasik the next day, but by the end of the month he decided to shift the ashram back to Meherabad. The women (Mehera, Mani, Naja, Walu, Vishnu's mother Kakubai, and Soonamasi and her daughter Khorshed) moved in the two rooms in the Water Tank building. Baba attended to the business of managing an ashram, and soon he began sleeping in his underground crypt. Disciples came to visit at Baba's invitation and left on his order to return home.

Filmwork in Switzerland

Baba's seventh trip to Europe would last more than seven months, from June 9, 1934, until January 7, 1935, longer than his interim stay in India. While he was in London, two more important women came into his orbit: Nonny Gayley and her daughter Rano. They had learned of Baba though their friend Ruano. Nonny knew him instantly from the photograph Ruano showed her. Now he called Nonny and Rano, as well as Ruano, to join him in London. He revealed that Ruano had been very kind to him in ancient Egypt. and that she, Nonny and Rano had close past connections from those times. Ruano and Nonny had been brother and sister, and Rano had been Ruano's son.

Like Baba's first female disciples from the West, Nonny and Rano had been sincere spiritual seekers before meeting him and had deep connections with him. They came from the crème de la crème of New York society, a world that they were happy to leave behind to pursue a spiritual life, and they became life-long devotees. 1647

Most of Baba's time during this trip would be devoted to filmwork. After three days in Paris he would return to London for a ten-day visit before continuing on to Zurich accompanied by a small group of English disciples, to engage in twelve days of preparations for another visit to Hollywood in December.

As with most film projects, the biggest hurdles now were honing the script and trying to find solid financial backing. To lower costs, the possibility of filming in India was discussed, instead of Hollywood. Baba even considered building a movie studio at Meherabad and sending the film to Bombay for processing.

The Westerners had wanted to make an additional feature film on Baba's life as the Avatar of the Age. But in January 1934, while still in India, he replied: "Producing a picture with such technical difficulties, special effects and production details would be quite impossible here. So an Indian production is being dropped in favor of filming in the West." Aw 18 (no. 1): 38

Bollywood, barely in its infancy and not remotely prepared to pull off such an elaborate production, would need another fifty years to come up to speed. Telegrams were fired back and forth through the spring of 1934 about Baba's return to Hollywood. Norina cabled Baba from Paris that her first husband, German stage and screenwriter Dr. Karl Vollmöller, had agreed to work on the script. Baba was familiar with Vollmöller's work and admired it.

Vollmöller had written a unique screenplay for *The Blue Angel*, the film that made Marlene Dietrich a star in 1930. He had also written the script for Norina's London great stage success, *The Miracle*. [30] On March 13 Baba replied to Norina: "Tell Karl to write two scenarios; one wholly for me and another for the producers using his superb imagination in both. My April coming depends on the scenario being ready. Otherwise, I cannot come."

Previously, while in London, Baba had seen and very much liked a film by the renowned Hungarian film director Gabriel Pascal. Norina contacted Pascal in Paris to discuss the project. He expressed great interest in Baba's proposed film and was immediately brought on board. 1593

But Pascal soon had misgivings. He would become frustrated with having to chase Baba all over Europe to sort things out. Although a cinematic genius, the director became impatient when he could make no headway with these "impractical" ladies.

Norina cabled him about financial backing and maddening, nitpicking script details. He began to blame Baba for the misunderstandings. In fact, he had had such a falling out with the ladies that when he heard Baba was coming to Paris he was determined to face him and tell him it was all a ridiculous waste of time.

However, as chance would have it, he was a day late arriving for his appointment, and by then Baba had already left for Switzerland. But being stubborn, Pascal raced to Zurich to personally have it out with the Master. He was a temperamental forty-year-old Hungarian from Transylvania, and by now he was seething, feeling Baba was just giving him the run-around.

Then, adding insult to injury, Baba had wasn't there when Pascal arrived for his rescheduled appointment in Zurich, and now he was livid. Suddenly, a phone call came instructing Elizabeth to give Pascal "a choice peach" and tell him Baba was on his way. This seemingly innocuous gesture profoundly calmed the man, who later confided his mother used to do the very same thing—save him the very best peach.

Baba returned shortly after and called for Pascal. As he entered the room, Baba's gentle smile instantly melted Pascal's anger. He meekly asked, "What do you wish me to do?" Baba sat him near, held his hand and asked about his work. Now peaceful, Pascal told Baba he wanted to bring out the expression of the deepest inner feelings by portraying the spiritual side of life in a way that had never been done before. Baba remarked:

> I caught one of your films in London and saw how subtly and beautifully you combine humor and pathos. I enjoyed it, and often indicated you're the man to direct my film. We have deep past connections and you will work for me in the future in films.
>
> That's why I've drawn you to me. You're my *Phoenix!* You've been with me for several incarnations. I'll help you fulfill my mission in the West, and your career will soar higher than ever before. 2934

And so it did, higher and higher. After meeting Baba, Pascal departed happier than he'd ever been in his life. "It was all wonderful—too wonderful for words. I went in like a lion and came out like a lamb, at once his devoted servant." Baba teased Pascal about knowing where the "missing link" in evolution was. Pascal's eyes popped. "I won't tell you now; maybe tomorrow." Up to his old mischief, however, the information simply became another missing link in his explanations.

Pascal enthused, "Anything Baba wishes, I'll do. I'll make this film my life's supreme task. I won't even need a script. I'll go out with my crew to the jungles and begin shooting. It'll be improvised on the spot, and show how God truly lives with men!" Aw 18 (no. 1): 39

Film discussions with Pascal and Vollmöller, who had recently arrived, went on for the next three days. Vollmöller had prepared the rough draft of a story about seven passengers in an airplane whose pilot represented the Master. Pascal even suggested Baba's hand be filmed as a special illustrating effect, to which Baba readily agreed. 1623–24

Baba asked Vollmöller to find an independent Western producer—European or American, promising to return and aid in explaining the minutest details about the film. The final scenario was to be based on reincarnation, as a group of three souls became involved with one another while changing roles over their next five lifetimes. Through intensely working through their karma and the Avatar's grace they achieve God-Realization at the end of those few lives. In it Baba gave an amazing explanation of evolution, reincarnation and involution. With a condensed version below, the full exposition can be found in the Supplement, entitled *The Creation of Consciousness—The Extraordinary Revelations on How it All Happened.*

Meher Baba with a group of female disciples at the time of his first meeting with Gabriel Pascal: Minta Toledano, Kitty, Delia, Anna Mertens, Anita de Caro (Vieillard) and Norina, Zurich, Switzerland, 1934

Next, Baba prepared a detailed illustrated chart for this film, explaining all about Creation, Evolution, Reincarnation, the Planes, Illumination and Realization. Aw 18 (no. 1): 38

> Creation, as you see it, has come out of me, from the minutest speck to the vastest expanse. Creation is made up of space and energy. When you go back to the Creation Point, even space doesn't exist—*no space, no energy, no time*. Beyond this point is the Infinite One in its real form. *That* is Baba. And I, from that Beyond State, look on this creation which has come out of the minutest point of me. That state of looking is the *Fourth Dimension.* 1560

Beginning on May 23, 1934, Baba spent ten days dictating *The Theme of Creation* on the alphabet board with stunning new revelations. Adi K. took down instructions for the accompanying charts and storyboard drawings on evolution to illustrate and assist the screenwriters. The five-by-seven-foot Film Master Chart displays the entire *Divine Theme* in a completely developed form.

The chart's bottom half expands on the earlier stages of the complex process – the original creation through subtle gases, the emergence of rocks, minerals and the first origins of life in the vegetable kingdom. This was the first time such cosmic secrets were revealed. What follows is a very condensed version of those explanations:

The Theme of Creation —
The First Revelation of How It All Happened

> Scientists understand evolution from the first life form to its last—human life. But none knows *why* this evolution of forms happens. After human life what is there? Scientists know nothing! Due to the evolution of consciousness all forms evolve. For example, take the *body* as consciousness, and *clothes* as the body. Now, the size of this shirt is according to your body. If a hand is cut off tomorrow, the shirt might be minus a sleeve. So, due to consciousness body changes. Now see this:
>
> The ocean was warm and still. With the presence of gas and air in the water it became rusty. Algae formed from this rust and sank from above to below. On reaching ocean bottom, it became seaweed. From the original algae [first plant form] came seaweed [second plant form] and from it evolved all the remaining vegetation on our planet.
>
> One of the first gross reptile forms was 175 feet long. It was fourteen feet wide and had three heads joined together, the middle one was six-feet round and the side heads two

feet in circumference. Its front snout partly resembled a reptile; the thin back resembled a fish. Its belly was ten feet round and tapered to a breadth of six feet at the tail. The middle head had a jaw. Its teeth were just like a fish.

But the side heads had only holes connected with the gills and no teeth. All three mouths were connected, one to another and breathed simultaneously with only one windpipe. Each head had an eye, so the creature had three eyes. Under a different class from prehistoric times birds have two eyes, evolving out of and beyond worms and fish.

There's a bird so peculiar no one can even have an idea of it even in his wildest imagination. This bird is half-bat and very large, about fifteen feet high with two legs like an ostrich. Its neck is about two feet in circumference, but its head is so small – about two feet compared to its body. With a six-foot wingspread, its beak is more like a vulture's with a thick end and a very thin point.

After this missing link, the first human form evolves [it is physically or sexually a eunuch – neither male nor female]. Scientists may find signs of this so-called missing link in Java, Sumatra or Indian jungles in the central provinces in Madhya Pradesh.

One cycle of time is 12,000 million years [12,000,000,000 = 12 billion years]. Scientists know nothing at all about cycles, but this hint just might open their eyes. The evolution of the world began two billion years ago, and evolution, which started from the nebula, will last until the completion of the cycle—when Mahapralaya, the total dissolution of the universe—will take place.

The human form has been evolving for millions of years and will continue to evolve. After a billion years, man will only be five inches in height at most, but will be very brainy. In the beginning of this cycle, man was fourteen feet tall and would live up to three hundred years.

About the gaseous structure of the universe, from the nebula came the four elements, though they were not produced simultaneously. First came heat, then crust, rocks and lastly, water. What is there in the universe? Billions and billions of nebulae. Every nebula contains millions of worlds and ours is the earth. What is there in the whole universe? It is gas in its 276 subtle states. Before gas turns into the first manifestation of the gross, it must evolve through 276 subtle stages.

No scientists know about these 276 subtle forms of gas before its first manifestation in the gross world. Subtle gas gradually turns into gross form as hydrogen, oxygen, etc. In the nebulae and in all heavenly bodies and planets there is evolution. All evolution begins from the nebulae.

The 276 subtle stages begin from the beginning of the nebulae, which are at the source of subtle energy (Pran) and subtle space (Akash), the gas left over after cooling turned into air. There is no air a hundred miles beyond our earth. This means even before the elements – not before heat, but before water – the electron had to evolve. In the beginning, our world was *very, very hot.*

After slowly cooling down, all the gas was solidified. As the planet became cooler, a crust formed. With the gradual cooling, the earth's crust became solid and the center remained hot. Rocks were formed from that crust. The center was full of gas and extremely hot. There are natural gaps in the crust, because rock forms were irregular. Then when the gas became cool, it turned into liquid.

And this liquid seeped in between the rocks. Rocks were turned into mountains and valleys, and the cool gas [water] filled them. This created the oceans and the seas.

Evolution of form begins with the oceans. As to the universe's gaseous structure, from the nebula came the four elements. Heat came first, then the earth's crust, rocks and lastly water. What's in the universe? Billions and billions of nebulae. Every nebula contains millions of worlds. Ours is the earth.... At first either show an ocean of dazzling light without a shore or deep darkness which then gradually vanishes into hollow emptiness.

From this darkness or dazzling light project a tiny point of light from which comes Akash (Full Space) and Pran (Primal Energy). These come together with a clash when at first there was more matter and less energy; then energy began increasing gradually.

Although the film would trace the lives of three characters through five lifetimes up to God-Realization, it takes far more than merely five, but countless, seemingly endless reincarnations for each soul to reach God-Realization. Illustrating this, Baba drew some storyboard sketches showing how the active [+] principle of Infinite Primal Energy [Pran], converged with the attractive [−] principle of Infinite Space [Akash], combining through the function of "clashing or colliding."

From the nebula came the four elements. Heat came first, then the earth's crust, rocks and lastly water to produce the result as the first primitive "spark of consciousness" in Creation. He then explained creation's beginning with the evolution of consciousness propelled forward by increasingly winding and complex atomic and molecular structures, winding *denser and denser sanskaric impressions* into the very fabric of matter itself.

This created greater and greater consciousness, passing through the earlier stages of evolution with those sanskaras winding on to higher forms, as yet another cast of actors evolved to fill the new stage, finally reaching the fullness of consciousness in *human form*. Baba continued:

From this whirling chaos, the subtle sphere comes into existence with the primal elements of fire, water, air and earth, nebulae and millions of heavenly bodies. Show billions of enormous, immense, hot, rotating bodies of masses spinning tremendously fast as millions of suns and planets.

Then show our solar system and earth being formed, bubbling over with very hot gases and liquids. Show the earth forming a crust as it cools, with uneven gaps and rocks in the middle—gas liquefying and evolving into oceans. From the ocean, evolution begins with algae and seaweed.

Show different forms of evolution from electrons, minerals, algae, to the vegetable kingdom and the formation of major species—seaweed, mushrooms, grass, neem trees and spinach; fish, birds, animals; then the missing ape link, and finally the story of the three characters in five lifetimes begins.

This film will actually demonstrate the entire purpose: creation, evolution, reincarnation, illumination and Realization – the whole process of inner and outer progression up to the point of the total fulfillment of all life, which is union with God. No ordinary human has any idea of these facts as real experience, but a God-Conscious Perfect Master *sees and experiences* it all in every moment.

The entire process will be portrayed and depicted as vividly as possible and personally supervised by me. The role of reincarnation and the seven planes will be shown with charts, animation and special effects. A perfect understanding of death will finally be given. Once man realizes it, he'll *never* fear the inevitable death that all without exception must undergo.

This film will uplift all humanity by illustrating the real purpose of life—union with God—and portray man's transformation of consciousness in fulfilling this purpose. The film will show people what life *truly is*, its goal, the mechanics of the universe, the nature of God, and how the inherent spiritual life ascends the divine ladder toward its very source. 1608–12; LBE 76–77

Whatever it meant for the future of spiritual film making, the project obviously kept the group of new devotees concentrating on Baba, trying to please him, accepting his constant plan changes as well as their own failures and disappointments with equanimity.

Seclusion at Fallenfluh

Nearing the end of his visit to Switzerland, Baba prepared to go into seclusion. Before he arrived he had already been in touch with Walter and Hedi, asking them to locate a "free and lofty place." As they lived in the shadow of the Swiss Alps, the spot they found was atop a mountain called Fallenfluh (Falling Rock), covered in wild virgin forest. The roads leading up to it were narrow and winding, and drivers had to stop to open and close cow gates in intervals. At the top was a cliff overlooking farms and fields and cowherds tending their animals against the backdrop of the Alps. Fallenfluh was isolated and quiet, a perfect place for Baba's seclusion. 1622

At 6:00 AM, Thursday, July 12, Baba left for the mountain, accompanied by his hosts and guides, Hedi and Walter, as well as Adi Jr., Kaka, Chanji and Quentin. They squeezed into a Buick meant for five passengers, with all their luggage as well. Hedi was at the wheel, knowing full well what a gift it was to be Baba's driver. She later recalled:

> We drove along the Lake of Zurich for about half an hour—all still quiet, almost no people on the road, passing village after village. Baba wanted me to drive quicker and

so I did. Before starting, I had adjusted my rear-view mirror so that I could see Baba's face. He was seated in the back between two of his mandali, his head deeply wrapped up in a big shawl—his face hidden in shadow. For a long moment, I could not look away. Although I kept the wheel well in my hands, I felt as if my own action was slipping off and as if we were driving on a cushion, the wheels scarcely touching the ground. I was keeping my eyes always fixed on Baba in the mirror. I then saw his face getting brighter, and at the same time, I was strongly drawn to the wheel . . . Again I saw Baba's face more clearly radiant. Then I felt as if I were discharged from a circle and I was driving easily once more. 1934

They reached the village of Schwyz two hours later and breakfasted on tea, buttered bread and fruit. There, Hedi spent the night. The men set off behind Baba, who walked to the mountain ridge. He was wearing a shirt, sadra and hat and carrying a raincoat thrown over his shoulder. He drew a fifty-yard boundary and ordered the men not to cross it unless called. Each man was given a two-hour shift, keeping watch and ensuring that no one disturbed Baba in any way: "While working, I leave my physical body which has become dead to all feelings of touch. I would not even feel it if my body were hammered or cut up into pieces." 1934

Baba began his seclusion at 9:30 AM. He lay down on a mattress holding a mosquito net against his chest, and disappeared beneath two sheets, all of which Kaka had carried and set up for him. After three hours he clapped for Kaka and asked him to sit closer. He then began sitting up once every hour. 1933

But by noon, the whole of Fallenfluh was obscured by black clouds and driving rain, all except for the place where Baba was lying bathed in rays of sunlight, which even Hedi could see from the village. Meanwhile the men became drenched, so they built a small fire. Their only disturbance was caused by a few Swiss farm wives who want to collect firewood. Walter deterred then by saying that they could not proceed any farther because dangerous electrical experiments were being carried out. He gave them a few Swiss francs and they returned to their homes.

Baba arose from his seclusion at 4:30 in the afternoon, much sooner than expected, radiant and completely dry. He explained to the men, "I am very happy. I am satisfied with the work done here. It was better than at Assisi. When I work like this, a meeting of large numbers of my agents is held; but you cannot see them with your gross eyes. Sometimes, though, you can hear a rumble like boot steps." He later called the storm "Maya's usual opposition." 1934

After eating the last of their provisions, Baba and the men walked down to the place where they were to meet Hedi, who had felt an "inner urge" to come and get them sooner than she had been instructed. On the way back they stopped for coffee at a small restaurant, where Baba was serenaded by yodelers, whose singing he very much liked. They reached Zurich by 7:30 PM. Baba called everyone to his room to explain that he had successful met with "advanced souls" of the spiritual hierarchy, and he spelled out on the board, "I have drawn circle around the country so that it will not be involved in the coming war." True to Baba's word, Switzerland remained neutral throughout the bloody conflict. 1631

Baba spent his last days in Zurich meeting with disciples and engaged in interviews with people who wished to meet him. On July 16 he departed by rail for Marseilles, accompanied by Norina, Elizabeth, Rano, Nonny, Ruano, Delia and Quentin, as well as the three mandali. Baba became uncomfortable in his Western suit and wanted to take off the jacket and pants. Even though he was wearing a sadra underneath he looked around the carriage full of Swiss passengers and ruefully gestured, "Yes, I guess I had better not." 1632

Baba's four days in Marseilles included rushed visits to parks and the zoo, and a trip to the bird market. There they purchased thirteen birds, but one escaped. Baba explained, "It is of great spiritual significance to take birds from the West to the East. Each one represents a person. The bird that flew away is symbolic of one of my close disciples who will realize me but die before I break my silence. It was my will that the bird flew away. It will die in a matter of days. My circle has twelve members, so the thirteenth bird had to go. The same thing happened at the time of the Buddha, who was given thirty-two birds by his disciples." 1633

On the evening of July 20, Baba boarded the SS *Strathnaver* bound for India and his ashram at Nasik. There he continued planning for his second visit to Hollywood.

Chapter Twenty-Two

Hollywood — Take Two

While Baba carried on in India, Norina, Elizabeth and Pascal remained hard at work in New York making arrangements for Baba's upcoming trip to Hollywood. In September they sent a cable informing him that filming would start in just two months, informing him that his presence was now essential for his projects to proceed.

Baba invited Rustom, Adi Jr. and Beheram to come with him, but finances were such that they had to stay behind in India. Kaka Baria, Chanji, Adi Sr. and Baba's brother Jal came instead. On November 15, 1934, they sailed from Bombay on the SS *Tuscania* for Baba's eighth visit to Europe, his third voyage to America and second working visit to Hollywood.

Arriving in Marseilles, Baba and his party took a train via Paris to London's Victoria Station. It was the wedding day of the Duke and Duchess of Kent, and grand celebrations were being held throughout the city. Baba mingled to watch the big parade and intimately contact the crowds. From Buckingham Palace he took a mile-long walk, cutting across Hyde Park to the West End where he was again staying at Hygeia House.

During their five days in London, Quentin assured Baba that he'd help Margaret with the film's "spirit dances." They were both scheduled to accompany Baba to Hollywood to choreograph the sequences under his supervision. But Quentin was signed to open a new musical revue on London's West End and there was no getting out of it. 1644–46

Finishing his primary work for war preparations in Europe and then bringing his films closer to fruition, Baba and his party left England on December 5. They sailed on the SS *Majestic*—fittingly named as it was for the time being the largest ship in the world. Baba was given a splendid stateroom on B deck.

As the ship neared America, Baba made clear he'd meet no outsiders in New York—no new persons, interviews or publicity. But Norina had already informed certain people about the Master's arrival. She had also planned a great publicity campaign for his visit. Cabling this to Baba aboard ship, he fired back instructions to *cancel everything*—he'd absolutely grant no interviews. As the ship docked in New York harbor on December 12, a group of frenzied newspaper reporters and photographers tried to invade Baba's cabin. He declined meeting with them and instructed Chanji to send them away.

As often happened with Baba's arrivals in foreign countries, there was a delay, again due to an immigration officer's suspicion about his silence. This was the second time for this to happen as the Avatar tried to enter the Port of New York. After a long wait, the press gave up and dispersed. Then after an endless delay, Baba and his party finally managed to clear customs.

They were all taken to the Hotel Shelton Towers on Lexington Avenue at 48th Street, where Norina had arranged Baba's stay. A production meeting took place there between Baba, Norina, Gabriel Pascal and Karl Vollmöller. But a working agreement between the men was proving difficult to achieve. 1644-48

As principal screenwriter, Vollmöller wanted the scenario prepared at his New York office, while Pascal, as the director, preferred they work in his Hollywood office. So Baba instructed, "Both of you should fly to Hollywood to meet me there. I'll be coming by train within days." They agreed to this and flew to the West Coast to await his arrival. 1651

In the meantime, Baba had a change of heart, for on Thursday, December 13, he allowed Norina's planned reception to take place after all, at the Stokes' double townhouse in Greenwich Village. Over two hundred people attended, including Tallulah Bankhead, who happened to be in New York. This was Baba's third and final visit to the grand old residence. 1653

After three days in New York, Baba and his entourage boarded a train for his second trip westward across the American continent. In addition to the men he had brought with him, he was accompanied by Elizabeth, Norina, Minta, Nadine, Ruano, Rano and Nonny. It was to be a three-and-a-half-day journey to Los Angeles, and Baba would use the time to review the script, refining plot points and characters.

Changing trains in Chicago, they boarded a Santa Fe Railway train that would be making stops in Omaha, Denver, Santa Fe and Albuquerque. But the train was delayed leaving the station in Albuquerque. Suddenly, Baba spelled out on his palm, "Indian," and bolted out of the train with Ruano on his arm. The men quickly followed, anxious that the train was to leave in moments. They panicked. All their luggage was aboard.

Baba walked rapidly and abruptly turned down a side street. He knew where he was going and stopped where two Native Americans were standing on a street corner. The one selling souvenirs quickly turned and walked away. Baba stood facing the other one, who was tall, stout and ruddy-faced, a red bandana tied around his forehead. Their eyes met.

Baba then turned and hurried back, re-boarding the train just as the whistle blew and it began to pull out of the station. When Ruano related the incident to the others, Baba added, "He's one of my direct agents in charge of all the Americas," further explaining that he was only one of four in the entire world with miraculous powers. 1655–56 This fourth-plane *abdal* with infinite powers was capable of changing his body. He was the direct agent for all of

North, Central and South America, controlling all spiritual agents in these regions.

Following Baba's contact in Albuquerque, he and his party continued west and de-boarded at the now familiar Pasadena station on December 18. He seemed delighted to be back in California and was driven with his group to a rented house at 1840 Camino Palmero in West Hollywood, where they would be staying for the next four weeks.

After a lapse of almost two and a half years, Baba's return to Hollywood was strictly focused on the film's development, and his presence was unpublicized so as not to attract people seeking to meet him and disrupt his work. He met daily with Norina, Elizabeth, Vollmöller and his assistant, Drake, as well as with Pascal and his screenwriter friend, Hy (John) S. Kraft.

Baba again explained in detail the theme of creation, reincarnation, the planes and God-Realization: "[Acting is] a very good art, and if expressed properly has divine qualities with a wondrous effect." But he added that if done improperly, "it could have very negative effects. . . . [However] when inspired with love, art leads to higher realms [and] it will open the inner life for you. When you are lost in it, your ego diminishes. Infinite love appears and God is attained. So you see how art can lead one to find God. Drama has always been used to portray spiritual truth. There is great power in the spoken word and when used with music and dancing it becomes even more potent." [22]

Baba went on to observe that not only film but the best live theatre can give us a kind of play that portrays spiritual life. Both can illustrate the art of co-operative teamwork. A play begins with producers, directors and actors, and it comes to life before an audience. And in special circumstances when all are in harmony, a magical unity can well be created. Aw 18 (no. 1): 21

Baba viewed the world as his stage and he employed many metaphors linking his Universal work to films and acting: "I enjoy my real state of being the Eternal Producer of the vast, ever-changing, never-ending comedic film called the Universe. Aw 18 (no. 1): 37

Baba's ideas were revelations to these worldly men, and they found it difficult to envision portraying everything as Baba wished. When he had first heard about Baba, Kraft had been extremely skeptical. But after their first meeting, he came away shaken and told Pascal, "There's such a tremendous power emanating from that man!" Kraft found it impossible to say no to Baba, so he was engaged to collaborate on the second script.

There were now two film scenarios being developed: Vollmöller and Markey's *This Man David*, and the other by Hy Kraft and associates, entitled *How it All Happened*, tracing the evolution of consciousness and reincarnation. Meanwhile, Baba continued meeting with studio executives, directors and producers, but many still found it difficult to wrap their minds around incorporating spiritual themes into the material aspects of production to create an instructive presentation that the public would find appealing. They repeated the same maddening question over and over: "But is it box-office? Will it sell?"

Though these men met with Meher Baba for business discussions, they were touched by his divine personality, and many of them invited him to their homes. He consented to only a few of their invitations. Learning that Baba was again in town, directors Ernst Lubitsch and Josef von Sternberg got in touch with him. Baba also returned to Paramount, Universal, Fox and Warner Brothers studios, where he met with celebrities, some for the second or third time.

These included America's adored Native American actor, Will Rogers. Just a year before Baba's first visit to Hollywood, Rogers had said publicly, "What a great time in the world for someone to come along who really knew something." He got his wish. He was so taken with Baba that he asked to visit him in India, but he died in a plane crash eight months later. 1657 footnote

One day actor Maurice Chevalier stopped by. So moved by Baba's touch and embrace when meeting him in 1932, he wanted to meet him again and again. He, too, wanted to go to India. With Baba's love shining on his face, Chevalier seemed a totally changed man. Baba was also photographed with popular actress and singer Alice Faye. Aw 18 (no. 1): 4

Baba and his party also saw several films, including *Imitation of Life*, at the famous Pantages Theater at Hollywood and Vine. They took evening walks along the Boulevard. One of the women recalled wistfully how gorgeous the sunsets were, but they were hard to enjoy. Baba walked so fast that they had to run to keep up. 1656

One day Norina phoned her old friend Mercedes de'Acosta, telling her there was someone in town whom she had heard of and now should meet in person. Mercedes was a Cuban-American socialite and screenwriter who had many close friends in the arts, including actor Marlene Dietrich, dancer Isadora Duncan, painter Picasso, sculptor Rodin and composer Igor Stravinsky. As a young girl, Mercedes had written impassioned letters to Jesus and Mary Magdalene, as well as to Joan of Arc and other Christian saints.

Mercedes had been deeply depressed lately and did not want to see anyone. But Norina told her she'd have no regrets meeting this person. She wouldn't say who he was; it was a surprise. She finally persuaded Mercedes to come to a very special New Year's Eve gathering on December 31, 1934.

Norina was waiting at the door when her friend arrived. Seeing Baba, Mercedes felt am overwhelming warmth radiating from him. She rushed into his open arms, asking, "Who on earth are you?" Baba gestured, "I am you." Then he spelled out on his board, "Go out and bring me your revolver." Mercedes was stunned, as she had told no one about the gun in her glove compartment. She recounted her recent feelings: "Leaving the hospital weeks earlier I was in bad shape—no job and very alone. The old unhappy spells attacked me again. So I got my revolver, went up into the Hollywood hills and shot at targets I hung on trees. As I held the gun, I felt this might be a way of escape." She went to the car and returned, handing the revolver to Baba.

He took the bullets out one by one and handed the gun back, explaining, "Suicide isn't the solution. It only entails rebirth with the same and even much *worse* problems all over again. The only solution is God-Realization—to see God in everything. Everything is easy then. Promise me you'll put this gun away and never again think of suicide." Aw 18 (no. 1): 15

De'Acosta and Garbo

Feeling his compassion, Mercedes promised. She then told Baba about her dear friend, Greta Garbo. Of course, he knew all about Garbo, commenting, "You were husband and wife in a past life in Italy. That's why there's such love between you now." Mercedes said, "So this explains why Greta said at our first meeting, 'Oh, I've been looking for you.'"

Baba also revealed that Garbo had been a yogi in a previous life and had died suddenly before attaining spiritual advancement: "She has latent yogic powers in this life, too, but no spiritual elevation. She both suffers and enjoys simultaneously and will be in the pangs of such agony one day she may commit suicide. She needs my contact. If she sees me, all this will change."

On hearing of this from Mercedes, Garbo was even more anxious to meet Baba. She had missed her previous opportunity in 1932. In anticipation of this one she stayed up all night before the meeting with the Master but fell asleep at the last moment, missing her appointment with him yet again. Aw 18 (no. 1): 14

Mercedes became truly happy after meeting Baba, and she presented him with a portable record player. Baba sent her a handkerchief as a New Year's gift, directing her to never give it away. She said that she would always sleep with it under her pillow. Mercedes also invited Baba to tea at her house. Although he was apt to decline most invitations, for her he consented.

The following day, when his group arrived at Mercedes' beautiful home, he entered and marched straight up to the top floor and proceeded to open every closet and drawer in the house, spiritually cleansing tangled sanskaric impressions from the atmosphere.

As he returned to the kitchen, Mercedes' cook, Millie, glared at him. She was highly irritable and kept on only because she was so good at her job. Beaming a smile, Baba gently patted Millie on the shoulder and sat down for tea. As he was about to depart, Mercedes and her friends gathered on the porch, while the cook peered curiously through the screen door. Baba suddenly bolted back up the steps, shook the cook's hand and headed towards to the car.

A few days later, Mercedes went away for a week. When she returned she found her Millie transformed into a mild angelic creature—meek as a lamb. Puzzled, Mercedes asked her what produced such a change. Millie explained: "You'll find it hard to believe, but while you were away, I woke up one night to find my room flooded with light. The Master who came to tea entered my room. I got up out of bed and touched him, and I swear I felt his robe in my hands. For some reason I can't explain, I've not felt angry since that moment." 1660-62

On the way back from Mercedes home, Baba had asked the driver to circle three times around Greta Garbo's house at 193 North Carmelina Avenue in Brentwood, where she had been living for the past six months. Reflecting on Garbo's missed opportunities to meet him when she cancelled their dinner engagement in 1932 and now slept through her appointment on this visit, Baba said she would now have difficulty balancing her inner psychic and spiritual needs with the demands of a very public life, both onscreen and off. He had wanted to save her that difficulty, and for that she needed just one minute in his physical presence and the necessary work would have been done. He spelled out on the board, "Well, it just wasn't meant to be. It was not her destiny to come to me.... She wanted to ask me something, but instead [she] sent her message through Mercedes, who carried my reply to her. 'Past life recollections, rare and fascinating as they may be, have nothing to do with the spiritual path and are as insignificant as recalling a dream experienced during one's sleep last night.'" 1146

It was Garbo's fate to disappoint Baba, but how much more she had disappointed herself. A year later, on November 15, 1935, Baba cabled Mercedes, "My love and blessings will enable Greta to see life as beautiful, pure, divine and everlasting." MM 1:242

Garbo's career lasted only a few more years, as she had increasing difficulty finding that inner and outer balance. Ironically, her iconic line from *Grand Hotel,* "I just want to be alone," became her credo. Garbo left Hollywood and became a recluse in New York City, but perhaps Baba's having driven around her house saved her from a far worse fate.

Later, in the 1950s, Tom Molinari, the Broadway dancer mentioned earlier, happened to encounter Garbo walking in disguise on a Manhattan side-street with her little dog. He stooped and petted the dog affectionately. On his complimenting her adorable pet, she smiled and thanked him. They exchanged a few words, without Tom mentioning Meher Baba, but perhaps he carried an unspoken a message of help from the Master. Greta Garbo died in 1990 at the age of 85.

Mercedes was destined to meet Baba three more times. The next time she saw him was was in 1937, when she was traveling throughout India searching for gurus and spiritual masters. Baba spoke to her plainly:

I have to make myself clear, not because I want anything from you, but because I feel for you, and as you've come all the way from Europe to see India. There are three kinds of spiritual beings in India: the sensational, the unassuming but deep and quiet, and then there's the Man-God [Perfect Master] or the God-Man [the Avatar]. . . . The sensational types just make a show of their knowledge of Vedanta and give lofty talks on higher ideals of life and spirituality.

But it's all on the surface and just an outward show. They seek to create an impression, and people who go to them are impressed by *seeming miracles*, which are really nothing more than tantric tricks. This is undesirable—a sort of bargaining. I absolutely don't want this kind of faith.

The other type, unassuming and quiet, has deeper knowledge and experience because they're advanced souls. Even a few are Perfect Ones. They prefer a quiet life, and doing their work in silence are little known. The Sadgurus and Qutubs experience Godhood and manhood both, simultaneously. They have attained the spiritual heights and have also come back down to human level to help mankind. Their methods are peculiar and not understood by ordinary people. 1956–57

Returning to 1934, as film plans continued to develop, Mercedes agreed to work for Baba on story continuity for one of the films, alongside Malcolm and Jean's screenwriter friend, Garrett Fort. Fort had been interested in spirituality even as a child, and he came to love Baba so deeply that he would later join him in India.

Starting out in silent films, Fort's first talkie was the groundbreaking 1929 Rouben Mamoulian musical production, *Applause*. But many of Fort's screenwriting projects were in the horror and melodrama genres, including *Dracula* and *Frankenstein* (1931), *The Lost Patrol* (1934), *Dracula's Daughter* (1936), *The Mark of*

Zorro (1940), and *Blood on the Sun* (1945). He already had sixty-two Hollywood screen credits to his name. 1664

Baba's collaborators continued to refine their work. In one scenario, Vollmöller envisioned a husband and wife achieving God-Realization together. Baba took Vollmöller aside on New Year's Day 1935 to explain that this could never happen: "Souls united in wedlock can never be Realized simultaneously together—never does it happen." Vollmöller asked why this was so, so Baba drew a diagram: "Because in the chain of births and deaths, each opposite sex changes simultaneously; that is, male becomes female and female becomes male." Baba drew a curving vertical line denoting the changing of male and female forms to illustrate his point:

> Changing their sex for many lifetimes, two souls reincarnate together until they drift apart at a point nearest their Realization. The secrets of life are completely unintelligible to the human mind, and so they're never revealed as they are, but in different methods and shapes. Love, real or divine, doesn't evolve, nor is it realized by temporal human love [lust]. Both are quite different. The best temporal human love cannot compare to divine love.

Baba said just as there are infinite shades of color in various flowers there are also diverse delicate differences in human love. He then dictated to Vollmöller the details of how the God-Realization scene should be portrayed on the screen.

He also gave instructions for a spirit dance and resurrection scene to be shown after the character dies, specifying, "This scene will have seven different movements accompanied by seven different musical themes, with seven different colors in the background"—the Divine Seven yet again.

Meanwhile, Margaret, Quentin and others were assigned the task of working out the choreography for this scene, and its development would continue in Nasik during 1937, after some of the

Westerners were invited to stay there. Baba assigned each one a very specific job. Margaret was given the themes for six dances that Baba wished her to create for the film. After each was rehearsed, it was performed before him. One was called "The Mirror Dance." 2527

When the time came for Baba to leave Hollywood and return to India with Gabriel Pascal, Hy Kraft shook himself awake from what he called an "Eastern maze" at the last minute and refused to go.

Standing: Brother Jal, Minta Toledano, unidentified woman, Meher Baba, Norina Matchabelli, Nadine Tolstoy, Elizabeth Patterson, Rano Galey and Adi K. Irani. Seated: Jean Adriel, Nonny Gayley and Ruano Bogislav, Hollywood, December 1934 — January 1935.

More Frustrations in Hollywood

Baba candidly revealed his Hollywood challenges in correspondence with Will and Mary Backett, an elderly Quaker couple who had met him in London in 1932. He dictated a letter to them from Hollywood:

My dear ones,   December 14, 1934

After a brief two-day stay in New York, I've come here. The seven days in rough seas, the busy time in New York, and again a long four-day cross-country train journey; the thought of the film and money hanging all the while in mind, the visits and interviews resumed ever since I set foot here with everyone who could help—all these things are so tiresome.

There are no hopes of getting any financial backing for an independent production of this type, which every businessman feels is a big enterprise involving such great risk. . . . So activities are directed to find a producer to whom the story could be sold, so those who invested in this project may get their money back.

If an independent producer buys the story, then of course there will be no need for me to stay, unless they themselves ask me to. So, for the present I've decided if during my stay, independent production isn't arranged for lack of funds or financial support, I'll hand over the script to dear Norina and Elizabeth telling them either to sell it or get it produced as they think best.

I can't stay here indefinitely. I have to see to my other affairs, the mandali and others on that side too; and if nothing is arranged, I'll leave here probably by early January. They're still trying their very best—Norina, Elizabeth and

Nonny—and many important people in the picture are brought in for interviews—nice people indeed, ready and willing to help, but couldn't for one reason or another.

In short, they all tried their best and are still trying, leaving nothing undone. I saw everyone brought to me for contact, and explained to each one my idea and object of making this film. And although they all sympathized, agreed and appreciated a splendid scheme like this, none could come forward with the financial help that is needed for a production of this kind. . . .

But I will still try for a few days to see as many as they bring, and explain the same thing over and over, however tedious and tiresome. After trying till the last moment of my stay here, if nothing is arranged for an independent production by January 8 or 9, I'll leave here for Vancouver, and sail by the Canadian Pacific liner, SS *Empress of Canada*. It leaves Vancouver on the twelfth.

Changing ships in Hong-Kong on February second to the Japanese *Fushimi Maru*, we arrive in India on the fifteenth or sixteenth after a month crossing the seas; then, as I told you, I go to the Himalayas for a year for great work that is ahead of me, and in which you all, my dearest ones, have to participate in the future—each in his or her capacity. . . . I know, my dears, how hard it will be for those who love me as you to be separated so long. But rest assured, dearest, I'll always be with you.

Just try to realize how I have to do it all, simply for the sake of the work which I wish you all to participate in, you, mine own, would take it all so willingly, so lovingly. I know you love me too deeply to need telling you this. This is my first Christmas in the West. I wish you all were here with me. I miss you so, but I am and will always be with you. With all love, [signed] M.S. Irani 1657–59; HT, Letter 181

This long, candid letter plainly revealed Baba's Hollywood frustrations. With all the studios closed for Christmas, he visited the bohemian colony in the Dunes of Oceano, about a three-hour drive up the coast from Los Angeles. This was the same place where he had exiled Meredith Starr and wife Margaret two years earlier. Although Starr's visit was to be only for a weekend, he had

L to R: Sam Cohen, Meher Baba, Hugo Seeling and John Doggett at the Dunes, Oceano, California, December 25 or 26, 1934

retuned there after Baba left for China, staying that entire summer attempting to turn the colony into his idea of an ashram, meaning of course, that everyone had to meditate and follow his regimen.

Baba would spending two days and one night among these bohemian artists who called themselves Dunites. They were a group of eccentric characters and spiritual seekers caring little for social conventions—a true early hippy colony established in the 1920s.

The renowned "Sufi Sam" Lewis was among them, as well as Sam Cohen, who would become a lifelong disciple. Baba stayed overnight in a nearby cabin.[23]

Sam Cohen later wrote a letter to Filis Frederick, telling her about an experience he had while sitting on the beach with Baba twenty years before: "He looked at me and pointed out to the Ocean. I said, 'Oh, yes, Baba, it's very big.' He shook his head and again waved his hand. 'Oh, yes, Baba it's beautiful.' Once again he gestured no. Then, a loud voice boomed, 'I AM AS BIG AS THE OCEAN.' Now, we all know Baba doesn't speak." Aw 11 (no. 3): 28

Baba returned to Hollywood to continue his work and make more new contacts. Among them was William Hurlbut, a friend of Norina's, as well as a prolific and successful Broadway playwright whose works included *Lilies of the Field*. He had moved to Hollywood in the early 1930s, where he became best known for his tenure at Universal Studios from 1933 to 1935. He adapted *The Bride of Frankenstein* novel as well as a new story, *Imitation of Life,* into successful screenplays that Baba had seen earlier at the Pantages Theatre on Hollywood and Vine.

Hurlbut met Baba on January 4. He said that he found it hard to live in the world, attending to his work and his spirituality at the same time. Baba said: "You mean spirituality made practical." "Yes," he replied, "that's it exactly!" Baba assured him, "It's very easy, very simple. Its very simplicity makes it so difficult."

"Is it really? How strange," Hurlbut replied. Baba explained: "People's ideas of God and spirituality are so far-fetched, fantastic and funny! Names and terms don't matter at all. It's *the feeling* that counts." "What should I do to feel and get a glimpse of it?" Hurlibut asked. Baba answered, "For a man in your position in modern times it's alright to live as you do, always keeping your mind on higher aspirations. Frankly, you're spiritual without even being conscious of it."

Hurlbut wondered if Baba really meant this, but he was reassured, "Yes, you're far more spiritual than even you yourself know. But there's still so much more you can do. Let me explain." Baba then told him to concentrate on a very particular thought several minutes every day.

On January 6, actress and drama coach Constance Collier came to see Baba at the house in West Hollywood. She lamented to him, "Oh, I have hundreds of friends, but none could be called a true one. I'm feeling so alone." Baba gestured, "I am your friend—the real one."

"Yes, I believe it. I don't feel alone since I've known you. Oh, please remember me," she begged. Baba assured her, "I am with and in you all the time." Collier's career continued for fifteen more successful years after meeting the Master, with twenty-one major Hollywood films.

Tullio Carminati, a screen actor Baba especially wanted in his film, came to see him that evening. Years before, Carminati had performed on stage in Europe with Norina in *The Miracle*. When he arrived, Tullio remarked to Norina, "My God, just look at you! You look so much better than you did before. There's really something so different—divine. I can clearly see it." Pointing to Baba, Norina replied, "It is his divinity you see in me. Just look at him and see for yourself."

Final Frustrations

After weeks of discussions, Baba finally acknowledged the futility of his Hollywood projects. Throwing up his hands, he decided return to India. All involved were shocked, pleading his personal presence was so necessary to inspire and guide them at every stage. Baba told them:

This picture could take months or even a year or more to produce. I can't stay here indefinitely. I have my work in India. Although important, this film is just a side-work. But I came all this distance in response to your requests and repeated cables to work with you and bring it to this practical stage. . . .

Make the film now as I've instructed, adhering to the points and spiritual themes I've dictated. Wherever I am, I'll always guide and help you internally. This is my work. And my guiding spirit will always enable you to tackle difficult issues that may arise in it.

So don't worry at all, and just go on with it, with everyone cooperating—each in his or her individual way. Remember, I'm always with you . . . but you must always *keep* me *with you, meaning you should never, ever leave me alone*. MM 3:363

Baba often used pets in his Universal work, and just before leaving Los Angeles, he asked for a "Hollywood" puppy to bring back to India. He was taken to a kennel to see a pedigreed tan cocker spaniel. He liked the puppy and bought him for $35, naming him "Chummy" after "Chum," an earlier dog he had in India. 1664-65

So ended Meher Baba's direct involvement with Hollywood. He departed on January 7, 1935, taking a train north to San Francisco, where he visited Golden Gate Park. He continued on by rail to Vancouver, Canada, where he arrived on the tenth. There he boarded the *Empress of Canada*, bound for Hawaii and the Orient.

It was an unbelievably painful voyage with little rest, as Baba's health had deteriorated alarmingly, and he was suffering from persistent chest pains and heart cramps. These had begun about the time that he arrived in London and lasted throughout his voyage to

Left: Baba petting his new cocker spaniel puppy, named Chummy, Hollywood, January 1935. Right: Baba and Chummy a year and a and a half later at Meher Retreat Ashram, Nasik, 1936

America and trip across the country to Hollywood. The pains continued until he reached India in mid-February 1935.

If such poor health didn't make for a terribly uncomfortable journey, the cross-Pacific weather was icy and windy, such that he was unable to take his accustomed walks on the deck. Compounding this was yet another new ailment—gum disease.

Gums and teeth need vital oxygen to remain healthy. Baba's determination not to speak deprived them of oxygen and they had deteriorated. The pain was accompanied by constant bleeding. It was difficult for him to rest for even a few minutes before he'd have to spit out blood and saliva throughout the night. Before long, his last teeth would have to be pulled. 1665–66

Weaknesses vs. Compassion

After setting sail from Honolulu, Baba told Chanji, "There's one soul aboard this ship I want to contact." The next day, Chanji went to the laundry room to iron Baba's pants. There he met a woman, Margaret Scott, who narrated her very troubled life, saying she was desperately thinking of divorcing her husband and even contemplating suicide.

Chanji spoke compassionately to her of Baba, who relayed to her through Chanji that she should not to get a divorce. Chanji talked with her for a few minutes each evening, until she became eager to meet Baba and receive his blessing. Baba agreed to see her when disembarking at Shanghai, providing no one else was around. As Baba left the ship, she was dismayed by the hordes of people at the dock. Then, to her amazement, the crowd suddenly dispersed, enabling her a precious few moments with Baba. He consoled her and made the sign of the cross on her forehead. 1668

Margaret met Baba again in 1952, when she told him, "I'm so sorry I caused you such suffering, Baba, for I know you've suffered for me." Baba assured her, "But your love has so compensated for all the suffering. I know deep down that you do love Baba so much. Baba loves you too." Margaret replied, "Sometimes I'm very naughty, just because I don't understand. But now, I think I understand." Baba explained:

> The most important thing is that we must be honest to God, to Baba, ourselves and humanity, in the sense that in loving God there's to be no compromise. I know exactly how you've tried, what you doubt and how you've tried to overcome this confusion, and how you've eventually come to me. And be sure of my love to help you. Baba helps you through his love. Love God and Baba, and leave the rest to Divine Will.

Margaret saw Baba again the following morning and asked, "Why did you say yesterday I hadn't changed?" Baba replied, "You loved me when you last saw me, and you love me *now*, so you've not changed. This means you've not failed me. . . . Everyone commits mistakes, unless one is perfect and one with God, but love for Baba wipes away all those mistakes."

"I thought I failed you and made you suffer," Margaret confessed. Baba further explained:

> As for suffering, I've suffered for myself and for the whole world and mostly for my intimate ones; so, definitely, I've suffered for you. But you love me, so this suffering has been compensated. I know exactly how you've tried, what you doubt, how you've tried to overcome this confusion, and how you'll eventually come to me. All that means you have not failed me.
>
> Everyone commits mistakes unless one is Perfect and One with God, but love for Baba wipes away those mistakes. We must remember that God is *all Truth, all Beauty*. And in our love for God, for Baba, we must be 100% honest. Purity, honesty and love; God wants these three things. And you love Baba, so don't bother about anything else.
>
> Love can wipe away every weakness, every mistake. When you love Baba one hundred percent, then God who's within you knows that love, and it's enough for Him. He's in all, He knows what we speak. He is wonderful, infinite, and the only one. He's real, and defects will go in sinners, in animals, in inanimate objects and in everyone. He's here now within those defects. He knows what we speak.
>
> He is wonderful, infinite, and only He is real. He knows you love Baba. So don't worry about your weaknesses or past-life sanskaras. They'll all go. And even if they linger on, love will one day totally consume them. In the Ocean of Love, everything disappears. However dirty our minds might be, the love we have in Him will cleanse it completely, like washing and being pristinely clear.

> Inside you is a lake of love for Baba. So for every difficulty or weakness that persists, you needn't bother. It's being totally washed off. Just honestly love with all your heart, thinking not so much of yourself but of the Beloved. So don't worry even you feel doubts or confusion and can't love me as I want you. Don't worry, because Baba loves you, and that's all that matters. 3061–62

Everyone whom Baba had chosen to help with his filmwork—writers, producers, directors and actors—underwent some form of spiritual transformation. In this way Baba directed their lives into vital new inner channels that they'd never experienced before.

Pascal and Alexander Markey nursed an ambition to film Baba's life. It was to be called *The Slippers of a Perfect Master*. Curiously, both decided to postpone this major opus to make a film on Gandhi's life instead. It was better box office in those days.

Markey had some property twenty miles northeast of Hollywood that he wished to dedicate to Baba, but the offer was graciously declined. Baba observed that it was not quite the right time. The property was subsequently used by Markey and Jean Adriel in 1946 for their *New Life Foundation*. It was sold when they found better property in Ojai, California, which later became Baba's west coast mountain retreat center known today as Meher Mount.

Markey travelled to India in 1954 and was present in a crowd of seven thousand when Baba delivered his shocking Final Declaration. Sadly, in the eyes of history neither he nor Pascal ever shot a single frame of the world's most incredible and photogenic hero. Aw 18 (no. 1): 1

The Odyssey of Gabriel Pascal, Baba's Phoenix

Always the adventurer, Gabriel had left Hollywood, traveling with Baba to India. But because none of Baba's films were ever made, Pascal was stranded there. A realistic man would have despaired, but Pascal welcomed the opportunity to be close to Baba. He donned pilgrim garb and traveled the dusty roads of India, visiting holy places with Baba on his journeys to contact the God-mad *masts,* a vitally important aspect of the Avatar's work in this Advent.

Baba later reminisced about Pascal, "His heavy Hungarian accent and pronunciations were often humorous. He'd say something and add, '*Balief* [believe] me, Baba, *balief* me!'" Pascal himself recalled his Indian pilgrimage and ashram stay with great nostalgia: "For the first time in my life I was really free. I was poor and desiring nothing, my poverty was pure."

Of course in time the old desires did return, and about a year later Pascal resurfaced in the Western world. However, he never gave up the thought that one day he'd return to India and become a renunciate or a monk.

Baba's disciple Eruch Jessawala said that as a farewell gift Baba gave Pascal a pair of sandals he himself had worn—a truly priceless gift. It's said the sandals and a small beaten-up suitcase were Pascal's sole possessions when he was put ashore in San Francisco by a sea captain he'd befriended in Bombay and hitched a ride with across the Pacific.

Pascal immediately went to the upscale St. Francis Hotel where he knew the Italian manager. It took a while for the manager to recognize him, bearded and dressed in Hindu garb. As always, Pascal chose the best room, sensing great changes were about come into his life. It was time to give Hollywood another try. But at checkout time, a different day-manager who didn't know Pascal demanded he leave his only suitcase in lieu of his unpaid hotel bill.

So he offered Baba's sandals in settlement: "Do you realize these sandals are worth millions? They belonged to a seer in India. I tell you they'll bring luck and you're fortunate to have them for my stinky little hotel bill." Pascal's dark eyes seemed to gleam with yogic power. Being a bit superstitious, the manager took the sandals and let him go.

Years later Pascal returned to the St. Francis Hotel to pay his old bill and collect his precious sandals. But it seems the previous day-manager was no longer there. He had become a multimillionaire shareholder in a mega-corporation. After being tracked down, he refused Pascal's offer, but did let him see the precious sandals, now kept in a safe-deposit box. A butler brought in the worn cowhide sandals, the work of an Indian village cobbler, displayed on a solid gold plate. ITS 89–90; Aw 18 (no. 1): 16

> By 1938, *Time* would name Gabriel Pascal one of the ten most influential people in the world.

Pascal then re-embarked on a brief but hectic career in the film industry, but although he was still a dynamic force and was greatly talented, he lacked discipline and often lost his head. Still, he was the only director George Bernard Shaw entrusted with his plays, even adjusting his stage scripts to the new cinema medium.

Shaw considered Pascal a genius and engaged him to direct his 1941 soon-to-be hit, *Major Barbara*—which curiously sounds like *Meher Baba*—as well as *Caesar and Cleopatra*. The $5.5 million epic was the most expensive movie produced at that time. Pascal filmed it by the seat of his pants in London under the noses of German bombers during the Blitz.

It is said that Pascal's cinematic genius did for film what Diaghilev did for Russian Ballet. He was the only producer ever to have major movie deals with seven countries on three continents:, including Hungary, Italy, Germany, China, India, England, and the U.S. [24]

Pascal managed to retain an option on Shaw's play *Pygmalion* by borrowing money from Margaret Scott. He successfully staged the play on Broadway and was nominated for an Academy Award for its 1938 film adaptation. Copies of the film were requested by Adolf Hitler as well as Mussolini, who promised to send it on to Pope Pius XI. But Pascal was unable to mount the musical version. Even Rodgers and Hammerstein tried for over a year to recast *Pygmalion* into a musical, but finally gave up, saying the material was simply not adaptable.

While he suffered due to his own erratic nature, Pascal loved Baba profoundly. And though it may appear he drifted away, he never lost his inner contact with the Master. In his last letters to Baba he talked hopefully of joining him again in India: "I'll bring my cameraman and crew to film two pictures—*Gandhi* and *The Slippers of a Perfect Master*. When you read the scenario of *Slippers* you will laugh tears. I'll bring it with me at the end of August. In your everlasting arms. I know you are always with me."

Pascal's final contact with Baba was for two hours in July 1952, in Scarsdale, New York, where Baba was recuperating from his automobile accident in Prague, Oklahoma. When they discussed his proposed biopic of Gandhi, Baba emphasized the need for a spiritual setting and said that he wanted it to be filmed in India. Aw 6 (no. 4): 46

Pascal promised to bring his new Cinemascope equipment to film Baba's birthday celebration in February 1954, as well as the Master's tour in India at Andhra, where he would ignite the hearts of over a hundred and fifty thousand devotees and announce to the world that he was the Avatar—Christ come again. Air India phoned Pascal twice to let him know where to find Baba on the tour, but he failed to arrive as expected. Baba appeared sad, since he had wanted that darshan filmed for posterity. [25]

Months later, Pascal had to cancel another trip at the last minute due to serious health issues. He was diagnosed with intestinal cancer and admitted to New York's Roosevelt Hospital, missing his final opportunity to film the God-Man's return in the new Cinemascope wide-screen process. He penned a final note from his hospital bed:

> Dearest Beloved Baba, my body is so weak as never before, but my spirit so bright as never before.
> You have the balance in your own hands, and I trust you're playing the Divine game as to human rules. I was a prince, a courtier and officer; a poet, great adventurer and artist. Maybe you'll give me back my wings. I hang now between heaven and earth on your grace. Your love is my only comfort in this valley of misery. Ever your *Phoenix,*—
> [signed] Gabriel

Pascal passed on July 6, 1954, just two days after posting this letter. He left the world heartbroken and penniless—not unheard of for those whom the Master had chosen as the apple of his eye. 2526

Baba was informed by cable. He remained still for a couple of minutes after reading it. He said, "Had Pascal come when I wanted him, he wouldn't have died." Still, he was Baba's to the end. Baba replied: "Pascal has come to me." 3538; Gi 127–28

Lyricist Alan Jay Lerner and composer Frederick Loewe were responsible for a succession of acclaimed Broadway musicals, including *Camelot* and *Brigadoon.* Following Pascal's death, they composed a brilliant musical version of *Pygmalion* in their 1956 landmark Broadway hit, *My Fair Lady.* Pascal himself had devised the plot point of elocution lessons with the famous line and musical number, "The rain in Spain stays mainly in the plain."

Pascal's estate, worth nothing at the time of his death, grew to $2,000,000 after his passing—a huge sum in the 1950s. Hollywood then optioned the movie rights for *My Fair Lady*, with George Cukor as director. The now-classic film was named 1964's Best Picture at the Academy Awards and received seven additional Oscars. In 1933, Baba had told Pascal, "You are my 'Phoenix,' and you will work for me in the future—particularly through motion pictures." And so he did. GM 126–27

Baba indicated that the real reason he had shown such interest in producing a movie was to draw Markey and others like Pascal and Garrett Fort to himself and give them his intimate spiritual contact. And although they didn't know it, all three were souls whom the Master had contacted in past Advents. The movies weren't essential, as his primary work with them was to renew that contact and push them forward to their next level spiritually.

Baba later disclosed to Markey, "Someday the themes we're discussing now will form the basis of an entirely new trend in motion pictures." But for all the time and effort the various writers, producers and actors devoted to Baba's projects, no completed screenplays ever emerged, only treatments. These included *This Man David*, about a messianic figure, David Lord, who comes to a southern American town.

Another treatment, *A Touch of Ma*ya, traced the evolution of consciousness to human form, and then through three people who played out their karma over a span of countless centuries. Although none of Baba's projects were ever brought to the silver screen, the synopses and treatments of the two final proposals are tucked away, preserved in film archives for future use. 5415-19

Baba's Western followers had invested heavily with shares in his film projects, having been assured of film roles. Years later, Elizabeth asked Margaret what she'd done with all her valuable shares. Quite matter-of-factly, Margaret replied "Oh, I burned them, of course." Elizabeth almost careened into a ditch. 1615

CHRIST COME AGAIN

Chapter Twenty-Three

The Ten Commandments

Cinematically, Baba's ideas for projects were well before their time in 1930s Hollywood, as well as being novel revelations even for sophisticated movie executives. Still, everyone in Hollywood with whom Baba worked was deeply impressed with the Master's divine personality.

As already mentioned, among the film luminaries Baba met in 1932 were Cecil B. De Mille and his wife Constance. She met him again in 1934. In May 1958, before leaving his home in New Jersey to be with Baba at his center in Myrtle Beach, devotee Harold Rudd wrote to DeMille to say that Baba had seen his latest movie, *The Ten Commandments,* and liked it very much. Baba had made a special trip to Bombay earlier in January, where reserved tickets were waiting.

DeMille's reply, in which he wrote of his great appreciation and the privilege of meeting Meher Baba, was forwarded to Harold at Myrtle Beach, just as Baba was there for his third and final visit. On May 6, he summoned Harold to the Lagoon Cabin to read the letter to him. The following day he had it read out to all of his disciples in the Barn. 4398

Messages of appreciation passed back and forth—Baba's appreciation for the film, and DeMille's happiness that this "venerable religious leader" remembered their meeting and for his "silent work and prophetic leadership" during his visits.

Meher Baba was an avid movie-goer, using the focused attention and emotions of the audience to conduct his Universal work, and on its completion, abruptly leaving the theatre. Almost always, he only saw as much of a film as he needed, after which everyone in his party had to follow him out. But in a rare move he allowed the men to see *The Ten Commandments* through to its end.

Another rare exception had occurred in Marseilles in 1934 with a few of the Western women, when he took them to see, not one, but two movies on the same day. But the film they went to see that evening turned out to be hopelessly boring. Everyone wanted to leave, but Baba insisted on sitting through it until the very end. The movie was French, and Baba kept nudging Rano to translate the dialogue. She was embarrassed, as it was so risqué that it was almost pornographic. Delia asked, "Baba, darling, are you *sure* your spiritual work isn't over yet?" It was so bad a few of them fell asleep. 1633

Baba also arranged for the women to see *The Ten Commandments*. He told them that Moses was a true seeker and had indeed heard the voice of God on Mt. Sinai. When he saw the burning bush, the "Light of God" and Divine *Noor* (Light) of the sixth plane, he was so overpowered that he instantly lost consciousness.

Baba commented on the fact that the film failed to show that particular scene, nor did it show Moses striking the rock with his rod for fresh water to quench the thirst of the desert wanderers. He revealed that this event in Moses' life foreshadowed his own life as Jesus, who would complete the work Moses had begun.

Baba also said that God didn't literally come to Moses and hand him actual stone tablets with the commandments carved into them, but that God has inscribed these rules on the inner tablet of every person's heart, experienced as an innate understanding of right and wrong: "People believe the Commandments were given from above. Little do they know that they are latent in every human being, and references to stone tablets are but symbolic representations. Each human is aware of the commandments, but human nature is such that every effort is made to circumvent them." Just as the Israelites gave themselves up to drunken orgies and idol worship, leading to Moses' symbolic breaking of the tablets, we give ourselves up to our lower selves and break the tablets of our own hearts. AO 96

Baba also commented:

> Moses was on the sixth plane, seeing God everywhere outside himself, but not yet merging in Him. His "seeing" the Promised Land of Israel, but not being able to enter it, is symbolic. Dropping his body, Moses *Realized* God, thus entering the real Promised Land.
>
> I liked this picture very much; it was well made and acted and has much to give those who are able to receive it. Ramses II in his very next life entered the Spiritual Path [the first subtle plane]. The old Pharaoh, Seti, received *mukti* [Infinite Bliss and liberation from future births] because he took Moses' name at the moment he was dying. 4239

Baba revealed that the Egyptians were not ignorant of Moses' spiritual level, and that he had been Abraham in a past minor Advent. Baba mentioned Moses again in the 1950s in Los Angeles, when a young Jewish devotee, Dana Field, asked how he could best serve him. Baba warned him that it was difficult: "I want your body, mind, possessions. My love brought you here. Moses and Peter served imperfectly, doubting and denying me, and so will you." 3569 "Moses prepared the way for Jesus, but didn't control his anger. Peter literally denied Jesus." SG 156; HM 435; AO 212

In the end, everything came down to Hollywood's reluctance to portray things the way Baba wished. Blending material production aspects and spiritual themes with audience appeal was an insurmountable challenge to the pre-digitalized and financially floundering Hollywood of the early 1930s.

Following this second failed attempt to get his movies off the ground, Baba left America and wouldn't return until seventeen years later, in 1952, to open his new spiritual center and "home in the West," in Myrtle Beach, South Carolina. But the Silent Master's visits to MGM, Paramount, Universal, Fox, RKO and Warner Brothers laid cables so that future generations of his "new humanity" would recognize that his work in Hollywood was enormously productive and is far from over.

"My Work is Universal"

Through his work in the world, Meher Baba came into contact with people of all castes, creeds and orientations—from the poorest peasant to the richest Hollywood tycoon. Each person had their own tendencies, temperaments, inclinations and weaknesses, as well as their good qualities.

In the beginning, Baba might overlook or even pamper some of those prejudices, tolerating weaknesses in temperament until his disciples gave them up, one by one, and came to see and live their lives from a more spiritual viewpoint:

> So if a Hindu comes to see me, I look to his caste—Brahmin, untouchable, etc., then talk and deal with him accordingly. In the case of a Parsi, a Muslim or a Christian, I explain things as the person likes best, pleasing their temperament, inclinations, prejudices, etc., so they can digest what I want to give, and gradually overcome and rise above prejudices.
>
> Thus, over the years Hindus, Muslims, Parsis, Christians, all my mandali have learned to live as one family. Their religious and other prejudices practically destroyed, and convinced now they were false and unreal; that real religion is One—Universal brotherhood and love for all alike. This is the spiritual end of life and my only mission. HM 476

The Next Voice You Hear

As a side note to this final Hollywood chapter, in 1950, almost two decades after Meher Baba's work in Hollywood, MGM produced a movie called *The Next Voice You Hear*. It was released during the Cold War era, a time of great unrest throughout the world. [26]

Helmed by William Wellman, a roster MGM director, the movie starred James Whitmore and Nancy Davis, a woman just two years away from marrying the man who would reach out to USSR President Mikhail Gorbachev, challenging him to "tear down that wall" in Berlin. President Ronald Reagan's challenge not only brought down the wall, but exactly coincided with Baba's most beloved Mehera leaving this world and passing to him forever in 1989.

The Next Voice You Hear was developed by Charles Shnee. According to the storyline, God would deliver an urgent message to humanity over a period of a week by "breaking His silence as His voice is heard on radios worldwide."

But of course that had been Meher Baba's plan: to break his silence on coast-to-coast radio from the Hollywood Bowl. *The Next Voice You Hear* was one of the first MGM "message movies," a concept spearheaded by Dore Schary, the new production chief at Metro Goldwyn Mayer.

In a striking 1951 coup originating from MGM corporate headquarters in New York, Schary toppled Louis B. Mayer from his twenty-seven-year term at the helm of MGM. Mayer had invented the great Hollywood "star system" during its golden years and was considered by many to be the iconic Godfather *and* Pope of Hollywood.

But these were also the tumultuous early days of television, and the landmark Supreme Court decision severing the monopoly of big studios from the theaters showing their films—a staggering revenue blow to Hollywood. New strategies were desperately called for. With his take-over, Schary insisted that the studio place less emphasis on its formerly successful musical and dance genres to focus on relevant *"message pictures"*—a term Louis B. Mayer scornfully derided.

Whether Charlie Shnee or Dore Schary ever met Baba in the early 1930s or had heard of him and his planned coast-to-coast radio silence breaking we'll never know. But the premise of this film had all the earmarks of having been poignantly inspired by Baba's silent impact on Hollywood a decade and a half earlier. So Hollywood had the final word by having God break his silence on the radio after all.

The theme so intrigued production chief Schary that he wrote a fascinating book based on the making of this "God-breaking-His-silence" picture. *Case History of a Movie* revealed the full story behind the film: how it was made, from its inception and screenplay development, casting, and pre- and post-production periods, right down to its final release. According to the book, the sneak preview of the film took place on a chilly, rainy Friday evening "with the smell of wet wool," in a Glendale, California, movie house. It was just before the final studio cut and public release in theaters nationwide.

The Next Voice You Hear received a Golden Globe nomination as best film in the category of "promoting international understanding." The performances and the story's characters are a bit corny by modern standards, and one's chances of catching it on television used to be as rare as an archangel appearing in human form. As of the publication of this book, it was available to stream on television.

Writer George Sumner Albee said, "Wouldn't it be something if God actually came on the radio and gave people such a scare they'd wake up and behave themselves!" That quote appeared in

Dore Schary's *Case History of a Movie*, elevating the movie yet more above its station.

It also placed the "germ" of the story in the days of radio, when the magical medium would be a natural place for God to speak to "Joe Smith, American." During the time it was written and filmed, this story must have seemed far less ludicrous than it might today. Reviewers observed:

> "It's a good idea that the audience never actually hears God's voice; it's all in reported speech, as it should be, because how could His voice be duplicated in a way worthy of Him?"

> "Would this be a movie about the Second Coming as seen through the eyes of those who created this film so many decades ago?"

> "A tenderhearted, wise movie . . . It did a wonderful job in getting across this wonderful news."

> "This movie should be required viewing for every man, woman and child in the world. It makes you think, as it was intended to."

> "Wonderful storyline, superb acting, tremendous direction with visuals at their best for those times. This movie needs to be remade . . . but very carefully."

It bears repeating that Baba said the Perfect Masters saw to it that the motion picture was invented and unveiled at his birth for his Advent, and he would use this powerful medium in his ongoing work toward spiritual globalization.

To that end, 1894, the year of Meher Baba's birth, saw the Thomas Edison Corporation establish the first motion-picture studio using the first movie camera built by William Kennedy Laurie Dickson under Thomas Edison's patent and commission. Edison's

Meher Baba sitting at a moviola viewing his first sound-filmed newsreel at London's Paramount Studios, April 1932.

assistant, Thomas Watson, had met Baba in England and financed the his first trip to America in 1931. Edison's camera was called the *Kinetograph*. Soon after, a Kinetoscope parlor opened at 1155 Broadway in New York's Bowery where spectators watched films for twenty-five cents. The next year, French brothers Auguste and Louis Lumière invented the Cinématograph, a camera and projector combo. Their first screening was of a film showing an oncoming train. Panicked theater patrons stampeded wildly out into the street.

That primitivism had changed radically by the 1930s, when Hollywood embraced the highest concentration of intellect and sophistication America had ever seen. But for all its intellectual bravura, its focus on the bottom line required finding the perfect "commercial cinema" equation, something Meher Baba repeatedly banged his head against from 1932 through 1935.

Visionless producers and writers who were offered true gold let it slip away with their catchy little caveat: *"But is it box-office?"* Adi K. Irani was present during all of the 1930s film discussions in Hollywood. In 1974, speaking at rock music's Pete Townshend's London recording complex, Adi recalled somewhat bitterly:

> We discussed the film over and over with screen writers and producers, but they couldn't agree on anything at all. They felt the entire material was so heavy and told me in a particularly strong manner there was enough material here to produce ten films. They started fighting over every word —"Maya—no Maya etc.," words Baba Himself suggested.
>
> All we learned from them were the words—*"Box Office! Box-office appeal!"* They didn't want it at all. I got fed up and told Baba it wasn't at all possible; we'd never get it produced. By then they had so diluted and simplified the theme it had lost all its flavor and charm and had become just one more box office story.

In the end, the film project was entirely given up. Hollywood historian Thomas Schatz commented on this problem

> By the mid-1930s studios were meshing into a vast interlocking system, unified by standardized production and marketing ... an increasingly stable system of technical and narrative conventions, but with a narrowed sense of audience interest and public taste.
>
> This limited what passed in Hollywood as viable property—"box-office." Prospects of anything truly innovative or distinctive being produced there were becoming more

and more remote, even at the competitive prestige level.
Tomas Schatz, *Genius of the System,* 198

Still, we can hope that one day Baba's work during those four incredible weeks—the first at the end of May 1932, the three others from December 18, 1934, to January 7, 1935—will have Hollywood reeling with tears and regret.

Filmmaker Paul Birchard wrote, "The whole notion that God Himself came down to earth, went to Hollywood and said, *'C'mon, guys! Let's make a movie!'* and they all just sat around arguing back and forth whether it would be *'box-office'* or not is just so totally mind-boggling." All those Hollywood types had to have been deeply veiled.

Historically, it would be interesting to be able to identify all the as-yet unnamed executives, writers and producers who were involved in Baba's film plans. Unfortunately the record doesn't include many of those details. In the 1960s, Baba's early English biographer, Charles Purdom, wrote, "This film *will be*, and will be done with Baba's inner direction and help. It will be the product of the combined lovers. It may be a great human love story, a great adventure story of struggle, challenge and achievement, incorporating the Divine Truths as laid down by Meher Baba in 1934-35." [27] Aw 18 (no. 1): 40

Quentin Loses and Regains

Despite his devotion and all the help he gave Baba with his Hollywood connections, Quentin Tod sometimes had difficulty obeying Baba's orders. After a couple of bad slip-ups in 1937, Baba took him aside for a long talk:

> Those who live near me must be very watchful. Knowing my love for you, Maya awaits an opportunity to use your weaknesses.
>
> The moment you neglect my instructions, Maya's purpose is served, and I must put up a big fight with it — not to destroy it, but to make you aware of its *nothingness*. The moment you fail to obey me implicitly, its grip on you tightens, adding to my suffering. EN 67

After this, Quentin began to cool down, and he eventually drifted away from Baba. Then came WWII. Margaret was very close to Quentin, and he contacted her following the war, after she had returned to England from India. They spent a wonderful afternoon at Kew Gardens talking lovingly of the Master, after which Quentin felt a resurgence of his love for Baba. Shortly after this, Margaret heard that Quentin had passed away. He had been suffering from malnutrition due to the ravages of the war years and the devastating London Blitz. But he had confided to Margaret that his love for Baba had grown stronger than before the break. DL 43–47

Even before young Merwan understood that the film that we know as "The Universe" emanated from himself as the Great Producer, he felt a connection with Hollywood. His best friend Baily said that in his senior year at St. Vincent's High School in 1911— two years before his first contact with Babajan—Merwan completed a two-hundred-page movie script and laboriously typed it in English. In late 1912, during his second year at college, he mailed it to the newly created Universal City Studios in North Hollywood, California. *Chanji's Dairies* 21 (vol. 22): 17, March 1927

Chanji later recorded a conversation with Baba's brother Jal, who said that Universal Studios replied with great interest, wanting Merwan to expand on his idea. But by then, Babajan had entered his life . . . and the rest became history.

Meher Baba Links Hollywood and Bollywood

While in Paris, Baba would see *Mr. Deeds Goes to Town* (1936), directed by Frank Capra and starring Gary Cooper. He liked it immensely and called it an outstanding example of film-making used to uplift mankind's consciousness, while providing solid entertainment. Capra, whose films were filled with such humor and wisdom, had been born three years after Baba. He was directing during both of Baba's Hollywood visits, though it is not known whether the great director had had any contact with Baba. [28] 1741

Whether it realized it or not, Hollywood was responding to the "push" Meher Baba gave it. As he had observed, the best movies are inspired by real people and events. In 1939, four years after Baba finished his work there, Hollywood produced twelve inspiring films. Baba saw many of them in India during the 1930s, 40s and 50s. Moreover, his film work was also intimately connected to Bollywood, the Bombay film industry.

Meher Baba promised to bring the East and West closer together. That promise included film, and it is evident in an extraordinary discourse Baba gave to a group of actors and executives from the Bombay film community who came for his darshan in the late 1950s.

This message reflects the sobering lessons he had received from his efforts to make a dent in the hard head of 1930s Hollywood commercialism. He had offered Hollywood spiritual gold, truths never before revealed to humanity, which was refused for the sake of the box office. Baba's message to Bollywood was even more incisive than the one he had given twenty-five years earlier to Hollywood:

> For better or for worse, the motion picture world has grown within the larger world of so-called realities. But the

film world is not foreign to the real world—they are affiliated so intimately that they can be seen essentially to be made of the same fabric. In a sense, everyone is an actor, and the world has often been compared to the stage by poets and philosophers.

Much of what passes for action in modern life is little but acting, and so the world needs to regard only the film world as being imitative. In the film world, the actor must think, feel and act as to the pattern held before him to temporarily mirror the personality of the character he is portraying.

This is also true to a considerable extent for those outside the world of motion pictures who struggle to follow the conventional pattern of living as they imagine it is expected of them, even if it cramps their inner individual style—not only figuratively but literally. While looking in the mirror, people often see themselves more through the eyes of others than through their own.

The reflected image evokes in their minds the impression they will make on others and the expectations others have of them. And the best that most can do is to try to look the part they are playing. Thus, the mirror literally and figuratively has become such a seemingly indispensable part of modern life that we might almost name this age as a *mirror-civilization*.

When the actor plays the part of a king, he knows it's an illusion and so has the advantage over the king in the outer world who is not necessarily aware of any illusion. Both, however, are equally helpless in their failure to find the Real. No one condemns as being a hypocrite the actor who plays the part of an emperor or reformer. Though he appears to be what he's not, his honesty is taken for granted as his audience *knows* he is acting a part.

But there are many outside the world of stage and screen who in actual life do not appear what they really are. The former are [actors] *on* the screen of their own creation; the latter are *behind* the screen of their creation. There are specific claims and privileges as well as specific duties and potentialities that no actor can afford to ignore. An actor who may be technically faultless in his part is yet trivial and worthless if he tries to evade his inherent spiritual potential.

The film world cannot escape its obligations to the larger world on which it makes so substantial an impression, and these obligations demand its spiritual potential take precedence over any money-making desires. The screenwriters, producers and actors should realize their spiritual potential instead of looking at their art merely or mainly as a business venture.

The more vividly they realize this, the more dignified and satisfactory will be the results of their efforts. Their inner account with themselves will be vastly gratifying, though the same might not be said of their bank accounts. If the film world cannot or will not give the greatest importance to this spiritual potential, it is a failure. The ordinary man's immediate need is to relax from the stress of life, to lessen the sense of insecurity and try to fill the emptiness within which greed and war are mostly responsible. He turns instinctively to the fleeting diversion of entertainment.

The film world affords this to a great extent. It has one of the greatest scopes influencing the lives of millions. It should ask itself whether it is utilizing its spiritual potential to the full so that man may be helped in his search for Truth, or is merely pandering to his pleasure of the false.

The industry should ask if is it encouraging and inspiring youth to face the responsibilities of tomorrow's world.

Or is it retarding youth's inner growth in an overdose of sex and violent crime films? Is it is striving after wealth and fame at the cost of man's inherent thirst for the spiritual and uplifting? The correct solution of every problem comes only from Indivisible Truth. There can be no artificial break in the unity of life by magnifying the false distinctions between theory, practice, the unreal and real.

The emphasis of every aspect of One Indivisible Life must be on the underlying unity, not apparent differences. This applies with as much force to those in the film world as to those in the outer world. The great initiator of the Truth of your being is *Divine Love* that burns the limiting self, disarms all fears, rises above all temptations, is deaf to the voices of lust and jealousy, but one which expresses the infinite spiritual potential. Those in the film world have also to play a part.

It is unreservedly in the divine game of life, aspiring to the highest within man. Then only can they find real beauty and fully express it. The spiritual potential of those in the film world, though in no way different from that of those outside it, must often be differently expressed.

Even as an actor you can experience and express divinity. In the motion picture world and by its means, you can learn and you can teach. But if you do not find love or happiness, truth or fulfillment in yourself, how can you impart them to your audience? You cannot inspire unless you are yourself inspired, nor can you awaken love in insensitive souls without yourself being pierced by it.

The actor has to realize real and living beauty is made manifest only by discovering and releasing the spiritual potential within himself. Artifice can no doubt do much to heighten the fresh and radiant beauty natural to youth. But this is artifice and not art, and such transient beauty is poles apart from real beauty. Without vision, your art will be shallow. Do not hesitate to glean that vision from the Great Ones. This will give you a living inspiration, bringing fulfillment in your life.

So, my message to the film world is: Play not to the gallery or for salary, but to the Infinite within. Live in God's presence even while acting your part so you can be true to yourself, to your partners, employers, and the larger and One Indivisible Life of which you are each an inseparable part. If the world is a stage, God is the only producer, and you can never be anything but a trivial player if you are not in unison with Him. 4350–52

Baba later addressed a group of prominent Bollywood directors who visited him in 1960:

Read *God Speaks* to get a wider view of the spiritual panorama—the Divine Drama revealing the secret of creation as a "Game of Love" or Divine Sport which God enjoys at His own cost! In films you should introduce spiritual truths, but do so gradually.

This is the need of the time. Doing it successfully, you'll profit materially and spiritually. Directing or producing such films, always keep in mind that except God everything is illusion. Then "works" will not bind you, and heart will become purer and able to reveal God's Treasure. 4670–71

Meher Baba's seminal work, *God Speaks*, reveals extraordinary details of the imaginary journey the soul makes through creation from its original unconscious state, to its final awakening in Divine

Self-consciousness. Baba said it will one day be clearly understood and accepted as the most authoritative book in the world.

"The Soul's Journey from Unconscious to Conscious God"
~ God Speaks

Evolution marks a series of temporary answers to "Who am I?" as the soul traverses a multitude of forms, beginning with simple gases and proceeding slowly through inanimate stone and mineral forms. These early evolutionary stages obviously have only the most primitive and lower, rudimentary consciousness and cannot provide a satisfactory answer to God's original question.

The original query thus provides a continuing momentum for the drop soul to develop new forms, each with greater consciousness, including the plant and animal beings. Each evolutionary kingdom reveals new dimensions of consciousness and experience to gain different kinds of awareness. As when the soul identifies itself with varied species of fish, it experiences the world as a creature living in water; conversely, as a bird, it enriches its consciousness by flying through air.

When the drop soul finally evolves a human form, consciousness is fully developed, but an individual is still unaware of the potential of his or her consciousness. So the original imperative question "Who am I?" persists and inaugurates the second phase: reincarnation. Since consciousness is fully developed, there is no longer a need for evolving new forms.

The individual's experience, gathered in early stages of evolution, is now humanized and expressed over countless lifetimes. The impulses gained in sub-human forms can play themselves out in broader context of intelligence, emotions, choices, diverse setting and interactions with people. But obviously no single lifetime can bear the burden of "humanizing" the entire evolutionary inheritance.

There must be a method for re-experiencing the pre-human legacy in manageable segments. The soul thus alternately experiences a series of opposites, organized as to themes. Accordingly, in different lives the soul becomes male and female, rich and poor, vigorous and weak, beautiful and ugly. Through exploring the potential of these many opposites, one eventually exhausts all possible human identities, and therefore has fully learned the entire range of human experience.

When the consciousness of the soul is ripe for disentanglement from the everyday gross world of matter and forms, it enters the spiritual path and turns inward and begins to see the inner world with the inner eye. During involution on the inner spiritual planes the soul returns to the full awareness of the Divine Force which created him. Like evolution, involution has certain states and stages, consisting of "planes" and "realms." But individuality continues along this spiritual path.

There is a Sufi saying "There are as many ways to God as there are souls." Each new plane denotes a state of being differing from the states that preceded it. The first three planes are within the subtle world or domain of energy —"pran." There follows the fourth plane, the threshold of the mental world, where misuse of great power for personal desire can lead to disintegration of consciousness, returning it to stone state and necessitating the entire journey through evolution once again.

The fifth and sixth planes represent true sainthood, which is understood to be increasing intimacy with God as the Beloved. On the sixth plane, the mind itself becomes the inner eye that *sees* God everywhere and in everything, but not yet in itself. The loving of God and the longing for His union is fully demonstrated in the sixth plane of consciousness.

The seventh plane marks true and lasting freedom in God-Realization. As false mind goes, impressions go and duality goes. The drops burst and again become the Ocean. God finally answers his question "Who am I?" with **"I am God."** The Infinite returns to the original starting point, now knowing with full consciousness and awareness he was, is and always will be infinite, realizing the entire journey has been an illusory dream, whose purpose is the full awakening of his soul.

Returning from Hollywood to India in 1935, Baba spoke candidly about happiness: "Just look at Hollywood movie stars. They have ample money, name, fame, everything – still they're unhappy. Why? Because money alone can't bring happiness." 1505

Chapter Twenty-Four

Balancing East and West: Nasik, Cannes, Meherabad and The Blue Bus Tours

After Meher Baba returned home from Hollywood in 1935, nearly all his work now would take place in India, much of it centered around Meherabad, where he would reside until the beginning of the Blue Bus Tours in December 1938. On October 5, 1935, Baba composed a poem which he had the mandali read aloud:

> O Damn good Meherabad,
> Mandali Mahal—Palace of the Circle,
> In face of storms, rain or gale,
> Attacked by thunder, lightning or hail;
> You must not fail, no, you must not fail!
> ~ 1660

Meher Retreat Ashram in Nasik

One of Baba's missions in this Advent was to balance the materialism of the West with the spirituality of the East. He wanted the Western women to meet his *gopis*—the women living in his ashram. But he especially wanted them to meet Mehera, the beloved of the Beloved. In 1933 he had brought ten of the women from Europe to India, where they met her for the first time and had the opportunity to mingle with the others.

He now wished to invite a group of Western men and women to India for an extended visit so that they could experience for themselves what ashram life was like.

In March 1936, He announced plans to establish an ashram in Mysore, India, but he began having second thoughts, observing that the people there were too "traditionally religious-minded and tangled up in Brahmin orthodoxy" for his ashram to operate in an uncontested atmosphere:

> I really like this place, but my movements here will be restricted. I can't freely move about due to such people. I don't like that. Time's past when I could dismantle a whole ashram in eight days as I did in Toka. Here it's different. To fix a definite plan so there won't be any difficulties in the future my sword must be in hand to enter the den of the lion and slay it.
>
> Then I might be able to do my work here among all this rigid orthodoxy. All these zealots should be sent to the battlefront! A scoundrel at least appears as he is, and is better than these people. People recognize and take precautions to stay away from a scoundrel. But these orthodox are dangerous devils, disguising themselves as saints!
>
> Even lazy, good-for-nothing loafers can courageously prepare for any eventuality, and are not afraid to die. But these zealots are cowardly hypocritical posers and all the more dangerous—black sheep wearing the clothes of a sadhu! 1706-07

With Mysore out of the picture, Baba chose Nasik as the location for his new ashram. In July, he wrote to to the Westerners to tell them of his plans so that they'd know what to expect:

> I have purchased the ideal property in Nasik. It is situated amidst beautiful surroundings with splendid scenery all around. With the Western group in Nasik, the Eastern group in Meherabad and myself in Rahuri, midway between Meherabad and Nasik, these will comprise the nucleus of my activities for the next five years.
>
> The center [in Nasik] has nothing in common with the accepted notions of ashrams, spiritual retreats and the strict, dry, rigid disciplines governing them. Its special feature will be its having my personal living guidance, as of Jesus to his disciples. . . .
>
> All possible arrangements have been made to make the physical life easy for you, and though it will not be a crown of thorns, it will not be a bed of roses either! You will be shown from time to time the three phases of my activities in the three different retreats: the modern—Nasik, the primitive—Rahuri [the mad and mast ashram], and the simple—Meherabad. 1751-52

On October 25, 1936, Baba departed for his ninth trip to the West. After traveling by rail to Karachi he boarded an airplane for his first flight, landing in Baghdad, where he fed one hundred crippled and diseased beggars. He continued on by rail to London, Zurich and Paris to meet with fifteen of his established Western disciples from England, France, Switzerland and the United States, inviting fifteen of them to his new ashram in Nasik, called Meher Retreat.

By Christmas Day, 1936, all fifteen Westerners had arrived in Nasik and were settled into two buildings, Manzil and Sarzat, which Baba had furnished with their comfort in mind, right down to the flush toilets. They were just in time for a gala Christmas dinner celebration. The Westerners laid out presents for Baba as he sat with them in the middle of the long dining table. His mood was joyful as he unwrapped their gifts and handed them back out to someone in the group.

After dinner he said, "My love flows eternally to all humanity, but at this particular moment we will remember those of the group who are physically absent." After a few moments of silence, Baba went on to comment, "I am crucified every moment. I am continually crucified and continually taking birth." 1760

Everyone was assigned duties at Meher Retreat, and schedules were laid out, including limits to which everyone was expected to adhere. It was their first experience of what Baba would come to call "freedom with clipped wings," and it was not an easy transition into the kind of life that the Easterners had been accustomed to since the 1920s. 1792

Try as they might, there was a constant atmosphere of disharmony and discontent ranging from petty squabbles to major misunderstandings among the Westerners. Baba admonished them:

> You want a million things. 'I want this, I want that.' If you were to keep an account of your wants—Oh God! Needs are not wants. Everything beyond needs is wants.
>
> Wanting inevitably leads to suffering. So try your very, very best to want less of what is beyond your needs.
>
> Try loving and loving more and more, and then you'll want less of what is beyond your needs, and want more of love. Try seriously. It'll all be bliss if you don't want anything. But you must try—consciously. The stone wants nothing, but wants nothing unconsciously. Begin by dying!
>
> Long for union. You really can't love each other! All right, but try at least to give in to each other. But even this you don't do. Why? Because you're not honest. That's why I love the mad at the Rahuri ashram. They're totally honest in their insanity. You come from far away to love and real-

ize me. But here you've turned into fighting cocks and hens!

I'll have to leave you all and go to Nepal, or send you all to the Himalayas. So, begin by wanting less. Try to love more. Try to have more tolerance. There's sublime happiness all around; yet everybody is sad, miserable and suffering.

So, will you all promise to begin dying? If there's disharmony and I find you unprepared to die, then it's better you all pack up and go. You haven't come here for name and fame. I've plenty of disciples from the West. I don't need anybody. I'm always alone and will be until eternity.

It is you who need me until you become me. But what's the use if you don't even try? So, all should begin to honestly try now, or seriously I'll tell you all to leave. Have real harmony, love and peace – not forced. If you're not what I want you to be, I can't give you what I want to.
1817–19

Among the challenges the Westerners faced was not seeing Baba when he was working at Meherabad or at the Rahuri mast and mad ashram. But Baba took them to visit Rahuri so that they could see him at work and observe his love for the inmates there. He also arranged for the women to visit his women's ashram on Meherabad Hill.

Baba marked his forty-third birthday in Nasik on February 17 and 18, 1937. It was a huge, breath-taking affair, happily caught on film. Shireenmai came from Poona for the joyful day to see the thousands of devotees and local villagers who had come to offer homage at her son's feet. Baba rose at five in the morning and spent the day supervising festivities as well as personally directing preparations for a feast for everyone. Smiling, he greeted each of the Westerners, remarking that he had that one bad Avataric habit of micro-managing every detail himself.

The program began at eight o'clock when Shireenmai washed Baba's feet with milk and honey, which was given out as prasad. The Westerns shared in this extraordinary ceremony. The Easterners were in seclusion on Meherabad Hill.

For eight back-breaking hours Baba bent and touched the feet of each his devotees and handed each a gift of prasad—a small bundle of grain tied in cloth. Baba said offering prasad to someone established his direct link and lifeline to that person and that it must work with the precision of a production line. "This is the first time I am touching the feet of those coming to pay me reverence," he observed. " I salute the divinity in them, as they salute the divinity in me." Gi 23; GG V:216

Splendid food was served throughout the two-day celebration. Throngs of lovers sat side by side on mats enjoying food served on banana leaves. Shireenmai and Gulmai, who discarded their differences for the festivities, showed the Westerners how to squat on the mats and eat from banana-leaf plates using their fingers. Music and singing continued throughout the event.

The Most Beautiful Film of Baba

Nasik 1937 is the name of the newsreel that was recorded at Baba's birthday celebration. Of all the moving images of Baba, this film captures Baba in his most Christ-like, compassionate glory. In one scene where he is seated on the ground, some of the more than-fifty-thousand devotees—young, old, rich, poor, healthy, ill, disabled—filed past him. With the grace of a dancer, he reached down with one hand to touch their feet and then his forehead while the other handed them their prasad. One poor, lame woman received her prasad and then hesitated ever so slightly, wishing for one more moment in his presence. With a barely perceptible tilt of his head to the right, Baba moved her gently on. In the next moment he flashed a glance at the camera—*that* moment, so filled with his presence, is perhaps the most breathtaking image of Meher Baba on film.

As the darshan progressed into the middle of the afternoon, someone asked Baba if his back hurt from all the bending and and reaching. Baba replied, "My back aches so much it doesn't ache at all." Then, smiling, he added, "The whole evolutionary scheme is passing through my spine today." 1785

As devotees passed by to receive the Master's gift of cloth and grain, their palms were marked with a red dye to stop them re-entering the line. Though music was playing and crowds milling everywhere, Baba's eyes missed nothing. How could eyes that sweep the universe in a glance miss something or someone so near?

And so, when one old woman eased back into line to have Baba's darshan a second time, Vishnu, seeing her red palm, was about to remove her. But Baba stopped, called Vishnu and slapped him. This moved the old woman to tears. "Oh God! Forgive my offense. It's not his fault, it's mine. I am coming to you for prasad a second time!" At this, Baba embraced her and directed Vishnu to feed her two grandchildren and to call them back with their mother the next day for more food. 1784-88

In One Ear and Out the Other

As things were still not going smoothly for the Westerners, on January 30, 1937, Baba held a meeting with them in Nasik on "a matter of great importance."

> Take all I say seriously. It's vital. I've not yet started working on you. I wanted to see how things went on here during the first month. Certain things must be decided to-

CHRIST COME AGAIN

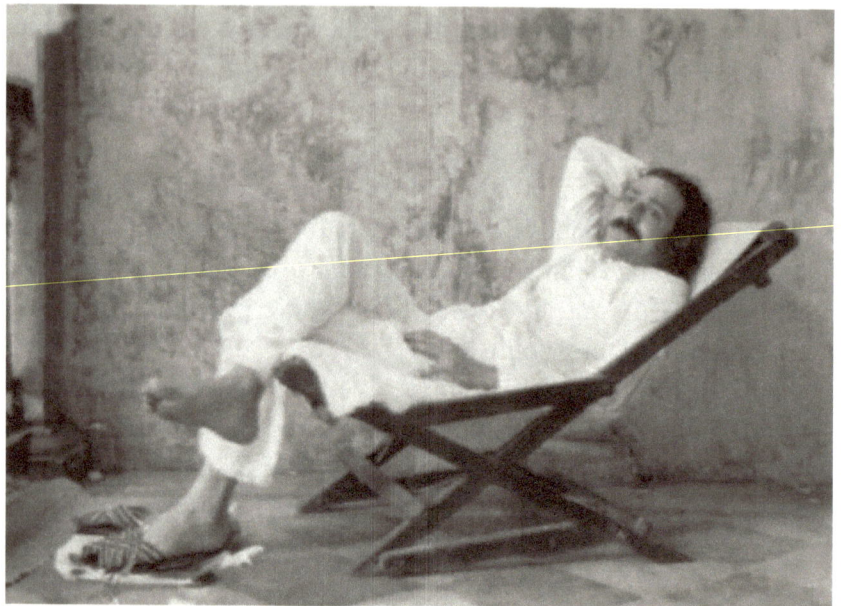

Meher Baba relaxing, late 1930s

day. Be honest in your replies. During the past month you've been living here together, and there's not been the harmony among you I'd hoped to see. As things now stand, I can't carry out the work I intend doing.

So either you must live harmoniously together and help me in my work, or the ashram must be disbanded and I'll have to do my work alone. Are you all prepared to live here harmoniously for five years? I would definitely prefer you to stay and help me, but if you really think you cannot stay, or there cannot be real harmony, then it had better be goodbye. I have not yet started the work.

Thorns are waiting to prick you. I'm talking plainly, so don't answer without thinking. Don't let sentiment and temporary enthusiasm sway you. Once agreed, your promise must be adhered to. There are bound to be differences, but one or the other must give in. That means all of you

CHRIST COME AGAIN

Meher Baba with (L to R) Delia DeLeon, Nadine Tolstoy, Margaret Craske and Norina Matchabelli, Nasik, India, February 17-18, 1937

who stay must be prepared to give in. I don't mind crises, I don't mind chaos, but I do mind disharmony.

At present, I have to spend my time patching up things, drawing both persons together on common ground, instead of spending it for the work and pushing you forward. I tolerate everything. So you must also. Be tolerant with everyone and when you feel like rising up in a fury and having an argument with your adversary, say: "I am here for Baba, and above all else Baba wants harmony."

You'll feel excited, jealous and proud at times. These qualities are there. Give in despite them! It's easier to go through fire than give in; more difficult than creating the creation to turn a selfish person unselfish; to turn stubbornness into flexibility. Your answer is a sacred promise to me. 1773-77

Baba then asked each to give his or her answer. He was pleased when they all answered that they were prepared to do their best to live harmoniously together. But then, facing an on-going lack of harmony among the Westerners, Baba had to read the riot act again and gave a final warning:

> Fix the situation—no ifs or buts about it. Mend your ways or go! You leave your home, your family to dedicate all to me, yet live a life of binding. You have no freedom to go out to the movies or shopping. You sacrifice for love in every way. You all love me, take me to be God – and I really *am* God—but the one thing that is a shortcoming in you all is this complete lack of control!
>
> If you had control, you'd be jewels as disciples! But control in all of you is so disastrously lacking, and it makes it very difficult for me to adjust all your other good points. This one lack makes the whole thing a total farce! There are only twelve [*sic*—there were fifteen] of you, and still no harmony.
>
> You don't love each other; you can't even *tolerate each other*. The slightest provocation shows your great weaknesses. Norina and Nadine tell the world, "We live with the greatest Master of the age!" But you don't say, "We stay with him, but fight like cats and dogs!" I warn you all very seriously, East and West—*control*. . . . Spiritually, it's not cowardly to give in.
>
> So if you can't love, at least have the decency and courage to give in. I've said it a million times, but it goes in one ear and out the other. This is the last time I'll tell you. If it goes, out you'll all go. You fight for sheer lack of control. This isn't yoga but *bhoga*—meaning taking with selfishness. Yoga implies giving in selflessness. Rano makes Norina mad. Kitty gets daily ill-tempered moods. In short,

you twelve [*sic*] raise hell every day over trifles that aren't even worthwhile.

    I might have put you all on silence, but you would've crushed each other! Very seriously, take practical steps the moment you feel excited. Remember me, and begin singing or dancing. You'll at once turn it into laughter. Think and speak only of me, and forget eating, drinking, sleeping and everything else in your ephemeral world! 2021–22

In June Baba shocked the Westerners by dissolving the Nasik ashram and sending them home early. But before they departed Baba promised to call them to an new ashram he intended to create in Cannes, France.

Cannes: A New Ashram on the Riviera

    In the late summer of 1937 Baba travelled to Cannes, France, inviting his closest Eastern and Western women to join him. Although the Eastern women were happy to accompany him, they were reluctant to leave India for the first time. Part of the voyage was through rough seas and several of them suffered from seasickness, especially Mehera. MM 1:377

    Late 1930s Cannes was a haven for the rich and famous, a parade of royalty and film stars who transformed the town with villas and palaces. It was the brightest, liveliest, most photographed spot in the world. [29] Competing with four princes from different parts of India, Norina Matchabelli managed to rent the elegant Villa Caldana for Baba, all the Easterners and a few of the Westerners—women only. The remaining women stayed in another large villa called Capo de Monte, along with the men and those disciples who would be called for short or extended visits.

    Baba also made one new important contact, a young woman named Irene Billo from Zurich. In fact, he had noted her absence at

Meher Baba dressed in a Western suit, Cannes, France, 1937

the reception where he had met Hedi, Walter and Helen. She arrived in the guise of a maid, invited by Kitty to assist with the housekeeping. She had known about Baba for quite some time and he quickly drew her close, but barely out of her teens, she struggled to be accepted by the older women.

By the summer of 1937, the world was on the verge of upheaval. The Spanish Civil war was raging, China and Japan had just declared war on each other, and Adolf Hitler was consolidating power in Germany. Everyone wanted to catch the Riviera sun before it was too late.

Baba and his party basked in quite a different light. The Queen of Romania was attracting a great deal of attention. Hearing of Baba through Norina, the she grandly sent him a telegram: "The Queen of Romania is prepared to receive Meher Baba." Without losing a beat Baba cabled back with a twinkle in his eye, "And Meher Baba is prepared to receive the Queen of Romania!" Needless to say, they never met. Aw 20 (no. 2): 16

Baba's usual attire when out and about was a suit, silk shirt and tie, with his long hair tucked up under a beret, and dark glasses to make his divinely penetrating eyes less conspicuous. But really, how was it possible to conceal such extraordinary beauty? People passing on the street would stop in their tracks and turn to gaze at his striking beauty and aura—royalty of a higher order.

Still, Baba wasn't especially comfortable in Western clothes. So on leaving Villa Caldana to walk to the men's villa, he'd leave in Western garb, and then halfway there Elizabeth would meet him in her car. He would get in and they would drive out of public view while he changed from Western slacks to his sadra, which he'd been wearing underneath, and a silk robe. One day, Irene Billo hitched a ride with them when Baba suddenly began taking his pants off. She was startled, but Rano assured her: "It's alright, Irene, Baba does this every day."

Meanwhile, Norina lost no time introducing the crème de la crème to "Shri Meher Baba." Mani explained: "With her background and lifestyle, Norina knew all the current, top people in every field of life, and she wanted nothing more than bring them *all* to Baba. She had the kind of personality that could charm and melt a stone." MM 1:371-72

Baba had not planned to meet many new people but he relented and gave interviews. He held court at Capo di Monte for an aristocracy that would all but vanish by the end of the war, as well as for his lovers—his new humanity. Still, of all the beautiful people in silks and diamonds, Baba himself was the crown jewel on the Riviera that summer.

Arriving in Cannes from Hollywood, Mercedes de' Acosta found Baba in a totally playful mood. One day, he spied a black cape hanging in her closet: "Draped in my cape and with a Spanish hat, he started doing a very serious flamenco dance from one side of the room to the other, snapping his fingers, clapping the rhythm with his hands and dancing with utter grace. It was absolutely glorious." As she began laughing, Baba beckoned her to join in. "I was delighted to see Baba so lighthearted and full of fun—what I so loved about him—always totally spontaneous and so unpredictable."

On August 21 Baba visited a casino in Monte Carlo with Norina and Elizabeth. He was truly stunning dressed incognito in one of Mercedes' berets and Norina's luxurious black Italian officer's cape with brass buttons and a silver clasp. Mehera recalled, "Baba came to our quarters to show us his regalia. He swept the cape back over his shoulder as he entered, looking so handsome in that outfit. With his fair skin he looked just like French aristocracy. We were floored."

Rano also remembered that night. "Baba grandly swept the cape over his shoulder as he came down the winding staircase, below which we waited gazing at him with mouths wide-open. He looked like a million—striking and utterly magnificent." The Godman blessed the casino that evening by going out dressed as royalty, completely blending into the chic, sophisticated Riviera atmosphere.

Among the Westerners invited for Baba's darshan in Cannes were the Mertens family, Helen Dahm, Margaret and William Donkin, who had been awarded his degree in medicine. Mercedes de'Costa was also given another chance to meet with Baba. He had earlier invited her to his Nasik ashram, but she hesitated, cabling she was afraid she'd miss her dear friend Greta Garbo too much. When Mercedes finally arrived in October Baba said, "Come to India as soon as possible, and bring Greta with you." Instead, Mercedes went there with another new friend, Consuela de Sides.

On September 30, Gabriel arrived in Cannes, having been called by Baba. He said to Baba, "I was surrounded by difficulties on all sides, but since meeting you, I've felt your inner help and my difficulties are slowly disappearing. Things have so adjusted themselves I'm now in a position to produce great films—all due to your inner help."

Meanwhile, Alexander Markey had decided to go to Cannes to begin writing a new play. After his arrival he received a cable from London saying that Baba was on his way to Cannes and wanted to meet Markey there. The man was stunned. Such coincidences only further strengthened his love and faith in the Master. Baba and

Markey discussed more possible film projects that the Universal Producer claimed were essential for his work. 1866

Norina brought a German gentleman named Mr. Seiber to meet Baba. Seiber seemed eager to work for his country's people, and, with war inevitable, he was granted a long interview. He wanted to know why conditions in Germany were so terrible. Baba smiled and explained:

> Chaos and destruction are essential for reconstruction. It is the spiritual law—create and destroy. Create chaos, confusion and misery—then destroy it so it may all be rebuilt anew. How can an old house be rebuilt unless utterly demolished? Your coming to me today is no coincidence, but my deliberate plan while Mussolini is now in Germany meeting Hitler.
>
> Important talks between them are going on at this moment! Your being here and my asking you to talk about the situation in Germany has a very significant purpose. I purposely brought you here today for this very reason. Hitler and Mussolini can never find a solution.
>
> They're surrounded by chaotic conditions and are simply adding to the misery. Only Christ can do it—and the time for that is very near. Perhaps you might be my sole working agent in Germany, but only if you stick to my instructions and do exactly as I say.

Baba gave Seiber the opportunity to join his disciples in Cannes, but he really never fit in. His long talks with Baba had little effect, prompting Baba to observe, "He's like an empty vessel which keeps throwing out whatever is placed in it!" As Jesus said: "New wine cannot be poured into old wineskins, lest they burst." Mark 2:21-22

Amongst all these interviews, Baba never let up his focus on his close ones, and he usually had his dinner with the women. One evening, Norina decorated the table with silver candlesticks. "Tonight, we'll have a candlelight supper with Baba," she announced grandly. They all thought it a splendid idea and dressed up for the intimate and charming occasion. Baba walked into the softly-lit dining room and said to the women, "It really looks wonderful! Beautiful! Who thought of it?"

The women said it was Norina's idea. Baba lovingly caressed her chin. "I'm so happy," he said. Then snapping his fingers he added, "Now let's put on the lights!" Norina's face fell, but she kept her cool and did as told. "Baba loved lights," Mehera explained. "He was never fond of dimly-lit rooms." Here was an occasion where Norina's old patterns surfaced, but Baba slashed her ego with words like a sword. One may wince at his reaction but ultimately bow to the Master's insight, as he lovingly embraced her thoughtful heart. Such were his ways. MM 1:364

This is how the new Christ moved in the new world. Baba explained, "Some like a quiet ashram life of solitude, silence and meditation. Others prefer a life of action and gaiety. I like the latter, but for my work, the former! So now I must deal with both." 1967

On September 19 Baba took a small group of the women to Paris, where they went boating on the Seine and visited an Art and Technical Exhibition where Baba accomplished some Universal work with the crowds. He also took them to the top of the Eiffel Tower. He later explained that, while at the top, he held a meeting with his agents and other members of the spiritual hierarchy, similar to the meetings held at Assisi in Italy and on Mount Fallenfluh in Switzerland.

It is extraordinary how Baba could be fully present with his disciples and still be in inner communion with agents and other advanced beings for a vital "inner-plane meeting." This meant carrying on two very divergent means of communication simultaneously, on both the gross and spiritual planes.

Jean Adriel narrated that on returning with them to Cannes, Baba appeared somewhat like a child, dazed by some unearthly beauty which no words could describe:

> I said to him, 'What is it, Baba dear?'
> Looking at me with eyes eloquent in anguished joy he spelled out: 'Hadn't you heard about the 'meeting?' 'No, dear, I hadn't.' Then he told me a most important meeting was held up in the Eiffel Tower, and ever since it had been difficult to hold himself in his body. He rested his head on my shoulder for a few moments. . . .
> Finally, at his signal, we helped him to the door where two of his Indian disciples were waiting to assist him. When I saw him an hour later, the painful transition had been accomplished, and he was his usual dynamic self, playing again his cosmic game with the forces of the universe." Av 232–33

But the high life of Cannes only provided a small break in the serious business of Baba's war work, as he declared, "My work here is uppermost. 1874–76

Baba even continued look for a "suitable boy." He told the women about the search and disclosed the profile he was seeking: that of a healthy, handsome, intelligent and innocent teenage boy in order to work for future youth.

He also continued his work with the women, explaining,

> Only the God-Man is consciously both God and man; so the God-Man is both Lord and the servant of the universe. Lord, in the state of helping all souls to progress toward Reality. As Servant, I consciously bear the burden of all. To serve him who serves all is serving the universe.

Selfless service and love are twin divine qualities. Only one who loves can serve. 1854c–55

Mohammed Comes to Cannes

A Renoir-like portrait of Mehera and Meher Baba taken during a picnic near Paris, France, 1937

In August 1936 Baidul had located a God-intoxicated soul named Mohammed. The *mast* had spent years wandering Bombay, pestered by gamblers looking for betting tips. Baidul brought him to the Rahuri ashram. Once settled, Mohammed took advantage of Baba's instructions that inmates be given all that they asked for—whatever their whims.

He took two hours to brush his teeth, demanding a full bucket of water to rinse his mouth, then sending it away only to demand it again a few minutes later. When Baba called him for his morning bath, it would take three men an hour to beguile him into cooperation. His daily diet included a dozen each of chapattis and bananas, six raw onions, four pounds of beets, two plates of rice, lentils and cooked vegetables, four ounces of pistachios, and six cups of tea in the morning and six more in the afternoon. He was habitually bent over to scratch the ground, looking for anything interesting, which he called *deesh*. W 44-45

When first brought to Baba, Mohammed was trapped between the third and fourth planes. Baba would push him across the fourth plane of subtle energy, with its dangerous powers, to the much safer fifth mental plane. This not only made his spiritual state more secure but made him much more manageable. A radical change began to take place as he became friendly, pleasant and cooperative. His love and affection for Baba, or "Dada" as he fondly referred to him, were truly great. He adored Baba and longed for his daily visits.

The fifth plane would give Mohamed the ability to know and change the thoughts of anyone in the Universe, and he became Baba's true secret agent, surpassing even sophisticated cyber encryption machines. With help from his spiritual agents, Baba took complete control of the approaching war. Hitler and Mussolini were coming into full military power, and when Baba was on the Riviera, Mussolini was heading for Berlin to confer with Hitler. Regarding their meeting Baba observed:

> No one will ever know what transpired between them, not even their closest, most trusted associates. . . . This will only be known to the world when the actual events take place to the world's great surprise. They share so much mutual confidence, but are bluffing each other and playing their own games.
> And the fun of it is *they both know it*. They have no idea what complications this will create. Such is the game when played for self-interest, greed and lust for power. See it all, and mark my words.

While these leaders were engaged in serious alliance talks, Baba had the *mast* brought by ship from India to Cannes. There he would conduct intense work with Mohammed involving the forces of Germany, with which Mohammed had a particularly strong spiritual connection. Baba called it a country which, now under Hitler's leadership, was experiencing total mass psychosis. But on November 19, he made the observation, "Hitler is a brave and great patriot who's done wonderful service to his country. But," he added, "as a human being, he is no good—cruel and hopeless! His treatment of the Jews is most heartless." 2048

It was next to impossible to obtain a European passport for Mohammed, as he was considered mad by the authorities and couldn't even sign his own name. So the excuse was made that he was being brought to France to undergo "mental treatment." Even so, getting him there was no game for the fainthearted. As Baba was already in Cannes, the almost impossible task was left to Adi Sr. and Baidul.

At first Mohammed was stable, but after a few days at sea he gave in to a foul mood and became a terrible nuisance. He began to abuse and curse his fellow passengers, flinging lit cigarettes in their faces. He walked hunched over collecting deck litter, his *deesh*, like a wayward child

The shocked and intimidated passengers complained so much to the ship's captain that Mohammed was nearly put ashore early. Everyone was relieved to disembark at Cannes. Baba commented, "Mast Mohammed represents Germany. How significant is his coming to France and the importance of my work with him here." 1875

Most visits were stopped while Baba worked with Mohammed for nine hours every day in seclusion. But one afternoon, taking a much needed break, Baba went out for a leisurely drive with Mercedes, and on a whim decided to take Mohammed along. They were driving a top-down convertible on a balmy Riviera day when the chauffeur slowed down for heavy traffic.

Suddenly, Mohammed began shouting wildly at the top of his lungs. They were pulled over by a policeman who glared at Baba and asked what all the commotion was. Baba put his hand to his mouth, indicating he didn't speak, while Mohammed started shouting louder and then singing at the top of his lungs. Poor Mercedes tried to explain things to the bewildered policeman. "Well, officer, these gentlemen are from India. . . . This one has taken a vow of silence and the other is a mentally-ill Hindu undergoing treatment here—but really, they're quite harmless!" The policeman who was speechless in the face of these strange tourists. Shaking his head, he waved them on.

It was at this time that Baba gave Mohammed the push across the fourth plane to the fifth so that he safely returned to India as a fifth-plane saint. On the fourth plane he had experienced perilous, infinite power. As a *mavali* (mischievous) mast there's no saying what sort of trouble he could have caused. His dangerous state was safely transcended and now replaced instead with unlimited knowledge.

Baba worked intensely with Mohammed for three weeks before returning to India. He had spent a full two and a half months in Cannes. Members of the group accompanied him to the port of Marseilles; among them was Margaret, who took him to visit an old church on a hill overlooking the Mediterranean, Our Lady of the Sea. Outside was a beggar. Margaret wanted to give him some money, but Baba stopped her, explaining, "Give it from *me*. If you give it, you'll receive sanskaric impressions from him."

In the church was a statue of the *Pietà*—Mary holding the battered body of Jesus after it was taken down from the cross. As Baba stood before it, Margaret silently wondered if Baba would actually be crucified this time. He responded by spelling out on his board, "It won't happen physically this time, but mentally."

Later that afternoon they went to a movie and saw a French film, *The Big House*. Margaret quietly translated the dialogue for Baba in English. Then she suddenly noticed he had slumped in his seat, seeming not to be listening. So she stopped. After a few minutes Baba sat up, gesturing, "I've just been to Vienna." 1341, 1894

Vichy Water

On November 3, Baba and the disciples accompanying him went to the docks to board the SS *Circassia* on her maiden voyage to Bombay. But just before boarding, Baba sent Norina out for some sparkling Vichy water. Then he put her through the strange ordeal of phoning back repeatedly to ask if the water was "alkaline or acidic," and was it one hundred percent or only partially alkaline, etc. Vichy water, a natural mineral tonic, comes from Vichy, a famous spa-city in central France. The government in German-occupied France was just about to be renamed and infamously known as the "Vichy regime." Thus the bottle of sparkling water became an agent of his war work.

The return journey was pleasant with smooth seas and sunny skies, just as Baba had promised. He continued working with Mohammed daily aboard ship, bathing him in his cabin bathroom. But it was no simple task and took hours each day—an hour just to get Mohammed's sandals off as he kicked his feet in protest. Though Baba's health was poor, he continued to pamper the *mast's* whims and moods. 1883

Arriving back in India, Baba continued his daily war work with this kingpin and others in the mast ashram at Lower Meherabad, bathing, feeding and cleaning their toilets, tasks so important that he hurried down the hill each day to the get started.

As Masaji handed him a broom, Baba rolled up his sleeves and pants to remove the pot from inside, carry it a distance, empty it in a pit, scour it with the broom and pour in phenol disinfectant. Then he brought the pot back and saw that the toilet area was sanitary. Baba observed, "Sadgurus in the highest state work like toilet-cleaners to abolish the bad sanskaras of sinners. Here I do this filthy work cleaning toilets and urinals. You'll never know how wonderful this work is to me! How can you ever understand my way of working?"

Meanwhile, in the bathing room Mohammed was being coaxed into a bath. He only relented after being humored with the promise of another "all expense paid voyage to Europe in a month" with the added ploy of maybe even finding him a wife! MM 1:383-84; 1887

The Master's Tomb

Before returning to Meherabad Baba had invited Norina, Kitty and Rano to become the first Westerners admitted to the women's ashram. He would soon invite more, but the existing space in the Water Tank building would not accommodate them. So he ordered a second story to be added to the structure to create dormitories on two floors.

The Dome, the small, stone structure where Meher Baba's body rests to this day, so tiny on the outside, but spiritually astronomical on the inside, touching the hearts of millions of his lovers

Additionally, he ordered the construction of a ten-bed hospital and a stone wall around the perimeter of the compound to provide more privacy for the women. He also instructed the mandali to build a dome over his crypt, the underground room on Meherabad Hill from the Prem Ashram days where he had secluded himself for six months back in 1927.

The British government had ordered the old Post Office building at Lower Meherabad torn down in 1933 as it was too close to the railway tracks for safety. The field stones were saved. Baba took advantage of this, telling the men to use the stones to build his tomb. Now everyone understood Baba's sacred intention for this humble structure, which would one day house his own physical remains. Baba had spent many nights in the crypt until the adjacent, aptly named corrugated Tin Cabin was built in 1935.

Because of the noise and presence of construction workers on the hill, Baba shifted the women to the hill station of Panchgani for the next four months. Also joining him at his invitation were Elizabeth and Nonny. At the end of that time Baba brought the group to a bungalow in Ahmednagar until they could move into their new dormitories, because the construction work was not yet complete. Joining the women there were Mansari Desai, a devotee who had repeatedly expressed her longing to join the women's ashram, as well as the entire Jessawala family.

The New St. Peter

Unbeknownst to Eruch Jessawala, he had been chosen from childhood, and in 1938 Baba called him to become one of his inner-circle companions. As the Avatar's new St. Peter, Eruch would become the voice and right hand of the Master, reading his alphabet board aloud, serving as his personal attendant, and from 1954 onwards, interpreting Baba's gestures after he discarded the board.

Eruch was nine, traveling to Meherabad with his family for their first visit with Baba in December 1925, when he fell off the carriage in which they were riding. Baba cuddled him, applying ash from the Dhuni to Eruch's bleeding elbow, holding him in his lap and kissing him. His kindness captured Eruch's heart. 632

When Baba visited the Jessawala family in Nasik five years later, he told Gaimai that before going school and returning in the afternoon, fourteen-year-old Eruch should meet Baba and have his meals with him. But the boy found this irksome and would hide from him.

On the first morning he left for school without seeing Baba. But in the afternoon Baba was standing outside waiting for him at the gate, and he had to spend the afternoon and evening playing what he called "children's games" with Baba. By the third day, Eruch was more cautious. Biking home from school and seeing Baba in the distance at his gate, he decided to sneak into the house by the back door, grab a quick snack, change his clothes and run off to play ball with his friends. But Gaimai caught him at his game and confronted him: "Baba was waiting for you so long. Don't you realize how blessed you are? He's our Zoroaster returned!" Though religious by nature, Eruch was skeptical of his mother's words.

How long I stood there—
waiting at your gate each day—
while you sneaked off to play
~ elf

Naturally Baba also caught on to the boy's ruse. So instead of waiting for him each afternoon, he'd ask Eruch in the evening how the games went and how the teams were doing. He'd ask by slowly pointing to the letters on his alphabet board. Now this was fun, unlike the earlier childish games.

Reading Baba's board was a challenge, but because Eruch became so good at it, Baba began to speed up and Eruch had to be on his toes. Eventually, he became Baba's best and fastest interpreters of the board. Only decades later did he realize how Baba had groomed him to fulfill this challenging lifetime role. TH 166–68

Although the Jessawalas were Zoroastrians, Eruch attended a Catholic school and had become far more interested in Jesus, having no idea that all the Avatars are one and the same Being. Eruch thought, "How much better had I been born in Jesus' time! How I'd love to be by his side. Will I ever see that day?" Little did he know that Christ had not only heard his longing, but waited for him daily at his front gate. Though being called to serve the Master was beyond his wildest dreams, for decades he remained unaware of Baba's divine state—that his Jesus had returned. 1187

Baba sealed Eruch's fate by having him spend one night alone in his Tiger Valley Cave. Elizabeth was so intrigued that she asked if she too could spend the night there. Baba replied, "Yes, but let me tell you when." The right time came on May 6, 1938. Baba and the women escorted Elizabeth to the cave, where she was to remain inside for twelve hours.

> At six p.m. sharp, Baba locked me in, handing me the key inside through the iron bars, and resting his hand upon my head in blessing. The moment all disappeared around the bend of the path, there was profound stillness. . . . On Baba's instructions, I lit a lantern at exactly ten minutes to seven. Then I lay down. Once, I heard heavy thuds, like steps on the path. I waited anxiously.
>
> Would someone appear? But the sound, though close, passed away—probably a cow or a buffalo grazing on the mountain side. In the shape of a kite resembling the Southern Cross, four stars stood out in the sky more vividly than the rest. By my watch it was close to midnight. Determined to remain awake, I continued thinking of Baba.
>
> Then, unexpectedly, a shock like electricity passed through my body from head to foot along the spine. It continued in waves of varying currents, and became so strong two or three times that it seemed to lift me, as would a rush of wind. I felt myself swinging out into space.
>
> The bedding unevenly swayed beneath me as if I were on a magic carpet. I felt if I could hold on I'd be carried safely. But it rocked so much I called out Baba's name;

immediately the troubled waters were stilled. Coming out of a daze, I found my arms folded across me, just as they cross the arms of the dead. They were so numb it took a while before I could even move them. Whatever state I passed through, I was consciously unconscious during it.

A seeming sense of time had passed, when I was aroused by the cheery sound of voices recognized as those of my friends. They appeared inside the cave, and called to me it was five a.m. and they'd been sent to summon me. I membered Baba telling me not to leave the cave until *exactly* six a.m. sharp. This seemed conflicting, and I was wondering what to do. At that moment, Baba glimmeringly appeared in the entrance, and light flooded the cave with unusual brightness. He smilingly answered my mental inquiry by saying, "Do as I said; leave only at six." Some time later, opening my eyes and looking at my watch, I found it was nearing six, and I rose to leave. I felt fresh and invigorated as daylight began faintly penetrating the cave.

Returning to the bungalow, I asked, "Was I dreaming?" Baba said, "No, it was more like a daze; neither awake nor asleep. You actually experienced these things physically." Then I inquired, "Was it symbolic?" "Yes," answered Baba. "In the future you'll know its full meaning." 1919–21

The Women's Ashram on the Hill

By mid-August the women were settled in their new quarters on Meherabad Hill. In addition to Mansari, they were joined by Eruch's mother Gaimai and his sisters Manu and Meheru. The Jessawala women were soon followed by more Westerners: Nadine, Hedi, Helen and Irene. By the beginning of September there were nineteen women living at Meherabad.

Baba assigned each Westerner her own set of duties, which included housekeeping and gardening, as well as work on the new *Meher Baba Journal*. He assigned Helen, who was an Abstract Expressionist artist, to paint murals on the interior walls of the Dome, as the structure was now called. Though Helen was sixty, she became absorbed, working precariously on her back on bamboo scaffolding, painting the dome's ceiling. Hedi, also an artist, assisted Helen by mixing her paints and holding her brushes.

When Baba opened the maternity hospital, he named Nadine chief matron and hired a Catholic female doctor. But if a woman went into labor in the middle of the night, the doctor refused to get up to attend. One night, a local village woman was brought to the hospital at 3:00 AM in the last hours of labor. Luckily, Shireenmai was visiting and she came came into the ward with one of the other women. While Baba himself boiled water, she delivered the child. After the infant, a girl, had been bathed, Baba held her and kissed her repeatedly. He was so pleased with Shireenmai's maternal instincts. Hadn't she been the mother of God's own blessed form? 1952

Astonishingly, Baba then named his next parents, telling Gaimai, "When I return after seven hundred years, you'll be my mother and Kharman Masi, my father." Kharman Masi had been one of Merwan's earliest female disciples, and Baba revealed to her, "You were also Buddha's aunt." Hearing this, Shireenmai cautioned Gaimai, "Never, ever be the Avatar's mother! What a miserable existence! You've seen my plight—how outsiders insult me and won't even let me live in peace." 2064

One day, Baba took the women to see Helen's progress inside the Dome. The women thought it would be a nice gesture to invite Shireenmai along. Always a quick-wit, she replied, "No thanks, dears, I've seen quite enough of Baba's *dome* as a child." Dome is the Parsi word for buttocks.

One day, Baba dictated to the women: "One day, there'll be airplanes large enough to hold four hundred people on which my lovers will come here for my darshan," adding as he swept his hand in front of him, "Many Americans will come to stay here, and take over this place with huge colonies." With his thumb and forefinger together, he concluded, "There won't be even *that much* space left. It will be like Jerusalem. For my spiritual work this is the best possible place, and will always be the center of my work." MM 1:339, 222

Baba also took the women to Sarosh Cinema on several occasions, but in order to avoid other theatergoers he had the movies run at 5:00 AM. The projectionist, Rustom Hathidaru, long in Baba's contact, had been telling his assistant, Bhasker Pawar, about the Master.

But the man had absolutely no faith in any "Babas." "I've never bowed my head to any man. I'm a Catholic—it's against my religion! Meher Baba commits grave sins letting people bow down to him. God will surely punish him terribly!" No sooner had he said this, when Baba appeared. Gazing at him, Pawar felt a shock and instantly fell at Baba's feet.

Baba helped the shaken man up off the floor. "These days I permit no one to touch my feet. You did it out of love, but it has disturbed my work. Now, I must touch your feet and you have to 'share with me in the sin.'" Baba gently placed his head on the man's feet and Pawar was deeply moved to tears. Rustom later asked, "You touched Meher Baba's feet against your religion!" Pawar said, "Don't ask. I don't know. Who can control the heart's outburst?" 2632

This was the second Catholic in the local area with the family name Pawar, moved to bow down to the Master. The first had been the poor carpenter, Ajoba, who had welcomed Baba and his men to Meherabad with freshly baked bread, and then helped build some of the new structures there over a decade earlier.

When Baba had visited the Jessawala family in Nagpur, he had pointedly asked Gaimai about Eruch. "Why not give him to me?" Taken aback, Papa Jessawala pleaded, "Give you our only son? Baba smiled, "No. He's my son. But I'll give you another one." 1198–99

The "another" was Eruch's yet-to-be-born younger brother, Meherwan, named by Baba himself and the first of a long line of Meherwans to come in the future. Baba would call eight-year-old Meherwan to join his mother and sisters after the beginning of the first Blue Bus Tour.

One of the first things Meherwan noticed was how Baba's men, who were very rough on the edges, always shouting and arguing with each other, were "meek and mild as lambs" in Baba's presence. He also saw how the Western women sometimes had trouble getting along. It was hard for them to see eye to eye, as Baba himself bitterly complained, but he needed to create a balance of very different temperaments.

Meherwan later observed that one way to identify the court of a Perfect Master or Avatar is that he requires all kinds of people in order to balance their different temperaments in his court. Only he can accommodate everything and everyone. Not even saints could do it. Mani explained:

> Each of us around Baba was a strong personality. Baba conducted the whole thing like a symphony, and we each played our own little tune according to his rhythm, each having different temperaments and ways of living and thinking . . . Italian Princess Norina, Russian countess Nadine, then Elizabeth, a savvy New York businesswoman.
> Nonny Galey was elegant and dainty. Rano was a finicky artist, Kitty was equally strong-willed, Irene Billo had her own Swiss ideas, and Margaret was a dancer. Only Baba could roll us all around to come up with unity.

The Meherabad Zoo

Ascending Meherabad Hill to return to the women when his work at Lower Meherabad was finished, Baba always seemed to find a baby bird fallen from its nest, or a tiny rabbit that had lost its mother, or a little squirrel that couldn't make it back up the tree to join its family. He would bring it to the women, urging them, "Quick, feed it. It's hungry!" After invariably over-feeding the tiny creature, Baba would gently push it across the floor with his hand, coaxing it to exercise its meal off. It was said that Baba fed his pets better than he did his mandali!

Mehera recalled, "Baba loved holding these little birds. He'd look at them with such love, like an old friend, petting each, blowing kisses and giving them his loving touch. When bigger, they'd fly away to freedom. Or Baba himself might hold one in his hand and release it to the sky with such a smile." 1671

Over time Baba and the women collected so many animals that they comprised a menagerie. Margaret once observed only half jokingly that Elizabeth loved animals more than people, so it was only natural that she would foot the bills for what everyone called the Meherabad zoo.

In time, Baba's zoo included two pigs dubbed Nutti and Gutti, a peacock called Moti, two peahens christened Idi and Jingi, an antelope named Lily and a lamb called Meher. There were also parrots, snakes, blackbirds, rabbits, dogs, hens and ducks. The women were responsible for the day-to-day care of this ever-growing menagerie.

Baba sent out word to his lovers in India that he wanted a pet monkey, but one that would immediately respond to him. Various animals were sent, including a clever chimpanzee. But none of them seemed especially drawn to Baba. Then one day, a small crate arrived. Inside was a tiny monkey not much larger than a baby squirrel.

Meher Baba flanked on his right by his material mother, Shireenmai, and on his left by Gulmai Irani, his spiritual mother. Others in that row, sitting from far left are Kitty Davy, Gaimai Jessawala (whom Baba said would be his mother in his next advent after seven hundred years), and to the right of Gulmai, Soonamasi and Valu Pawar, whom Baba cured of blindness. In back row standing left to right Rano Galey, sister Mani, Mehera (holding alphabet board), Norina Matchabelli, Nadine Tolstoy, Helen Dahm (whose wall paintings adorn the inside of Baba's tomb), Irene Billo and Hedi Mertens. Front row sitting left to right, Manu and Meheru Jessawala, Khorshed Irani and Mansari Desai, Upper Meherabad, 1938.

Baba was called, and as usual, he had the men sit in a circle around the cage. If the monkey ran to Baba and jumped right into his lap, it was the lucky one. As soon as the cage was opened, like a streak of lightning the little rascal scampered straight to Baba, ran up his shoulder and began chattering wildly in his ear. "Listening" to the monkey's message, Baba smiled and nodded his head. And this is how Lucky got his name. He had huge sparkling eyes and long, soft eyelashes. He was so small that Katie Irani called him a "pocket monkey." 2011-12

Baba would take him on his lap and lovingly hold and caress him, and Lucky would kiss Baba's neck and then hide under his jacket or in his pocket. Baba hand-fed him bananas and other choice fruit. Then he would jump up on Baba's shoulder to inspect and groom Baba's hair. He couldn't get enough of Baba's warmth and light. The tiny creature was also getting a tremendous push forward in his evolution.

But Lucky was also mischievous, prancing around Baba's feet when he approached to play. Baba gave him to Norina to care for, and he proved anything but lucky for her. She was confined to bed in the upper Meherabad dormitory healing a strained foot ligament. She recalled:

> Our part-time life under the mosquito net became strained. Lucky slept in a box at the head of my bed, snoring all night, and insisted sitting on the palm of my hand for his afternoon nap. He'd escape from under the net and make havoc with tooth paste, powder boxes and fountain pens, all squeezed open and scattered wherever....
>
> To trick him down from rafters near the ceiling I'd put my arms around my neighbor and give loud, *spectacular kisses*, arousing Lucky's jealousy. When he quickly jumped between us I'd catch him and put him back in his cage. Aw 1 (no. 3): 21-22; 2424; HM 550

Lucky loved to interrupt Mansari, who was translating *Meher Baba Journal* articles into Gujarati, overturning her ink bottle and grabbing her pens and paper and running off with them. The little rascal was finally given away to a "lucky" family of devotees. 2143

A Traveling Ashram

The 1930s were drawing to a rapid close—a decade in which the Master had set the stage building up to a devastating world war, and another coming decade to deal with it and its aftermath. Looking back, it was also the period during which Baba attempted the bold experiment of blending his Eastern and Western female disciples together in a unique ashram.

In December 1938, Baba embarked on the first of four tours of India, which would continue for a period of three years, through 1941. Accompanying him would be the nineteen women living at Meherabad, as well as Katie Irani. This was the first and only time he would work so intensively with the women. He wanted to give them the chance to see the countryside and to experience lifestyles other than what they had known in Meherabad and Nasik. He intended to take them to visit important pilgrimage sites, many of which were associated with his previous Advents, as well as the shrines and tombs of saints and Perfect Masters. He also wished to locate a site for his Universal Spiritual Ashram.

He told them, "As you're well aware, all my movements and journeys have significance. Compare them to a king's personal inspection tour of a state to see how his work is progressing in different places. . . . Travelling with me involves great privations, and even greater when my greatest work is being accomplished." MM 1:220, 222

Baba's main focus, however, would be the search for *masts*—the God-intoxicated souls who would act as agents for his critical work throughout the war. The great mast tours that would occupy him into the mid-1940s began during the Blue Bus Tours. He declared, "Masts are my best medium for work in the world; so I exert myself to contact them." 2408

Baba designed the vehicle himself, which was painted two shades of blue, giving the bus its name. Its drivers would include

The Blue Bus, nearly packed and ready for the road, India, late 1938 or 1939. Eruch can be seen on the right, while Kaka is loading the roof.

Elizabeth, Eruch and Dr. Donkin. The roof was loaded with luggage, bedding rolls, cooking gear and provisions. The interior of the bus held perishable food, the buckets Baba used for bathing masts, baskets, fragile clay food containers and small personal items belonging to the women. Built to accommodate fifteen passengers and two people in the cab, in reality, the bus had to accommodate twice as many passengers on occasion. Packed and loaded, Rano said that it resembled a gypsy caravan. 1960

The Blue Bus carried Baba and the women thousands of miles throughout the country as well as into Ceylon (now Sri Lanka). On several journeys it was sent on ahead filled with luggage while the rest of the party traveled by rail. Men invited to accompany him travelled ahead to secure accommodations in many of the locations where Baba planned to halt. Although the tours were challenging, they were also delightfully rewarding for the women.

Baba routinely woke them before dawn so that they could eat and be on the bus when it was still dark. Elizabeth, who hated early risings, had to be wide awake to drive the bus. She found it almost impossible to be bright and cheery, and, unable to focus, she sometimes wept out of sheer helplessness. But she always did it and never said no to Baba. He'd clap his hands to awaken the women at 4:00 AM, and a few minutes later he'd say to her, "It's late now. Come on, get up! The others are having their tea and you haven't even washed your face."

> Even when the women returned to Meherabad between tours, Elizabeth was unable to function early in the morning. The other women would watch her come down the steep stairs from the upper floor of the dormitory, eyes closed, carrying a lantern, holding their breath until her feet safely touched the ground. M 137

Like a zombie Elizabeth would dress, saying, "Don't hurry me, Baba dear, I'm coming, I'm coming." Kitty would make her feel worse by proclaiming the exact time to the minute. Elizabeth said that she could bear it more easily if she just didn't know how early it was.

One morning, just before they were to pull out, while everyone else was rushing about in the dark, Elizabeth sat, dazed, on a bedroll with, tears rolling down her cheeks. Baba passed by and snapped his fingers as if to ask, "Elizabeth, what's this?" "I'm not crying, Baba," she replied. He held her head to his chest, telling her, "You know, Elizabeth, from those I love I take everything and then I give to them—high blood pressure, arthritis, lumbago," continuing with a long list of ailments. Elizabeth then got up and climbed into the driver's seat, laughing. MM 2:32

Many of the roads in India at this time were unpaved, and the women were always covered in the dust that rained in through the open windows of the bus. But worse than this, Gulmai always sat near the front holding her grandson Jangoo, who was just a toddler, on her lap. When he had to go to the bathroom, she would hold him up and tell him to pee out the window. Those behind him got sprayed if they were sitting by a window. Sometime he was carsick and had to vomit out the window.

The women were often disheveled from riding in the bus for hours on end, and sometimes when they stopped in a town, a crowd would gather, shouting, "Oh, a traveling circus is in town!" Or they might be mistaken for a film company scouting locations.

On October 14, 1939, during Baba's eight-month halt in Bangalore, Rano's mother Nonny, age sixty-four, succumbed to heart failure. Baba was out of town that day, but on his way back, he kept asking the time. At 6:40 PM, he gestured to Chanji, "Nonny has just expired." When they arrived at the Links Bungalow, where they were staying in Bangalore, Baba went straight to her room. Looking at her intently, he placed two fingers on her closed eyelids. As he did, Nonny gave a final sigh, dropping her head to one side—the final release. Her final words had been, "What beauty! What beauty!"

Baba took Rano in his embrace and spelled on his board: "Nonny was one of my greatest lovers. She always gave spontaneously for my work to serve mankind's greatest need." He also said that it was the first time he had been present at the death of one of his disciples, revealing to Rano that he had given her mother mukti. Her soul had merged into his ocean of love forever in infinite bliss. Nonny's body was cremated outside Bangalore and her ashes were sent to Meherabad, where they were interred on the hill. 2040

Baba often escorted the women to sites connected with his earlier Advents. One day during the second tour they visited Mathura, where Lord Krishna was born, before continuing on to Gokul, where he spent his childhood, and to Vrindavan, where he lived with the cow herders—his gopis. Near a temple in Vrindavan, a young mast playing the flute became ecstatic seeing Baba, and exclaimed, "Here comes my Murlival—the Flute Player! I've been waiting for you!"

Visiting these places associated with Krishna, Baba told the women, "When I see these places, I remember my old haunts where I used to play with the gopis and steal milk and curds. Here, I played my flute and my Radha would come running to me! Today I've brought my new gopis, and Mehera is my new Radha. Now, let's go see where Krishna ate his last meal." The women were surprised and delighted when Baba took them back to the dak bungalow for tea where they and their Krishna had earlier eaten lunch. 1983

The most disturbing event of the second tour took place on Christmas morning 1939, when Baba had a sudden heart cramp. He told the mandali to mark the time: 9:27 AM. The pain lasted three minutes. Tremors warning of a devastating earthquake in Turkey had begun at that exact moment, lasting exactly three minutes. Two days later Turkey experienced a disastrous earthquake, which took thirty thousand lives and affected thousands more. 2067

When the group returned to Meherabad at the end of the second tour, the mandali had to escort twenty-five men from the Bangalore *mast* ashram, only six of whom were true *masts*, five dogs, three monkeys, two pet birds and several geese, as well as a gazelle, peacock, lamb and white rabbit. They were all crammed cheek to jowl in a single third-class railway compartment, with trunks, packing cases, tables and chairs that had been brought to Bangalore.

As soon as the train left the station, Shariat Khan, a *mast* who wore bells tied around his ankles, began dancing to rhythms he beat out on an empty kerosene tin, making Eruch and Baidul join him "like circus bears," Eruch related decades later. "Strangers would try to enter the compartment, but quickly changed their minds, appalled seeing this mad entourage.

Baba and the women made two more journeys in the Blue Bus. The third tour was the longest, taking Baba's entourage south to the island nation of Ceylon, then west to Goa and Panjim, north to Jaipur and then on to Dehradun. From there they traveled west to Quetta, now in Pakistan, before making their way east and south back to Meherabad. Its most memorable event involved a crossing of the Indus River during a raging rainstorm, on a pontoon bridge consisting of wooden planks nailed onto teak boats that rose and fell with the waves in the river.

In addition to masts, Baba continued to look for a suitable boy. He sent Papa Jessawala out on one occasion to find and keep a boy ready for him to work with when he arrived in Lahore.

> Papa brought nearly sixty boys, whom he had stand at attention in a row on the railway station platform. He proudly told Baba, "Select whomever you like. You've no idea how difficult it was to find such fine boys!" This made Baba laugh, and giving a rupee to each boy, he sent them all back home.
>
> Papa couldn't believe it. "Didn't you like even one?"
>
> "It's not a question of liking. My work is over."
>
> "Your work is over? How could it be over by paying a rupee to each? I could have done that, and it would have saved me all the trouble of rounding them up and bringing them here."
>
> Baba smiled, "It's my work; how could you possibly understand it?"
>
> "Strange—very strange work indeed! With so much effort, I found and brought so many boys—and you sent them all back. Is this the way you work?"

Again, this made Baba laugh, and he calmed him, "Don't worry. You'll reap the fruit of your labor. This work was given to you solely for the purpose of allowing you to serve me." 2208–09

The last tour was the shortest, taking them south to the seaside town of Karwar, and after the previous tour's events, this one felt like a real seaside holiday. They returned home again in in exactly one month.

Wartime gas rationing forced the Blue Bus into retirement, but Baba's mast work would continue to consume much of his attention throughout WWII and well into the 1940s. The Blue Bus Tours have come to be recognized as one of the most important phases of his work in this Advent, and Baba said, "This Blue Bus is like Krishna's chariot, and after my manifestation people will worship it!"

A few years later, in a moment of extreme frustration, Baba said, "I've worked twenty-one years; seven with men, and how much I enjoyed that; the next seven with boys, which I both suffered and enjoyed; then seven with the women. You don't know how sick and fed up I am with that! But thank God, that phase is ending."

Mani later recalled, "Baba worked for years with the men mandali, Prem Ashram boys, the mad and masts, and then the women. Oh, working with the women! He never actually said it, but certainly implied, 'Never, ever again!'" MM 1:292; 2:185

Life with the Master was so challenging that Baba said only half-jokingly that it was harder for Him to manage an ashram full of women than to oversee WWII. Fortunately, he was blessed with what Mani called a "God-sized" sense of humor to get him through undoubtedly his most difficult advent of the past five thousand years. Baba said it himself: "Divinity includes all that's beautiful and gracious. How can you expect a Perfect Being to have no sense of humor?" 1755; MM1:454

Chapter Twenty-Five
War Clouds

Baba decried organized religions, maintaining that they were dried-up riverbeds. They were inflamed with age-old prejudicial tensions, hatreds and wars. He poignantly remarked that even the Himalayas, once so highly revered as the home of great sages and saints, were no longer spiritual:

> Spiritually, they're just masses of stone. They have no more importance than huge heaps of rock.
> Man wants God but is given stone in the form of churches, temples, idols and images! They are now all corrupt! They were once considered places of worship. The places of God's prayer and love have turned into pitiable business centers for their caretakers.
> Thus, the names of God and religion are besmeared, bringing humanity utterly disastrous natural calamities . . . with untold miseries suffered in their wake.
> This is why the Avatars' and Sadgurus' teachings caution not to give importance to such places and forms of worship. Their spiritual work is to diminish and destroy all these piles of stone which keep humanity away from God rather than drawing it closer." 1912

Baba emphasized that all this suffering, these wars and natural calamities, would inevitably come. Discordant energies had to be allowed to rise up to the surface of humanity's consciousness and be played out during the Avatar's physical presence on earth. He added that some such wars would continue long after he dropped his physical body; but promising that after his Manifestation a very long period of peace was to come.

The Disease of Selfishness Leads to War

Whereas WWI was under the control of the Perfect Master Sai Baba of Shirdi, WWII would come under Meher Baba's direct charge. Baba declared:

> In spite of its attendant evils, this war over which no earthly power has control shall play its part in my Mission of helping humanity fulfill the Divine Plan on Earth to inherit the coming era of Truth and Love, of Peace and Universal Brotherhood, of Spiritual Understanding and Unbounded Creativity. This war is a necessary evil and in God's plan to awaken humanity to higher values. If humanity fails to profit by the lessons of war, it will have suffered in vain. GD 15

These kinds of events are meant to true humanity's course toward its real but forgotten collective needs and goals. After Meher Baba returned from Hollywood, the laser-like focus of his work would be on the preparation for and waging of a horrific but spiritually necessary second world war; a conflagration he said would draw in both hemispheres of the global brain: East and West, and would be fought on land as well as in the sea and air. His comments likewise became focused on the coming war:

> Man alone is responsible for war. Through greed, vanity, selfishness and cruelty he brings this recurring evil upon himself. In His Grace, God transmutes this man-made tragedy into a channel for the quickening of humanity to

recognize higher values. Appalling as it is, man's war is thus saved by the Infinite from remaining an unmitigated evil. MW 1

Killing over one quarter of a billion people since 1900, 263 wars have been fought as the inevitable explosive gross manifestations of mankind's collective egocentric false minds. With WWII about to erupt, Meher Baba commented on how conflicts between nations are unavoidable until that false ego-self is tamed and eliminated.

But he also said that as man faces the truth and begins to appreciate how all humanity and all creation are one, the problem of wars will start to disappear. Wars must be so clearly seen by all to be both unnecessary and unreasonable that the immediate problem will not be to stop wars, but to wage them spiritually against that attitude of mind which generates them. In light of the truth of the unity of all, a cooperative and harmonious life becomes inevitable. Thus, the chief task for those tasked with rebuilding after a great war is to do their utmost to dispel the ignorance enveloping humanity. LH 129-30

Meher Baba during the pre-war years, 1930s

If it is man who creates war, it is God who takes on that chaos and suffering, using them as a vehicle for massive purification and spiritual growth; thus providing opportunities for bravery, loyalty, patience, love and after a long end-run, eternal redemption. Countless numbers of people whose lives are sacrificed to war and disasters may receive mukti.

Or, if they must reincarnate, they quickly return billions of impressions lighter to a new life on a more direct path toward the realization of their ultimate spiritual destiny. Since this is the only reason we reincarnate, all other considerations are secondary, however horrific a war may be. Some may be shocked and have difficulty accepting this.

The analogy of a disastrous forest fire burning everything in its path for millions of acres is one way of trying to comprehend these events. Richer, more fertile forests quickly grow to replace old, dying trees which have to be destroyed for the good of the entire forest. Life is ever renewing and no one and nothing is ever lost.

As Baba explained, "It is better that men forget their petty selves under the pressure of a collective calamity than be permanently encased in the ignoble pursuit of personal safety in their ruthless attempt to perpetuate their own separative existence and interests." GD 13

Once, in 1934, while in Paris, Baba explained to a man who had come to take his darshan:

> World War I wasn't enough to bring a change of heart in man. The world, purged of its pride, will listen to reason only after an even more terrible purgatory. A global holocaust will engulf the world. And that's not an opinion; I *know*!
>
> Every day, hour and minute of a man's life is a sort of minor war between the heart and mind, emotion and intellect, good and bad. When these individual conflicts spread out and develop, the collective result eventually takes the shape of a big, worldwide war cloud which can never be

avoided by any number of peace conferences, unless and until the very root cause is removed. 1615

War as Divine Diplomacy

From the mid-1930s onward, the Avatar geared up intensely for the onslaught of WWII, which he'd direct like an orchestra conductor. In 1936, an Associated Press reporter asked the Master, "Will there be a war before you speak?" Baba replied, "Yes, it is necessary—unavoidable. None will win, none will lose. But it will create an awakening for a better and higher ideal. These false ideas—race, color, nationality, nationalism, etc. will be eradicated and destroyed with universal human brotherhood and real idealism established. I shall lead the way for those true seekers." 1748

As early as March 1936, newspapers foresaw war between Germany and France, and on March 14, Baba confirmed their predictions, "It is definite that a war will break out involving the whole world. It's better it not start now. The instant war begins, my work will also begin." 1703

In March 1938, signaled by a spectacular aurora borealis over European skies, Hitler made the final move to mobilize *Anschluss*, the annexation of Austria into the German Reich. This was the first definitive step towards the beginning of WWII.

In June 1939 Baba spoke about his advent as Avatar Krishna, saying that had Krishna not brought about war, he wouldn't have given the Bhagavad Gita. Had Krishna said, "Don't fight," who would have listened? Everybody was in a fighting mood. When he said, "Fight!" he brought the real meaning of Truth into the world. Baba said the world was going back to that same barbarous state as in the time of Krishna, and now there would be a truly horrific battle.

Later, however, after the outbreak of the war, Baba would return to this theme, saying, "Go to war if you can't avoid it, but *never* fight for the sake of killing. Just help and kill detached or be killed without fear or anger toward the killer; few can do it. I want this war to make things right for spiritual progress and advancement." 2018

When asked in 1939 by a reporter about his interest in politics, Baba repeated what he had said in the *London Sunday Express*, "I don't concern myself with ethics, science or politics. Self-knowledge includes *everything*. He who gains Self-knowledge gains everything." He also spoke of worldwide corruption by so-called leaders craving power by fair means or foul: "So much deception is purely for the sake of almighty power, while politicians and bankers aren't the least interested in the truth, lest their selfish ends put them completely out of the picture." 2055

Why do the God-Man's acute observations ring even more alarming to us today in the early twenty-first century than when he made them over eighty years ago? As the Hindus say, "Before dying, a cobra's venom is at its most deadly poisonous state."

> To be in the public eye, politicians invent lies, concoct stories and distort facts in the name of public service. They present these lies to mislead the public either because they are big names or by the very tricks of the originators who have the ability to misrepresent facts with sensational words to influence weakness in the mass mind. It is the same all over the world.
>
> It's a game of winning and losing—the inevitable struggle for existence is played out in all departments and aspects of life. The struggle goes on and on in religion, politics, morality, ethics, business, industry, etc. at different times, places and in different ways according to conditions. 2055

By the late 1930s Baba's work had become so intense that it affected the women living on Meherabad Hill. On many nights, just before falling asleep, Hedi would feel a rapid tingling, like tiny electric shocks. Then suddenly, she would realize that it was morning, her eyes still open as if no time had passed; nor would she have moved until the moment of her awakening.

One morning she found Norina bent over her with a puzzled expression. Hedi announced, "Oh, I've just been to Chartres." Norina exclaimed, "Chartres! That's in France!" "Yes," Hedi replied, "I've been in France." Norina ran right to Baba to tell him. He explained, "Yes, I've sent her to France on the past twenty-six nights to do important work for me there. . . . Life is a series of experiences needing innumerable forms. Death is but *an interval* in that one long life. And as I've said before, '*Life is wife, knife and strife!*' [lust, violence and anger]." 2033

Meher Baba conveyed to Irene Billo that war was *de facto* "divine diplomacy" of another kind, necessary to avert a worse disaster—the death of half the planet's brain by the complete collapse of Western civilization. He would be on tenterhooks until war was declared, actively working with the mad and *masts* as his battlefield chessmen. It's impossible to comprehend the excruciating actuality of war in one with a universal mind, as when Baba revealed, *"I am daily, continuously crucified, as none of you can ever begin to know."* Of course, nails were never driven into his hands and feet. He was referring to his mental crucifixion as his consciousness was connected with the unimaginable suffering in the world's second, ultimately nuclear, war.

On September 30, 1938, Baba remarked, "With all the talk of peace, spiritually speaking both war and peace are nothing. Externally war is most dreadful, and unless absolutely necessary for the spiritual upheaval, I'd never allow this war to be. For years I've predicted a far more terrible war than the last one was definite." GM 133

Three days later he wrote to Delia DeLeon in London:

> The world is in such a state of fear and perplexity that no one knows what will happen. But wait and see. I know all—present and future. Nothing can stop the work I am here to do. Am I not the Avatar? The world will soon know and see me as such. Be patient and firm as a rock in your faith and love. Then I can use you to channel my work of divine love for the upliftment of humanity. 1953

An Ashram Skit Foreshadows the War

On May 3, 1939, near the end of the first Blue Bus Tour, the women staged a play on Manu Jessawala's birthday at Baba's behest, based on the "plot points" he had given Mani to incorporate. Talented at mounting productions for the women to perform for Baba, Mani had written a pantomime skit parodying world leaders. She cast herself as Adolf Hitler, Katie as Benito Mussolini, and Rano as Prime Minister Neville Chamberlain. Meheru and Naja portrayed other politicos. 2005; M 133

While the women were performing their own silent, Chaplinesque skit for Baba, Chaplin himself was filming *The Great Dictator*—his own parody of Hitler and one of Baba's favorite Chaplin films. After seeing *The Great Dictator* on its release the following year, Baba praised Chaplin's acting as Hitler and Billy Gilbert's role as Col. Buckshot, portraying Hitler's successor, Herman Göering. The men and women all saw the picture. Baba commented, "It's the only film I'd liked to have seen seven times!" MM 2:145

In June, Baba told the women:

> People want war—either a bloody war—worse than WWI, affecting every part of the world, including America and Persia [Iran], or an economic war throughout the world

which would be far *worse* than a bloody war and would result in internal civil revolutions everywhere, Germany fighting with Germany and killing Hitler, Italy fighting with Italy and killing Mussolini and so on. It would be better to have war. If not, everywhere there will be bloody civil revolution.

Do you know what happened in the French Revolution? It will be just like that everywhere.

The "No God—No Religion" campaign is flourishing and the "God and Religion" campaigns are low. Russia, France, Italy and Germany are internally and unconsciously becoming "Non-God" believers. So are Persia, Turkey and India.

Germany believes Hitler to be its Savior; Italy, Mussolini as its Savior. What about Russia?

Can you believe how horrible it will be when war starts? London, Paris, Berlin—in a few days like a desert. Women and children— all will suffer.

On September 1, 1939, nine months after Baba began his historic Blue Bus journeys, Hitler invaded Poland. There was great excitement when, exactly four months to the day the women had performed their pantomime, Prime Minister Neville Chamberlain officially declared war on Germany. The horrific game of WWII was officially on—just what Baba had been waiting for.

That same day he began sending Adi Sr., Jal, Elizabeth and Donkin in turns to a nearby shop that had a radio, so that they could listen to war news and report back. Donkin recorded in his diary, "Baba was peeved on the previous days over the delay. He's so relieved now that the war is on." After a few days more they rented a small radio to listen throughout the day. DD 18

Baba felt relieved and greatly unburdened. In the suspense of these leaders' indecision he felt deep responsibility: "England has kept her word and won't rest till Hitler is crushed. Now comes a long fight with Germany and Nazism." Baba said Hitler was mad —crazy and brutal, and Mussolini a mean, poor wretch who'd be crushed. 2269

Now, only selfless love could win the day:

> Only through selfless love is it possible for humanity to eradicate greed, intolerance and exploitation. These three demons are responsible for war in all its gross and subtle forms which they assume in civilized life. In no other way can the mass mind be purged of its age-old war-psychosis. Only with redeeming clarity will the truth be truly perceived.
>
> War is not only abominable, but *never* necessary to adjust differences of any nature between nations. The chief task of those deeply concerned with humanity's regeneration is to wage a holy war against this *pernicious state of mind that justifies aggression in any form.* This can be accomplished only by dispelling the spiritual apathy and ignorance which hold mankind hostage in total bondage.
>
> If humanity is to redeem itself, it must emerge from this dreadful cataclysm of war with unimpaired spiritual integrity, with hearts free from the poison of malice and revenge, with minds disburdened of blows given and received, with souls unscathed by suffering and filled with the spirit of unconditional surrender to the ultimate Divine Will. MW 4-5

Even the All-knowing One kept up with the world's perspective on the war. If he himself didn't skim the newspaper, Baba would have one of the men read out selected articles—-tragic and comic—-from what he fondly referred to as the "bogus news." Afterwards, wanting to hear letters from his lovers, Baba would gesture:

> Now let's have the real news! . . . You see me sitting here quietly; how can you know what I'm really doing quietly in this corner. . . . You can't even imagine the conditions of the people in Europe now—no rest, no sleep—a state of continued anxiety and tension. It isn't like the last war—fought on land and water; now not so much a shooting-war, it will mostly be bombing from the air.
>
> Hitler isn't so mad as to rush to distant places like India without the aid of Russia. But Japan certainly has her eyes on India and wants it. My blessings to England. Had it failed now, it would be the end. It's impossible now for Hitler to withdraw at this stage. Even if he says "Stop!" the other countries won't, for they're determined to destroy Nazism. Let's hope America helps now—with money and supplies, if not with men; it will help a lot. When the last Munich Peace Pact was signed, I told you definitely there'd be a war. I'm glad it's begun—not because I said so, but because it's inevitable as an essential prelude to the great upheaval in the world. If the war runs its full course, the world will witness devastating destruction such as it has never known since the creation.
>
> It will spread everywhere and be full of surprises, changing the entire history and world map, affecting countries far removed from the war zone—India, Persia and Afghanistan. . . . They're frightened and in panic preparing for it, but they don't know what I've decided. I'll give you a big surprise. I do things suddenly; this surprise will be sudden and soon. 2033–34; Mani's 1938 *Red Letter Book*

Despite calling it bogus, Baba continued to read the news on a daily basis, tracking world events, and he kept a map where troop movement and battles could be charted. Throughout the war Rano subscribed to *Time Magazine*, receiving each weekly issue by mail. Initially Baba took little interest in it, but later he'd have her read out certain articles. Then if an issue didn't come, he'd have her send for a replacement.

In fact, throughout the Blue Bus Tours, Baba spoke to the women about world events and encouraged them to keep up with the news, all except for Mehera, who wasn't allowed to read. When the women read articles aloud in front of her, they had to remember to substitute "Mrs. Hitler" for Hitler, "Mrs. Mussolini" for Mussolini, and "so-and-so" in reference to lesser known players. It drove the Westerners crazy.

Much of Baba's coming work would be aimed at drawing America into the fray. He said that Roosevelt had a good heart, was sincere and capable and wanted to help, but faced great odds at home with a majority of Americans sick of war and wanting neutrality. They felt the countless lives lost in WWI were sacrificed to no avail, and now they thanked God for the separation afforded by the Atlantic and Pacific Oceans.

Baba quipped to Donkin, "Chamberlain should prod that fat-chinned, big-bellied Roosevelt with his umbrella." Later, just before America entered the war, Baba commented that Roosevelt's speech meant war, and America would play a very great part in humanity's battle. 2206

"All are mine," he said, "you as well as they. How do you know God doesn't work through these leaders? Churchill's the right man for his place. Gandhi is weak, but honest; Hitler strong, but dishonest. Only God works through, leads and knows them all!" 2161

Baba once used the metaphor of boiling cane reeds in the sugar-making process to describe the cleansing of hearts. When the sugar cane is cut, put in big vats and boiled, a thick black, stinking froth rises to the top of the vat. In order for the heart to be cleansed, the "scum and impurities" of sanskaras must rise to the top to be skimmed off by the Avatar.

But by the end of the boiling process, after the froth has been skimmed away, what's left is a pure sweet golden liquid that crystallizes into sugar. Likewise, the Avatar's work, including the direction of wars, brings to the surface the scum of humanity's unconscious, collective past, which has accumulated since the previous advent.

As it had been fourteen hundred years since Avatar Mohammed's advent, a double, seven-hundred-year cycle had passed, and so a much deeper cleansing than usual is taking place. The Avatar allows and encourages humanity's accumulated impressions to manifest, as in the current machine age, the Kali Yuga, enabling him to skim them off to produce the pure crystal awareness of God.

CHRIST COME AGAIN

Chapter Twenty-Six

Baba's Wayfarers

In 1942, while searching the Himalayas for *masts*, Baba revealed:

> There are two lakhs [200,000] *masts* in India, one thousand in Russia and one thousand in China. Europe has only a few. *Masts* in India are the original spiritual "office holders"; those in Europe are agents drawing spiritual force from Indian *masts*. In Rome, there is one very advanced *mast*. The agents are linked with the original office bearers. Indian masts are officers in charge of regions.
>
> They also control the European regions through agents. The Rome agent gets "power" from India and distributes it to European agents. Russian and Chinese masts are like Indian original workers and also help European masts through the distributor in Rome.
>
> The Russian, Chinese and Indian *masts* render reciprocal help. Spiritually degraded people from India are reborn in the West. Meritorious souls from the West are reborn in India, as are the Indian meritorious souls so that they may advance spiritually. 2294

Donkin described the qualities of *masts*:

> *Majzoob*s can be on the fifth or sixth plane; *Pirs*—sixth plane; *Wali*—fifth plane; *Masts*—third, fourth or fifth plane; God-mad—first or second plane; and the world-mad—zero plane! In the past, *masts* were little known outside the Muslim world. But since Baba contacted so many, others in the East are coming to know and recognize these God-intoxicated jewels." DD 271; 2187-88

Baba said that the mind of one advanced on the spiritual path works very, very slowly. The mind of one who is simply mad works very, very fast. That's the difference. Outwardly, there may be little difference; inwardly, there is such a vast difference. Only a true Master can tell that difference.

The Search for *Masts*

Traveling the length and breadth of India, Baba contacted thousands of God-intoxicated souls, using their spiritual energy to direct the war, moving them symbolically like pieces on a chessboard to accomplish the inner aspects in his war work.

Baba frequently engaged his agents, who had complete use of their faculties, but he would often enlist *masts* to stand in an agent's place like a relay switch to carry out important Inner work connected to specific places and events in the world. But it was difficult work, both for Baba and the *masts*:

> It is most difficult for a spiritually intoxicated *mast* to come out of the self-sufficiency of his state, as he is so immersed in bliss he has no need to get linked with anyone and has no wants. Just as a *mast* becomes completely indifferent to his body or physical conditions of his life, he can

also become indifferent to the physical or spiritual conditions of others, and may get walled-in by his own self-sufficiency. In such desirelessness, only the Master can draw him out of his choice of isolation.

The Master can awaken within him an expansive love breaking through all limitations to prepare him for shouldering the responsibility of rendering service to others in need of spiritual help. Stationed on the inner planes and free from limitations and handicaps in the gross world, a mast is often in contact with a far greater number of souls than is an ordinary person.

Because a *mast's* mind has such countless far-reaching links, he can be a more effective agent for spiritual work than persons with only gross world awareness. A *mast's* mind is often used directly by the Master to send his spiritual help to different parts of the world. W 10

Just prior to the outbreak of WWII Baba's priority became contacting these advanced souls. He traveled more than seventy thousand miles to hunt down these precious spiritual jewels, whom he thought of his most beloved children. "If man is God playing an ignorant fool, then a *mast* is God playing the child. When the Master submits himself to the sordid limitations of physical existence, it's not for his own sake but for mankind." MM 2:226

Few had any idea of the hardships Baba and the men underwent in this work over the years, traveling thousands of miles , often without luggage or bedrolls, spending sleepless nights on hard wooden benches at railway stations or in third-class train carriages. It was difficult to find decent food and they had no place to bathe. Only Baba's status as the God-man enabled him to maintain his health while laboring so hard.

Among the mandali, Eruch and Baidul were most often responsible for locating *masts*, although all the the men assisted at one time or another. Day and night, often for many days at a time,

Eruch and Baidul traveled from one remote place to another on Baba's order. Baba gave Baidul an uncanny sixth sense to perceive the spiritual scent of true *masts*. He could detect a subtle fragrance that enabled him to locate them. It was a unique service to Baba. No one else could do it. Baba gave him the title of Sardar, meaning "Chief of the *Masts*."

Finding a *mast*, Baidul and Eruch often spent hours and sometimes days using all means possible to cajole him into meeting Baba. Sometimes Baba had to come to the *mast*. He once spent days seeking out a *mast* named Krishna. Seeing Baba on the road, the young man leapt into Baba's arms in ecstasy, kissing him profusely, and exclaiming, "You are Allah! Allah!" They fell down on the ground, rolling in the dust. "What a sight for the heavens to see the lover and Beloved locked in a divine embrace!" 2424

Eruch recalled, "After a good *mast* contact, Baba was never happier. Even walking there was triumph in his stride, such radiance and happiness." TH 288

As more and more of these *masts* and mad souls came into Baba's orbit, he decided to create safe havens for them, where they could be cared for properly. In 1936, at the same time that the first rumblings of war were heard in Germany, Baba established the strange and wonderful Rahuri ashram for the insane and the truly God-mad. It was the first of a series of *mast* ashrams that he would create, each one dissolved when the work was finished.

Even the mad were kept alongside the few truly intoxicated souls as the Lord of the Universe became a companion to the afflicted. From 4:00 AM daily, Baba gave himself over to tending them. He washed their faces, shaved them, cut their hair, emptied and cleaned their latrines, hand-fed them their meals, and embraced and kissed them. He even arranged musical entertainment for them. Rahuri ashram became the safe house for those suffering mental affliction, and the Lord of Creation welcomed them to his refuge. Baba's work gave the *masts* a spiritual push forward. He explained their agonized state:

> Masts are desperately in love with God—agonizingly overcome by intense spiritual energies that are too much for them, forcing them to lose contact with the world and shed the normal human habits and customs of civilized society. While in a state of spiritual splendor, they may live in physical squalor. Drowned in ecstasy, only the divine love embodied in a Perfect Master can reach them. 1734
>
> All *masts* are intoxicated by divine love for God. A normal person on alcohol or drugs enjoys this sensation so long as the intoxicant is sufficiently concentrated in his blood and tissues. A drunkard feels happy, cares for no one or anything and has only the sensation of drunkenness; past, present or future have practically no meaning. But as soon as this ordinary intoxication passes away, the drunkard suffers a crash—a hangover. . . . The God-intoxicated experiences the same sensation. Like a drunkard he enjoys and cares for no one and nothing, in proportion to the extent of his inner intoxication; the vast difference is the *mast's* [far higher] intoxication is continual; it may increase, but never decrease or becomes harmful. It's an inner state of permanent and unalloyed intoxication, independent of anything external. Creation is full of bliss and the *mast* enjoys this bliss.
> He becomes intoxicated to an almost unlimited extent, virtually consuming and absorbing him, making the world around him totally vanish. Absorbed in God alone, such a one is continually preoccupied in thinking of God [as the Beloved], and with that comes a lightning-bolt of pure love,

consuming him even further in the state of divine intoxication.

How does one become a *mast*? They have minds unbalanced through ceaselessly dwelling upon God and neglecting normal human requirements . . . or unbalanced by sudden contact with an advanced spiritual being. There are those who've sought spiritual experiences or have met with a crisis from which they're unable to recover. What characterizes all real *masts* is their utter and ultimate love of God. 1733–34

Despite the filthy living conditions where they are found and not having bathed for years, an other-worldly light shines from their fierce, beautiful eyes. Baba said, "Their love is such that I bow down and serve them, bathe, shave and feed them—I'm so happy when I'm with them. I'm just like a kid, a child." Mani's Diaries, 1962-63

Masts become permanently unconscious in part or in whole of their physical bodies, actions and surroundings. Their principal sensation is their permanent enjoyment of divine intoxication. As spiritual drunkards, they experience themselves as God. Enjoying a permanent state of spiritual intoxication makes them dazed and unaware of their bodies or surroundings. Intense love for God overcomes and drowns them in ecstasy; only Divine love can reach them. They are not approachable by any other means. They are drowned in the pure oceanic bliss of God's presence everywhere.

The film *Nasik 1937* captures Baba inside the *mast* ashram at Rahuri looking radiantly happy as he shaves and feeds the *masts* and the mad. Nowhere does he look more gloriously like Jesus than in this scene. Even when he was still a mile or more away, these *masts* could detect the scent of his approach. Crouching on the ground, they would peer under the bamboo fence, eagerly awaiting his arrival.

Baba's Scribe

While it was the Eastern men who assisted Baba with the *masts* most of the time, there was one Westerner who was vital to his work with the God-intoxicated. William Donkin had met the Master in London in 1933 while still in medical school, studying to be an orthopedic surgeon. Entering Baba's room, he saw a blinding light and became dazed, not knowing who Baba was or how he even got in and out of that room. Baba expressed great happiness in meeting him and remarked, "I'm opening a hospital at my ashram in India and I'll need a doctor who knows surgery."

After this polite interview, with Donkin's hand on the doorknob, Baba struck him with an arrow of divine Love. The shock changed the course of his life forever, for in that instant he knew Baba was God. Baba invited Donkin to join him in India after he had completed his medical degree.

William Donkin, intimate disciple and member of the mandali for over thirty years, and author of *The Wayfarers*, documenting Baba's extraordinary *mast* work during this Advent

Like Lawrence of Arabia, Donkin, at age twenty, had made a six-month expedition mapping routes across the Sahara Desert on camelback. He embarked on an even more adventurous journey in 1939, turning his back on England, his family and any hopes they had for him as a doctor. Arriving in India, he joined Meher Baba to

Meher Baba explaining a point to his disciples

live and travel throughout India as one of Baba's personal physicians and an intimate disciple for the next thirty years. LL 4:7; 1558–59

During the war's early days, he would serve in the British army, setting up a base hospital in Bangalore for facial burns for wounded soldiers from the North African and Burmese theaters of war. Fluent in Italian, he treated Italian prisoners of war in the 160-bed hospital. Aw 13 (no.1): 34

Donkin also learned Urdu, Persian and Hindi while creating an extensive record of Baba's work with God-intoxicated souls—*The Wayfarers*—-a groundbreaking account containing descriptions of *masts* and advanced souls accompanied by many rare photos. One day Donkin observed, "You know, Baba, your *mast* work is so important. It's fascinating and beyond significant! Yet there's no record of it. If an account were written down it would be so useful and interesting for future generations."

Two days later Baba pitched the idea back to Donkin, saying, "That was an excellent idea. *You write it.* You're the only one who could do it. I'll help you." Thus, *The Wayfarers* was born. Baba began giving him explanations and describing all the different kinds of *masts*.

"So I did it," Donkin wrote, "my aim being to faithfully record Baba's visible work with *masts* and others. His real *Inner work* with them he'd just not reveal to us." Baba's *mast* work showed the world that the Lord of the Universe is the slave of his divinely intoxicated ones, and a pure testament to the reality of Meher Baba's Avatarhood. The book *The Wayfarers* is so unique that the US Library of Congress calls it "the most unusual book we have ever received and likely the first book of its kind in the world." Aw 1 (no. 1): 3; 2557–58

Baba explained to Donkin that, when attaining consciousness of the subtle and mental planes, if the soul isn't mercifully "veiled" as to its state, and doesn't choose a non-stop express route like a train, it may be lured into taking "side-trips" through the backstreets of what are called the heavens of the inner spiritual planes. In these heavens souls becomes so enchanted that they lose the normal consciousness that ordinary people experience.

Becoming stuck in these heavens leads to all sorts of peculiar, erratic, endearing and even hilarious behavior. In a sense, *masts* become so comfortably marooned in this intoxicated state that they don't want to leave it. But to continue their spiritual progress, they cannot remain here and need a "push" out of their comfortable rut into a higher plane. Baba's work was to provide that push, stating, "*Masts* are my best medium for work in the world and why I exert such effort to reach them."

During his life, Baba said that he contacted ninety percent of the world's higher-plane *masts,* who can only be found in certain regions of the East. In 1941 he travelled eighteen thousand miles. The following year he traveled fifteen thousand miles, which included a trip to South India to re-contact the great sixth-plane *mast*, Chatti Baba. On that same day, the ultimately victorious Allied push at El Alamein began in North Africa. In only two years, the Avatar traveled nearly thirty-five thousand miles seeking out those he called his dearest children. 2303, 2408

The following excerpts from *The Wayfarers* offer insights into the unusual phenomenon of *masts*:

> One wonders if *masts* are found in other parts of the world; and if not, then why India alone is gifted with such souls? In explaining this paradox, Meher Baba said that India was nearest to the "creation point," the Om point, and

so is the most significant country in the world of spirituality—a point to be remembered.

For this reason, Baba explained, there are very few advanced *masts* outside India, and none in Europe or America; though there were mystics, saints and lovers of God here and there in the West. He said there were also a few *masts* in Arabia and Egypt.

There are a very few in Iran, and [fewer] in Tibet. So it's not surprising in the West there are no traditions about these God-intoxicated souls, such that when first confronted by a *mast's* eccentric characteristics, a Westerner's reaction is disbelief or total abhorrence. W 32

These ragged, eccentric men and women who pass their lives in filth and squalor and talk apparent nonsense, who often roam about naked and may abuse and strike others; who do no worldly work, who smoke and drink tea and chew tobacco in unnatural quantities —are we to believe these people are *truly* spiritually advanced and closer to God than intelligent, civilized men and women?

The reply is yes, they are, and with the help of some extraordinary notes dictated by Meher Baba it is possible to understand why these God-intoxicated souls are the way they are. He said:

> There's no such thing as good or evil. Morally speaking, this difference exists so worldly affairs may be conducted according to limitations imposed by society. But from the spiritual standpoint, both are bindings. Standards of good and bad are established as contemporary norms varying with the times. In spirituality, often what the masses understand as good is spiritually *bad*.
>
> And what is understood as bad by the masses is often *good* from a spiritual point. Robbery is generally bad, but if one robs to help a starving mother who has just given birth,

it's good. By general standards, beating others is also bad, but if you beat someone with the motive of correcting his life and do so without the slightest malice or anger, this beating is a blessed virtue. By society's standards of religion, health, morality, etc., cleanliness of body and mind are indispensable

It's fairly easy to keep the body clean; but cleanliness of mind—oh, very difficult indeed. The more one is attached to bodily cleanliness for merely selfish reasons, the less chances of having a truly clean mind. But if one is given up wholly to mental cleanliness—becoming free from low, selfish, impure desires and thoughts of lust, greed, anger, backbiting, etc., the less one's mind is attached to bodily needs and bodily cleanliness. All this applies to ordinary persons. W 33; 2283–84

Five Types of *Masts*

Baba identified five types of *masts*: 1) God-merged, 2) God-intoxicated, 3) God-absorbed, 4) God-communed, and 5) God-mad. According to *The Wayfarers*:

> The God-absorbed and God-communed can more or less keep their bodies clean. Their minds are almost automatically clean due to being absorbed and in communion with God. But the rest—the God-merged, God-intoxicated and God-mad all invariably have dirty bodies, live in dirty surroundings and may have dirty physical habits. One who is God-mad has a clean, pure mind.
> The God-intoxicated [soul] has a mind but no thoughts and simply enjoys that enchanted state. A God-merged [soul] has no mind—he is fully merged in God. So in these cases their mental cleanliness and purity can't be ques-

tioned. Then why should their bodies or environments be dirty? It's not that they purposely choose an unclean place but tend to gravitate towards it, indifferent either to physical plane cleanliness or dirt. For these souls, a palace, a hut, or filthy railway urinal are the same.

Masts are driven into any of these places by circumstance. It's natural for a mast to have a dirty body and to be driven to dirty surroundings; but if a *mast's* devotee happens to offer him comfort or cleanliness, he may or may not take it, but he is indifferent to it all. In these three types also, greed, anger, avarice and lust are simply non-existent.

The minds of the God-mad and God-intoxicated are always turned towards God, and the God-merged simply have no mind; their bodily actions are not under their control. As they are indifferent to everything, so their actions are either indifferently controlled or directly controlled by God. Whatever they do, good or bad from worldly standards, has no personal, selfish motive.

So, if they laugh, cry, are happy or morose, caress or beat others, they're unconscious of how they behave. Still, their acts of anger help those on whom this unconscious anger is spent, as their selfless anger *destroys* those very anger sanskaras of the recipient.

If *A* gets angry and beats *B*, *B*'s red sanskaras of anger become attached to *A*; *A* loses and *B* gains. If *B* also gets angry and beats *A* in return, then both are equal. If a *mast* hits either *A* or *B* their anger sanskaras are destroyed and do not recoil on the mast. If *either A* or *B* hits a *mast*, watch out.

It's a terrible binding. Now, why does one mast become *jalali* [fiery-tempered], another *jamali* [mild], or another *mahbubi* [having effeminate ways or clothing]? Everyone has to pass through innumerable lives. If a man, who in his past life lived in an environment of strife and great activity, becomes in this lifetime a mast, he's a fiery, jalali type. W 32–35

    Jalali is always hot-tempered, abusive to others and talks at random. He's restless and will likely beat those who come near him. He lives in an environment of filth and squalor, and is almost always dressed in rags. . . . He never asks for gifts except tea and tobacco. If given clothes, money and so forth, he'll just throw them away. . . . He's happy in crowded streets and bazaars, and sometimes enjoys the company of dogs, while the presence of small children annoys him. . . .
    If another led his past life in a quiet village or in a dull and idle environment in this life becomes a *mast*, he's of the mild or jamali type. If in his earlier life a man was a bachelor, who may or may not have engaged in the sexual act and becomes in this life a *mast*, he is a mahbubi type because love for women sanskaras were unexpressed in his past life. In this life it finds expression in wearing some part of a woman's dress or acting like a woman. W 28–29

Baba said that four of the five Perfect Masters during his Advent had mixed jamali/jalali personalities: "Narayan Maharaj was a pure jamali, while Tajuddin Baba, Sai Baba and Babajan were both jamali/jalali types. Upasni Maharaj was pure jalali."

Baba would contact several truly high *masts* to employ in his war work, and their inner states were worlds apart from ordinary madness. Only Baba could see the distinction, explaining, "A fast mind is sick. A slow mind is sound. A *still* mind is *divine*."

Those gifted with divine minds always recognized Baba. In May 1939, Baba had a high *mast* named Mai Bap brought to Meherabad. When Baba lovingly patted his back, the *mast* cried out, "There's intense burning! You've set me on fire!" Baba lovingly calmed, bathed and fed him. Later that evening before Mai Bap was driven back to his home, Kaka Baria asked where he had been. The mast's eyes brightened: "Oh I've come to the court of God and dined at his palace!" 2009

The Divine Art of Contacting *Masts*

Meher Baba in a rare moment of repose, Rahuri Mast Ashram, 1936

There was a divine art to approaching a *mast*. Baba instructed the men to remain apart at the beginning to observe how local people offered reverence, and to note the particular food or fancy of each, such as tea, *pan* or cigarettes. Only then would they approach and mollify them, above all avoiding any action that might offend one of Baba's beloved children. Sometimes a *mast* was persuaded to come to Baba; if not, Baba himself might come to them. SG 39

Even then they might run from him, inwardly sensing that they were about to get "spiritually drenched," like a mischievous child running from its mother at bath time. They sensed some *duty* would be given if they agreed to his contact. If the contact was good, it was clearly reflected long afterwards in Baba's mood.

Early in 1939, during a long halt in Ajmer during the first Blue Bus Tour, Baba explained about God-Realized majzoobs. "These are most advanced seventh-plane masts, drowned in divinity but with little consciousness of their own body. How exceptionally rare they are in the world, and here in Ajmer such a one is nearby!" Baba added there was only one other majzoob in India at that time.

Baba sent Adi Sr. and Kaka Baria to bring this extraordinary seventh-plane mast from his tiny, filthy two-room hovel near the tomb of a Perfect Master. He was called Cha-cha because all day long he would call out *"Cha, Cha!"*—"Tea, Tea!" His devotees brought him endless cups of chai, which he often just poured down over his head and chest.

Adi Sr. and Kaka Baria spent days trying to convince Chacha to come with them. He adamantly refused, but Baba wasn't content with the refusal. So again after a few days he asked Adi, "Can't you try just once more to *somehow* bring Chacha?" "It's totally futile, Baba," Adi replied. "He won't even budge!" Still, Baba sent him back a final time. On February 14, Adi walked up to Chacha with no expectations and gently held his arm, saying, "Why not come with us today?"

To Adi and Kaka's's amazement, the *mast* rose slowly to his feet without argument. Barely able to walk, he stumbled along between them. With difficulty they got him into a *tonga* (a small, single-horse-drawn carriage). Adi got into the back with Chacha and Kaka rode up front. Seeing this, Chacha's Muslim caretaker and followers became suspicious, asking where they were taking him. "To see our elder brother. Don't worry, we promise we'll bring him back," Adi replied.

When they reached the *mast* compound, Chacha was unable to get out of the tonga. Baba himself came out, gently took his hand and helped him struggle down. Chacha hadn't moved from his abode for so many years that his legs no longer functioned. Kaka and Adi took his arms and helped him to slowly make his way as God's light shone brilliantly from his eyes. Upon Chacha's arrival, Baba was radiantly happy and remarked, "Chacha alone is worth a hundred *masts*!"

Baba revealed that Chacha hadn't bathed in thirty years. He had ordered Rano to keep hot water at the ready to bathe this most extraordinary *mast*. As Rano brought bucket after bucket of hot water, Baba carefully poured cup after cup over his clothes to dissolve the sugar in them before trying to remove them. He finally had to cut the clothes away with scissors, carefully, piece by piece.

Meanwhile, Adi was still trying to remove Chacha's old red fez cap, which was fused to his head under his turban. Tenderly, Adi continued the delicate task as Baba gestured, "Gently, gently . . . don't hurt him." Finally, the cap lifted away. Adi was aghast to see white skin, so raw that after bathing he could only pat it dry. Baba bathed the rest of Chacha's body with mild soap and warm water. Afterward, he presented Chacha with a new white *kafni* (robe).

Chacha had no consciousness of his body—only the consciousness of *Himself* as God. This God-Realized, seventh-plane majzoob saw Baba as God; he knew only Baba as God. It was a glorious time—God being with Himself as God with no veils in between! Baba was in a glorious state as well, while Adi was completely

The extremely rare God-Realized seventh-plane majzoob, Chacha, whose name was Nur Ali Shah Pathan

exhausted.

Chacha immediately asked for tea, but instead of drinking it he poured it all over himself. When Baba asked if he'd stay a bit longer, Chacha softly uttered, "I'll stay, if you'll help me." Baba then lovingly hand-fed him. Chacha was later delivered back to his hovel and caretakers in another tonga. Baba visited Chacha at 3:30 AM in the coming days to come to avoid crowds to meet with him in total privacy. What extraordinary work was done with Chacha for the sake of the world.

Baba's external, gross world care for the *masts* was frequently followed by hours of seclusion, working with them individually. Who could guess what was accomplished? Baba never fully explained the workings or results of these intimate contacts. But he did reveal that certain *masts* represented specific nations in the war-torn world. To behold a *mast*, one would never suspect they could possibly carry out any kind of work, so dazed and oblivious to the world and their bodies they were.

But after such apparently exhausting work with Baba they would emerge utterly radiant, as if coming from an international summit of world leaders, confident in the work accomplished. Baba declared, "These *masts* are God's true soldiers!" By contact with the Master they were given a push from their trapped places on the inner planes to continue their spiritual journeys on a more direct path toward the goal of God-Realization. MM 2:17

Baba explained that a *mast* assumes a subtle body, or in the higher planes, a mental body—each being a far higher vibration than the gross body:

> A *mast's* divinely intoxicated state neutralizes heat, cold and disease without worrying to keep their bodies healthy. They possess strong physiques. It's impossible for scientists to know of this power even though they've discovered ether, electrons and protons. They cannot reach even the

fringe of the subtle *energy* world or *mental thought* worlds. 3163

    The soul has immense powers to the degree of advancement it has attained. The power itself sustains the physical body even in the hardest strains and trials. That's how even oblivious to the world and their physical needs, they live fresh and strong as ever. An ordinary man would drop the body even under a thousandth of a part of the strain they experience. 2090

When Baba worked with a high *mast* who fully co-operated, the drain on his vitality was immense, such that he'd emerge from seclusion pale and apparently exhausted, his clothes drenched in perspiration, but joyous as well. He became so engrossed as to forgo meals, sleep, contact with the men and women, and, it seemed, the gross world. Nothing made Meher Baba happier than a successful session with such a being. Donkin recorded a rare glimpse of Baba resting after such work:

    He looked so radiantly noble, his unbraided hair hanging down. His phenomenal strength of character and mysterious spiritual beauty were astonishing as he sat on the couch, his face in repose with a fusion of spiritual bliss and serenity, yet sadness, giving it such dignity and grandeur. His face surpasses nature's scenery and rapid changes of mood.
    Like time-lapse photography with clouds morphing and racing quickly across the sky, Baba's facial expressions similarly changed in rapid sequence, as he experienced the sufferings of the universe, working with rapidly changing conditions in countless places all over the world. MS 93

It's absolutely impossible for an ordinary man to understand my work. With my universal mind working on an unlimited scale for the universe, what I do is outside the bounds of human intellect. . . . I visit places, see different sights. I go to plays, movies and do a hundred and one other things.

But I don't enjoy these things as you do. They are the medium of my Inner work. My every breath constantly does this work, while outwardly you find me doing nothing special. You can never grasp the internal mystery. I must do great work for the welfare of humanity; it is my universal duty.

As Emperor of the spiritual kingdom, each second I receive inner reports—messages from my agents in every corner of the globe due to the troublesome times we face. I inwardly receive only distressing reports, like the China and Japan conflict—news pouring in each moment from various parts of the world, and I must issue instructions to my agents.

You can't see outwardly my managing an infinite number of things inwardly which no one knows. But the effect of my work appears outwardly. You find me abruptly changing moods—one moment happy, jolly; the very next, serious, irritable—utterly morose. 1295–96

Meeting Two Secret Agents in Goa

After an eight-month halt in Bangalore during the second Blue Bus Tour, Baba and the women set out for a tour of India's west coast, through Goa. Baba loved Goa's spiritual atmosphere and Portuguese customs, calling them "such a pleasant change from British India." The afternoon they arrived at their hotel, Elizabeth stopped the car to enter a restaurant next to the Basilica of Good

Jesus. A white-bearded old man in a *topee* (safari hat) emerged looking like what Donkin called "Moses in an old suit." Elizabeth asked him when the Basilica would be open. He said it was always open. He and Baba stared at each other for a moment before the man left. MM 2: 47

The Basilica contained the tomb of St. Francis Xavier (1506-1552. He and St. Ignatius of Loyola, along with five other veterans, underwent a spiritual conversion and formed the French Catholic order known as the Jesuits (Soldiers of Christ) to become apostolic educators and missionaries. St. Francis spent the last years of his life as a missionary in Southeast Asia, Japan and India. He died in Goa.

Baba took the women inside the Basilica. Emerging after paying their respects, they ran into the old man again, who explained to Elizabeth that he had just arrived from Karachi. He was a playwright, but until now none of his work had been performed. He had come to Goa to continue writing, mentioning modern dramas and the works of George Bernard Shaw. Baba signaled his brother Jal to ask the old man if he needed anything—especially money. "No, thanks," he said, glancing back at Baba.

Back at the hotel Baba told the women, "You're all blind. He's spiritually advanced—a conscious agent. All this talk about plays had a hidden meaning only for me. I gave him internal instructions; now he'll leave Goa."

The next day Elizabeth encountered the man a third time. He said cryptically, "I don't know why, but I feel all on fire. I planned to be in Goa some months. But now I must leave for a colder country up north." Elizabeth related the strange meeting to Baba. He explained, "As Elizabeth was first to meet him, so she must be the last." Later that day, they heard on the radio that Germany had invaded Denmark and Norway without prior warning—"cold countries in the north."

Another of Baba's Goan agents was a Christian *mastani* (female *mast*), found striding along the highway, not in rags, but in a black chiffon blouse and long pleated skirt. As she was walking past Baba's hotel, Norina tried to coax her in to meet him. The *mastani* refused, but she looked up at him on the hotel balcony before continuing on her way. Like all female *masts*, she was known as Mastani Mai (Mastani Mother), and Baba said she held the key to the spiritual affairs of Goa. 2096–98; MM 2: 47

The Last *Mast* for Now

Chatti Baba, a jamali sixth-plane *mast,* was so named because he always carried a clay water jug called a *chatti*. Baba had first contacted Chatti Baba in South India, and he had the sweetly tempered *mast* brought to Meherabad. Baba worked intensely, bathing him with one hundred fifty to two hundred buckets of water daily. After his baths, Chatti Baba liked sit on the ground pouring handfuls of earth over his head, so Baba ordered baskets of dirt to be brought to him each day.

Baba brought Chatti Baba along on the third Blue Bus Tour, but the mast traveled by rail with the men. Dr. Nilu, another Baba's personal physicians, had absolutely no faith in *masts*; in fact he referred to them as "innocent madmen." But one winter morning in Quetta he saw that Chatti Baba had sat outside all night long on the icy ground, dressed only in his thin cotton *lungi* (a long piece of cloth wrapped around an man's lower torso), not leaving his seat even in a raging hail storm. Nilu had spent the entire night wrapped up in his overcoat under four woolen blankets and had still been cold. Seeing Chatti Baba sitting nearly naked on the ice profoundly impressed Nilu and finally convinced him that the *mast* was no ordinary man.

In fact, during Baba's month-long stay in Quetta, Chatti Baba never came indoors, but roamed about all night in freezing weather, continuing his daily bucket baths of icy water while maintaining perfect health. One day, Baba gestured to Krishna Nair, the young disciple who attended Chatti Baba, to ask if he felt cold. The *mast* replied, "Cold? I'm on fire! I'm burning up!" Puzzled, Krishna asked, "You're having a cold bath, yet you feel you're burning?" Chatti Baba nodded toward Baba. "His fire is burning me!" 2203–04

Prior to his spiritual awakening, Chatti Baba had been a railway station master, and sometimes he tapped out Morse Code messages on his window. At irregular hours of the night or day he called out orders in English to his imaginary railway subordinates. Baba loved Chatti Baba dearly, and, as if in a divine game, he fulfilled his slightest whim. Mercurial as a child, the *mast* had an enchantment about him and a soft, delightful laugh that was contagious to all who knew him.

Of his beloved *masts* Baba said:

> In my own way, I make love to these lovers of God who have no consciousness of the world and are blissfully indifferent to physical wants. They have only love for God without worldly consciousness. The world's people love Illusion, cry and beg for more Illusion! They're immersed in lust, anger and greed. But these masts are brave heroes who've kicked off Illusion and now live only for their Beloved. 1986–88

Endnotes

[1] From talks given by Espandiar Vesali at the Los Angeles, CA, Baba Center, Summer 2003. Espandiar eventually moved to California, where the author knew him for a few years and visited his home for some Baba meetings. He also did some healing massage work on his crippled feet. They were both in Oklahoma in 2002 for the fiftieth anniversary of the automobile accident during which Baba shed his blood for America and the world in 1952. He witnessed how Baba truly manifested in Espandiar's heart. Though Espandiar barely spoke English, his love for Baba was palpable. Just being in his presence, receiving an embrace and his soft kiss on the cheek with such light from his eyes, was a wonderful experience. Espandiar left Los Angeles in 2006 to return to Iran, feeling he'd soon be going to Baba. He passed soon after, fulfilling a wish to die in his homeland. Espandiar passed to Baba Christmas Eve 2009 at over ninety years of age, the last Prem Ashram student in Iran.

[2] Gandhi had been deeply influenced in the late nineteenth century during his university years in London by American Henry David Thoreau's revolutionary work, *Civil Disobedience*. Thoreau's philosophy inspired Gandhi's non-violent, anti-British, "Quit India" campaign in his active political years from the 1920s to the mid-1940s. How fascinating to think that the influence of an American dropout from society would one day manifest in the freeing of India's freedom and its independence from British rule..

[3] Minoo Kharas said he was writing his memoir to include his Gandhi and Meher Baba stories and other anecdotes of their interactions over a span of fifteen years. However, Minoo's health and

eyesight were failing, so many of these stories were never published.

In the early 1990s the author was advised by Baba's sister, Mani, that some of Minoo's material was still considered by some in India to be "politically very sensitive," and perhaps it wasn't the best time to publish it.

Minoo died before finishing his book [and] Naosherwan Anzar became its custodian. In 2013 he published *The God-Seeker, Diaries of Minoo Kharas.* Several of the wonderful Gandhi stories that Minoo told the author do not appear in this version of Minoo's life, even though they were included in his diary.

[4] Margaret Craske studied with the famous Enrico Cecchetti in the private London studio he ran from 1918 to 1923, when he taught for the Diaghilev Ballet Company. The Maestro gave her a certificate qualifying her to carry on his teaching tradition—a rare honor. She was considered the world's leading authority in the Cecchetti technique.

Margaret established her own school in London and danced with the Ballet Russe and Royal Ballet. She co-authored what is now a classic reference on the Cecchetti method, which, as of 2015, was still in print. Her own book is entitled *The Theory and Practice of Allegro in Classical Ballet,* published in 1920.

Margaret gave away her school in 1940, after Baba called her to India. She spent seven years in the women's ashram at Upper Meherabad and traveling with Baba, until he sent her to America, saying "You must go; I've made you my link in America . . . go and spread my love there!"

Margaret toured with New York's American Ballet Theater. She also taught at the Metropolitan Opera Ballet, the Juilliard School and Manhattan School of Ballet until 1983. Some of her students were destined to follow Baba. She brought a group of them to Myrtle Beach to meet him during his three visits in the 1950s.

[5] In 1911, West London's Olympia Exhibition Hall was transformed into a massive Gothic cathedral mounting the huge medieval pageant. According to *The London Times*, "*The Miracle* is a work of art London has never seen the likes of." 1307 and footnote

[6] Filis Frederick later observed: "It was easier in the 1930s with the skeptical rationalism of Freud, Marx, Wittgenstein, Russell, etc. Men held Western thinking, such that a group of Western women stepping outside conventional religious roles to follow an 'Eastern guru' emphasized the way of the heart." Aw 20 (no. 2): 12

Filis came into Meher Baba's orbit in the 1940s. She founded *The Awakener*, the first American magazine devoted to him. She was psychically aware and conscious of many past lives. She once revealed her memory of Baba as Pharaoh Akhenaton, Filis further recalled being Akhenaton's daughter, Meritaten, known as Scota.

[7] Greenwich Village was a unique neighborhood whose street plan followed nature—the original animal trails used by Native Americans and, later, Dutch farmers with close ties to the earth. Village residents refused to conform when the steamrollers of progress began leveling New York City neighborhoods to create one vast standardized metropolis.

In the absence of clean-cut vertical N/S and horizontal E/W lines to accommodate four-wheeled vehicles on village streets, this unusual geography became something of a refuge. Here lived literary and artistic free-thinkers, writers and poets, including Edgar Allen Poe, Walt Whitman, Henry James, Edith Wharton, Edna St. Vincent, O. Henry and Upton Sinclair, who was a close friend of Graham Stokes.

The area was home to countless others who left their mark on America's history—simple bohemians who thrived in its free atmosphere. As such, Greenwich Village was a natural magnet for Stokes and would be for the Avatar as well.

Graham Stokes' personal papers went to Columbia University Library. Stokes' diary is still owned by the family.

[8] See Forman's *New York Times* article, published on April 24, 1932, in its entirety, in the Supplement.

[9] You can view the newsreel made during this garden interview at www.youtube.com/watch?v=PBOuFcpMdAY.

[10] Lettice Stokes, Graham's widow from his second marriage, recalled how crowds gathered in front of their townhouse for just a glimpse of "the Baba." For decades after Baba was gone, the Stokes' doorbell would ring at all hours of the day and night with people asking, "Is this the house Meher Baba stayed in?"

The author became the weekend gardener for Mrs. Stokes during his three years living in New York from 1979 until 1981. Lettice Stokes had lifetime box seats at Lincoln Center and would often ask him to join her for concerts on Friday afternoons, with Leonard Bernstein or Zubin Mehta conducting. He also pushed her in her wheelchair through the museums she and Graham had funded with large endowments, and which she had been unable to visit on her own for so long.

Later he would visit this historic house, befriending the new owners after telling them the remarkable story of their treasured home.

[11] Adapted from a talk given by Philip White, published in *The Broken-Down Furniture News* (September-October 1992 issue), a newsletter produced by the Denver, Colorado Meher Baba community.

[12] See www.lordmeher.org, p.1416–17 for the full text of Meher Baba's message given on this day. Also see: www.youtube.com/watch?v=rt4xVI2odKw for Baba's first filmed Paramount newsreel interview with Charles Purdom.

Just days after this garden filming, a third newsreel was shot during his return to Croton-on-Harmon, forty miles up the Hudson River from New York City, very close to where the author would be ordained a priest thirty-two years later.

An extensive list of videos with and about Meher Baba can be found at www.youtube.com/playlist?list=PLOuSCdGZXPBpqyS-LLeeaxritg2YO65iNy.

[13] Baba said his name and image might end up being used like Sai Baba's, as cheap propaganda: "'Sai this and Sai that, Baba this and Baba that.' Such things are done in India by the same worldly-minded ones who after his passing made a travesty of Sai Baba's life."

[14] In 1962, the author, age twenty six, visited the home of Helen Hayes, another great actress whom Baba saw in her 1931 performance in *The Good Fairy* at New York's Henry Miller Theater on Broadway. He was invited to her Hudson River estate in Nyack, New York, to record her reading select scripture passages for a seminary project. The seminary was directly across the river from her sprawling waterfront property. This was his first experience of how the Avatar works indirectly. Those whom Baba touches "tags" others. The tag from Helen Hayes wouldn't manifest for fifteen years. He believed that this contact with her may have helped set him up for a powerful revelation of Baba's presence in London in the mid-1970s, when he gazed at a large, stunning photograph of Baba in the living room of Pete Townsend of *The Who:* "I was totally floored by Baba's intimacy, [and] could have gazed at him forever."

CHRIST COME AGAIN

[15] Baba would later reveal that Napoleon reincarnated in the twentieth century as his disciple Vishnu Deorukhkar.

Sadly, Pickfair was demolished in 1990 when actress Pia Zadora purchased it and claimed it was haunted by "supernatural occurrences." https://en.wikipedia.org/wiki/Pickfair

[16] As a teenager growing up in 1950s Boston, the author made tape recordings of *The Big Show* each week on his Revere tape recorder—the first such recorder ever made for home use: "I lived for Sunday nights."

[17] Tallulah Bankhead carried her inner connection with Baba for the rest of her life. She is immortalized with him in a mural on the dining-hall wall at the Meherabad Pilgrim Center in Meherabad, India, just a short distance from Meher Baba's Samadhi.

You can listen to Tallulah Bankhead singing her theme song with a few of her NBC guest stars at www.youtube.com/watch?v=ZC7k70-HTbc. She told one of the author's friends about singing to Baba.

[18] Many Baba lovers have observed that Baba's use of the alphabet board pre-figured computer and laptop keyboards, cell phone texting, and perhaps even the Internet.

[19] The author retraced Baba's voyage thirty-two years later on his own first Pacific crossing to stop off at these same two Japanese port-cities, en-route to his mission assignment as a newly ordained priest to serve the people of South Korea.

[20] Theresa of Avila (1515–1582) was a Carmelite nun and mystic. She was endowed with great personal charm, tact and boundless good will. Her writings, notably *The Life and Way of Perfection,* are among the greatest in Christian literature. 1567 Footnote

To this day, the Carmelite convent that St. Theresa founded in Avila has photos of Baba deep inside their cloister, unseen by others, commemorating his 1933 visit.

[21] This house would stand in as the exterior for the home of *Ozzie and Harriet* for the popular 1950s TV series.

[22] Baba also used the analogy of drama in his discourse on reincarnation and karma, describing the individual soul's continuing life through countless acts and scenes until finally it becomes conscious of the Truth—that the author of the drama becomes the actors so as to enter into full, conscious possession of His own creative infinity in the great cosmic drama.

[23] In later years the cabin was incorporated into the compound of a homeless mission called "Just As You Are Ministries." 1659–60; Gl, February 2005, 7
On June 8-9, 2013, the town of Oceano put on its first *Dunite Days Celebration* to raise funds to restore the cabin, which was moved to the Oceano Depot.

[24] You can view Pascal on a film set at www.youtube.com/watch?v=a9iLtivLQjA. You can also see a fascinating five-part documentary, *"Who was Gabriel Pascal?,"* running ten minutes per part and featuring George Bernard Shaw, Pascal and his beautiful wife Valerie.
Part 1: www.youtube.com/watch?v=kKvxoQjA-og
Part 2: www.youtube.com/watch?v=ueSHXUP1gtE
Part 3: www.youtube.com/watch?v=6No_-k67w4w
Part 4: www.youtube.com/watch?v=5KjLjH5v980
Part 5: www.youtube.com/watch?v=AcWhWtSrfhY

[25] Had Pascal come to Andhra he might have captured the following touching scene. People were informed of Baba's willingness to see them through newspaper notices and handbills with Baba's photo, one of which was seen by a four-year-old boy.

Returning home from school, the boy excitedly asked his parents to take him to see Baba. But being strict Hindus, they weren't about to visit a "Parsi saint." They tried to distract the child, but he persisted and refused to eat his dinner unless the father took him to Baba. So the boy went to bed that night hungry and crying with the handbill tucked under his pillow. The next morning, still heartbroken, he reluctantly went to school, despairing of seeing Baba. But his longing continued.

Baba's program that day was to visit a couple of schools and then the homes of a few select followers. Suddenly Baba ordered the driver make an unscheduled stop at the boy's school. He walked straight into the boy's classroom, and the child gazed up in wonder at seeing Baba standing there. Before the teacher and students realized what was happening, he rushed and flung himself into Baba's waiting arms. When Baba picked him up and lovingly embraced him, the boy dissolved into tears of joy, Baba then left the school, his work complete.

When the boy returned home that afternoon and told his parents what had happened, the father was deeply touched by Baba's love for the child. That evening, the whole family went for darshan, with the father asking Baba's forgiveness.

[26] The film, *The Next Voice You Hear*, inspired the author to visit Hollywood and follow in Baba's steps.

[27] Charles Purdom's son Edmund went on to be a major British and Hollywood film actor in the 1950s, 60s and 70s.

[28] Besides *Mr. Deeds Goes To Town*, Capra's other remarkable films included: *You Can't Take It WIth You* (1938), *Mr. Smith Goes TO Washington* (1939*), Meet John Doe* (1941), *It's A Wonderful Life (*1946), and *Pocketful OF Miracles (*1961)

[29] The idea for the heralded annual Cannes Film Festival was formulated by Jean Zay right around the time Baba was in Cannes, but it didn't come to fruition for another decade, in 1946, after WWII. Baba used Cannes as his home base for eighty-two days, almost as much time as he spent at his "home in the West," the Meher Spiritual Center in Myrtle Beach, South Carolina.

Multivolume Table of Contents

Avatar: The Life and Teachings of Meher Baba 1894 – 1969
and the Avatar's revelations on his hidden life as Jesus

VOLUME ONE

Preface, Synopsis–Overview
Chapter Contents
Introduction
1 The Avatar's Last Seven Major Advents
2 Christ's Return to Earth in the twentieth century
3 Beyond Religion
4 The Birth of Merwan—All Merciful Light
5 Merwan's Friends and Early Life
6 The Kiss of Infinite Radiant Light
7 A Mother's Agony
8 First Disciple—First Ashram
9 Meherabad and Persia
10 The Avatar's Circle
11 Meherabad Flourishing.
12 In the Kingdom of Silence
13 The Second Long Stay at Meherabad.

VOLUME TWO

14 Prem Love Ashram Blooms
15 Lust and Love
16 Secret Visits to Persia and the West.
17 The Avatar Reaches America's Shores
18 Baba's Return to the West
19 Realization through the Medium of Film
20 Breaking His Silence in the Hollywood Bowl

21 Italy, Egypt, Spain and Switzerland
22 Hollywood—Take Two
23 The Ten Commandments
24 Balancing East and West: Nasik, Cannes, Meherabad and the Blue Bus Tours
25 War Clouds
26 Baba's Wayfarers

VOLUMES THREE and onward
27 A Remote-Controlled War
28 From the Holocaust to D-Day
29 The Intrepid Mother Shireen
30 The Universe as the Mind's Dream—The Secret of Sleep
31 Angels and Life on Other Planets.
32 Meher Baba's Final Declaration on Global Devastation
33 The New Heaven on Earth
34 The Three Sanskaric Veils Obstructing Divine Consciousness
35 Natural and Un-Natural Impression
36 Non-Natural Impressions
37 The Afterlife
38 Miracles Attributed to Meher Baba
39 The Avatar's Spiritual Consort
40 Jesus' Fifty-Year Exile in India after His Crucifixion
41 Meher Baba's Seclusion at Jesus' Tomb in Kashmir
42 The Curtain Rises on The New Life
43 Gypsy Beggars
44 A Terrorist's Mistake
45 Manonash —Annihilating False Mind
46 Manonash Seclusion Postscript—The *Hijras*
47 The Trail of Tears
48 Oklahoma—"Oh, What a Beautiful Morning"
49 The Fiery Free Life
50 Grinding Down His Disciples' Minds

51 Revisiting Hamirpur and Andhra
52 The Avatar's First TV Appearance
53 Another Tragedy for the Sake of the World
54 Real Life—Real Obedience
55 A Last Visit to the West
56 Investing in Loss and Dealing with Ghosts
57 The East-West Gathering
58 More of Baba's Favorite Things
59 The Beginning of the End
60 Selfish and Selfless Service
61 The Final Decade—Fighting a "Drug-net" of Illusion
62 Lost in Rajasthan
63 The Last Deep Seclusion
64 Baba is Filmed for a Documentary
65 My Time Has Come
66 "Remember This"
67 The Eternal Moment
68 Inconsolable Grief
69 Mehera's Visions and Dialogues with Baba

CODA

St. Peter's Gate: Rome
The 3rd Fatima Secret and Two Suspicious Papal Deaths

Supplement

April 24, 1932, *New York Times* article by James Forman
On Fate and Destiny
For the Sake of Love
Food for the Lion of Love
A Letter to Children.
How to Love God
The Universe—An Illusory Holograph

The Dream of Creation
Existence is Substance and Life is Shadow
12 Ways of Realizing Me
Creation of the Universe and Consciousness
Be Like a Stone
Life Eternal
The Soul's Amazing A to Z Journey
Manonash Discourse
The Travail of the New World Order
On Love Divine and Profane
Dream State and Divine Knowledge—*Swayambhu*
Meher Baba's Manifestation
The Aura and Halo
Demystifying Death and the Afterlife
Evolution and Human Consciousness
A Love Poem by Meher Baba
Baba's Favorite Things and Pets
Poem to the Blue Bus
Praising His Disciples
Real Light and False Darkness
Repeating God's Name
Mohammed and Meher Baba's Lineage
God Speaks: Amazon's favorite Book
You Alone Exist
101 Names of God

Reference Codes and Copyrights

See note below for * symbols

Permission for the use of the quoted material in this work has been obtained both orally and in writing, except where unnecessary due to the brevity of quoted passages. Words of Meher Baba reprinted by permission, © 1956, 1967 and all subsequent years, by the Avatar Meher Baba Perpetual Public Charitable Trust, India, cited as AMBPPCT, including source material from Lord Meher, by Bhau Kalchuri and AMBPCCT. This includes photographs with additional permission given by Lawrence Reiter and photos from the MSI (Mani S. Irani) collection, Meherabad, India. Permission has also been given by the following copyright holders as well as permissions quoted at the start of this work.

Please note: Free online works cited in this book, *Christ Come Again*, are on this site: http://ambppct.org/library.php. This site lists alphabetically all books written by Meher Baba, noted in the Appendix below by a single *. Double ** denotes online books written about Meher Baba. These are found at the same site, from which you can select the book and then click on "Read Me." *Lord Meher* and *The Awakener Magazine* have their own online address given below under their reference. Also see: https://sites.google.-com/site/babawebsites/.

A	Answers: *Conversations with Meher Baba*, ed. Naosherwan Anzar from *The Silent Teachings of Meher Baba*, © 2001, Beloved Archives, Hamilton, NJ
**AA	*Avatar of the Age: Meher Baba Manifesting*, Bhau Kalchuri, © 1985, Lawrence Reiter
AO	*The Ancient One*, Eruch Jessawala, ed. Naosherwan Anzar,

© 1985, AMBPPCT
ASL *The Advancing Stream of Life*, Meher Baba, ed. Adi Irani, © 1969, AMBPPCT
**Av *Avatar*, Jean Adriel, © 1947
AW *Awakenings*, Bhau Kalchuri, © 2011
Aw *The Awakener Magazine* (www.theawakenermagazine.org), © Universal Spiritual League in America, Inc. All quotes used by permission of AMBPPCT
*Be *Beams from Meher Baba on the Spiritual Panorama*, ed. Ivy Duce, © 1958, Sufism Reoriented, Walnut Creek, CA
BG *Best of the Glow,* 1984, edited and © 1984, Naosherwan Anzar, Beloved Archives, Hamilton, NJ
CD *The Combined Diary* [of Five Early Baba Disciples], © AMBPPCT
Dar *Darshan Hours*, ed. Eruch Jessawala and Rick Chapman, © 1971, Meher Baba Information
DC T*he Die is Cast*, "Compiled by a Disciple," © 1955, Meher Spiritual Center, Myrtle Beach, SC
DD *Donkin's Diaries,* © 2011, AMBPPCT
DH *The Divine Humanity of Meher Baba*, ed. Bill LePage, © 1999, AMBPPCT
*Di D*iscourses,* Meher Baba, 7th Edition, © 1987, AMBPPCT
DL *Dance of Love*, Margaret Craske, © 1980, Sheriar Press, Inc,. Myrtle Beach, SC
elf Author's initials, Edward Louis Flanagan for couplets, poems and haiku in the text
*EN T*he Everything and the Nothing,* Meher Baba, © 1989, AMBPPCT
FL *82 Family Letters, 1956-69*, Mani Irani, © AMBPPCT
GB *God-Brother*, Mani Irani, © 1993, AMBPPCT
*GD *Gems from the Discourses of Meher Baba,* © 1945, Circle Productions, Inc.
**GG *Glimpses of the Godman*, Bal Natu, Vols. 2, 5 and 6

cited), © 1979, AMBPPCT
Gi   *Gift of God*, Arnavaz Dadachanji, © 1996, AMBPPCT
Gl/Gl   *The Glow* and *The Glow International*, ed. and © Naosherwan Anzar, Beloved Archives, Hamilton, NJ, Meher Baba quotes © AMBPPCT
**GM   *The God Man*, Charles Purdom, © 1971, AMBPPCT
*GMMG   *God to Man and Man to God*, ed. Charles Purdom, © 1975, AMBPPCT
*GS   *God Speaks,* Meher Baba, 1955, 1973 (2nd Edition), © Sufism Reoriented, Walnut Creek, CA, online: www.ambppct.org/Book_Files/godspeaks_r.pdf
GuG   *Growing Up with God*, Sheela Fenster, © 2009, David and Sheela Fenster
HGO   *He Gives the Ocean*, Najoo Kotwal, © 2006, AMBPPCT
HM   *How a Master Works*, Ivy Duce, © 1975, Sufism Reoriented, Walnut Creek, CA
HT   *Heart Talk,* © AMBPPCT
*INF   *Infinite Intelligence*, Meher Baba, © 2005, AMBPPCT (cited as *Intelligence Notebooks*)
IS   *It So Happened*, ed. Bill LePage, © 1998, AMBPPCT
ITC   *In the Company of Avatar Meher Baba*, M.R. Dhakephalkar, © 1999
ITS   *Is That So*, ed. Bill LePage, © 1985
JLH   *Just To Love Him,* Adi K. Irani, © 1985, AMBPPCT
JOG   *Jesus among Other Gods*, Ravi Zacharias, © 2000, Nashville, TN: Word
LA   *Love Alone Prevails*, Kitty Davy, © 1981, Meher Spiritual Center, Myrtle Beach, SC
*LB   *Life at Its Best*, Meher Baba, © 1957, Sufism Reoriented, Walnut Creek, CA
LBE   *Lord Buddha's Explanation of the Universe*, trans. and ed. Lawrence Reiter, © 2004
LFM   *Letters from the Mandali*, ed. Jim Mistry, © 1983, AMBP

	PCT
LGM	*Let's Go to Meherabad!,* © 1985, AMBPPCT
LH	*Listen Humanity*, Meher Baba, ed. Don Stevens, © 1982, AMBPPCT
LJ	*Life is a Jest*, pub. R. P. Pankhraj, © AMBPPCT
LL	*Lives of Love*, Judith Garbett, © 1998, AMBPPCT
LM	*Lord Meher,* Bhau Kalchuri, © 1979, L. Reiter and AMBP PCT online www.lordmeher.org
LOL	*Letters of Love*, Jane Barry Haynes, ©1997, EliNor Publications
M	*Mehera*, compiled from tape recordings; pub. Naosherwan Anzar, ©1989, AMBPPCT
MC	*The Mystic Christ,* Ethan Walker, © 2003, Ed Flanagan
MBC	*Meher Baba Calling,* © 1964, AMBPPCT
MeM	*Meher Message Magazine,* © 1929, AMBPPCT
MM	*Mehera—Meher*, David Fenster, First English Printed Edition, © 2003, Ed Flanagan
MS	*Much Silence*, Tom and Dorothy Hopkins, © 1974, Meher Baba Association, London
MW	*Meher Baba on War*, ed. K.K. Ramakrishnan, © 1972, AMBPPCT
MZ	*Memoirs of a Zetetic,* Amira Kuman Hazra, © 1987, Ed Flanagan
**NE	*The Nothing and The Everything*, Bhau Kalchuri, © 1981, Lawrence Reiter and AMBPPCT
NL	*Meher Baba's New Life*, Bhau Kalchuri, co-publisher Ed Flanagan, © 2008, AMBPPCT
NW	*Nowhere To Now Here*, Michael Da Costa, © 1999, Ed Flanagan
OL	*Ocean of Love*, © 1991, Meher Baba Association
OY	*Over the Years with Meher Baba*, Bill Le Page, © 1999, AMBPPCT

PA	*Poems to Avatar Meher Baba*, ed. Ben Leet and Steve Klein, © 1985, Manifestation, Inc.
*PL	*The Path of Love,* ed. Filis Frederick, © 1986, AMBPPCT
PM	*The Perfect Master*, Charles Purdom, © 1971, Meher Spiritual Center Inc., Myrtle Beach, SC
PS	*Practical Spirituality*, John Grant, © 1985, AMBPPCT
QA	*Shri Meher Baba, The Perfect Master, Questions and Answers,* ©AMBPPCT
RD	*Ramjoo's Diaries*, Ramjoo Abdulla, © 1979, AMBPCCT
RT	*The Real Treasure, Volumes I-IV*, Rustom Falahati, © 2008, Ed Flanagan
S	*The Samadhi,* Bal Natu, © 1997, Sheriar Foundation, Myrtle Beach, SC
Sa	*The Sayings of Shri Meher Baba*, © 1933, AMBPPCT
**SG	*Stay With God*, Francis Brabazon, © 1977, Ed Flanagan, co-held by Bill LePage, Australia
SH	*Surrendering to Him*, Rhoda Adi Dubash, © 2002, AMBPPCT
SL	*Seekers of Love*, Amiya Hazra and Keith Gunn, © 2008, Meher Mownawani Publications
SOF	*Souls on Fire*, William M. Stephens, © 1998, Oceanic Press
SS	*The Secret of Sleep*, Meher Baba, © 1983, AMBPPCT
*ST	*Sparks of the Truth*, ed. C.D. Deshmukh, © 1967, AMBPPCT
STP	*The Spiritual Training Program,* Bhau Kalchuri, © 2005, AMBPPCT
TNL	*Tales from the New Life with Meher Baba*, ed. Don E. Stevens, © 1973, AMBPPCT
T	*Treasures from the Meher Baba Journals*, compiled and ed. Elizabeth Patterson and Jayne Barry Haynes, © 1980, Meher Spiritual Center, Myrtle Beach, SC, and AMBPPCT
TGS	*The God-Seeker, The Diaries of Minoo Kharas,* © 2013, Beloved Archives, Hamilton, NJ

TH	*That's How It Was*, Eruch Jessawala, © 1995, AMBPPCT
TK	*Turning the Key*, Bill Le Page, © 1999, Ed Flanagan
TIW	*Three Incredible Weeks*, ed. Malcolm Schloss and Charles Purdom, © 1979, AMBPPCT
TY	*Twenty Years with Meher Baba,* © 1975, Avatar Meher Baba Poona Centre, Pune, India
**W	*The Wayfarers*, William Donkin, © 1948, AMBPPCT
WK	*Words of Kabir and Other Stories,* by Sam Kerawalla, © 2006

CHRIST COME AGAIN

www.ingramcontent.com/pod-product-compliance
Lightning Source LLC
Chambersburg PA
CBHW031228290426
44109CB00012B/201